Fodor's

SECOND 2nd EDITION

The Rockies

GW00630727

FODOR'S TRAVEL PUBLICATIONS, INC.
New York & London

Published in the United States by Fodor's Travel Publications, Inc., a subsidiary of Random House, Inc., New York, and simultaneously in Canada by Random House of Canada Limited, Toronto. Distributed by Random House, Inc., New York.

ISBN 0–679–01818–2

Fodor's The Rockies

Editor: Andrew E. Beresky
Contributors: Stephen Allen, Curtis W. Casewit, Jeremy Schmidt, Ena Spalding, David Wishart
Research Assistants: Cecelia Caso, Su Wright, Kereen Allord
Maps: David Lindroth Inc., Jon Bauch Design, Pictograph
Illustrations: Brian Callanan
Cover Photograph: Peter Guttman

Cover Design: Vignelli Associates

Special Sales

Fodor's Travel Publications are available at special discounts for bulk purchases (100 copies or more) for sales promotions or premiums. Special editions, including personalized covers, excerpts of existing guides, and corporate imprints, can be created in large quantities for special needs. For more information, write to Special Marketing, Fodor's Travel Publications, 201 East 50th Street, New York, NY 10022. Inquiries from the United Kingdom should be sent to Fodor's Travel Publications, 30–32 Bedford Square, London WC1B 3SG.

MANUFACTURED IN THE UNITED STATES OF AMERICA
10 9 8 7 6 5 4 3 2 1

CONTENTS

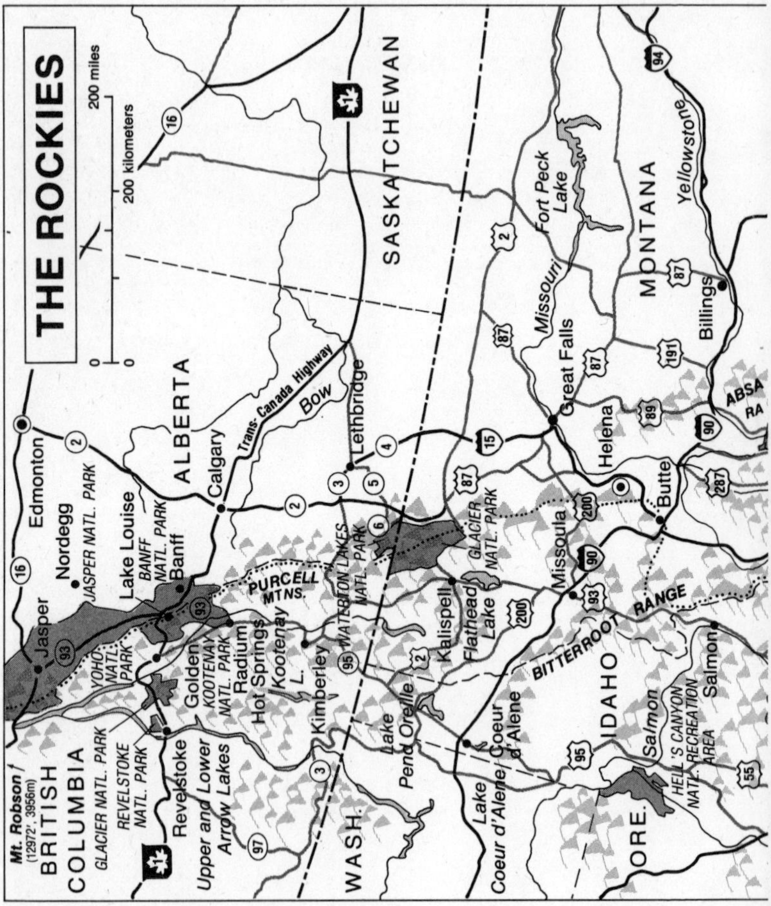
THE ROCKIES
0 200 miles
0 200 kilometers
Mt. Robson (12972'; 3956m)
BRITISH COLUMBIA
GLACIER NATL. PARK
REVELSTOKE NATL. PARK
Revelstoke
Upper and Lower Arrow Lakes
Golden
YOHO NATL. PARK
Jasper
JASPER NATL. PARK
Nordegg
Edmonton
Lake Louise
BANFF NATL. PARK
Banff
KOOTENAY NATL. PARK
Radium Hot Springs
Kootenay L.
Kimberley
PURCELL MTNS.
ALBERTA
Calgary
Trans-Canada Highway
Bow
Lethbridge
WATERTON LAKES NATL. PARK
SASKATCHEWAN
WASH.
Lake Pend Oreille
Kalispell
Flathead Lake
GLACIER NATL. PARK
Lake Coeur d'Alene
Coeur d'Alene
BITTERROOT RANGE
IDAHO
Salmon
HELL'S CANYON NATL. RECREATION AREA
ORE.
Missoula
Helena
Butte
Great Falls
Missouri
Fort Peck Lake
MONTANA
Billings
Yellowstone
ABSA RA
2
3
4
5
6
15
16
55
87
89
90
93
94
95
97
191
200
287

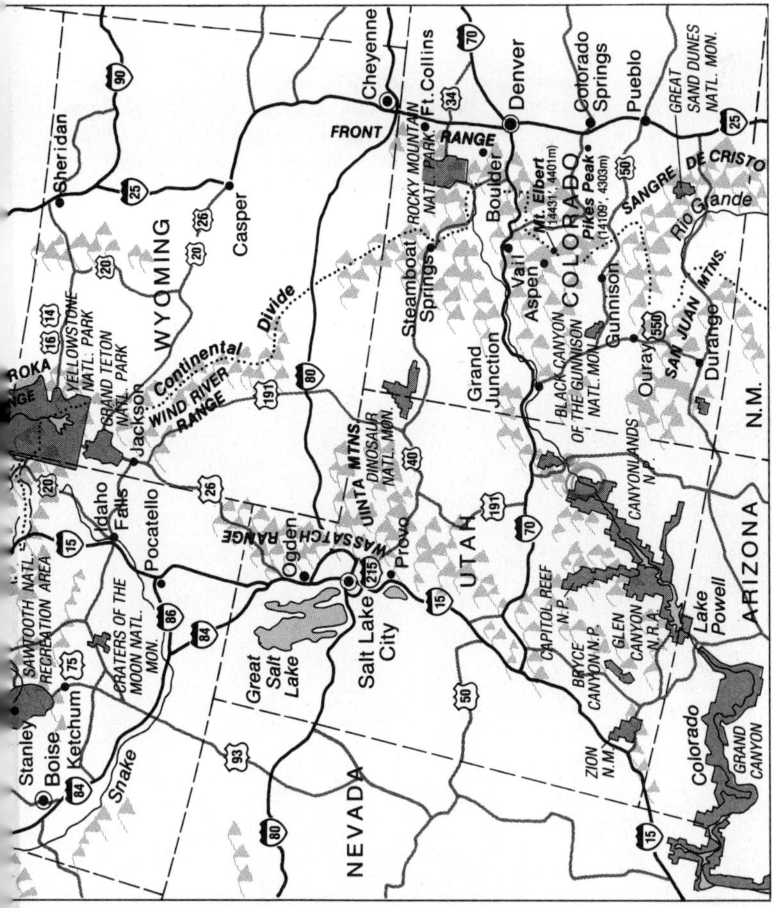
Stanley
Boise
Ketchum
Snake
SAWTOOTH NATL. RECREATION AREA
CRATERS OF THE MOON NATL. MON.
Idaho Falls
Pocatello
YELLOWSTONE NATL. PARK
GRAND TETON NATL. PARK
Jackson
WIND RIVER RANGE
Continental Divide
WYOMING
Sheridan
Casper
Cheyenne
FRONT RANGE
Ft. Collins
ROCKY MOUNTAIN NATL. PARK
Steamboat Springs
Boulder
Denver
Colorado Springs
Pueblo
Vail
Aspen
Mt. Elbert (14431', 4401m)
Pikes Peak (14109', 4303m)
COLORADO
Grand Junction
BLACK CANYON OF THE GUNNISON NATL. MON.
Gunnison
Ouray
SAN JUAN MTNS.
Durango
SANGRE DE CRISTO
Rio Grande
GREAT SAND DUNES NATL. MON.
N.M.
Great Salt Lake
Ogden
Salt Lake City
Provo
WASSATCH RANGE
UINTA MTNS
DINOSAUR NATL. MON.
UTAH
CANYONLANDS N.P.
CAPITOL REEF N.P.
BRYCE CANYON N.P.
GLEN CANYON N.R.A.
Lake Powell
ARIZONA
ZION N.M.
Colorado
GRAND CANYON
NEVADA

FOREWORD

The Rocky Mountains, extending from Alaska through Canada and to northern New Mexico, embrace the most rugged terrain and some of the most awesome scenery in North America. This guide takes you through the U.S. Rockies—including Colorado, Utah, Wyoming, and Idaho—and the Canadian Rockies of Alberta and British Columbia. Along the way, the guide offers you suggestions on enjoying the activities in this great outdoors, along with lists of places to eat, to stay and to camp.

While every care has been taken to assure the accuracy of the information in this guide, the passage of time will always bring change, and consequently the publisher cannot accept responsibility for errors that may occur.

All prices and opening times quoted here are based on information available to us at press time. Hours and admission fees may change, however, and the prudent traveler will avoid inconvenience by calling ahead.

Fodor's wants to hear about your travel experiences, both pleasant and unpleasant. When a hotel or restaurant fails to live up to its billing, let us know and we will investigate the complaint and revise our entries where the facts warrant it.

Send your letters to the editors of Fodor's Travel Publications, 201 E. 50th Street, New York, NY 10022.

AN INTRODUCTION TO THE ROCKIES

by
JEREMY SCHMIDT

Mr. Schmidt, a Wyoming resident, is an acclaimed travel journalist, and the author of Adventuring in the Rockies.

In the oft-quoted and appropriate words of John Muir, "Climb the mountains and get their good tidings. Nature's peace will flow into you as sunshine flows into trees. The winds will blow their own freshness into you and the storms their energy, while cares drop off like autumn leaves."

This is the reason people visit the Rocky Mountains. They are not the highest in North America, nor the most spectacular to look at; these honors must go to mountains in Alaska and the Yukon. Yet for sheer scale, for continental-sized bravado, the Rockies rank first. They form a unified, elegant, 2,000-mile-long rampart above the western plains. They divide the rivers that flow toward the Pacific Ocean from those that flow to the Atlantic, create their own local weather patterns, determine what sorts of plants can grow and which animals can live in a given area, and provide a natural geographic and scenic climax for the entire continent.

The Rockies begin with the Sangre de Cristo and Jemez mountains near Santa Fe, New Mexico. They achieve their highest altitude in Colorado, their greatest width across Idaho and Montana, and their grandest scenery in Canada. Finally they ease gently into the foothills of northern British Columbia near the Yukon border. In that distance, they span an astonishing range of landscapes, including some that you wouldn't expect to find in mountains at all: in Colorado, huge sand dunes and dry desert valleys; in Wyoming, a basin, hundreds of square miles in extent, with no river outlet; in Idaho, a vast field of broken lava from a flow less than two million years old, into which entire rivers disappear from view; and in Montana, rain forests dripping with water and moss. Added to the apparent anomalies are the expected sights: the immense Columbia Icefields and the near-Himalayan scale of the Canadian Rockies; hundreds of crystal rivers and turquoise lakes; deep valleys filled with morning mist; the sharp pinnacles of the Grand Teton Range, standing across Jackson Hole from the gentler contours of the Gros Ventre Mountains; the geysers of Yellowstone; the spectacular wildflower displays everywhere you travel between July and September; the even more profligate colors of autumnal aspens in Colorado, or of alpine larch in Canada; and a thousand other natural wonders.

Within the Rockies are dozens of smaller, constituent ranges with separate names. Colorado has the Gore and Collegiate ranges, the San Juan, the Sawatch, the Park, the Elk, the West Elk, and others. Driving through Idaho you will see the Salmon River Range, the White Clouds, the Sawtooths, the Bitterroots, the Lost River Range, and more. These sub-ranges stand separated from each other by deep valleys, major rivers, and open areas many miles wide. They are made of different types of rock, and they support different plants and animals. Yet all of them are classified under the broad heading of the Rockies. A traveler will have little trouble distinguishing them from ranges such as the Cascades of Washington State, or California's Sierras, which lie far to the west, separated from the Rockies by deserts and distance.

North of the border, however, the distinction is less clear. Here, the Rockies are crowded by neighboring ranges. In contrast to what you see in Colorado, the Rockies in Canada form a dramatic but relatively narrow band of summits, about 60 or 70 miles wide. This line of peaks carries the Continental Divide, which in turn marks a long portion of the boundary between the provinces of British Columbia and Alberta. On the west side of the range lies a long, deep valley called the Rocky Mountain Trench. No peaks west of that trench, however spectacular they may be, are considered part of the Rockies, and for good reason—they are much older, and made of different rock.

Geology

The Rockies began their spectacular rise about 70 million years ago from the flat floor of an ancient inland sea. It was a dramatic event, geologically speaking, but that initial uplift was the first of a series of occurrences which, taken together, tell the story of the Rocky Mountains. Each subrange has its own history, and one of the joys of traveling in the region lies in learning how to recognize the differences between one set of mountains and its neighbor.

In very general terms, the rock of the Rockies is of three types. The first is sedimentary rock, formed from sand and mud that settled millions of years ago into basins and hardened from chemical action and the weight of overlying layers. Examples include sandstone, limestone, and shale. Beneath them is metamorphic rock, very hard and very old, annealed by heat and pressure; granite, schist, gneiss, and marble are examples. The third type is volcanic rock, ranging from ancient to barely cooled. One lava flow in Yellowstone National Park was liquid scarcely 40,000 years ago.

All three types are well-represented in Colorado, where the geologic story is one of tumult and continual change. As you travel north, the rock structures become simpler and easier to read. You can form a picture, oversimplified but useful, by imagining the region before the Rockies were born. The surface of the land was flat then, and made of sedimentary rock, layer upon layer of it, miles deep, all having been deposited in the inland sea over the previous period of about 400 million years. Far below the sedimentary beds lie the older, harder rocks. Once they had been near the surface, but the immense weight of the overlying sediments had buried them.

Then came the uplift, powered by the forces of drifting continents. North America has been moving slowly westward, away from Europe, pushing as it goes against the floor of the Pacific Ocean, creating enormous pressures that relieve themselves from time to time as earthquakes along fault lines like California's San Andreas. It was the same sort of force which broke out dramatically some 70 million years ago. The area that is now the Rockies cracked, buckled, warped, and rose, the way ice buckles in the middle of a frozen lake. The sediments, exposed on top, began to erode away, filling adjacent river valleys. In some high areas, these sediments were stripped entirely away, exposing the harder rocks that lie beneath.

These are often laced with veins of mineral ore; visit a gold- or silver-mining town anywhere in the Rockies, and you'll find shafts blasted into hard rock, not sediments. Although placer mining, which started the gold rush, is done in the gravel and silt of riverbeds, the gold obtained this way was eroded out of hard rock at some time in the past, and, being exceptionally heavy, settled beneath the gravel.

To complicate the story in Colorado, volcanoes erupted from time to time, spewing out vast quantities of lava and building whole mountain ranges; the San Juan Range is one of these.

Similar events happened farther north, but with variations. Wyoming's Wind River Range is composed of old, hard rock, while the Absarokas just north are volcanic and relatively young. Yellowstone is practically one huge volcano—actually a collapsed volcano, or caldera—but the neighboring Tetons, long since stripped of their sediments, are made of granite. From the middle of Montana northward, in Glacier, Banff, and Jasper National parks, you'll see almost nothing but vast layers of sedimentary rock; look closely and you will find fossil seashells. Travel west from Banff on the Trans-Canada Highway, across the long valley called the Rocky Mountain Trench, and ascend into the neighboring range, and you'll suddenly find yourself in hard rock again. These are the Selkirk Mountains, not the Rockies. They are about three times as old and lost their sedimentary burden in the distant past. If they could think about it, they might consider the Rockies to be young upstarts that blocked their view of the Alberta plains.

As soon as mountains start to rise, erosive forces begin tearing them down. Wind, water, frost and, most dramatic of all, glaciers, have spent millions of years shaping the landscape we see today. You can see these processes at work throughout the Rockies and even hear the glaciers grinding as they move.

The landscape is far from finished. Some parts of the region appear to be still rising. Volcanic activity could start up again—most likely, according to geologists, in the Yellowstone area. Rivers cut ever deeper, rocks fall from cliffs, and floods change the faces of whole valleys. West of Yellowstone Park is Quake Lake, created during the summer of 1959 when a strong earthquake dropped the side of a mountain into the Madison River Valley. Under raw scarps up to 20 feet high, you can still see the old highway disappearing into the lake.

History

No one knows when the first humans walked the foothills of the Rockies, but it appears there were people throughout the region as long as 20,000 years ago. They were hunters and gatherers, nomads who lived by following the movements of game animals. Eventually, some groups learned agriculture and established civilizations based on the growing of corn, beans, and squash. These were the people who built the cliff dwellings of Mesa Verde and whose descendents still live in pueblo villages in northern New Mexico.

To the north, in the Rockies and on the Plains, the nomadic lifestyle survived into the late 19th century among the Sioux, Shoshone, Blackfoot, Arapahoe, Cheyenne, and Ute. Theirs was a culture based on the hunting of large animals, primarily the American bison, or buffalo, which once roamed the plains in numbers estimated as high as 60 million. From these animals the tribes derived food, shelter, clothing, and much more.

Then came the slowly growing influence of European culture, beginning with Coronado, who marched into what is now northern New Mexico in 1540. The Spanish brought horses, which in turn brought profound changes to the lives of the Indians who acquired them. Along with horses came manufactured goods like metal tools, beads, textiles, liquor, and rifles. These trade items were eagerly assimilated into the native way of life, altering it in sometimes important ways, but not destroying it. Some historians say that nomadic culture in North America reached its peak after the introduction of horses and metal tools. If true, it was a short-lived success, which came to an end with the arrival of gold-seekers in the 1860s.

The prospectors weren't the first non-Indians in the mountains. Spanish soldiers and missionaries had ridden as far north as central Colorado. French-Canadians, too, had glimpsed the Rockies from the western plains, and there can be little doubt that a few unnamed adventurers found their way into the Rockies but never lived to tell the tale. In the early 1800s, explorers crossed the northern Rockies—notably the Americans Lewis and Clark and the Canadian David Thompson. The fur traders who followed ushered in one of the more colorful episodes in western history—the time of the mountain men, who included Jim Bridger, Kit Carson, John Colter, and Jedediah Smith. Their moment in the sun, lasting a bare 20 years, ended when beaver had been trapped nearly to extinction in the 1840s.

The mountain men were followed by settlers bound for California and Oregon, people who for the most part saw the Rockies as nothing more than obstacles in their trail; the sooner behind them, the better. The first group with clear intentions to stay were the Mormons, who began settling near the Great Salt Lake in 1847. Two years later, they watched, and profited, as a stream of prospectors, the "Forty-Niners," hurried through Salt Lake City toward the California gold fields. More than a few of the gold rushers must have wished they had stopped and done a little prospecting along the way, because nine years later, in 1858, gold was discovered in Colorado. The announcement set off a frantic rush of gold-seekers, who poured into the new city of Denver and the surrounding countryside, until nearly every valley in the Rockies had felt their impact.

Things would never be the same again. With mining and miners came the need for ranches and farms, for lumber, coal, railroads and communication lines, and banks and government services. But inevitably the mines were played out, or the market failed. Exploitation of other primary resources—timber, coal, uranium, oil, hydroelectricity—filled the need in places, and continues to do so to a large degree. But these are industries characterized by cycles of boom and bust. Communities without broader means of support have suffered hard times or dried up entirely. This is still happening, as the current instability of energy prices adds another chapter to the region's bumpy economic history. The Rocky Mountain economy is now in a period of transition as it struggles to diversify. Tourism plays an ever-increasing role, as a visit to one of the region's many restored gold-rush towns clearly demonstrates.

Climate

Mountain weather varies with location. In the thin air at high altitudes, the sun may feel hot, but when you step into the shade or a cloud passes overhead, you realize that the air is chilly. It can be raining on one side of a mountain range and sunny on the other; snowing on the peaks, but dry and warm in the valley; blowing a gale in a river canyon, but breathlessly calm in an adjacent alfalfa field. Mountains are big enough to create their own local weather conditions.

As a rule of thumb, the higher you go, the cooler the air becomes—on average, the change is about three degrees Fahrenheit per 1,000 feet of elevation. Altitude, in this regard, can be equated with latitude; climbing a mountain is similar to traveling north. As you go higher, you pass through different types of forest until trees give way to frozen tundra, bare rock, and finally ice or snow, and you find yourself in an environment similar to that of the Earth's polar regions. During hot summer days, the arctic heights can feel like paradise. Conversely, while skiers bundle warmly against winter conditions at the resorts of Colorado or Alberta, residents of Denver and Calgary might be basking in 70° sunshine.

The mountain year is dominated by winter. Ask a resident of the region about summer, and he's likely to make a crack about how you've already missed it. In fact, winter never seems far away in the Rockies. It can snow on any day of the year, even in mid-July, which seems terribly unfair, considering that the snowbanks of the previous winter usually last until late July. But overall, summer in the Rockies is a beautiful season characterized by warm, sunny days and pleasant nights. It lasts, depending on elevation, from early June to late August. During this time, flowers burst into bloom, covering whole mountainsides with sheets of color. Animals graze day and night, storing up the fat they will need to see them through the long winter. Streams and rivers swell with runoff, only to quiet down again as snowfields disappear.

By September, nights become frosty, fall colors appear, and animals display their new winter fur. Snow dusts the high country, but disappears in the still-strong autumn sun. To many, this is the most pleasant time in the Rockies. Summer crowds are gone, but the weather remains good, and there is a sense that these are halcyon days—peace and warmth before the harshness of winter sets in.

Winter begins in November, when permanent snows block high passes and pile up in the valleys. Ski areas are usually open by early December. January brings the coldest weather most years—minus 50°F and below, in the extremes—but intense cold rarely lasts for long. Even after the most frigid nights, daytime temperatures often rise to near freezing in the rays of bright high-altitude sunshine. Winter in the Rockies feels less severe than winter in the upper Midwest, but it seems to last twice as long.

People who live in the mountains begin thinking about spring in March, during times of thaw; but winter always returns and seems to last for several more months, severely testing everyone's patience. There is something profoundly disheartening about seeing two feet of snow in the middle of May obliterate the greening landscape. However it may feel to one's winter-weary nerves, winter loses its punch after March. Higher elevations stay cold and soggy well into June, but valley bottoms and south-facing slopes enjoy warm conditions from April onward. Denver, Cheyenne, and Calgary are gifted by spells of balmy weather throughout the winter—even in February. These, however, always end with a storm dumping snow and sleet to remind everyone that these are the Rocky Mountains, after all, and that when it comes to weather, the mountains are in charge.

Speaking of long winters, and considering that the Rockies stretch all the way from northern New Mexico to just south of the Yukon, it would be reasonable to think that spring must come earlier to the south end of the range than to the north. Ironically, this is not the case. The summits of Colorado and New Mexico are thousands of feet higher than those of Canada. Higher altitudes compensate for lower latitudes, and seasons are just about the same throughout the range. True, the winter sun is stronger in Colorado, and the summer days are a little longer in Canada, but the seasonal landmarks are not much different from place to place. High alpine passes in Banff National Park open for hiking in early July, just as they do in the mountains above Telluride, Colorado.

Wildlife

The Rockies are home to a great variety of fauna, but of particular interest are those associated with wilderness: elk, moose, deer, bison, mountain goat, bighorn sheep, coyote, wolf, cougar, black bear, and grizzly; and birds such as eagles, osprey, various hawks, trumpeter swans, and whooping cranes. To see any of them is worth a little effort. Your chances are best in protected areas like national parks, especially early in the morning and at dusk. Wild animals rarely pose any threat to a careful observer—one who is quiet, who moves slowly (but not stealthily; wild animals get very uncomfortable with our clumsy attempts to "sneak up" on them), and who keeps far enough away that his presence does not affect the behavior of the animal. This distance varies with the animals involved and might be hundreds of yards. In places like Yellowstone, you can see a lot from your car. Some animals have become so accustomed to the presence of autos and their passengers that only when you leave the imaginary boundaries of vehicle and pavement will they feel threatened, and become aggressive. A word of warning should be sufficient: Apparently calm animals can in fact be very nervous and therefore dangerous.

During summer, many animals keep to themselves. Some require secrecy to avoid predators; others disperse simply because there is so much range available to them after the snows melt. For this reason, animals you see in July and August will usually be alone or in small groups.

Fall is probably the best time to view wildlife. Animals appear healthy and fit after a summer of plenty. Elk, bison, and bighorn gather for the annual mating rituals. Flocks of migrating birds wing past. Even coyotes, finished with the business of keeping their young safely hidden, seem bolder as they hunt for mice in brown meadows. In winter, game animals stay in valley bottoms and are easily seen in certain places; the Jackson Hole Elk Refuge is a notable example.

Bears deserve a special word. There are two species in the Rockies: black bears and grizzly bears. Of these, the grizzly is the larger, the fiercer, and the less able to adapt to human presence in its wilderness home. Ultimately, it loses any conflict with human beings, and its survival—already limited to a shrunken range from Yellowstone Park north—hangs in the balance. Administrative policy in grizzly country aims at avoiding conflict, but this is often not possible. Black bears are more abundant than grizzlies and are found throughout the Rockies. Despite their name, they come in a variety of colors, from jet black to brown to light cinnamon. Because bears are secretive creatures, the chance of a traveler seeing either black or grizzly bears is small. To avoid seeing them in the wrong situation—that is, at close range or in your camp—it is important to follow the advice of park rangers and wardens, especially in the matter of keeping food securely locked away between meals.

Mosquitoes shed far more human blood than any of the big-name predators. It is possible, especially in early summer, to find yourself enveloped by dense clouds of these pests. Repellent helps; the spray kind lets you treat clothing as well as skin. But if they are really bad, you just have to move indoors, into the tent, or to another place entirely. You'll learn quickly to avoid wet areas, which usually harbor the densest populations. In many other places, you won't notice mosquitoes until just around sunset, when they appear out of nowhere, as if some sort of insect dinner bell had been rung.

Seeing the Territory

Driving a personal vehicle is generally the most satisfying way to get around in the Rockies. Whether you take a car, a motor home or a car-trailer combination, having control of the wheel gives you infinite freedom to choose your own route. Even the busiest highways serve up generous portions of scenery. The Trans-Canada Highway, for example, cuts straight through Banff and Yoho National parks. Interstate 70, west of Denver, starts with a quick tour of historic gold-rush towns, dives through a long tunnel near timberline, crosses Vail Pass, and finishes with a splendid tour of Glenwood Canyon and the upper Colorado River.

Of course you'll want to get away from the main routes from time to time, and even if you turn off at random you can hardly lose. There's no shortage of secondary and tertiary roads in the Rockies. Most are well-marked and indicated accurately enough on ordinary highway maps. Just be sure to keep the gas tank supplied, as it can be a long way between towns, some of which may have only one service station, which happens to be closed for the weekend. Chambers of Commerce and tourism offices throughout the region can provide descriptions of driving tours, complete with maps, mileages, and suggested stops.

Adventurous drivers should consider the real byways of the Rockies—forest access roads. These are usually gravel and almost always lead to interesting, uncrowded places. If you seek quiet campgrounds, isolated meadows, and untrampled river banks, pick up the appropriate forest maps from district national and provincial forest ranger stations. Unless otherwise indicated, such back roads are usually passable by normal vehicles. Motor homes may have clearance problems, and some roads are not suitable for trailers. Those marked as "primitive" or "four-wheel drive only" should not be attempted in passenger cars. Pay attention also to signs warning that a road may be impassable in bad weather.

All this should not discourage visitors who would prefer not to drive. Excellent bus tours are available, and train routes, while limited, can be spectacular. The major national parks are all served by public transport, and you could easily spend your entire holiday in any one of them without exhausting the possibilities. For example, Yellowstone Park has four centers of interest: Mammoth Hot Springs, Grand Canyon of the Yellowstone River, Yellowstone Lake, and Old Faithful. By staying two nights at each location, and partaking in any of the various tours and activities offered, you would occupy more than a week and barely scratch the surface. And never have to drive anywhere. This holds true for resort areas and guest ranches as well as national parks. Increasingly, winter resorts cater to summer visitors, offering a wide range of mountain activities all in one place, at package prices that families will appreciate, and with the added benefit of superb restaurants and interesting shopping.

Ultimately, however, the best way to see the Rockies is to walk in them. Backpackers, who spend days or weeks on trails, develop a unique perspective, attuned as they are to the slower rhythms of the wilderness. But the same sense of peace can be felt closer to civilization, even if only a hundred yards from the road at a creekside picnic table or on a wooded path between the cabins and the main lodge at a guest ranch. The possibilities are endless, and while trails exist to challenge the most experienced mountaineer, many others are perfect for an afternoon or evening stroll. No special equipment is required beyond comfortable walking shoes and a desire to be out of doors. A few easy walking areas, all in national parks, stand out: Lake Louise, where you can walk to an alpine teahouse; Many Glacier in Glacier National Park, a lake-filled basin ringed by steep-walled mountains; the Upper Geyser Basin in Yellowstone, where boardwalks lead to hundreds of thermal features and geysers more powerful than Old Faithful; and Jenny Lake in Grand Teton, connected by a crystalline stream to several others like jewels on a necklace.

The areas mentioned above, and many others, are famous for good reason—they are supremely beautiful at all seasons, and in all sorts of weather. They can be crowded to the point of distraction from mid-morning to late afternoon. Early morning, however, is always a peaceful time, and evenings are only a little less so. It goes without saying that there are innumerable alternatives to the best-known places, which you can find with a little imagination, or simply by asking rangers and wardens for advice. They'll be only too happy to steer you to less-traveled areas.

It isn't important how far one goes, or how deeply into the wilderness one penetrates. The important thing is to spend a little quiet time away from vehicles and the sometimes frustrating details of travel. It is amazing how quickly the cool, fragrant air beside a mountain stream can rejuvenate the ragged spirits of a tired traveler.

FACTS AT YOUR FINGERTIPS

FACTS AND FIGURES. The Rocky Mountains span a distance of 2,000 miles and 25 degrees of latitude, from northern New Mexico to northern British Columbia. Seven states and two provinces claim parts of the range. There are no large cities *in* the Rockies; all cities of size—including Denver, Salt Lake, Calgary, and Edmonton—are located on the plains nearby. Denver is the largest population center in the Rockies, with about 1.6 million people in its metropolitan area, accounting for more than half of Colorado's population. For the most part, the 10.6 million residents of Alberta, British Columbia, Idaho, Montana, Wyoming, and Colorado live in far smaller communities, or on ranches and farms. The biggest town in the Montana Rockies, for example, is Missoula, with a whopping 33,388 people—far bigger than any town in the Canadian Rockies. Wyoming has only 4.8 people per square mile.

Ranching, mining, timber, and tourism (which includes sports activities like skiing) are the major industries.

Colorado claims the highest point in the Rockies, Mt. Elbert, which rises to 14,433 feet. In fact, all 54 Rocky Mountain summits over 14,000 feet are in Colorado, but this can be a misleading figure, as the state is generally at a high altitude. The Canadian Rockies are no less spectacular, with the 12,972-foot Mt. Robson being their highest point.

Timberline, the altitude beyond which trees do not grow, is around 12,000 feet in northern New Mexico. Due to the effects of latitude, timberline drops to around 7,000 feet at the Canadian border, so that even as the summits get lower, the entire range has bare and snow-covered peaks, and well-forested valleys.

PLANNING YOUR TRIP. For most people, driving a private vehicle is the best way to see the Rockies. Having your own car or camper allows for a spontaneous, adventurous style of travel. All you need are good maps, a guidebook, such as this one, and a small library of supplementary material that you can pick up along the road or send for in advance at the addresses listed in *Tourist Information.*

An auto-club membership can be useful for both advance planning and dealing with problems you might have along the road. Contact: the **American Automobile Association,** 8111 Gatehouse Rd., Falls Church, VA 22047; the **Canadian Automobile Association,** 999 W. Broadway, Vancouver, BC V5Z 1K5 (604–733–6660).

MONEY MATTERS. The Canadian dollar, like its American counterpart, is divided into 100 cents. As we go to press, the Canadian dollar is worth about 78 cents in American currency. All prices in this guide are listed in the currency of the country they are in—Canadian dollars in Canada, American dollars in the United States.

Most tourist towns have several places where you can change money. Banks usually provide this service; hotels generally only change money for guests. American dollars are readily accepted in many Canadian stores, and prices can be adjusted to the exchange rate. Canadian money is less readily accepted in the United States.

On the road, avoid carrying large amounts of cash. Travelers' checks are one way of doing this, and you'll have no trouble cashing the major brands in the Rockies. Automatic Bank Teller machines, open 24 hours a day, can give you cash from your account at home. Many also give cash on major credit cards.

TELEPHONES. Each of the states and provinces covered in this book has one three-digit area code. except Colorado, which now has two. Other than Colorado, area codes are not given in any listings in this book, unless they refer to numbers outside the state or province being covered. Area codes are:

Alberta: 403
British Columbia: 604
Colorado: 303 and 719
Idaho: 208
Montana: 406
Utah: 801
Wyoming: 307

SOURCES OF INFORMATION. The state and provincial authorities listed below all provide some form of vacation planner with comprehensive listings of things to do, routes to follow, hotels, campgrounds, and other basic facts. Most include an up-to-date highway map. Make your request well in advance, as it may take as much as six weeks to get these materials by mail.

Alberta: *Travel Alberta,* Box 2500, Edmonton, AB T5J 2Z4 (800–222–6501 in Alberta; 800–661–8888 in rest of Canada and the United States).

British Columbia: *Tourism BC,* Parliament Buildings, Victoria, BC V8V 1X4 (phone local travel information centers within the province; 800–663–6000 outside BC, and in the United States).

Colorado: *Colorado Tourism Board,* 1625 Broadway, Suite 1700, Denver, CO 80202 (800–433–2656; 592–5410 in Colorado).

Idaho: *Idaho Travel Council,* Hall of Mirrors, 2nd floor, 700 W. State St., Boise, ID 83720 (800–635–7820; 334–2470 in Idaho).

Montana: *Travel Montana,* Department of Commerce, Helena, MT 59620 (800–548–3390; 444–2654 in Montana).

Utah: *Utah Travel Council,* Council Hall, Capitol Hill, Salt Lake City, UT 84114 (801–538–1030).

Wyoming: *Wyoming Travel Commission,* I–25 at College Dr., Cheyenne, WY 82002 (800–225–5996, 777–7777 in Wyoming).

These and other materials are also available at local Chambers of Commerce and information centers across the region.

TIPS FOR BRITISH VISITORS. Passports. To enter the U.S. you will need a valid passport (cost £15). You will not need a visa if you are staying for less than 90 days, have a return ticket, and are flying with a participating airline. There are some exceptions to this, so check with your travel agent or with the *United States Embassy,* Visa and Immigration Department, 24 Grosvenor St., London W1 (tel. 01–449–3443). No vaccinations are required for entry into the United States.

Visas are not required to enter Canada, but you must, of course, have a valid passport. (British Visitor's Passports are also valid for entry into Canada.) Passports are valid for 10 years and cost £15; British Visitor's Passports are valid only one year and cost £7.50. No health certificates are required for entry.

Customs. If you are 21 or over, you can take into the U.S.: 200 cigarettes, or 50 cigars, or 1 Kg of tobacco; one liter of alcohol. Everyone is entitled to take into the United States duty-free gifts to a value of $100. Be careful not to try to take in meat or meat products, seeds, plants, fruits, etc. And avoid narcotics like the plague.

If you are 18 or older, you may import duty-free into Canada: 200 cigarettes and 50 cigars and three pounds tobacco; one bottle (40 fl. oz.) of liquor or 24 pints of beer; a small amount of perfume; plus other goods to the value of $40. Do not take in meats, seeds, plants, fruits, etc.

Insurance. We heartily recommend that you insure yourself to cover health and motoring mishaps, with *Europ Assistance,* 252 High St., Croydon CRO INF (tel. 01–680–1234). Their excellent service is all the more valuable when you consider the possible costs of health care in both the United States and Canada.

Tour Operators. The price battle that has raged over transatlantic fares has meant that most tour operators now offer excellent budget packages to the U.S. and Canada. Among those that you might consider as you plan your trip to the U.S. are:

Albany Travel (Manchester) *Ltd.,* 190 Deansgate, Manchester M3 3WD (tel. 061–833–0202).

American Airplan, Marlborough House Walton-on-Thames, Surrey KT12 2TJ (tel. 0932–246166).

Caravan Abroad Ltd., 56 Middle St., Brockham, Surrey RH3 7HW (tel. 07–3784–2735 or 01–939–2735 from London).

Speedbird, 152 King St., London W6 OQU (tel. 01–741–8041). Also operates tours to Canada. For Canadian tour operators, contact:

Thomas Cook, Ltd., Box 36, Thorpe Wood, Peterborough PE3 6SB (tel. 0733–63200).

Jetsave, Sussex House, London Rd., East Grinstead, Sussex RH19 1LD (tel. 0342–28–231).

Trek America, Ltd., Trek House, The Bullring, Deddington, Oxon OX5 4TT (tel. 0869–38777).

Airfares. We suggest you explore the current scene for budget flight possibilities, including *Virgin Atlantic Airways.*

Some of these cut-rate fares can be extremely difficult to come by, so be sure to book well in advance. Be sure to check on APEX and other money-saving fares, as, quite frankly, only business travelers who don't have to watch the price of their tickets fly full-price these days—and find themselves sitting right beside an APEX passenger!

Tourist Information. More information is available from the following sources:

United States Travel and Tourism, 22 Sackville St., London W1X 2EA (tel. 01–439–7433).

Tourism British Columbia, 1 Regent St., London SW1Y 4NS (tel. 01–930–6857).

Alberta Tourism, Alberta House, 1 Mount St., London W1Y 5AA (01–441–491–3430).

WHEN TO GO. Something is happening all year-round in the Rockies. Snow sports are generally in season from early December to early April, with Christmas seeing the largest crowds at ski resorts. Spring is perhaps the most limited season, with snow blocking the high country well into June most years. Hikers intent on spending much time above treeline should plan to visit after July 1, but comfortable weather lasts until mid-October. Rivers are best for white-water rafting early in the summer, when ample runoff makes them exciting. Fishermen, however, look forward to the lower water levels of late summer. Mountain meadows burst with wildflowers in July and August, while fall colors steal the show during September and October. Wildlife viewing is good in the spring, when the year's young wobble along behind their mothers. During summer, large animals disperse to remote places, and birds are busy with nesting; spotting animals in July requires careful attention. In fall, elk and other animals, healthy after a summer of plenty, reappear for the mating season. Most hunting seasons open in the fall.

PACKING. Informality reigns in the Rockies, and casual clothing is acceptable—even expected—in most places. Dressier clothing is appropriate for certain elegant restaurants and performing events at resorts and in larger cities, but these are the exception, not the rule. Jeans, sport shirts, and T-shirts fit in almost everywhere, for both men and women. If you plan to spend much time outdoors, and certainly if you go in winter, choose clothing appropriate for cold and wet weather. Cotton and denim, although best for the warmth and dryness of summer, can be uncomfortable when dampened by cold air. Wool, the old standby, remains a good choice, but recently synthetic fabrics have made great advances in comfort and warmth. If you don't find appropriate clothing at home, you can buy it easily in almost any town in the Rockies.

If you attend dances and other events at Indian reservations, dress more conservatively—skirts for women, long pants for men—or you may be asked to leave.

Even in summer, nights can be cold and high passes windy. Pack a sweater and a light jacket, perhaps a wool cap and gloves. You'll want shorts during the day. Sunglasses, skin cream with a sunblock, and a sun hat are important for high-altitude conditions. Sturdy footwear is a must for hiking: Look for the new lightweight walkers, which are essentially beefed-up running shoes with lugged soles. If you plan to go out into the wilds, you'll need higher boots with more ankle support. Don't forget rain gear, and keep it near the surface of your pack. A camera, plenty of film, binoculars, a compass, rucksack, spare eyeglasses, and mosquito repellent will not go unused. Good nature guides are available throughout the region, but don't forget your favorite bird book.

CLIMATE. Summer in the Rockies begins in late June or early July. Days can be warm with highs in the 80s or 90s, while nighttime temperatures fall to the 40s and 50s. Afternoon thunderstorms are common over the higher peaks, but overall, the summer climate is sunny and pleasant. Fall begins in September, often with a week of unsettled weather around the middle of the month, followed by four to six weeks of gorgeous Indian Summer—frosty nights and warm days, a delightful time to be in the mountains. Winter creeps in during November, with deep, permanent snows arriving by December. In January, overnight temperatures dive to as low as –60°F in particularly cold places, although the common winter low is much warmer than that. Daytime temperatures during winter are often near freezing under the surprisingly warm mountain sun. Winter tapers off in March, with snow lasting into April on valley bottoms and into July on mountain passes. The Rockies have a reputation for extreme weather, but that cuts two ways: No condition ever lasts for long. Generally speaking, the Rocky Mountain climate is pleasant, moderate, and eminently livable. Below are approximate *average* temperatures for the region (in degrees F). As for extremes, temperatures in the upper 90s are considered very hot; in the winter, people start talking when the mercury reads –40F°.

Month	Average Maximum (°F)	Average Minimum (°F)
Jan	25	5
Feb	30	10
Mar	40	20
Apr	50	28
May	65	36
Jun	70	48
Jul	81	55
Aug	80	50
Sep	70	40
Oct	57	34
Nov	40	21
Dec	30	10

ALTITUDE. The air is noticeably thinner in the mountains than at sea level, and this can affect how you feel. Dizziness, lack of strength, and heavy breathing are subtle signs that you aren't getting your normal dose of oxygen. Going slow and resting often for the first few days is all that most people need to do to allow their bodies to produce more red-blood cells. However, severe headaches and nausea are more serious symptoms, and should be viewed as such. Altitude can kill, and has done so when its victims, even experienced mountaineers, failed to heed the warnings. It is easy, especially in Colorado, where highways climb to 12,000 feet and higher (the 14,264-foot summit of Evans Peak, for instance), to go too high too fast. The remedy is to go down quickly, into heavier air. Other altitude-related problems include dehydration and sun exposure.

WHAT WILL IT COST? The amount you spend obviously varies with your style of travel, but generally costs are moderate throughout the region. Students, sharing expenses, traveling by auto, camping out, and preparing their own meals, can live on as little as $10 per day per person. The scale goes nowhere but up from there. Whatever their needs, two people can certainly travel comfortably on about $100 per day, not counting vehicle costs.

Even if you aren't camping out, you can keep costs down by carrying an ice chest and buying groceries instead of eating all your meals in restaurants. You benefit more than your pocketbook this way. No restaurant has better ambience than a shady streamside picnic area along a quiet mountain road. As for lodging, it is possible to find a room for around $25 or less, remembering that the closer you get to resort areas, and to peak season, the higher the prices will be. In general, food and lodging costs are a notch higher in Canada than they are in the United States, although many things, like skiing, are cheaper in Canada. The current exchange rate tends to even things out.

HINTS TO THE MOTORIST. Maximum speed limit in the United States is 65 miles per hour on rural highways. In Canada, where distances are expressed in kilometers, speed limits are similar. Canada requires the use of seat belts. Radar detectors are illegal in Alberta.

Mountain Driving. Modern highways make mountain driving safe and generally trouble-free. Keep in mind that altitude affects carburetors; if your car runs rough, you can have it adjusted for thin air. Climbing long grades can be hard on engines; check the coolant level as often as you check your oil. If the engine overheats, pull off to the side of the road and let it cool with the engine running. Descending from a pass, use the transmission as a brake, downshifting to third or even second gear as the steepness requires. Avoid riding the brakes. Observe speed limits for curves. Remember that conditions vary with altitude and exposure. Rain in the valley can be snow up high, and a road that is dry in the sunshine can be icy in the shade.

In winter, snow and ice make driving more demanding, but road maintenance is generally good, and plows are prompt. Snow tires and chains are a must. In stormy weather, carry an emergency kit containing warm clothes, some food, and perhaps a sleeping bag. If stalled by deep snow, do not leave your car. Wait for help, running the engine only if needed. Assistance is never far away.

For road condition reports, call the following numbers: Colorado, 303–639–1111; Wyoming, 800–442–7850, out of state, 307–733–9966; Idaho, 208–334–3664; Montana, 800–332–6171, out of state 406–444–6339; Utah, 801–964–6000; in British Columbia, check the phone book for the number of the local Royal Canadian Mounted Police; in Alberta, 800–222–6501, outside Alberta and in the United States, 800–661–8888.

Back Roads, Gravel Roads. The dirt and gravel roads of the Rockies are a joy to explore. They take travelers to remote, beautiful places, and, given a few rules, you should not hesitate to follow one, even in an ordinary passenger car. Use regional forest maps (available locally from provincial and national forest offices, and from some tourist offices) as guides. They show roads, campgrounds, rivers, and more, all in excellent detail, covering adjacent private lands in addition to forest lands. A rule of thumb for drivers: If there's a maintained campground on a given road, it is suitable for passenger vehicles. Others are marked as primitive roads; pay heed to these and other warnings. Don't set off on an unmaintained road in a heavy autumn snowstorm; you could get stranded.

Pulling a Trailer. If you plan to pull a trailer and have never done so before, you will need a whole new set of driving skills—starting, stopping, backing up, cornering, passing, and even being passed. Try to practice these things in advance. Learn to use side mirrors, especially when backing up. Remember when pulling a heavy load that everything takes more room and more time. Acceleration is slower; so is the maximum speed that you should travel. It takes longer to stop with a load pushing from behind. When cornering, swing wider than usual, paying attention to where the trailer wheels are. Never leave a heater or stove pilot light on while fueling.

Mountain conditions make trailer driving even more difficult. Watch out for engine overheating on uphill grades; conserve your brakes going down. Units with propane cooking stoves or heaters are not permitted in long tunnels. On certain passes with tight curves and narrow roadways, trailers or vehicles over a certain length are prohibited; other passes are closed to trailer traffic in winter.

TOUR GROUPS. If you prefer to leave the driving to someone else, consider a package tour. Although you will have to march to the beat of a tour guide's drum rather than your own, you are likely to save money on airfare, hotels, and ground transportation. *Personalized! Tours & Travel* (Box 17513, Portland, OR 97217, tel. 503–283–4866 or 800–248–0414) offers 12-day escorted camping tours for small groups to the American Rockies and 11-day camping tours to the Canadian Rockies. Meals, camping accommodations, and activities such as white-water rafting are included. Tours are available, departing from Portland, June–September.

BORDER CROSSING AND CUSTOMS. Major border crossings between Canada and the U.S. are open 24 hours, seven days a week; others have limited hours, or close during winter. If in question, ask locally or check with the appropriate tourism office.

American citizens do not need passports to visit Canada, and vice versa, but some form of identification is required. Canadian and U.S. driver's licenses and international licenses are valid in both countries. If you drive your own vehicle, carry registration papers; if driving a rented vehicle, be sure to carry a copy of the rental agreement. Americans visiting Canada should have a special inter-province liability insurance card, available from most insurance companies.

Citizens of the United States or Canada are permitted to bring home certain amounts of acquired goods duty-free; ask when crossing. For valuable items like cameras and electronic equipment, you should get customs receipts before leaving your country to prove you did not buy them abroad. Firearms for hunting are allowed entry to both countries, but specific regulations apply. Revolvers, handguns, and fully automatic weapons are not permitted in Canada. For more information, contact: **Revenue Canada,** Customs and Excise, 1166 W. Pender St., Vancouver, BC V6E 2M8 (604–689–5411); or the District Director, **US Customs,** 300 2nd Ave. S, Great Falls, MT 59405 (406–453–7631).

TRAVELING WITH PETS. When traveling with a dog or cat, check ahead when making hotel and motel reservations. Don't leave pets in cars parked in the sun.

Animals must be kept on leashes in national parks; in addition, they are forbidden on back-country trails. This does not usually pertain to wilderness areas and forest lands, although the same reasoning could apply, as dogs have been known to provoke bears and even elk. Think carefully before exposing a city dog to the dangers of wilderness conditions.

If you plan to cross the border with a cat or dog, carry proof of rabies vaccination. Complete information is available from: **Veterinary Inspection Directorate,** Agriculture Canada, Room 801, 1001 W. Pender St., Vancouver, BC V6E 2M7 (604–666–0575); and **U.S. Customs Service,** Box 7118, Washington, DC 20229 (202–633–2000).

ACCOMMODATIONS. During the summer season, especially in resort areas, accommodations are often booked solid early in the day. Try not to get stuck looking at No Vacancy signs at 9:00 in the evening. Use this book, or the accommodations guides provided by tourism offices for each state and province, to help with your planning. Many hotels and motels in the United States belong to national chains which provide central reservation services. Generally, you can reach them on toll-free (800) numbers listed in brochures and phone books, or by calling 800–555–1212. Among the chains are Holiday Inns, Ramada Inns, Best Westerns, TraveLodges, Quality Inns, Hiltons, and Marriotts. Budget chains include Budget Host Inns, Days Inns of America, Friendship Inns International, Imperial 400, La Quinta Motor Inns, Motel 6, Regal 8 Inns, and Super 8 Motels.

Hotels and motels are divided into five categories, arranged primarily by price. Although the names of the various hotel and motel categories are standard, the prices listed under each category may vary from area to area. This variance is meant to reflect local price standards and takes into account that what might be considered moderate in an urban area might be quite expensive in a rural region. In every case, however, the price ranges for each category are clearly stated before each listing of establishments. In some instances, prices reflect the inclusion of a certain number of meals. *Full American Plan (FAP)* includes three meals daily. *Modified American Plan (MAP)* means breakfast and dinner. *Continental Plan (CP)* offers European-style breakfast (roll or croissant and tea or coffee). *European Plan (EP)* means no meals are included in the quoted price.

Free parking is assumed at all motels and motor hotels; you must pay for parking, however, at most city hotels, though certain establishments offer free parking, frequently for occupants of higher-than-minimum-rate rooms. Baby sitter lists are always available in good hotels and motels, and cribs are always on hand—sometimes free, but more frequently at a cost of $1 or $2 per night. The cost of a cot in your room, to supplement beds, is around $3 per night, but moving an extra single bed into a room costs around $7 in better hotels and motels.

Women Guests. Hotel chains in general are becoming more cognizant of the requirements of women guests. Inquire at reservation time if interested in "female" amenities, such as skirt hangers or "women only" floors, which may require a special key. If security is a concern, it's often wise to take rooms above the first floor and to be sure that hotel personnel do not announce your room number at the front desk. Many women traveling alone prefer to stay only in rooms that do not have direct access to the outside.

Guest Ranches. Guest ranches are a specialty of the West, catering to people with a keen interest in the outdoors who plan to stay a few days or more. Along with meals and lodging, guest ranches offer a variety of activities, including trail rides, cookouts, wilderness excursions, boating, skiing, fishing, hunting, and even such unranchlike sports as tennis. Some are working ranches; many are beautifully located in remote areas and operated by families who have lived and worked there for two or three generations. All of them are unique; so far, there are no guest ranch chains. Staying at one can give you a different perspective on life in the Rockies. Costs range from $250 to $800 per person per week, including meals. Reserve at least two months ahead. Listings are available from the state and provincial tourism offices (see *Sources of Information,* above) or from local Chambers of Commerce.

Youth Hostels and Other Budget Lodgings. Youth hostels are common in Canada and becoming more so in the United States. Not limited to young people, they welcome anyone, although nonmembers may pay a dollar or two more than members. Sexes are segregated, and you may share a room with strangers, but the atmosphere is friendly, you have access to cooking facilities, and the price is right. Rates are usually under $10 per person. Membership information and directories are available from **Canadian Hosteling Association,** Pacific Region, 1515 Discovery St. Vancouver BC V6R 4K5 (604–224–7111); or **American Youth Hostels,** Box 37613, Washington, DC 20013 (202–783–6161).

Budget lodging can also be found at YMCA and YWCA locations. For information, contact: **YMCA,** 101 N. Wacker Dr., 14th floor, Chicago, IL 60606 (312–977–0031); **YWCA,** 726 Broadway, New York, NY 10003 (212–614–2700); YMCA, 955 Burrard St., Vancouver, BC V6Z 1Y2 (604–681–0221); or YWCA, 580 Burrard St., Vancouver, BC V6C 2K9 (604–683–2531).

Bed and Breakfasts. Bed-and-breakfast accommodations are growing in popularity in the United States and have long been common in Canada. Prices for double rooms start at under $30. Check with services such as those listed below.

The accommodations booklet available free from BC Tourism contains a list of B&B booking services for the province. A useful book, *Bed and Breakfast USA: A Guide to Guest Houses and Tourist Homes,* is available from Tourist House Associates of America, Inc., Box 355-A, Greentown, PA 18426.

Bed and Breakfast/Rocky Mountains, Box 804, Colorado Springs, CO 80901 (303–630–3433).

Bed and Breakfasts of Idaho, Box 7323, Boise, ID 83707 (208–336–5174).

RESTAURANTS. The great variety of cuisine available in what appears to be such a rugged and remote area may come as a surprise to travelers. Yet, encouraged by the great diversity of visitors to this region, restaurants of all types and price ranges have opened, with sophisticated menus and kitchens to match.

Regional cuisine centers around beef, which is often superb. The Mexican influence so common at the southern end of the Rockies is working its way north, and just about every town now boasts a Mexican restaurant, where meals are never expensive. It is possible to have a sit-down dinner for as little as $6 per person, including tip (15% is customary), at numerous good local cafes and family restaurants, and at chain restaurants like Big Boy, Denny's, Bonanza, and Village Inn.

Restaurants listed in this book fall into the price categories *Deluxe, Expensive, Moderate,* and *Inexpensive.* These vary from location to location, to reflect the fact that moderate prices for a big city or five-star resort may be expensive for less-traveled areas.

SENIOR-CITIZEN DISCOUNTS. With a "Golden Age Pass," available free from United States national parks, seniors get free admission to areas administered by the National Park Service and pay only half-price for camping. Discounts also apply at many hotels and motels, privately run campgrounds, and admission to a wide range of facilities. For information, contact organizations such as the **American Association of Retired Persons,** 3200 E. Carson, Lakewood, CA 90712 (213–496–2277); and the **National Council of Senior Citizens,** 925 15th St. NW, Washington, DC 20005 (202–347–8800).

DRINKING LAWS. Each state and province has its own laws. In some, packaged liquor is available only from official stores that may be closed one day a week, not necessarily Sunday. In others, you can buy beer and wine at grocery stores, but liquor only at an official outlet. The minimum drinking age in the United States is 21. In Canada, the legal drinking age is 18 in Alberta, and 19 in British Columbia.

TIME ZONES. The entire region, including eastern British Columbia and excluding the northern panhandle of Idaho, is in the Mountain Time Zone. This is two hours behind the Eastern Zone (New York/Toronto), one hour ahead of the Pacific Zone (Los Angeles/Vancouver), and seven hours behind Greenwich Mean Time. Between the first Sunday in April and the last Sunday in October, Daylight Saving Time is in effect, during which clocks are advanced one hour.

BUSINESS HOURS. Banking hours are similar to those in the rest of Canada and the United States, generally 9 A.M., to 3 P.M., although some have longer hours, and drive-up tellers are often open until about 4:30 P.M. Electronic tellers, open 24 hours, are found in most towns. Shops open at 9 A.M., shopping centers at 10 A.M. Most close by 5:30 P.M., but hours are extended during summer in resort areas. Most convenience marts and gas stations are open late.

SUMMER SPORTS. Hiking is natural to the Rockies and need not be strenuous (see *Hiking and Backpacking* and *Rafting* below). But there's a lot more to do in the mountains than that. Swimming is possible, if invigorating, in quite a few lakes; hot-spring pools are found throughout the region. Waterskiing, sailing, and sailboarding are practiced on large lakes and reservoirs. Many rivers and lakes are suitable for canoeing and rowing. Bicycling increases in popularity each year, especially with the growing popularity of "mountain bikes," with fat, lugged tires and extra-strong frames designed for use off the pavement, which are available for rental at outlets throughout the Rockies. Resort areas and municipalities offer golf, tennis, and other club sports.

SKIING. In a region of spectacular mountains and generous snowfall, skiing is naturally a popular sport. When you say "skiing" to a Rockies resident, you need to qualify the term: Do you mean cross country or downhill? If cross country, do you mean super-light equipment meant for groomed, silky-smooth trails, or heftier gear intended for back-country touring? If downhill, do you expect to ride a helicopter, a snow cat, or a more traditional ski lift? The opportunities are unlimited.

Many visitors will choose a full-scale resort that offers all types of skiing and other activities in one convenient package. Of the big ones, Sun Valley, Idaho, established in 1936, was the first; Aspen, Colorado, known for glitz, is arguably the most famous, and Alta and Snowbird, in Utah, have some justification for claiming the most reliable powder snow in the United States. Jackson Hole, Wyoming, with the greatest vertical rise of any ski area on the continent, has what many serious skiers consider the best mountain, while Lake Louise, in Alberta, is embedded in what may be the Rockies' grandest scenery.

In addition to the large resorts, many smaller areas offer superb skiing at lower prices, and these should not be overlooked, especially by families and people who place less value on sparkling nightlife. Cross-country fans can choose from a variety of quiet lodges and guest ranches in sometimes remote, spectacular places.

Snowmobiling is popular with some visitors, who find hundreds of miles of groomed trails prepared for their use. Ice skaters enjoy manicured rinks and big frozen lakes.

For information, contact the addresses listed under *Visitor Information* (above). Most of them will provide a winter activities guide filled with details as well as snow reports. **Colorado Ski Country USA,** 1560 Broadway, Suite 1440, Denver, CO 80202, will send you an 80-page guide to the state's ski areas for $2 (free at tourism offices in Colorado).

ROUGHING IT. To many visitors, outdoor living is the best part of a visit to the Rockies. Campgrounds in national parks, national forests, and provincial forests are basic but well-designed and beautifully situated. They offer parking, picnic tables, tent spots, drinking water, and toilets, many without running water, in exchange for a nominal user's fee. Try to arrive early in the day; because in the busy season, campgrounds fill up by early afternoon. National and provincial forest areas are less crowded. For information, call the individual parks. Maps showing their locations are available from local offices.

Private campgrounds, including national chains like Kampgrounds of America, are usually equipped with showers, laundromats, utility hookups for RVs, and other amenities. Some accept reservations if you call ahead.

Booklets listing all campgrounds are available from state and provincial tourism offices.

SPECIAL CAMPS AND SCHOOLS. A number of schools and camps offer programs in mountaineering, backpacking, natural history, photography, skiing, and horseback riding, with sessions lasting from two days to a month. These include:

Audubon Ecology Camp, Trail Lake Ranch, Dubois, WY 82513 (307–455–2457).

Yamnuska Mountain School, Box 7500 TA, Canmore, AB T0L 0M0 (403–678–4164).

Yellowstone Institute, Yellowstone National Park, WY 82190 (307–344–7749).

HUNTING AND FISHING. For current regulations, write to the following addresses:

Alberta: *Alberta Fish and Wildlife,* 9920 108th St., Edmonton, AB T5K 2C9 (403–427–3590).

British Columbia: *Ministry of Tourism,* Parliament Buildings, Victoria, BC V8V 1X4 (800–663–6000).

Colorado: *Division of Wildlife.* 6060 Broadway, Denver, CO 80216 (303–291–7227).

Idaho: *Idaho Department of Fish and Game,* 600 S. Walnut, Box 25, Boise, ID 83707 (208–334–3700).

Montana: *Montana Department of Fish, Wildlife and Parks,* 1420 East Sixth St., Helena, MT 59620 (406–444–2535).

Utah: Wildlife Resources Division, 1596 W. North Temple, Salt Lake City, UT 84116 (801–533–9333).

Wyoming: *Wyoming Game and Fish Department,* Cheyenne, WY 82002 (307–777–7728).

Fishing permits are required in all state, provincial, and national parks. Hunting is prohibited in Canadian national parks, and firearms must be unloaded, dismantled, and securely wrapped for transport.

HIKING AND BACKPACKING. Hiking trails give the most intimate view of the mountains. While some demand a high level of fitness, many provide easy strolls along crystal-clear rivers or through open wildflower meadows. Backpackers carry their camping gear, enabling them to make extended trips into remote places. In national parks and a few wilderness areas, you need camping permits for overnight trips; over most of the range, you need only to sign in at the trailhead.

Those without experience should start with short distances in supervised areas, where trails are clearly marked and someone will come looking if you don't return on time. You can get advice, guidebooks, lightweight food, equipment, and (very important) maps at mountain sports stores throughout the region; the same stores will help you with guided trips and equipment rental. Two books with useful trail descriptions are: *Adventuring in the Rockies,* by Jeremy Schmidt; and *The Canadian Rockies Trail Guide,* by Brian Patton and Bart Robinson.

RAFTING. Exhilarating rafting trips last anywhere from half a day to two weeks. You can float down a calm river watching for wildlife or crash through exciting white water. Day trips can be booked on short notice; longer trips should be booked well in advance. Rafting companies provide meals and specialized equipment—life jackets, paddles, wet suits if appropriate, etc. You can either rent tents and sleeping bags or bring your own. For information, contact state and provincial tourism offices or local Chambers of Commerce. In Colorado, write to the **Colorado River Outfitters Association,** Box 20281, Denver, CO 80220 (303–751–9274); in

Idaho, **Idaho Outfitters and Guides Association,** Box 95, Boise, ID 83701 (208–342–1468); in Montana, **Montana Outfitters and Guides Association,** Box 631, Hot Springs, MT 59845 (406–741–2811); and in Utah, **Utah Guides and Outfitters,** Box 21242, Salt Lake City, UT 34121 (801–943–6707).

STATE, PROVINCIAL, AND NATIONAL PARKS. Some of the world's most spectacular scenery is preserved in the many parks of the region. The most famous national parks are Banff and Jasper in Canada; and Glacier, Yellowstone, Grand Teton, and Rocky Mountain in the United States. In all of them, mountain scenery is exceptional, wildlife is abundant, rivers run clear, and lakes sparkle. Private concessionaires provide a complete range of amenities, from guided trips to full-service lodging. However, don't overlook the huge variety of other parks, large and small, ranging from historical monuments like Big Hole National Battlefield in Montana, to large recreational areas like Kananaskis Country, just east of Banff National Park in Alberta. Many of these lesser-known places offer the same natural splendor as the big-name parks, but without the crowds.

In visiting the big parks, try to avoid the most crowded times. These include Memorial Day, Independence Day (July 4), and Labor Day (first Monday in September) in the United States; and Dominion Day (July 1) and Labour Day (same as United States) in Canada.

Information on parks is given throughout this guide. You can also write to the **National Park Service,** Rocky Mountain Regional Office, Box 25287, Denver, CO 80225 (303–969–2000); and **Parks Canada,** Regional Information Advisor, Room 520 Box 2989, Station M, 220 4th Ave. SE, Calgary, AB T2P 3H8 (403–292–4440). State and provincial parks are listed in materials available from state travel offices (see *Sources of Information,* above).

HINTS TO THE DISABLED. A visit to the Rockies means contact with nature, even for travelers with handicaps. Numerous parks have trails negotiable by wheelchair. These include the best and most scenic places—Lake Louise in Banff National Park, Going-to-the-Sun Highway in Glacier National Park, Yellowstone's Upper Geyser Basin, Rocky Mountain's Trail Ridge Road, and hundreds of others. The *National Park Guide for the Handicapped* is available from the U.S. Government Printing Office, Washington, DC 20402. Other sources of information are *Travel Ability* by Lois Reamy, published by Macmillan Publishing Co., Inc., 101K Brown St., Riverside, NJ 08370; *Access to the World: A Travel Guide for the Handicapped,* by Louise Weiss, available from Facts on File, 460 Park Ave. South, New York, NY 10016; and *The Wheelchair Traveler* by D. R. Annand, Ball Hill Road, Milford, NH 03055, which gives valuable access information about motels, hotels, and restaurants. The Air Transport Association (ATA), 1700 New York Ave. NW, Washington, DC 20006, publishes a free pamphlet, *Air Travel for the Handicapped.* In Canada, contact the **Canadian Paraplegic Association,** 780 S.W. Marine Dr., Vancouver, BC V6P 5Y7 (604–324–3611), or **Southern District Office,** 200 Rivercrest Dr. SE, #185, Calgary, AB, T2C 2X5 (403–236–5060).

POSTAGE. Letter rates within the United States and from the U.S. to Mexico are 25¢ for the first ounce and 20¢ per additional ounce. Postcards cost 15¢. Letters from the U.S. to Canada cost 30¢ for the first ounce and 22¢ per additional ounce. Within Canada, letters and postcards both cost 38¢; to the United States, 44¢. Overseas postage costs are higher; check with a post office.

EMERGENCY TELEPHONE NUMBERS. In many U.S. and Canadian localities, the emergency number for police, fire, ambulance, and paramedic help is 911. This and other local emergency numbers are often displayed on pay phones in the United States and Canada. If in doubt, dial "0" for operator and ask to be connected.

SECURITY. Theft is on the increase in tourist areas. Vehicles seem to be the most common target, especially at remote trailheads, where thieves can be confident that the owners are miles away. Yet even at scenic overlooks, where you'll be away from the car for only a few minutes, you can return to find something missing from the front seat. Lock your car. When leaving it for more than a few minutes, put valuables in the trunk, out of sight.

THE COLORADO ROCKIES

by
CURTIS W. CASEWIT

Mr. Casewit has written many travel guides, contributed travel features to some 40 international newspapers, garnered several best book awards from the Colorado Authors' League, and taught journalism at the University of Colorado-Denver Center. He has been a contributor to Fodor's for many years.

"These mountains move us in some way which nothing else does," wrote a 19th-century Englishman. And to be sure, these powerful ranges draw millions of visitors year-round.

On a good day, you can see the Colorado Rockies from the western borders of Nebraska and Kansas. The wavy silhouette grows and sharpens as you approach Colorado; by the time you reach Denver, the Continental Divide is all glitter and sheen.

With tens of thousands of square miles of national parks and monuments, state parks, and other public land, Colorado is a tourist's state *par excellence.* Of the 54 peaks that exceed 14,000 feet in the Rockies, *all* are located in Colorado. As a result, the state has more major ski resorts than New Mexico, Utah, or Wyoming, giant resorts with up-to-date gondola cars, triple and quadruple chair lifts, mountain restaurants, nurseries, and comfortable base facilities that also welcome those who don't ski. This tourist-happy state has more guest ranches, stables, hunting guides, white-river-rafting operators than you could count; and campers, hikers, hunters, anglers, nature worshippers, bird watchers, and rock climbers all find happiness here.

From his final resting place on Lookout Mountain, Buffalo Bill looks westward over the mountains to the Continental Divide. About 150 miles south you'll see Pikes Peak, altitude 14,110 feet, where Katherine Lee Bates was inspired to write "America the Beautiful." The famous Air Force Academy and Garden of the Gods are nearby.

North, south, east, and west of Denver are well-advertised enticements. Once you've left Denver, the air is a joy to breathe. And Denver itself numbers among its own attractions the best of theaters, concert halls, museums, shopping places, historic sites, and parks.

The Quality of Life

Mountains are foremost on Coloradans' minds. According to one Denver executive, "Every day when I drive to the office, I take a fresh look. I can see Mt. Evans. How lucky I am! To live here near those mountains!" The wife of a rancher, transplanted from Oklahoma to Colorado's glowing high country, agrees. "Each time I look out of that window and spot those peaks, I must grin," she says.

On Friday afternoons and Saturday and Sunday mornings, Denver's main artery west—Interstate 70—comes alive with automobiles, pickups, and jeeps heading to the beloved Rockies for the weekend. Some of the drivers have fulfilled the Denverite's Great Dream: a mountain cabin in a nearby place like Conifer, Evergreen, or Eldorado Springs. The very, very rich buy themselves condominiums in Vail, 110 miles west of the Mile-High City. Others fly to sporty weekends in Aspen in their private planes.

In Colorado, recreation has a capital R. Some mountain-bound vehicles transport kayaks; you see them pulling horse trailers, boats, and tent campers. In winter, almost everyone seems to own a ski rack.

Colorado History

Colorado's recorded history begins in the cliffs and canyons of Mesa Verde (now a national park), where Indians later known as the Basketmakers left evidence of a civilization that originated in the eighth century A.D. and flourished until the 13th century, when it died mysteriously, the apparent victim of drought. Other Indians roamed the state's eastern plains for centuries thereafter.

In the early 18th century Spanish prospectors traveled through. They were followed a century later by English and French trappers and fur traders in search of beaver.

The U.S. government acquired much of what is now Colorado in 1803 as part of the Louisiana Purchase from France (at a mere 3½¢ an acre). This set the stage for exploration by Col. Zebulon Pike in 1806, Maj. Stephen Long in 1820, and Lt. John C. Fremont from 1842 to 1852. In 1855, the Irishman Sir George Gore showed up in Colorado with a retinue of 40 hunters and porters; his caravan eventually comprised 112 horses, 21 carts, six wagons, and a dozen hunting dogs. Sir George roamed the Colorado Rockies for many months, shooting grizzly bear, antelope, and other

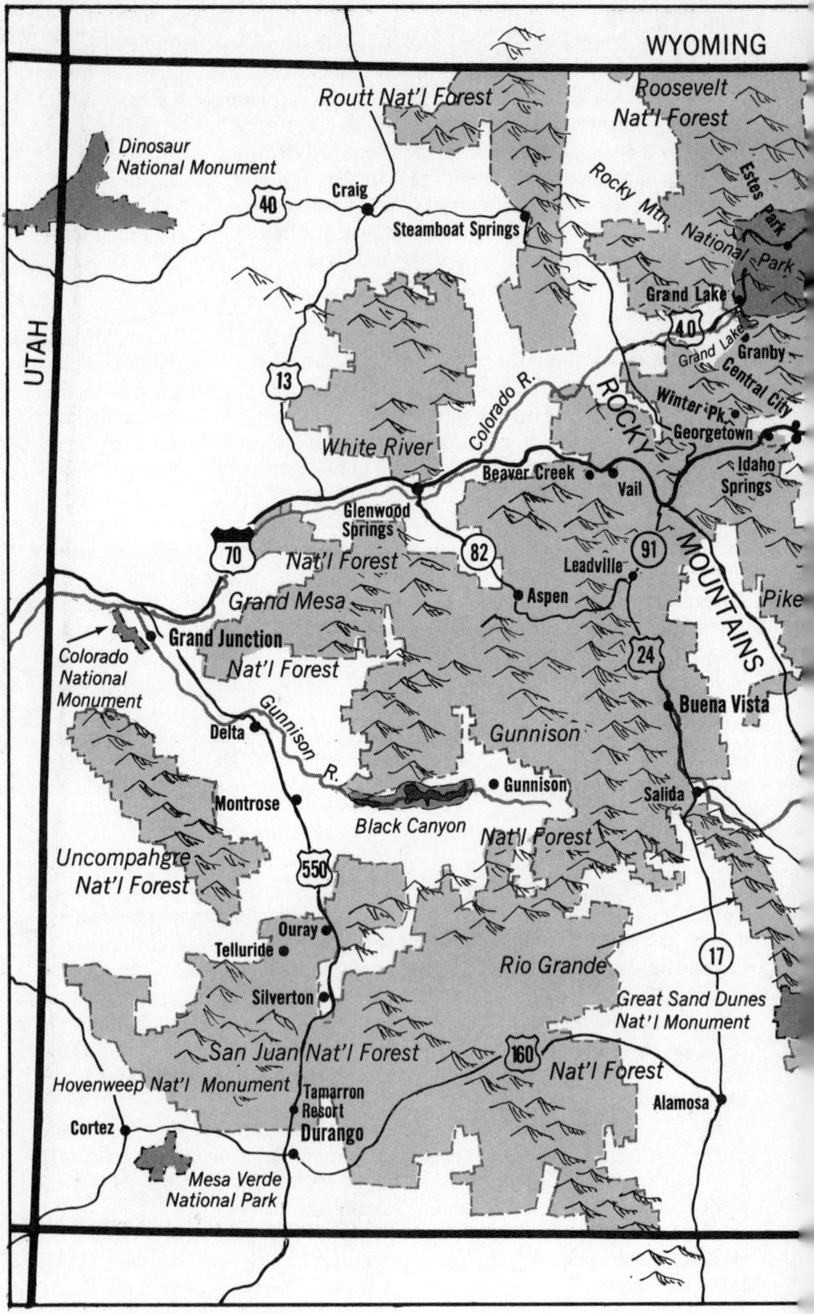
WYOMING
UTAH
Routt Nat'l Forest
Roosevelt Nat'l Forest
Dinosaur National Monument
40
Craig
Steamboat Springs
Rocky Mtn. National Park
Estes Park
Grand Lake
40
Grand Lake
Granby
Central City
Winter Pk.
Georgetown
Idaho Springs
13
Colorado R.
ROCKY MOUNTAINS
White River
Beaver Creek
Vail
Glenwood Springs
70
Nat'l Forest
82
91
Leadville
Aspen
Grand Mesa
Grand Junction
Nat'l Forest
Pike
Colorado National Monument
24
Buena Vista
Gunnison R.
Delta
Gunnison
Gunnison
Salida
Montrose
Black Canyon
Nat'l Forest
Uncompahgre Nat'l Forest
550
Ouray
Telluride
Rio Grande
17
Silverton
Great Sand Dunes Nat'l Monument
San Juan Nat'l Forest
160
Nat'l Forest
Hovenweep Nat'l Monument
Tamarron Resort
Alamosa
Cortez
Durango
Mesa Verde National Park

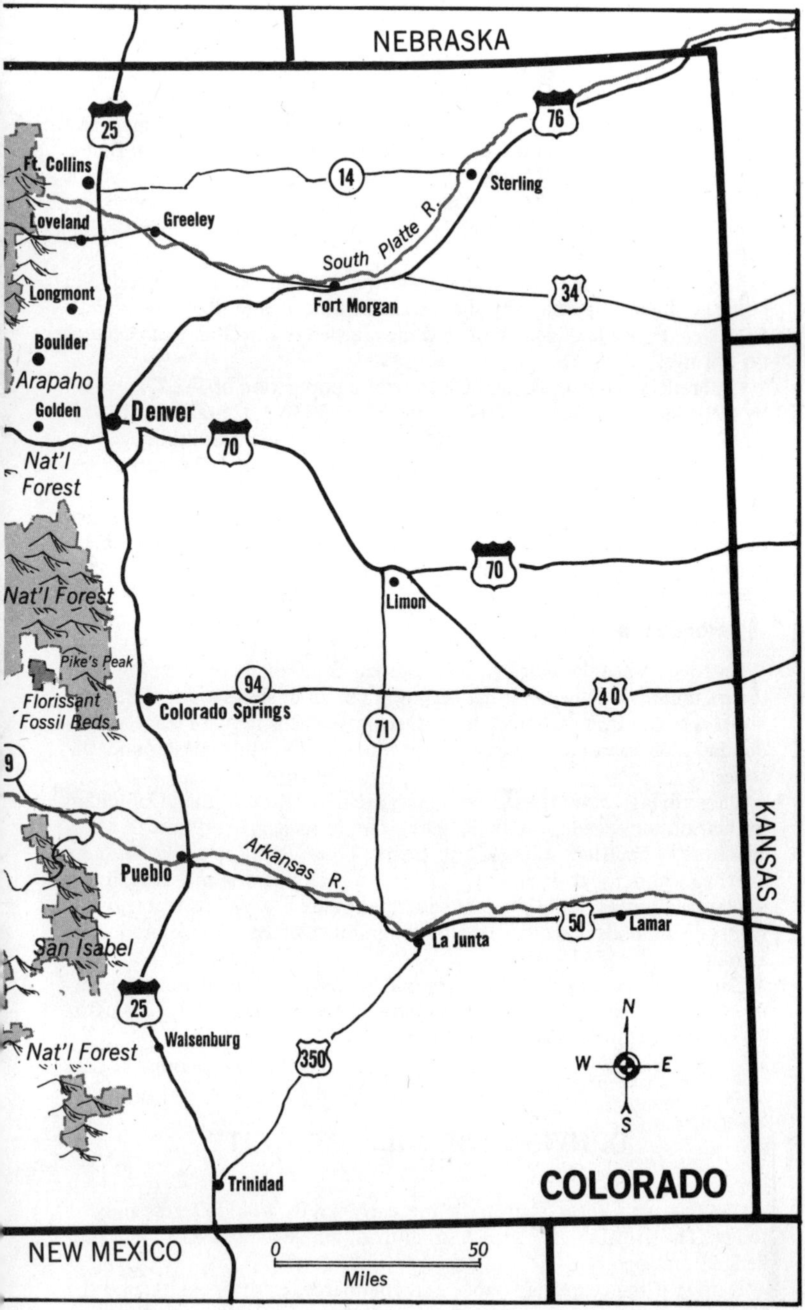
NEBRASKA
25
76
Ft. Collins
14
Sterling
Loveland
Greeley
South Platte R.
Longmont
Fort Morgan
34
Boulder
Arapaho
Golden
Denver
70
Nat'l
Forest
70
Limon
Nat'l Forest
Pike's Peak
94
Florissant
Fossil Beds
Colorado Springs
40
71
9
KANSAS
Arkansas R.
Pueblo
50
Lamar
La Junta
San Isabel
25
Walsenburg
Nat'l Forest
350
N
W
E
S
Trinidad
COLORADO
NEW MEXICO
0
50
Miles

animals for his elegant nightly dinners, complete with silver service and rare wines. The Gore Range on the west side of Colorado's Continental Divide still bears his name.

A century to the day after the signing of the Declaration of Independence, Colorado entered the Union, receiving its nickname "The Centennial State."

Spanish and Indian names alternate with those of frontiersmen and early settlers as place names in Colorado: such names as Alamosa, Buena (pronounced "byoona") Vista, Cheraw, Durango, Gunnison, Kiowa, Kit Carson, Manzanola, Meeker, Ouray, and Saguache. The mining boom contributed the names Gold Hill, Gypsum, Leadville, Silverton, and Telluride.

The word Colorado itself came from the Spanish word for "ruddy," a choice influenced perhaps by the terrain of what is now Red Rocks Park near Denver, Redcliff near Vail, and the Garden of the Gods near Colorado Springs.

Colorado's first census, in 1860, showed a population of 342,770, which by 1910 had increased to 800,000, and by 1950 to 1,325,000. By 1980 it was 2,889,000, and the current figures put it just over three million. Colorado is the nation's eighth largest state in area, with 104,247 square miles, but only the 27th largest in terms of population.

If the mountains divide the state into western mountains and eastern plains, the weather divides it less distinctly into pleasant summers, brisk autumns, uneven winters, and balmy springs.

Coloradans

As for the people, you can characterize Coloradans by their love for the mountains, but beyond that they don't seem to share many traits, unless it is a consuming interest in the Denver Broncos football team, whose Sunday-afternoon games attract a prodigious TV audience around the state.

Those living out on the eastern plains are more Kansan than Coloradan in their outlook, and those living along the Front Range or in its foothills are more urban than mountain in theirs. Those living in the mountains are the most outdoor-oriented, interested in such pursuits as fishing, hunting, horsemanship, and skiing. In general they are hearty, hospitable types, whose livelihoods are often tied to the number of visitors Colorado can attract.

During the past two decades Coloradans have become increasingly international: French symphony conductors, Swiss pastry chefs, and Austrian ski instructors are not out of place here.

DENVER: THE MILE-HIGH CITY

Anyone who knew Denver in the early 1970s wouldn't recognize it today. The growing city with a small-town ambience has become a full-fledged metropolis.

Denver is the center of finance and commerce for the Rockies, and the city's population has grown with arrivals from New York, Dallas, San

Francisco, and other cities. The new families have reclaimed dilapidated downtown neighborhoods, such as historic Capitol Hill, and restored the old brick and frame homes.

The new Denverites have brought with them their favorite shopping, dining, and entertainment from around the world. City stores offer wares from antique clothing to Oriental jade, computers, even Greek and Thai groceries. Lovers of haute cuisine will find their pleasure in scores of restaurants, such as the award-winning Chateau Pyrenees or the Normandy Restaurant Français, which rival standards set by prestigious restaurants of both U.S. coasts.

Denver's ethnic cuisine reflects its varied populace, and there are now restaurants with authentic French, German, Swiss, Italian, Spanish, Greek, Mexican, and assorted Oriental cooking. You can even find Afghan and Moroccan places.

Thanks to a more and more sophisticated public, the Colorado state capital also excels in its cultural life. The Denver Symphony and the Denver Center Theater Company are at home in ultramodern performance halls in the heart of downtown. The Denver Art Museum regularly hosts top international exhibits and foreign motion pictures garner large audiences.

The Heart of Downtown Denver

You will understand Denver's layout best by keeping in mind that there are two major thoroughfares: Broadway, which runs north and south; and Colfax, which runs east and west. East of Broadway is East Colfax, which leads all the way to Aurora, a suburb. West Colfax travels west to Lakewood and Golden. South Broadway, meanwhile, allows you to reach the suburbs of Englewood and Littleton. Street names run in alphabetical order west of South Broadway and east of Colorado Boulevard.

In the heart of downtown Denver, thoroughfares run diagonally to the normal grid. Numbered streets are in this section; the rest of the city has numbered avenues (17th St., for instance, is immediately downtown—17th Ave. is not).

You can pick up assorted pamphlets from the city's Visitors Bureau at 225 W. Colfax, at the edge of the Civic Center complex downtown. The center is directly across the street from City Hall (distinguishable by the clock tower and chimes), which Denverites call the City and County Building.

The Civic Center Area

The U.S. Mint, 320 West Colfax, is across from the Visitors Bureau. More than five billion coins are stamped here each year. The mint is open for weekday tours all year, except the last two weeks in June (usually until July 5) when it closes for inventory. The second-largest cache of gold bullion is on display, too. Tourists often purchase souvenir coin sets and other collectors' items.

The mint stands on the west side of Denver's Civic Center, a three-block stretch of lawns and gardens. It's the inner-city oasis where office workers and tourists picnic, stroll, or just rest. The area is rich in statuary.

The Civic Center was inspired by the Mall in Washington, D.C., and leads visitors to the Capitol Building, modeled after the nation's Capitol.

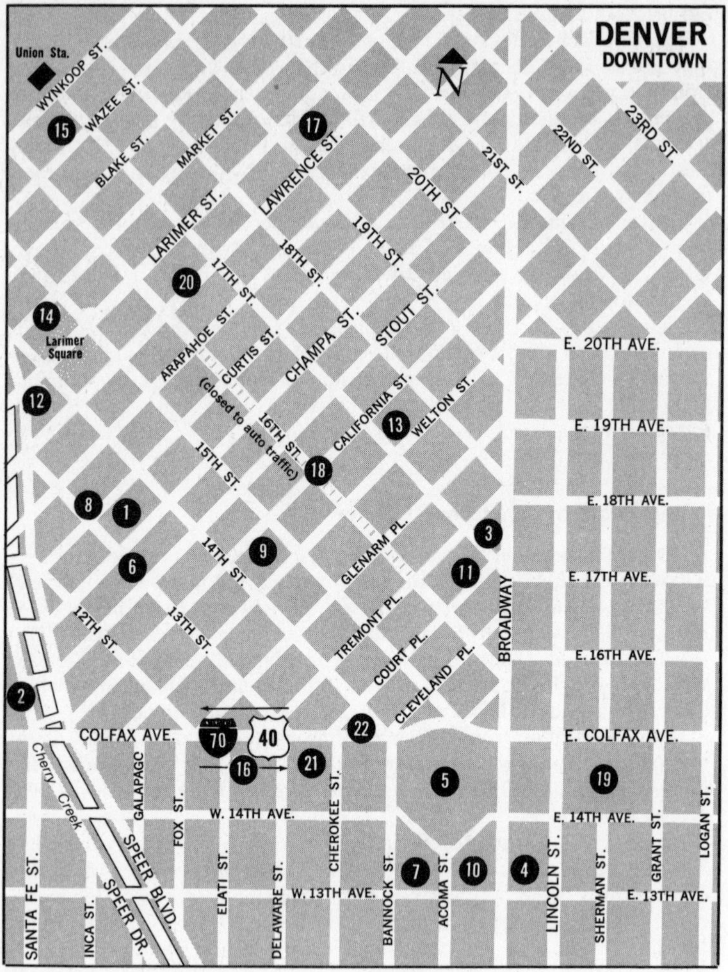

Points of Interest

1) Auditorium Arena & Theater
2) Auraria Campus
3) Brown Palace Hotel
4) Colorado History Museum
5) Civic Center
6) Convention Center, Currigan Hall
7) Denver Art Museum
8) Denver Center for the Performing Arts
9) Denver Post Building
10) Denver Public Library/Main
11) Denver Radisson Hotel
12) The Tivoli
13) Hyatt Regency Denver
14) Larimer Square
15) The Oxford-Alexis Hotel
16) Rocky Mountain News Building
17) Sakura Square
18) Sixteenth St. Mall
19) State Capitol
20) Tabor Center Shopping Mall and Westin Hotel Complex
21) U.S. Mint
22) Visitor's Bureau

The 160-room building was completed in 1894, with gold leaf hammered from Colorado ore covering the dome. From the balcony just below, visitors can see a 150-mile panorama of the Rockies to the west.

The Denver Art Museum towers behind the library. You won't overlook the angular gray-tiled building with windows in seemingly random sizes and shapes. The exhibits span cultures as well as eras: African, Oriental, pre-Columbian, and early American, with one or two masterpieces by Rembrandt, Picasso, Matisse, Renoir, Rubens, and others. There's also a good collection of contemporary art, textiles, costumes, pottery, jewelry, period rooms, and antique furniture. The Native American exhibit is excellent.

Two blocks away at 13th and Broadway is the Colorado History Museum, which houses treasures collected by the Colorado Historical Society. Artifacts and photos from Denver's early life, ancient Mesa Verde Indian pieces, and a fascinating diorama of Denver as it was in 1860 are among the exhibits.

The Denver Public Library is across from the History Museum at 1357 Broadway. Of special interest is the fourth-floor Western History Department.

Not-to-Miss Downtown Sights

The Buckhorn Exchange at 1000 Osage Street is worth a visit just before lunchtime. Several generations have enriched this museum-*cum*-dining emporium, whose contents include hundreds of historic photos (some of the Tabors, for instance, a local mining family whose rags-to-riches story is part of local lore), antique western guns, trophies, antlers of every description, stuffed animals, Indian mementos, and paintings. Admission is free.

One block behind the Visitors Bureau is the Denver Firefighters Museum at 1326 Tremont Place. Old hand pumps, uniforms, photos, and other items are housed in Fire House No. 1, built in 1909. Nearby, Currigan Exhibition Hall, at 14th and Champa, hosts many shows, conventions, and festivals.

The highlight of downtown Denver sightseeing is Larimer Square, on Larimer Street between 14th and 15th. This is the city's original business block. Denver had abandoned lower Larimer Street in the early 1900s, leaving it to vagrants and disrepair, until a local preservation group rescued the buildings and restored them as Denver's first Historic District. Here are all manner of shops and exotica, including bistros, fine restaurants, silversmiths, and leatherworkers' studios. Consider lunching in the charming old dining room of the nearby Oxford-Alexis Hotel.

Another outstanding downtown shopping and strolling spot is the 16th Street Mall, a mile-long section closed to traffic. Browse, listen to the street musicians, try one of the excellent restaurants, or visit the ultramodern Tabor Center, which features over 70 retailers and restaurants. A free shuttle bus runs the length of the mall.

Financial District

The heart of Denver's business community is 17th Street, where *Fortune* 500 companies occupy sleek offices in towers of glass, chrome, and steel.

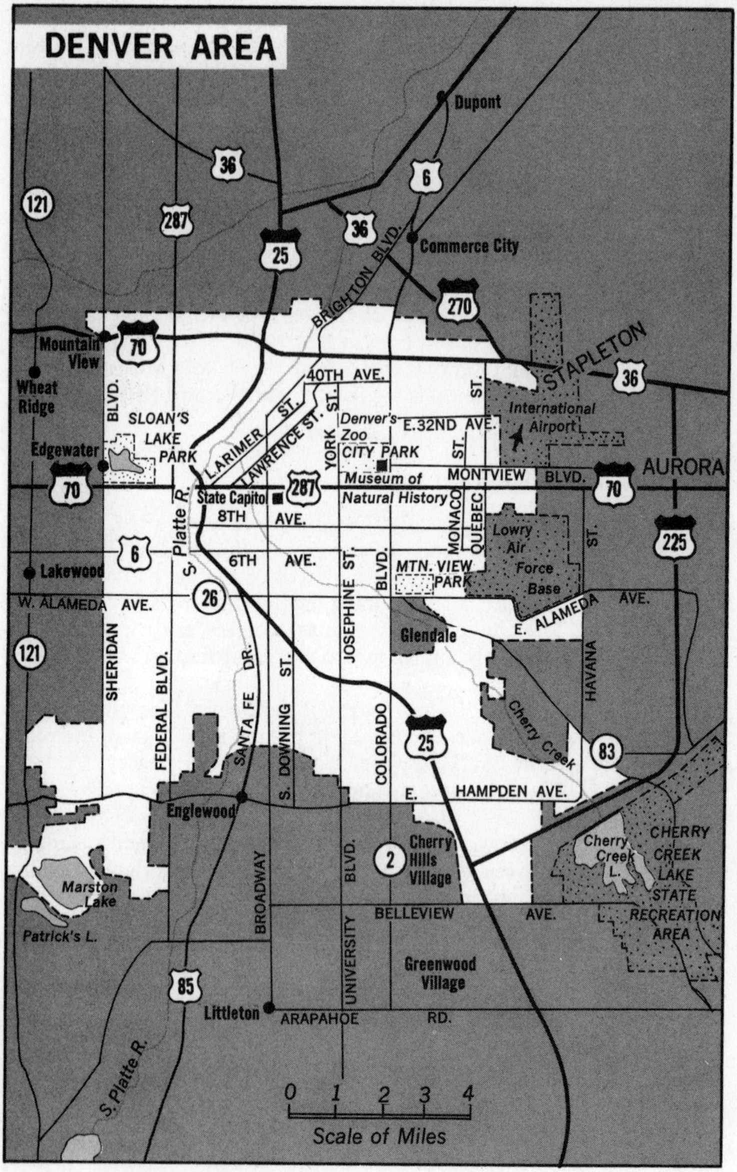
DENVER AREA
Dupont
36
6
121
287
36
25
Commerce City
BRIGHTON BLVD.
270
Mountain View
70
STAPLETON
36
Wheat Ridge
BLVD.
40TH AVE.
ST.
International Airport
SLOAN'S LAKE PARK
LARIMER ST.
LAWRENCE ST.
YORK ST.
Denver's Zoo
E.32ND AVE.
Edgewater
CITY PARK
ST.
70
AURORA
Museum of Natural History
MONTVIEW BLVD.
70
S. Platte R.
State Capitol
287
8TH AVE.
MONACO
QUEBEC
Lowry Air Force Base
ST.
225
6
6TH AVE.
Lakewood
MTN. VIEW PARK
W. ALAMEDA AVE.
26
E. ALAMEDA AVE.
121
SHERIDAN
FEDERAL BLVD.
SANTA FE DR.
S. DOWNING ST.
JOSEPHINE ST.
COLORADO BLVD.
Glendale
HAVANA
Cherry Creek
25
83
E. HAMPDEN AVE.
Englewood
Cherry Hills Village
2
CHERRY CREEK LAKE STATE RECREATION AREA
Cherry Creek L.
Marston Lake
Patrick's L.
BROADWAY
UNIVERSITY BLVD.
BELLEVIEW AVE.
Greenwood Village
85
Littleton
ARAPAHOE RD.
S. Platte R.
0 1 2 3 4
Scale of Miles

Although the oil business is no longer booming in Denver, there is no shortage of skyscrapers built with oil money, or of men and women in various fields carrying on Denver's commercial tradition.

Just west of Speer Boulevard is the sleek Auraria Higher Education Center. Metro State College, Denver Community College, and the University of Colorado all use the ultramodern educational village. Tucked behind the classroom buildings, Ninth Street Historic Park is a block of Victorian working-class houses in one of Denver's oldest neighborhoods, now restored as college offices.

The finely restored Tivoli Denver Mall Complex at Larimer and 10th streets is an ornate white building with a distinctive blue roof. This one-time brewery is now a Denver landmark, featuring three atrium levels of elegant shops and restaurants. There are also 12 small movie theaters and daily live entertainment. You'll find plenty of parking nearby.

Across the Platte River on 15th Street is the Forney Transportation Museum, filled with vintage vehicles, "pufferbellies," historic railroad cars, old-time airplanes, and more.

A free trolley shuttle makes a loop downtown, stopping at Lawrence Street, Larimer Square, the 16th Street Mall, and 17th Street.

East of Downtown

The Denver Botanic Gardens, at 909 York Street, offer seasonal displays, an alpine house, and a two-acre Japanese garden. The bubble-shaped conservatory shelters a tropical/subtropical forest with streams, paths, and foot bridges.

City Park, northeast of the Botanic Gardens along 17th Avenue, between York Street and Colorado Boulevard, is the centerpiece of Denver's 25,000-acre city park system, with 640 acres for recreation and learning. Start at the Museum of Natural History, which has many floors of dinosaurs, Indian artifacts, insects, birds, and animals from around the world. Don't miss the moose and elk displays and the whale exhibit. Visitors can rent headphones that plug into outlets at each display for brief talks. The Gates Planetarium, attached to the Museum, offers laser-light concerts projected onto an overhead 50-foot dome, while the audience watches from reclining chairs. The complex is also home to the Imax Theater, with its four-and-a-half-story screen.

A short walk west takes you to the Denver Zoological Gardens, where several thousand animals are housed in their native habitats. The Children's Zoo sports a monkey island and cavorting seals. There are also an exciting polar bear exhibit, arctic wolves in natural habitat, and a renowned walk-through aviary.

PRACTICAL INFORMATION FOR DENVER

HOW TO GET THERE. Most airlines, bus companies, and trains serve this western metropolis, offering a large number of choices and price ranges. Generally, if you arrive from far away, flying is the least expensive way to go. For shorter trips and travel within the state, buses have the edge.

By air. Denver's *Stapleton Airport,* the fourth-busiest in the world, is served by most major carriers. Among these are: *American, Continental, Delta, TWA, United,* and *USAir. American West Airlines* has expanded its Denver hub, as has *Continental.* Regional lines include *Air Midwest, Chicago Air,* and *Northwest.* Among commuter carriers are *Continental Express, Mesa Airlines,* and *United Express.*

Numerous airlines offer discount fares with certain restrictions. For example, Continental Airlines offers lower fares during off-peak hours and during light travel periods. Other carriers offer Super-Saver tickets. These must be booked in advance and may be nonrefundable and restrict the length of stay and departure/arrival dates. These special rates change almost weekly, so consult your travel agent for the best deals.

By bus. *Greyhound* serves Colorado and has a terminal in downtown Denver. Discounts are available for children.

By train. *Amtrak* offers service from Chicago, San Francisco, Seattle, Portland, and Los Angeles. Amtrak also serves Glenwood Springs, Winter Park, Granby, Grand Junction, and other Colorado towns.

By car. Main highways into Denver are I–25 from Wyoming in the north and New Mexico in the south; I–70 from Utah in the west and Kansas in the east; and I–80S from Nebraska in the northeast.

TOURIST INFORMATION. *Denver Metro Convention and Visitors Bureau,* 225 W. Colfax Ave., Denver 80202 (303–892–1112), provides an official *Visitors' Guide* that lists area attractions, events, shopping areas, and provides a map. Open Mon.–Fri. 8 A.M.–5 P.M., Sat. 9 A.M.–1 P.M.; Saturdays until 5 P.M. in summer.

TELEPHONES. The area codes for Colorado are 303 (Northern Region) and 719 (Southern Region). Directory assistance in Denver is 1–411; from outside the city dial 303–555–1212. Pay phones require 20¢ or 25¢.

Emergency telephone numbers. In metropolitan Denver, dial either 911 or 0 for *ambulance, fire,* or *police.* The *State Patrol* number is 239–4501. The *Poison Control Hotline* can be reached at 629–1123. For *road conditions,* phone 639–1111 (Denver area) or 639–1234 (statewide).

ACCOMMODATIONS in Denver range from the world-famous Brown Palace, through its sister lodgings in the deluxe and expensive categories, on to the many fine hotels scattered along highways and side streets. Many of the latter are connected to national chain operations. Cost figures here are generally for the minimum- or moderate-priced rooms, unless a range is indicated. Listings are in order of price category.

The price categories in this section, for double occupancy, are as follows: *Deluxe,* \$100–\$250; *Expensive,* \$60–\$99; *Moderate,* \$45–\$60; and *Inexpensive,* under \$19–\$45. All motels and hotels accept major credit cards unless otherwise indicated.

Deluxe

Best Western Regency. 3900 Elati St., 80216 (458–0808 or 800–528–1234). I-25 at W. 38th Ave. Large hotel in north Denver, popular for conventions. Two pools, saunas, exercise rooms, barber and beauty shops, restaurants, and cocktail lounge.

Brown Palace. 321 17th St., 80202 (297–3111). Downtown. One of the world's well-known hotels, with good service, 500 guest rooms, and tasteful decoration. Elegant dining in the *Palace Arms* or *Ellyngton's,* relaxed meals in the *Ship Tavern,* where prime rib reigns. Beauty and barber shops, florist, drugstore.

The Burnsley. 1000 Grant St., 80203 (830–1000). Distinguished small hotel close to downtown and state capitol. Some penthouse suites and kitchenettes. Panoramic views. Music, entertainment. Favored by upper-echelon business executives.

Cambridge Club Hotel. 1560 Sherman, 80203 (831–1252). Luxurious one- and two-bedroom suites are available here, with Continental breakfast, 24-hour room service, health club privileges. Appeals to business travelers.

Clarion Denver Airport. 3203 Quebec, 80207 (800–325–6064). At airport. A well-run 579-room motel with large indoor pool, sauna, and outstanding dining facilities. Complimentary airport limousine.

Denver Marriott City Center. 1701 California, 80202 (297–1300 or 800–228–9290). Centrally located 42-story 612-room hotel, with 42 luxury suites, in downtown financial center. Indoor pool. Ballrooms. Restaurants and bars. Ideal for conventions.

Denver Radisson Hotel. 1550 Court Pl., 80202 (893–3333 or 800–333–3333). Downtown. A 750-room hotel catering to conventions. Five dining areas and handsome cocktail lounge. Heated pools, saunas, radios, barber and beauty shops, airline counters, drugstore; airport bus available.

Hyatt Regency Denver. 1750 Welton, 80202 (295–1700 or 800–233–1234). Downtown Denver's elegant $44-million 550-room convention hotel. Formerly the Fairmont. All amenities. *Marquis* dining room. Sunday brunches. 24-hour *McGuire's* restaurant and cocktail lounge. Rooftop pool, "sky court" tennis.

Loews Giorgio Hotel. 4150 E. Mississippi, 80222 (782–9300 or 800–223–0888). This skyscraper hotel has 200 rooms and 20 suites, all with Italian country villa decor. Complimentary breakfast is featured, and there are superb restaurants. The nearby Cherry Creek Sporting Club is available for use. Convention facilities are available.

The Oxford-Alexis Hotel. 1600 17th St., 80202 (628–5400). Downtown. Slick $8-million renovation of a small, grand 82-room hotel near Union Station. Restaurant, bar, entertainment. Charming Sunday brunches.

Sheraton Denver Tech Center. 4900 DTC Parkway, 80237 (779–1100 or 800–325–3535). 640 rooms at Tech Center, 12 miles southeast of downtown Denver. Built in 1980. Conference and banquet facilities, shops, health club.

Westin Hotel. Denver Tabor Center, 1672 Lawrence St., 80202 (572–9100 or 800–228–3000). Luxurious 430-room 19-story hotel with rooftop pool. Seventy shops, plus access to mall meeting facilities.

Writer's Manor. 1730 S. Colorado Blvd., 80222 (756–8877 or 800–525–8072). Southeast Denver. A spacious 350-room motel with two heated pools, sauna. *Churchill* gourmet restaurant, coffee shops, and bars.

Expensive

Best Western Inn at the Mart. 401 E. 58th Ave., 80216 (297–1717 or 800–528–1234). I-25, Exit 215. Popular with sales reps. Shops, cafes, post office on premises. Convention site.

Compri-Lakewood. 137 Union Blvd., 80228 (969–9900 or 800–426–6777). Cable TV, heated pool, health club. Free breakfast, late snacks, and beverages. Meeting facilities.

The Doubletree Hotel at Heather Ridge Country Club. 13696 E. Iliff, 80014 (337–2800). This large hotel has many amenities, including golf, tennis, health club. Handicapped facilities, nonsmoking rooms. Meeting rooms.

Embassy Suites Denver Southeast. 7525 E. Hampden Ave., 80231 (696–6644 or 800–525–3585). This is an outstanding hotel for the discriminating, with 208 well-appointed suites. Free breakfast, airport transportation.

Holiday Inn Downtown. 1450 Glenarm Pl., 80202 (573–1450 or 800–423–5128). 400-room hotel in excellent downtown location. Free indoor parking.

Holiday Inn Southeast. 9009 E. Arapahoe Rd., Englewood, 80112 (790–1421). At Denver Tech Center, I-25. Suites available. Indoor pool, sauna, exercise room, steam room. Live entertainment and dancing Tues.-Sat. Dining room, cocktail lounge, and coffee shop. Good location south of city.

Howard Johnson South Motor Lodge. 6300 E. Hampden Ave., 80222 (758–2211 or 800–654–2000). Exit 201, I-25 South. Modern chain motel. Restaurant, cocktail lounge, hot tubs, meeting and banquet facilities.

Raffles Hotel. 3200 S. Parker Rd., Aurora, 80014 (695–1700). I-225 and S. Parker Rd. Large, comfortable, well-designed hostelry with all amenities, including indoor jogging track. Large convention area with ballroom. Good restaurants. Famous for Sunday brunch.

Ramada Inn Foothills. 11595 W. Sixth Ave., Lakewood 80215 (238–7751 or 800–2–RAMADA). Attractive establishment at Sixth Ave. and Simms, on the way to the ski areas. Pool and sauna. Elegant lobby, plush rooms.

Rodeway Inn. 4590 Quebec, 80216 (320–0260 or 800–228–2000). Five minutes from Stapleton International Airport, courtesy car provided. Special rooms offer private steam bath, recliner chairs, office-size work desks. *Bijou Revue* restaurant and lounge. Entertainment.

Sheraton Denver Airport. 3535 Quebec, 80207 (333–7711 or 800–325–3535). At Stapleton International Airport. This modern hotel offers heated indoor pool, sauna, health club, restaurant, and cocktail lounge. Free airport bus.

The Warwick Denver. 1776 Grant St., 80203 (861–2000). Former Governor's Court Hotel.). Near downtown. Within walking distance of museums, the Denver Mall, and the city's business section.

Moderate

Broadway Plaza Motel. 1111 Broadway, 80203 (893–3501). Four blocks south of State Capitol. 40 rooms. Rooftop sun deck, free coffee. Cafes nearby.

Colburn Hotel. 980 Grant St., 80203 (837–1261). Close to downtown area. All rooms with baths. Some kitchenettes and facilities for permanent guests. *Charlie Brown's* dining room, cocktail lounge.

Continental Inn Denver. 2601 Zuni St., 80211 (433–6677 or 800–525–8110; from Colorado, 800–332–8767). Convenient to town at Valley Hwy. and N. Speer Blvd. Large heated pool, free coffee, dining room, coffee shop, cocktail lounge, dancing. Nicely renovated.

Days Inn. 1680 Colorado Blvd., 80222 (691–2223 or 800–633–1414). This chain has standard but comfortable rooms with free HBO, indoor pool, and covered parking. Special weekend rates, seniors' discount.

Holiday Chalet. East Colfax at High St., 80218 (321–9975). Clean, comfortable apartment hotel in eastern section of the city.

Kipling Inn. 715 Kipling St., Lakewood, 80215 (232–5000). 9½ miles southwest, off Route 6. Heated pool, playground, restaurant, cocktail lounge. Some units have kitchens.

La Quinta. 3975 Peoria, 80239 (371–5640 or 800–531–5900). Chain motel with 112 rooms, not far from airport. *Denny's Cafe.* A good value.

Sands Motel. 13388 E. Colfax, Aurora, 80011 (366–3581). Located across from Fitzsimmons Hospital, near Lowry and Buckley. Water beds available. Some units have kitchens.

Inexpensive

American Family Lodge—North. 5888 Broadway, 80216 (296–3100). Standard motel four miles north at I-25 exit 215, near Merchandise Mart.

American Family Lodge—West. 4735 Kipling St., Wheat Ridge, 80033 (423–0800). Eight miles west on I-70 Exit 65. Heated pool. 24-hour cafe opposite.

Anchor Motel. 2323 S. Broadway, 80210 (744–3281). Four miles south on State 87. Small motel, free coffee, pets allowed, sun deck. 24-hour cafe nearby. Good value.

Comfort Inn-Airport. 7201 E. 36th Ave., 80207 (393–7666 or 800–228–5150). Convenient but standard airport motel offers free breakfast, exercise room, and a pool.

Franklin House. 1620 Franklin St., 80218 (331–9106). This comfortable, European-style guest house is in east Denver, 15 walking minutes from downtown.

Motel Six. 480 Wadsworth Blvd., 80226 (232–4924). West Denver. Bargain rates for simple, clean rooms. Fills up early in the day. En route to mountains.

Rosedale Motel. 3901 Elati, 80216 (433–8345). I-25 at 38th Ave. in west Denver. A modest motel with clean rooms.

Six Pence Inn. 9920 W. 49th, Wheat Ridge, 80033 (424–0658). At I-70 and Kipling. Across from *Furr's Cafeteria* and *Denny's.*

BED AND BREAKFASTS. Affectionately known as B & B's, these guest homes provide the personal touch in accommodations and are becoming more popular in the United States every year. A B & B offers the warmth of sharing someone's house in rooms set aside for that purpose, a delightful home-cooked breakfast, and the chance to get to know a local family. Rooms are infinitely varied—you may have to head down the hall to the bathroom, but you will often find antique furniture and fresh flowers on your bedside table. For a directory of guest homes in Denver send $4 to *Bed & Breakfast Colorado,* Box 12206, Boulder [illegible]. This service will assist you with reservations. Rates for doubles run $50–$150.

Here is a sampling of Denver's bed-and-breakfast establishments:

Queen Anne Inn. 2147 Tremont Pl., 80205 (296–6666). This elegant, three-story 1879 home is near downtown. The inn offers 10 rooms with varying decor. Afternoon tea and wine is served.

Victoria Oaks. 1575 Race St., 80206 (355–1818). A Victorian-style residence, with nine rooms (some with shared baths), that serves free breakfast and afternoon tea.

YMCAS AND HOSTELS. Located in most major cities, these provide basic, economical lodging.

YMCA. 25 E. 16th Ave., Denver, 80202 (861–8300). Downtown. Small coffee shop in lobby; lobby open 24 hours. Check-in is 11 A.M.–10 P.M. on a first-come, first-serve basis. Rooms are small but clean and have telephones. Separate floor for women. Doubles with bath are $31.25.

Denver International Youth Hostel, 630 E. 16th Ave., Denver, CO 80206 (832–9996). No limit on stay. Dormitory-style, communal kitchen, any age welcome. Bring sleeping bag or rent linens. Men and women on separate floors. Rates are $6. Membership not required. Reservations with half deposit.

RESTAURANTS. The 1,700 restaurants in the Denver metropolitan area are often underestimated, but offer every type of fare from haute cuisine to the simplest cowboy chow. Foreign restaurants proliferate. Western steak houses are abundant, and you can get excellent mountain trout practically anywhere.

While many excellent restaurants go in for international cuisine, those serving steak and lobster are prevalent and popular. Most good restaurants prefer that you make dinner reservations. Dress is usually casual, and ties are rarely required. Prices listed here are for medium-priced meals on an establishment's menu, unless a range is indicated. For other worthwhile restaurants, check hotel listings. Restaurants are listed according to price category.

Restaurant categories are: *Deluxe,* $55 and up; *Expensive,* $30–$55; *Moderate,* $18–$30; and *Inexpensive,* under $18. These prices are for two meals, including appetizer and soup or salad, but exclude drinks and tips. All restaurants listed accept major credit cards unless otherwise noted.

American and Western

Deluxe

Adirondacks. 901 Larimer (573–8900). Bright California import, featuring southwestern cuisine. Stylish decor, fine linens and glassware. Views of Denver skyline. A favorite with business people. Sun. brunch.

Buckhorn Exchange. 1000 Osage St. (534–9505). A Denver institution since 1893. Friendly, informal, truly Western eatery. Famous bean soup and steaks of several sizes; also buffalo meat, quail, and trout. Nightly specials. Sociable bar. Hundreds of pictures, animal heads, and stuffed creatures decorate the walls.

Ellyngton's. Brown Palace Hotel, 17th and Tremont (297–3111). Excellent trout and salmon, filet mignon, mixed grill, pork chops. Exquisite table linens and silverware. Dancing Fri. and Sat. Also in the hotel, the **Palace Arms** is the choice of Denver's old guard. Known for local steaks.

McGuire's. At the Hyatt Regency Hotel, 18th and Welton (295–5831). Snazzy coffee shop with long hours. Chicken in the pot, enchiladas, Cajun specialties, and even a diet menu.

Mostly Seafood. 303–16th St. (892–5999) and 2223 S. Monaco Pkwy. (756–5541). A seafood shop and restaurant, with long list of fresh catches, rich desserts, and delicious bread pudding. Takeout and catering are available.

Wellshire Inn. 3333 S. Colorado Blvd. (759–3333). Elaborate menu served against a baronial manor backdrop in southeast Denver. Overlooks golf course. Specialties include fresh salmon, spinach salad, veal Verona, chicken with almonds, Cantonese duck, elegant desserts. Fabulous Sun. brunch. Recommended.

Moderate

Apple Tree Shanty. 8710 E. Colfax (333–3223). Pit-prepared ribs a house specialty. Sizable dessert menu. Waitresses in Dutch-style garb. No reservations.

Healthy Habits. 865 S. Colorado Blvd. (733–2105). The leading health food buffet offers 80 salads and a pasta bar, but no meat. Open 10:30 AM–10 P.M. No smoking, no tips. Beer and wine available.

North Woods Inn. 6115 S. Santa Fe Dr., 12 miles southwest on U.S. 85 in Littleton (794–2112). This locally popular restaurant serves steak, beef stew, and logging-camp food with home-baked sourdough bread. Decor is north woods. Good value for big eaters.

Tabor Grill. Westin Hotel. 1672 Lawrence St., Tabor Center (572–9100). This lively eatery has good chops, chicken, and fresh fish. Bar. Open seven days.

White Fence Farm. 6263 W. Jewell Ave., between S. Sheridan and Wadsworth blvds. (935–5945). In a meadow en route to mountains. Great American food with a southern accent—ham, turkey, chicken, ribs—prepared Colonial style and served by waitresses in historic dress. Liquor. Excellent quality food. Mostly local clientele. Dinner only.

Inexpensive

Furr's. 3215 S. Wadsworth, Lakewood (989–9188). Clean and modern cafeteria. No credit cards.

King's Table Buffet. 12600 E. Colfax (341–5363). All-you-can-eat buffet at this place, which is popular with seniors. No liquor.

Wyatt's Cafeteria. W. Alameda and Wadsworth (934–5663). Prettily presented quality foods at reasonable prices. No liquor.

French and Continental

Deluxe

The Augusta Room. Westin Hotel, 1672 Lawrence (572–9100). One of Denver's most elegant gourmet outposts. Good service; dishes prepared with an eye for color. Smoked sturgeon, pheasant mousse, poached salmon, Long Island duckling.

Churchill's. Writers' Manor, 1730 S. Colorado Blvd. (756–8877). Candlelit and cosmopolitan. Fresh fish daily. European chef prepares fine veal, Cornish game hen, lamb chops. One of Denver's best with superb service.

Deluxe to Expensive.

Normandy Restaurant Français. 1515 Madison (321–3311). A cozy east Denver restaurant with a fine reputation among local gourmets. Interesting appetizers include smoked trout, escargots, duck terrine, and mousseline Neptune. Frogs' legs, veal entrees and coq au Beaujolais. Fresh fish daily; roast goose at Christmas. Wine cellar with many vintages, including rare imports. Large selection of European desserts. Several private rooms. Under longtime ownership-supervision of M. and Mme. Gerstlè.

Quorum. 233 East Colfax Ave. (861–8686). Across from the state capitol, an elegant favorite with local aficionados and politicos. Rack of lamb, sweetbreads, steak Diana, duckling "Elle," fresh scallops, Dover sole, chateaubriand. For smaller appetites, the "light menu" includes marinated chicken, braised lamb, fresh fish, duckling strips. Multilingual owner/personality Pierre Wolfe is always on hand. Excellent choice for European visitors. Open for lunch.

Tante Louise. 4900 E. Colfax (355–4488). Creative European-style east Denver restaurant. Excellent veal and lamb shanks. Splendid appetizers such as pâtés, oysters, mussels; out-of-the-ordinary desserts; house wines. Intimate setting.

Inexpensive

Le Central. 112 E. Eighth Ave. (863–8094). Genuine French restaurant at fair prices; good wine list. Extremely busy. No credit cards.

German and Swiss

Moderate

Gasthaus Ridgeview. 4465 Garrison, Wheat Ridge (424–2161). Genuine German offerings for hungry clientele. Sauerbraten, schnitzel, *Kassler, Rindsrouladen,* milk-fed veal dishes, goose (in December), duckling, strudel. Peter Hellerman, proprietor and chef, is from Germany; hostess Elizabeth Hellerman is from Switzerland. Imported beers. Outdoor area for lunch.

Inexpensive

Das Essen Haus. Belmar, 1050 S. Wadsworth Blvd., Lakewood (936–7864). American version of German restaurant. Modest, bright, clean. No liquor.

Swiss Bells Restaurant. 7340 W. 38th Ave., Wheat Ridge (421–6622). Ernie Eugster's longtime Swiss-American cafe. Fair value. No liquor. No credit cards, but checks accepted.

International

Deluxe

Bay Wolf. 231 Milwaukee (388–9221). One of Denver's "in" restaurants. Ingenious dishes, beautifully displayed. Intimate booths. Excellent service. Bar. Jazz. Private banquet room.

Chateau Pyrenees. 6538 S. Yosemite Circle, Englewood (770–6660). Grandeur in furnishings, chandeliers, splendid French chateau ambience, tuxedoed waiters (*and* waitresses). Colorado's most elaborate menu, in French. Outstanding Swiss chef. Hors d'oeuvres include escargots, lobster, delicacies in champagne sauce; entrees feature venison medallions, chateaubriand, roast rack of lamb, fish, and elegant fowl, such as baby poussaint and roast quail, all beautifully presented. Classical piano music; international wine list. Austrian proprietor Conrad Trinkaus, a perfectionist, always on premises. Reservations essential.

Expensive

Windows. At Radisson Hotel, 1550 Court Pl. (893–3333). Prime rib, shrimp, many chicken entrées are available here, with a seafood buffet on Fridays and a Sunday brunch.

Moderate

The Market. 1445 Larimer St. (534–5140). Gourmet deli, cafe, bakery, and grocery. Small sit-down area. Interesting atmosphere.

Italian and Mexican

Expensive

Campari's. Sheraton Hotel, 4900 DTC Pkwy. (779–8899). Northern Italian cuisine is featured in this place with an Old World country inn atmosphere. Fare includes homemade pasta, fresh seafood, gelati, and sorbetti. Long wine list. Reservations are recommended.

Josephina's. 1433 Larimer, downtown (623–0166). Roaring Twenties decor in a historic building, with foods such as spaghetti, pizza, chicken. Excellent lasagna. Bar. Attracts a young crowd.

The New York Connection. 11th and Ogden (832–1414). Small east-Denver Italian restaurant attracting neighborhood aficionados of southern Italian cooking.

Tuscany. At Loew's Giorgio Hotel, 4150 E. Mississippi (782–9311). Elegant Italian fare, prepared by a chef from Bari, is offered here along with poached seafood, grilled fish, marinated pork, and superb lamb. For dessert, try fresh raspberries or pastries baked in-house. European background music softens the touch.

Moderate

Casa Bonita. 6715 W. Colfax Ave. at JCRS Center (232–5115). A busy Mexican restaurant for Americans. Tasty food in multi-tiered surroundings decorated with murals. Entertaining mariachi music. Fun for the kids.

La Fontanella. 1700 E. Evans, near Denver University (778–8598). Popular Italian restaurant for lunch and dinner. Young clientele. Large menu.

Garcia's of Scottsdale. 1697 S. Havana (755–2670). All the south-of-the-border favorites. Mexican background music.

Inexpensive

Don Quijote Restaurant. 35 Federal Blvd. (934–9753). This is a long-time neighborhood establishment, with authentic Mexican and Spanish food and margaritas.

El Noa Noa. 722 Santa Fe Dr. (623–9968). This casual, popular Mexican restaurant has a patio. The food is good and the ambience very pleasant.

Old Spaghetti Factory. 1215 18th St., downtown (295–1864). Pasta served in the old Denver Cable Car Company. Lively and crowded. Great value.

Moroccan and Jewish

Deluxe

Mataam Fez. 4609 E. Colfax (399–9282). East Denver's Moroccan restaurant. Genuine couscous, lamb dishes, *pastella.* Dim lights, heavy pillows. Good Moroccan wines. Plan on several hours for a complete supper.

Moderate

Bagel Deli Restaurant. 6217 E. 14th Ave. (322–0350). Outstanding Kosher foods are served here for lunch or early dinner. Carryouts are available. Large portions.

Oriental

Expensive

Gasho. 5071-C S. Syracuse, I-25 and E. Belleview (773–3277). Dramatic tableside hibachi cooking. Good beef, chicken, sole. Popular with tourists. *Sake* and plum wine available.

Moderate to Inexpensive

Canton Landing. 6265 E. Evans (759–1228). Three Chinese cuisines under one roof are available at a luncheon buffet or dinner dailyuntil 10:30 P.M. Chinese beer is featured.

Imperial. 1 Broadway (698–2800). Popular Chinese restaurant. Open seven days a week. Small bar. Extremely busy. Reservations for large groups only.

Lotus Room. W. Ninth Ave. and Speer Blvd. (534–7918). Busy family restaurant, frequented by Denverites. Excellent chop suey, Chinese duck, and countless other dishes. Good value. Informal.

New Saigon. 630 S. Federal Blvd. (936–4954). In southwest Denver. Small but outstanding Vietnamese cafe, with dishes from *Mi Tom Cua* to *Bo Vien* and *Goi Cuon.* Friendly atmosphere. Closed Mon.

Yuan Mongolian Barbeque. 7555 E. Arapahoe Rd. at Heritage Place Shopping Center (771–6296). Denver's only help-yourself, all-you-can-eat Mongolian barbecue, with 50 Chinese dishes. Enormous portions. Mixed drinks, wines, Chinese beer. Longtime owner Yuan Hsin is always on premises. Popular lunch place; superb dinner value.

Seafood

Expensive

Fresh Fish Company. 7800 E. Hampden (740–9556). Variety of fresh fish broiled over mesquite. Delicious catfish fillet. Sourdough bread. Bar.

Moderate

Red Lobster. 6166 W. Alameda, Lakewood (922–3694). Long seafood menu, some fresh catches. Popular with families.

DRINKING LAWS. Colorado Law requires that anyone purchasing hard liquor, wine, or beer must be 21 years of age. Drinks must be off the table at closing hour. Packaged liquor is not sold in bars, but may be obtained in liquor stores, open until midnight, Mon.-Sat. No sales when election polls are open and on Dec. 25. Children may sit at a table in the bar if they are accompanied by an adult. In recent years, the state has introduced stiff drunk-driving laws.

NIGHTLIFE AND BARS. Denver's teeming nightlife can offer a visitor—even a resident—many choices.

Basin's Up, 1427 Larimer (623–2104), has Denver's best rock and blues bands, seven nights a week.

At **The Comedy Works,** 1226 15th St. (595–3637), young comedians perform in Denver's original all-comedy nightclub.

El Chapultepec, 19th and Market (295–9126), is the favorite of Denver's jazz lovers. The **Denver Art Museum** has live jazz or contemporary bands and a cash bar on Wed. evenings.

The rock and disco scene centers in Glendale, a nearby suburb that has now been completely surrounded by Denver expansion. Leetsdale Drive east from Colorado Blvd. is the main area for action. Places to try include **Lauderdale's,** 2250 S. Monaco (756–4555), Big-name rockers appear regularly in summer at **Red Rocks,** Morrison (575–2637), and **Fiddler's Green,** 6350 Greenwood Plaza Blvd. (741–5000), and year-round at **McNichols Sports Arena,** 1635 Clay (575–3217).

Funplex, Coal-mine Rd. and Kipling (972–4344), features dance bands on Sunday evenings.

HOW TO GET AROUND. From the airport. Downtown is seven miles from Stapleton International. Taxi service is about $10; see *By taxi,* below. Limousines (398–2284) to major hotels run $5 to city center; $7 to southeast area. Cabs, limousines, and city buses leave from lower level, door 5. Rental cars are also available at the airport; see *By car,* below.

By bus. The *RTD (Regional Transportation District)* operates the city's buses. Buses run not only within Denver, but also in the suburbs and to Boulder. Route and schedule information is available by calling 778–6000. Basic city fare: 75¢ peak hours, 50¢ off-peak; exact change required. Seniors over 65 ride for 10¢. A free shuttle runs along the 16th Street Mall downtown. A first-time rider's kit with system maps and information can be obtained by writing RTD, Department of Marketing, 1600 Blake St., Denver, CO 80202.

By taxi. Cabs in Denver may be hailed or requested by phone. Taxis are usually plentiful in the city. *Yellow Cab* (777–7777) is one of the major operators, as is *Metro Taxi* (333–3333). Cabs operate on a "live meter" system; rates change from by-the-mile to by-the-minute in bad weather or heavy traffic.

By car. Two interstate highways, I-70 and I-25, intersect near downtown Denver. Traffic usually flows smoothly, except from 6:30 to 8:30 in the morning and 4 to 6 in the afternoon, when traffic can be stop-and-go, especially on I-25. Most AM radio stations provide traffic updates during these hours. Parking downtown is hard to find and ranges from 75¢ a half hour to $6 a day. Parking is usually easy in the suburbs. The designated Snow Route signs around the city indicate streets on which parking is not allowed during a snowstorm. On these roads during heavy storms parked cars will be towed. Handicapped parking is indicated by blue-and-white signs.

Rental cars. All major agencies have offices in Denver, including *Avis* (800–331–1212) and *Hertz* (800–654–3131). The city has hundreds of other rental companies, from *Rent-A-Lemon* to offices that specialize in Porsches and other sports cars. There are also many companies renting limousines in the city. Try *Colorado Limousine* (832–7155), or *People's Choice* (398–2727), with one-hour service available.

TOURS. *Gray Line* offers a deluxe city and mountain tour that includes a drive to mountain parks, the main sights of Denver, and a lunch stop in Evergreen. Departs daily at 9 A.M., returning 3 P.M., at a cost of $15. Children receive a discount. They offer special trips to Pikes Peak, Central City and, in summer, Rocky Mountain National Park. Your hotel will contact Gray Line for your pickup, or call 289–2841. Mailing address is Box 38667, Denver 80238.

The preservation group, *Historical Denver, Inc.,* arranges tours of "old Denver." Walking tours cost $7, $5 for children and seniors. Van tours are $12, $10 for children and seniors. Each is two hours long. Contact Historic Denver at 1330 17th Street, 80202 (534–1858).

SPECIAL-INTEREST TOURS. *The U.S. Mint,* 320 West Colfax (844–3582). Tours depart at 30-minute intervals every weekday, except the last two weeks in June. 8:30 A.M.–3:00 P.M. Free.

Colorado State Capitol, Broadway and Colfax (866–5000). Free guided tours. Open 9 A.M.–4 P.M. Mon.-Fri. Call (866–2604).

Colorado Governor's Mansion, at Eighth and Logan streets downtown (866–3682), is open for tours at announced times of the year.

The Denver Center for the Performing Arts, 14th and Curtis (893–4200). Tours on Wed. and Fri. at 12:10 P.M., or by appointment. Phone.

ZOOS. Denver's **Zoological Gardens** are located in City Park (575–2754). Several thousand animals are housed in native habitats. The Children's Zoo here sports a monkey island and cavorting seals. There are walk-through bird houses and impressive polar bear and arctic wolf exhibits. Hours are 10 A.M.–5 P.M. Adults $4, children and seniors $2.

PARKS AND GARDENS. Denver Botanic Gardens, 1005 York St. (331–4010). Outdoor gardens and a conservatory offer beautiful arrangements of native and exotic plant life. Eight hundred species of tropical and subtropical plants thrive year-round in the steel and glass conservatory with trickling streams, waterfalls, and tall royal palms.

Elitch Gardens has some of the best displays in Denver. Many of the area's parks, particularly *City Park* at 17th and York streets, and *Washington Park* at S. Downing and E. Virginia, also have outstanding gardens.

THEME AND AMUSEMENT PARKS. Elitch Gardens, 4620 W. 38th Ave. (455–4771). May be one of the most delightful amusement parks in the nation. Loosely patterned after Tivoli Gardens in Copenhagen, Elitch Gardens charms with its colors, impeccable maintenance, and imaginative rides. One of these, Mister Twister, is rated the second most exciting roller coaster in the world. Also a "Miniature Madness" section for tots, a well-known summer-stock theater, and many refreshment stands. Open daily June-late Aug. 10 A.M.–11 P.M.; special hours at beginning and end of season.

Hyland Hills Water World, one of America's largest water parks, in Federal Heights (427–SURF), has two wave-tech pools and 14 water slides. Open daily May-Aug. 10 A.M.–11 P.M.

Lakeside Amusement Park, 4601 Sheridan Blvd. (477–1621), is not far from Elitch's. Lakeside has a different character altogether, somewhat noisier and faster and aimed more toward large crowds. The park is located next to a lake, and the lights reflecting on the water are mesmerizing. Open June-Sept. Mon.-Fri., 6–11 P.M.; Sat., Sun., and holidays, noon–11 P.M.

CAMPING. The Denver area offers a number of excellent camping sites. Here are a few of the better campgrounds in the area:

Barr Lake Campground. Box 264, RR 3 Brighton, CO 80601 (659–6180) 15 miles northeast on I-76. Store, good fishing. Open year-round. Near State Park.

Chatfield State Recreation Area, 11500 Roxborough Rd., Littleton 80215 (797–3986). Summers only. On lake, with swimming, fishing, hiking trails. 150 sites. $10 per night. Fills up quickly during holidays.

Cherry Creek Reservoir State Recreation Area. Eight miles southeast of Denver on Route 83 (690–1166). 102 trailer spaces. Rental includes electricity hookup, running water, flush toilets, and laundry facilities. Rental plus small State Recreation Areas fee. Tent camping also permitted.

Chief Hosa Campgrounds. Route 3, Box 282, Golden 80401 (526–0364). A pleasant campground in the mountains 20 miles from Denver on I-70 West. Laundry, groceries, pool. Open mid-May-Sept. Reservations accepted.

Denver East KOA. Box 597, Strasburg, CO 80136 (622–9274). 91 sites, some cabins, pool, laundry, grocery. Open year-round.

Denver North Campground. Route 1, Box 149, Broomfield 80020 (452–4120). 15 miles north on I-25. 157 sites, year-round. All amenities. Reservations accepted.

SPECTATOR SPORTS. The Denver area's **auto racetracks** offer everything from Indianapolis-type formula cars to motorcycle competition. Nearest is *Lakeside Speedway* at the amusement park, W. 44th Ave. and Sheridan (477–1621). The Sunday night stock car programs run from early May through Labor Day.

Next to the stadium, the *Denver Nuggets* **basketball** team is based in *McNichols Arena* from October to May. Tickets are $8–$20. Call 893–DUNK.

If you've never seen a **dog race,** try the *Mile High Kennel Club* at Colorado Blvd. and E. 62nd Ave. (288–1591). The greyhounds run six nights a week, June through August, with matinees on Saturdays. Betting is legal for persons 18 or over. Admission is 50¢, programs cost $1, and parking is free.

The 74,000 seats of *Mile High Stadium,* Federal Blvd. and 17th Ave. (433–7466), are never enough to hold all the fans of the *Denver Broncos* **football** team. The team has done well in recent years and is now a city-wide passion. Fans wait years for tickets and brave traffic jams around the stadium at game times.

Each January Denver hosts the *National Western Stock Show,* northeast of Denver at I-70 and Brighton Blvd., with a rodeo, cattle displays, and a myriad of contests. Phone 297–1166 for ticket information.

SEASONAL EVENTS. January: *The National Western Stock Show and Rodeo,* the world's largest single livestock exhibition, takes place for 12 days in mid-month. Millions of dollars in business deals are settled here each year. Events include professional and amateur rodeo, several horse shows, and the judging of champion cattle. All stock show events are held at the Denver Coliseum, at I-70 and Washington Street. **February:** *Garden and Home Show,* Currigan Hall. The Hyatt Regency Tech Center presents *Jazzfest.* **March:** *Denver Symphony Run* (marathon benefit). *St. Patrick's Day Parade* downtown. **April:** *Easter Sunrise services* at Red Rocks. *Boulder Symphony spring concerts* open in Boulder. **May:** *Cinco de Mayo* Mexican celebration in Skyline Park with food and entertainment. At Lakeside Amusement Park and Elitch Gardens, *theater and bands* begin performances to run throughout the summer. **June:** *Greyhound racing* at Mile High Kennel Club throughout the summer, with pari-mutuel betting. Annual *Cherry Blossoms Festival* in Sakura Square. *The People's Fair* is held in Civil Center Park. *Colorado Renaissance Fair* runs through July in Larkspur. **July:** *Colorado Indian Market,* Currigan Exhibition Hall, with Indian dances, food, artwork. The *Drums Along the Rockies* competition is held at Mile Hi Stadium. Fresh produce at the *Denver Farmers' Market,* 16th and Market Sts., lower downtown, on Saturdays through October. **August:** *Coors International Bike Classic* race. **September:** *Denver Broncos* professional football season opens. The *Festival of Mountain and Plain* is held Labor Day. **October:** Early in the month is the *Larimer Square Oktoberfest.* The *Denver Symphony,* opens a season filled with classical, pops, and children's concerts. **December:** The *Annual Parade of Lights* features brilliantly lighted holiday floats, bands, and Santa. Larimer Square has the yearly *Christmas Walk,* and art, dance, and food highlight the *Colorado Indian Winter Market,* Currigan Hall.

HISTORIC SITES AND HOUSES. The Molly Brown House, 1340 Pennsylvania Ave. (832–4092), was home to "the unsinkable Molly Brown," a *Titanic* survivor who bought the house in 1894. It has been beautifully restored. Open Tues.-Sat. 10 A.M.–3 P.M.; Sun. noon–3 P.M. Cost is $3 adults, $1 children 6–18, $1.50 seniors.

Grant Humphries Mansion, 770 Pennsylvania Ave., near downtown area (866–3507), is an architecturally interesting 1903 house on 2½ acres. Tours Tues.–Fri.

Ninth Street Historic Park, Auraria Campus, is a picturesque block of early Denver homes, now used as academic offices.

Denver has other beautiful Victorian homes. See *Tours* above for a walking tour that will acquaint you with the city's rich past. **Pearce-McAllister**

Cottage, 1880 Gaylord (322–3704), is a historic home built in 1899. Guided tours on Wed.–Sun., 10 A.M.–4 P.M. **Larimer Square,** downtown, includes Denver's oldest streets, with courtyards, gas lamps, and Victorian buildings. Virtually every desperado in the West once walked this street, which today houses restaurants, galleries, and nightclubs.

MUSEUMS. Denver is a multifaceted city with a rich history, and its museums reflects Denver's personality. **Arvada Center for the Arts and Humanities,** 6901 Wadsworth Blvd., Arvada (431–3080). Overlooking the city, 12 miles from downtown. Art and history exhibits. Hours are Mon.-Fri., 9 A.M.–9 P.M.; Sat., 8 A.M.–5 P.M.; Sun., 1–5 P.M. Free.

The Buckhorn Exchange, at 1000 Osage St. (534–9505), is a nice lunchtime stop. Several generations have enriched this museum and dining emporium, which houses hundreds of historic photos, ancient western guns, trophies and antlers of every description, stuffed animals, Indian mementos, and paintings. Free.

The Children's Museum, 2121 Crescent Dr. (433–7444), offers story hours, hands-on displays, health screening, and much more. Open Tues.-Fri. and Sun., noon–5 P.M.; Sat. 10 A.M.–5 P.M. Admission $2.25, $1.50 for seniors.

Colorado History Museum, 1300 Broadway (866–3682), houses artifacts and photos of early Denver, ancient Mesa Verde Indian pieces, and a fascinating diorama of Denver in 1860. Contains the treasures collected by the Colorado Historical Society, including many permanent exhibits.

The Colorado Railroad Museum, 17155 W. 44th Ave., Golden (279–4591), houses many early Colorado railroad items in a depot-style building. Open daily 9 A.M.–5 P.M. Family admission is $5.50.

The Denver Art Museum, 100 S. 14th Ave. (575–2793), houses a collection that includes African, Western U.S., Oriental, and pre-Columbian items, with some works by Rembrandt, Picasso, Matisse, Renoir, Rubens, and others. There are also textiles, costumes, pottery, jewelry, period rooms, and antique furniture. Sun. noon–5 P.M., Tues.-Sat. 9 A.M.–5 P.M.; closed Mon. Cost is $2.50 adults, $1.50 for seniors, students, and children.

The Denver Museum of Natural History, Montview and Colorado blvds. (370–6300), in City Park, features four floors of dinosaurs, Indian artifacts, insects, birds, and animals from around the world. Don't miss the moose and elk displays and whale exhibit. Headphones can be rented to plug into outlets at each display. *IMAX Theater,* in the museum, is "the cinema of the future." Images explode on the huge screen with elaborate acoustics.

The Forney Transportation Museum, 1416 Platte (433–3643), features antique cars, carriages, and trains. $3 for adults, $1.50 for children 12–18, 50¢ for children under 12.

The Museum of Western Art, 1727 Tremont Place (296–1880), fits Denver's western image. Open Tues.-Sat. 10 A.M.–4:30 P.M. Admission $3 for adults, children under 7 free, $1.50 for seniors.

MUSIC. Denver has a variety of music, from bluegrass to opera. Check the entertainment sections of the *Denver Post* and *The Rocky Mountain News* for up-to-date listings.

Arvada Center for the Arts and Humanities, 6901 Wadsworth Blvd., Arvada (422–8050), books everything from jazz to chamber music.

Denver Symphony Orchestra, Boettcher Concert Hall, 950 13th St. (592–7777). The DSO imports world-renowned conductors and musicians, and also performs a jazz series, pops series, and special outdoor concerts.

The Paramount Theater, 1621 Glenarm (534–8336), presents classical soloists, Gibson Jazz concerts, and various entertainers.

DANCE. Dance in Denver takes many forms, with an emphasis on the modern. **Arvada Center,** 6901 Wadsworth Blvd., Arvada (431–3080), imports nationally known troupes for its fall-to-spring program.

Colorado Ballet, 999–18th St. (298–0677), is Denver's premier dance troupe. Christmas *Nutcracker* performances are a traditional local event.

Colorado Contemporary Dance, 14th and Champa (697–8977), advertises performances by well-known companies several times each year.

New Dance Theater, 2006 Lawrence St. (295–1759), is home to the Cleo Parker Robinson Dance Troupe. Ultramodern dance performances take place at various times during the year.

THEATER. At **The Denver Center for the Performing Arts,** 1050 13th St. (893–4100), the Denver Center Company performs in repertory Mon.-Sat., fall through spring. **The Source,** a 158-seat theater, stages premieres of locally written plays. **Stage West,** in the Galleria of the Denver Arts Center, offers professional off-Broadway-type productions in a 250-seat cabaret with bar. Weeknight performances are less expensive than weekends, and the first week of a production sees tickets at almost half the regular price.

The Arvada Center (see *Music* above) features a variety of attractions in fall and winter.

The Changing Scene, 1527½ Champa (893–5775); the **City Stage Ensemble** at Jack's, 1553 Platte St. (433–8082); and **Germinal Stage,** 2450 W. 44th Ave. (296–1192), rank among Denver's best small theaters.

Center Attractions/Robert Garner at the Auditorium Theater, 14th and Curtis (573–7151), brings in Broadway touring companies.

The Avenue Theater, 2119 E. 17th Ave. (377–1720), presents original works with lots of witty improvization.

Opera Colorado, 695 S. Colorado Blvd. (778–6464), performs at Boettcher Concert Hall in the Denver Arts Center, April and May only.

ART GALLERIES. Denver has many fine galleries throughout the city, with the Cherry Creek and downtown areas boasting the largest concentration. **Brigitte Schluger Gallery,** 929 Broadway (825–8555). Fine art, folk art, sculpture. Hours Mon.–Sat., 10 A.M.–6 P.M.

Camera Obscura Gallery, 1309 Bannock St. (623–4059). Contemporary and vintage photographs.

Mudhead Gallery, 555–17th St., in the Hyatt Regency Pavillion (293–0007). This gallery specializes in Western and Southwestern art and Indian jewelry. It also displays a permanent collection of Kachina dolls and pottery. Open Mon.–Sat, 9 A.M.–9 P.M.

COLORADO'S FRONT RANGE

As you climb into the foothills of the Rockies, you enter the early pioneers' world of mining camps, boomtowns, hot springs, and past splendors. The Old West lives on in meadows, forests, geologic wonders, and striking unspoilt panoramas.

Golden

Golden, Denver's westernmost suburb, spread along the banks of Clear Creek as a pioneer camp in 1859. It became the capital of Colorado Territory in 1862, and still boasts many buildings from pioneer days. According to a banner over the main street, Golden is "Where the West Remains."

The Railroad Museum, at 17155 West 44th Ave., has an 1880s-style depot, historical exhibits, old narrow-gauge locomotives, and railroad and trolley cars.

The Foothills Art Center, 15th and Washington, was built as a Presbyterian church in 1892. It opened as an art center in 1968.

The Colorado School of Mines Geology Museum is nearby at 16th and Maple. The 1940 structure displays mineral ores, fossils, mining equipment, meteorites, and even a replica of an old gold mine.

Around Golden

Lookout Mountain, just west of Golden on I–70, has the grave of Buffalo Bill Cody at the summit. Here also is a museum displaying relics of his cavalry and Wild West show days. Free.

Hikers and nature worshippers should drive up to the Jefferson County Conference and Nature Center at 900 Colorow Rd. It offers a small botanical museum and trails.

On the way to Lookout Mountain, you may wish to leave I–70 and visit the Mother Cabrini Shrine, devoted to Saint Francis Xavier Cabrini. The setting includes a large number of meadows, summer flowers, forests, and quite a few steps that will make young walkers happy but can cause older ones to puff a little.

Also consider a trip to Heritage Square, a mile west of the intersection of routes 6 and 40. The village has shops with metal smiths, jewelers, and candy makers. There is an alpine slide, a stable for horseback rides, a narrow-gauge train, and a large melodrama theater.

Red Rocks

Red Rocks Park lies above the small town of Morrison on Denver's western edge. The red sandstone formations, thrust skyward by the upheaval of a prehistoric ocean bed, make an impact on the first-time viewer. There's lots of space for hiking and exploring, but casual climbs on the rocks are not advisable.

Everything is giant at the Red Rocks Park, including the natural amphitheater. For years, the theater was used for ballet and classical music performances. The cost was formidable, however, and mountain gusts would carry away the sound. Now, with modern improvements, Red Rocks is the site of well-attended summer rock concerts. Although expensive, tickets often sell out weeks in advance. It takes about 30 minutes to reach Red Rocks from Denver. Best route: the Sixth Avenue Freeway west to I–70; turn south and get off at the next exit so you'll be driving south on Hog Back Rd. towards Morrison.

Evergreen

Evergreen, 30 miles west of Denver on I–70 or Route 74, was settled in 1859 as a lumber and supply center for the local mining camps. Today it provides a mountain retreat for city dwellers and a quiet home for Denver workers who don't mind the commute. Lots of specialty shops here in a busy, but small-town atmosphere. Evergreen is surrounded by several mountain parks, and nearby Evergreen Lake is a favorite spot for visitors, with boating in summer and ice skating in winter.

Idaho Springs

Idaho Springs, above Evergreen on I–70, has been called "the buckle of Colorado's mineral belt." Families find a wealth of history here, and the community's hot springs—where the Ute Indians brought their old, sick, and wounded—are open year-round. The springs flow through two separate tunnels, one for men and one for women, carved into the mountains. You may wish to reserve a private bath for your family for an hour. Swimming pool, sauna, and whirlpool are available, too. The dramatic Bridal Veil Falls is a short hike away. Idaho Springs is also the gateway to the nation's highest auto road, which climbs to 14,260 feet at the top of Mount Evans.

Nearby is the Indian Springs Resort. Built in 1869, it is now a complete tourist facility, with tennis courts, restaurants, and, of course, hot mineral baths.

For an adventurous side trip from Idaho Springs, drive up Fall River Road (Exit 48 from I–70) for an intimate look at various mountain terrains. The road ends at St. Mary's Lake, and a 30- or 40-minute climb up a well-marked footpath will bring you to St. Mary's Glacier, which has snow all year long. The glacier is popular with summer skiers.

Central City

Central City, once known as "the richest square mile on earth," can be reached from Golden on Route 119 via Route 67 west. It was here, on a spot now marked by a modest plaque, that John Gregory first struck gold in 1859 and began the rush to the Rockies. In summer, Central City and nearby Blackhawk come alive, looking like reborn boomtowns of a century ago. Winding Eureka Street sports saloons with swinging doors, gift shops and candy stores in a gaudy old-west manner. A great number of the brick buildings erected in the old boom days and some of the old mines can still be visited.

Central City is most renowned for its summer operas held in the old 1878 Central City Opera House, with solid stone walls four feet thick. Fine murals and crystal chandeliers decorate the Victorian interior. Artists from the New York Metropolitan Opera and other leading companies fly out on occasion to sing here. The operas are often followed by hit Broadway musicals and plays, frequently with the original casts.

Boulder

Boulder is a half-hour drive north of Denver on Route 36 from I–25. As you approach, you'll see the much-photographed reddish sandstone formations known as the "Flatirons," the abrupt border between the plains and the Rockies. The Flatirons are also a gateway to webs of popular hiking trails in the hills that rise behind the college town. And rock climbers favor these same rocks.

Boulder's tree-lined campus is worth visiting, especially in summer, when the University of Colorado stages its yearly Colorado Shakespeare Festival. Several Shakespeare plays are performed here in repertory mid-July–mid-August.

Boulder is headquarters to the National Center for Atmospheric Research. Perched on a mesa southwest of town, the futuristic complex sits in a nature preserve open to hikers and picnickers. The National Bureau of Standards is also located in this university town.

PRACTICAL INFORMATION FOR COLORADO'S FRONT RANGE

HOW TO GET THERE. By bus. *RTD* (778–6000) travels between Denver, Boulder, Golden, and Evergreen. *Greyhound* (292–6100) travels to Idaho Springs.

By car. Boulder can be reached most quickly on Route 36 from I–25. This route affords a good view of the city nestled in its valley, the Flatirons towering above. Golden can be reached from Denver by taking I–25 North to I–70 West. Evergreen and Idaho Springs are west on I–70. To reach Central City head west on Route 6 from Golden, then pick up Route 119. No commuter buses currently travel this route.

ACCOMMODATIONS. Rates for double occupancy average as follows: *Deluxe,* \$100–\$215; *Expensive,* \$75–\$100; *Moderate,* \$40–\$75; and *Inexpensive,* under \$40.

Boulder

Hotel Boulderado. *Deluxe.* 2115–13th St., 80303 (442–4344 or 800–433–4344). This elegant 1908 downtown hotel has been restored to Victorian splendor. Genuine antiques in rooms, many suites, beautiful lobby. Health club privileges, banquet facilities, entertainment. Three restaurants.

Best Western Boulder Inn. *Expensive.* 770 28th St. 80303 (449–3800 or 800–528–1234). Across from University of Colorado. Restaurant, bar, pools, 100 attractively furnished rooms, private baths, Chinese restaurant.

The Broker Inn. *Expensive.* 555 30th St. 80303 (444–3330). Near University of Colorado. Pool. Elegant *Old West Restaurant* on premises.

Clarion Harvest House Hotel. *Expensive.* 1345 28th St. 80302 (443–3850 or 800–CLARION). A modern high-rise motel with landscaped grounds, dining facilities, cocktail lounge, swimming pool, 15 tennis courts. Shopping center nearby.

Holiday Inn Holidome. *Expensive.* 800 28th St. 80303 (443–3322 or 800–HOLIDAY). In addition to the chain's rooms, there are a pool, exercise room, restaurant. Across from University of Colorado.

University Inn. *Expensive.* 1632 Broadway 80302 (442–3830). TV. Pool. Free Continental breakfast; cafe nearby.

Central City

Gilpin Hotel. *Moderate.* 111 Main, Blackhawk 80427 (582–5012). Tiny historic miners' hotel built in 1900 and well-restored.

Golden Rose Hotel. *Moderate.* 102 Main, Blackhawk (825–1413 in Denver, or 582–5060 local). Small Victorian-style hotel, built 1874 and restored with elegant furniture. Hot tub, sauna.

Evergreen

Bauer's Spruce Island Chalets. *Expensive.* 5987 S. Brook Forest Rd., Box 1678, 80439 (674–4757). One- to four-bedroom houses, in a restful mountain atmosphere.

Davidson Lodge. *Expensive.* 27400 Hwy. 74 (674–3442). Featured here are comfortable cabins along scenic Bear Creek. Open year-round. Fishing, skiing, sightseeing.

Golden

The Dove Inn. *Expensive.* 711–14th St. (278–2209). This is a pleasant 1889 Victorian home, some with private baths. Delicious breakfasts are served.

Days Inn West. *Moderate.* 15059 W. Colfax (277–0200 or 800–325–2525). Handsomely renovated rooms are available here, along with suites with kitchens. Conference areas, restaurant, exercise room, free cable TV.

Idaho Springs

Argo Motor Inn. *Expensive.* One mile east on I-70, 80452 (567–4473). Modernistic motel near mine. Tennis courts not far away. On river.

Indian Springs Resort. *Moderate.* 302 Soda Creek Rd. 80452 (623–2050). Old resort hotel with mineral pool, baths, exercise room, small cafe. Off the beaten track and good value.

H & H Motor Lodge. *Inexpensive.* 2445 Colorado Blvd. (567–2838). This lodge has nicely appointed rooms, some kitchens, hot tub, cable TV, laundry.

Winter Park

Information on lodgings is available through *Central Reservations,* Box 36, Winter Park 80482 (453–2525).

Creekside Condos. *Deluxe.* 145 Arapahoe Rd., 80482 (726–9461). Charming, quiet units with modern amenities, overlooking creek. Close to cross-country skiing.

Hi Country Haus Resort. *Deluxe.* Route 40, 80482 (726–9421). Spacious condos, indoor pool, cross-country skiing, shuttles to ski area. Liquor store, cafes, movies. Meeting room for 120; full of large groups in winter. Largest complex in the area.

Beaver Lodge and Beaver Village. *Inexpensive–Moderate.* Box 43, 80482 (726–5741 or 800–525–3304; in Denver 449–4135). Lodge rooms and condos; horses in summer. Condos offer sound-proofed walls, handsome stone fireplaces. Balconies, recreation center.

Alpenglo Motor Lodge. *Inexpensive.* Route 40, 80482 (726–5294). Acceptable accommodations on highway.

BED AND BREAKFASTS. In the area around Denver, a number of residents are opening their homes to travelers.

The Briar Rose. *Expensive.* 2151 Arapahoe, Boulder 80303 (442–3007). Country-style brick home. Fruit and flowers in your room. Very hospitable.

Greystone Guest Ranch. *Expensive.* Near Evergreen (674–3328). On a 500-acre wooded estate with lodge and cottages. Library, horseback riding.

Pearl's Place. *Moderate.* 497 Pearl (442–2242). This is a pleasant, centrally located establishment.

For additional listings write or call: *Bed and Breakfast Colorado, Ltd.,* Box 6061, Dept. V., Boulder, CO 80306 (494–4994).

RESTAURANTS. The influences of academia and tourism have combined to bring fine dining to Colorado's Front Range. Our price ranges are: *Deluxe,* \$60 and up; *Expensive,* \$25–\$50; *Moderate,* \$15–\$25; *Inexpensive,* under \$15. These rates are for two full meals with appetizer, exclusive of tax and tip.

Boulder

Flagstaff House. *Deluxe.* Flagstaff Rd. (442–4640). On Flagstaff Mountain, with fine views. Award-winning Continental/American menu including oven-smoked salmon, venison, filet à la Wellington, duck, Alaskan king crab. Prime rib a specialty. Cocktail patio, free appetizers. A treat in summer.

Boulder Dinner Theater. *Expensive.* 5501 Arapahoe (449–6000). Cheerful young actors, singers, and dancers regale you after a well-cooked supper.

Franco's. *Expensive.* 2115 13th (in Hotel Boulderado) (449–4818). Elegant Italian restaurant boasting pasta specialties. Choose from any of six sauces made fresh daily. Spaghetti, linguine, fettuccine at the pasta bar. Liquor.

Harvest Restaurant and Bakery. *Moderate.* 1738 Pearl St. (449–6223). Specializes in natural foods. Own baking. Beer and wine served. Background music and outdoor seating.

Pour La France. *Moderate.* 1001 Pearl St. (449–3929). This European-style cafe and bakery has special blend coffees, amazing pastries, gourmet pizzas, and late-night dining. Outdoor patio. Bar.

Furr's Cafeteria. *Inexpensive.* 2880 Diagonal Hwy. (443–9211). In large shopping center. Excellent value. No bar.

Central City

Black Forest Inn. *Expensive.* 260 Gregory, Black Hawk (279–2333). Bill Lorenz's well-managed Bavarian restaurant, just east of Central City on Route 279, offers goose liver pâté, elk, venison, pheasant, and other native game. Wiener schnitzel, calves liver à la Berlin, Canadian snow-goose, fresh trout, herring, berries in season. Beer garden with accordion player in summer. Owner always on premises. Open noon–9:30 P.M.

The Teller House Eureka Room. *Expensive.* 120 Eureka (582–3200). Laden with romance and history, the Teller House has been restored to its former splendor. Cocktail lounge. *Teller Bar* with "Face on the Bar-room Floor." Restaurant open only during summer.

Evergreen

El Rancho Colorado. *Expensive.* I-70 Exit 252 (526–0661). Steak, prime rib, fresh rainbow trout. The rustic atmosphere includes a cocktail lounge with a fireplace. In the heart of the mountains.

Evergreen Inn. *Inexpensive.* 27845 Route 74 (674–5495). Friendly local pub with reasonably priced food.

Golden

Briarwood Inn. *Deluxe.* 1630 8th St. (279–3121). Elegant country inn. Fine tablecloths, china, cutlery. Classical background music. Lazy Susan with free appetizers; great variety of American and Continental dishes. Reservations recommended.

The Chart House. *Expensive–Moderate.* 25908 Genesee Trail Road, I-70 Exit 254 (526–9813). Famous Sun. brunch. Dinner menu offers many cuts of meat. Mountain views.

Idaho Springs

Indian Springs Resort. *Moderate.* 302 Soda Creek Rd. (623–2050). Home cooking.

Beau Jo's. *Inexpensive.* 1517 Miner's St. (567–4376). Features mountain pie and great pizza. Incredible menu selection; beer, wine. Rustic atmosphere.

The Buffalo Bar. *Inexpensive.* 1617 Miner St. (567–2729). Western-style dining with old-time atmosphere and buffalo specialties are featured here.

Winter Park

Chalet Restaurant. *Moderate.* U.S. Hwy. 40 (726–5402). Ambitious Continental fare, with some American items and crepes. Chef-owned; friendly and reliable.

Last Waltz. *Moderate.* Route 40, Kings Crossing Center (726–4877). This modest place has great Mexican-American food and prompt service. Bar. Good value.

TOURS AND SPECIAL-INTEREST SIGHTSEEING. The Mountain Men, 3003 S. Macon Cir., Aurora 80014 (750–5200), conduct summer and winter four-wheel-drive tours which include Georgetown, Idaho Springs, and Central City. The Georgetown tour focuses on Guanella Pass and does not stop in town. Another tour includes a guided drive through both Idaho Springs and Central City, with a brief stop in the latter town for exploration of its many shops and historic buildings.

Boulder

The *Bureau of Conference Services and Cultural Affairs,* 2440 Pearl 80302 (442–1044), offers pamphlets describing self-guided tours of the town.

Boulder Beer Brewery, 2880 Wilderness Pl. (444–8448) gives guided 45-minute tours of the facilities, culminating in a visit to the newly opened tasting room, where visitors receive a free sample. Thurs., 11 A.M.; groups of five or more may make special arrangements.

National Center for Atmospheric Research, 1850 Table Mesa Dr. (497–1000). Self-guided tours of the southwest Boulder facility are offered Mon.–Sat. Brochures, exhibits, and trail maps for the Center's nature preserve are available.

Central City

Brochures for a walking tour of this famous mining town are available at most hotels and from *City Hall,* 117 Eureka St. 80427.

Golden

Adolph Coors Brewery, 13th and Ford (277–BEER). Free tours of the "single largest brewery in the world," Mon.–Sat. Special tours for the disabled.

PARKS AND GARDENS. Colorado's Front Range has a number of places to enjoy the *urban* outdoors.

Boulder

Chautauqua Park, Ninth and Baseline; at the base of the Flatirons. Dining room, auditorium, music programs, tennis.

City Park. Next to Boulder Creek at Canyon and Broadway. Bandshell has summer music performances.

Flagstaff Mountain. At the western end of Baseline Road, in the mountains. Beautiful views.

Idaho Springs

Riley Cooper Park. Colorado and 23d aves., on Clear Creek. Tables.

OUTDOOR ACTIVITIES. The magnificent outdoors offer a wide range of sporting choices in Colorado's Front Range.

Boulder

Boulder is an extremely health-conscious town, and **jogging** and **cycling** are popular even in the worst of weather. Many trails are available throughout town. Rental bicycles are available from *University Bicycles,* 839 Pearl St. (444–4196). Free bike trail maps are provided by the *Bank of Boulder,* 3033 Iris Ave. (443–9090); they may also be picked up in person at the *Chamber of Commerce,* 1001 Canyon Blvd. (442–1044). Other maps are available from the *Bicycle Racing Association,* 821 Acoma St., Denver 80209 (820–2453), and from the *Colorado Department of Highways,* 4201 E. Arkansas, Denver 80222.

For **hiking,** the Boulder Mountain Park system beckons with 6,000 acres of open space; the "Mesa Trail" is especially enjoyable. For trail maps contact the *Chamber of Commerce,* 1001 Canyon Blvd. (442–1044). Other hiking spots include Boulder Canyon (at the end of Canyon Blvd.), Eldorado Canyon (off Hwy. 93, seven miles south of town), and Flagstaff Mountain, at the west end of Baseline Road. The parks also provide good spots for **cross-country skiing.** For **swimming, racquetball, weight lifting** and other sports, try one of Boulder's fitness centers, listed below. Hours and fees differ for each activity: *North Boulder Recreation Center,* 3170 N. Broadway (441–3444). Pool, gym, racquetball, tennis. *South Boulder Recreation Center,* 1360 Gillaspie (441–3448). Usual activities and lake with boating. *YMCA,* 2850 Mapleton, near Cross (442–2778). Pool, gym, weights, classes.

Golden

For **hiking** around Golden try *Golden Gate Canyon State Park* on Route 93, with its beautiful rock formations and 100-mile panoramas of the Continental Divide.

Idaho Springs

Echo Lake, on Mt. Evans, outside Idaho Springs, attracts **anglers** and overnight campers. Also outside Idaho Springs is St. Mary's Lake; a climb from it leads to St. Mary's Glacier. The year-round snow makes it a perfect spot for summer **skiing.**

Winter Park

Cross-country enthusiasts head for nearby Idlewild, with a *Nordic Center* (726–5564) in the town; *Snow Mountain Ranch/YMCA of the Rockies* (887–2152), with 26 miles of groomed trails; *C Lazy U Ranch* (807–3344) near Granby for outstanding trail systems; *Silver Creek Resort,* 30 minutes north of Winter Park (887–3384); or *Devil's Thumb Ranch,* north of Fraser (726–5632).

Snow tubing at *Fraser Valley Sports Center* (726–5954) is uncontrolled fun; $5 an hour for an inner tube and rope tow.

Snowmobiling is available from *Beaver Village* (726–5741). $40 for a half-day guided tour up to the summit of the Continental Divide; also available from *Trailblazer Rental* (726–5290).

Ice skating is available at *Snow Mountain Ranch* (887–2152) and at public rinks in Winter Park and Fraser.

Sleigh rides are scheduled from Meadow Ridge, Beaver Village, Idlewild, and from McLean Real Estate Office by *Winter Park Sleighrides* (726–5557 or 9461).

Racquetball, swimming, and **weight lifting** can be enjoyed by guests of Snowblaze, Meadow Ridge, and Iron Horse. **Roller skating** and **basketball** are available year-round at Snow Mountain Ranch.

In summer, people head off for day **hikes, backpack trips, bicycling** (mountain bikes are for rent at many ski shops, including *Sportstalker,* Cooper Creek Square, 726–8873, and *Ski Depot,* Route 40, 726–8055), and **windsurfing.** The *Alpine Adventure Program* (726–5514) at Mary Jane has instruction in **rock climbing, rappeling,** and **windsurfing,** and will help you organize self-guided mountain hikes. **Volleyball** and **horseshoes** are popular at the Mary Jane base area. The Alpine Slide swings under the Arrow Lift on the Winter Park side.

The **golf** course at *Pole Creek* (726–9225) has spectacular vistas, long fairways, challenging greens. Open June–Oct. Greens fees are $32 for 18 holes, $20 for 9 holes. Five miles from Winter Park. *Grand Lake* public course (627–8008) is 30 miles away.

Half- and full-day rafting trips are popular on the Colorado River. Try *Alpine Whitewater* (627–3538), *Mad River Fish and Float* (726–5290), or *Timber Rafting* (726–9550).

DOWNHILL SKIING. Winter Park. Box 36, Winter Park 80482 (726–5514). Take I–70 to Route 40; 67 miles from Denver. Popular with families. 18 lifts; 97 trails (36% beginner, 48% intermediate, 16% advanced skiers). Vertical drop 2,220 feet. Lift tickets are $28.

MUSEUMS AND HISTORIC SITES. The area surrounding Denver is rich in the history of the country's western expansion.

Boulder

Boulder Historical Society, 1206 Euclid (449–3464). Harbeck House, built at the turn of the century by a banker and his wife as a summer residence, houses the society's collection, which focuses on local history. Hours are Tues.–Fri., 10 A.M.–4 P.M.; Sat., noon–4 P.M.

University of Colorado Museum of Natural History, Broadway between 15th and 16th streets (492–6165 weekdays, 492–6892 weekends). Biology, anthropology, and earth science halls, along with changing exhibits.

Central City

This Victorian "gingerbread" tour boasts a wealth of historic sites.

Central City Gold Mine and Museum. 126 Spring St. (582–5574), offers a 20-minute mine tour and a mining and railroad display.

St. James Methodist Church on Eureka Street is the oldest church in the state, dating to 1859. The interior has been restored; if the door is open, look in at the intricate stenciling that decorates the sanctuary.

The Teller House, 110 Eureka St. (279–8306) was built in 1872 at the staggering cost of $107,000. It became the most opulent hostelry of the gold fields, hosting Ulysses S. Grant, Oscar Wilde, Baron de Rothschild, and other notables. The famous "Face on the Barroom Floor" in the saloon is one of the highlights of the 45-minute tour, which also includes the renowned *Central City Opera House* next door. Tours are available daily from 11 A.M.–5 P.M.

Evergreen

Downtown, take some time to visit the **Hiwan Homestead Museum,** 4208 S. Timbervale Dr. (674–6262), a pioneer display in a 17-room log house that offers tastes of the past, including a reconstructed 1880s assay office. Free afternoon tours Tues.–Sun.

Golden

Colorado School of Mines Geologic Museum, at 16th and Maple (273–3823). The 1940 structure displays mineral ores, fossils, mining equipment, meteorites, and even a replica of an old gold mine. Open Mon.–Sat., 9 A.M.–4 P.M., Sun. 1–4 P.M. Free.

The Railroad Museum, 17155 W. 44th Ave. (279–4591), has an 1880s-style depot, historical exhibits, old narrow-gauge locomotives, and railroad and trolley cars. Open daily 9 A.M.–5 P.M.; family admission $5.50.

The Buffalo Bill Museum, Lookout Mountain, Route 40 (526–0488), features the famed Westerner's grave and personal possessions. Closed Mon. Small entrance fee.

Idaho Springs

Don't miss the **Clear Creek Museum** and the **Argo Gold Mill,** 2515 Riverside Dr., downtown. Equipment and mining displays are shown inside an actual gold mine. There are tours of the shaft and adjoining ore mill, May–Labor Day. Small entrance fee. For information write Argo Town U.S.A., Box 1498, Idaho Springs 80452 (567–2421).

Underhill Museum, 1400 Miner St., is a historic old home with original furnishings, old mining relics, and maps. Open Tues., Thurs., and Sat.

MUSIC AND THEATER. At **Red Rocks Park,** near Morrison, rock concerts are performed in a natural amphitheater formed by jutting red sandstone formations. Call 572–4704 for concert information. Open June to Labor Day.

Boulder

Boulder Public Library, 1000 Canyon (441–3114), has free concerts throughout the year featuring both local and national performers in a broad range of styles. The *Budapest Takacs String Quartet* performs Sept.–April (492–8008). *Colorado Music Festival,* mid-June through July, sells out quickly. Contact them at 1245 Pearl, 80302 (443–1397), for reservations.

Macky Auditorium, Box 285, University of Colorado, Boulder 80309 (492–8424), hosts performances by the *Boulder Philharmonic,* the *College of Music,* visiting musicians participating in the "artists series," and concerts by nationally known groups.

Boulder is home to the *Colorado Shakespeare Festival* each July and Aug. For information, write University of Colorado Department of Theater and Dance, Campus Box 261, Boulder, CO 80309 (492–7355). Other performances are hosted by the **University Drama and Dance departments,** Campus Box 261, Boulder 80309 (492–7355). **Nomads,** 1410 Quince St. (443–7510), is a modern, experimental theater.

Central City

Summer performances at the **Central City Opera House** are world-famous and definitely worth a visit. Write Central City Opera Association, 1615 California, Suite 614, Denver 80202 (623–7167).

Evergreen

Colorado Philharmonic Orchestra, Box 975, 80439 (674–5161). Young musicians in summer repertory.

Longmont

Longmont Symphony Orchestra, Vance Brand Auditorium (776–5295). Good local orchestra with well-known guest soloists.

PIKES PEAK COUNTRY

Like Mount Rainier, it is awe-inspiring even when seen from a half-day's drive away. Like the Matterhorn, it stands as an affront and a challenge to all mountaineers. Lofty Pikes Peak is not the tallest mountain in the Rockies, but it is certainly the most monumental. It positively towers over nearby Colorado Springs, and is clearly visible from Denver, 75 miles away, when the smog lifts there. Visitors flock to the best-known peak in the Rockies, and with good reason: Pikes Peak is not only breathtaking in its own right, but the centerpiece of some of the state's best sightseeing as well.

Colorado Springs

Colorado Springs is leaping out of its resort-and-retirement beginnings to become a hotbed for the high-tech military, space, and research industries. With over 35 museums to match every taste, natural wonders, and a variety of other attractions, it remains one of Colorado's most popular vacation areas.

The military is a strong presence here. Military retirees account for the largest single income source in the El Paso County (Colorado Springs) area, and the active payroll from the United States Air Force Academy, NORAD (North American Air Defense Command), and army base Fort Carson gives the town a special flavor.

NORAD itself, located in the bowels of Cheyenne Mountain, can be visited with advance reservations. Information on the tour is available from the visitors' center, south of Route 24 and Petersen Boulevard.

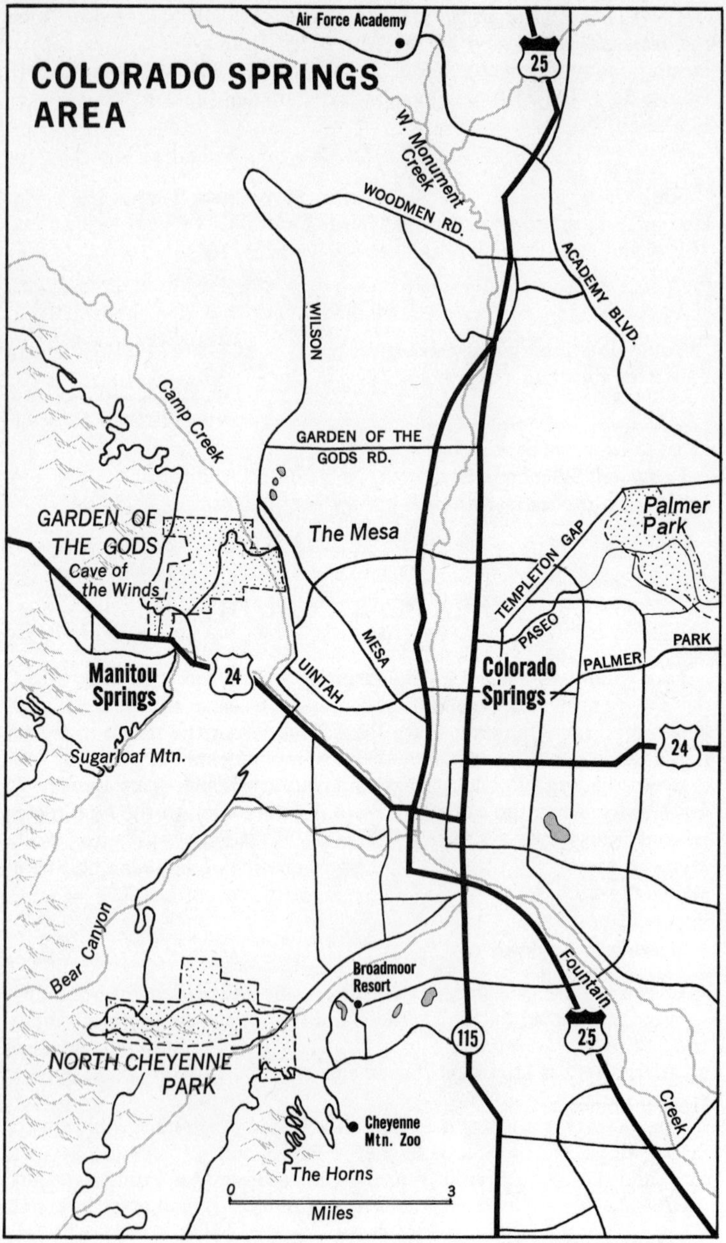
COLORADO SPRINGS AREA
Air Force Academy
25
W. Monument Creek
WOODMEN RD.
ACADEMY BLVD.
WILSON
Camp Creek
GARDEN OF THE GODS RD.
Palmer Park
GARDEN OF THE GODS
Cave of the Winds
The Mesa
TEMPLETON GAP
PASEO
MESA
PARK
Manitou Springs
24
UINTAH
Colorado Springs
PALMER
24
Sugarloaf Mtn.
Bear Canyon
Broadmoor Resort
Fountain
115
25
NORTH CHEYENNE PARK
Cheyenne Mtn. Zoo
Creek
The Horns
0
3
Miles

The Air Force Academy is one of the state's top tourist draws, and the U.S. Olympic Center is open to the public. Athletes from all over the country come to train and test at the facilities of the OTC and to compete against each other in excellent sports facilities.

The town retains the attractions that first drew travelers to "the Springs," as it is known in Colorado: the red sandstone cliffs of the 940-acre Garden of the Gods, the Cave of the Winds, Seven Falls cascading 300 feet through a deep canyon, the Cheyenne Mountain Highway and, of course, Pikes Peak.

Pikes Peak

Those who have seen it are amazed that Pikes Peak is actually accessible. From May to October, a mountain toll road runs from Colorado Springs to the summit. The Pikes Peak Incline Railway runs to the summit from Manitou Springs during the same months.

Up the road from the railway is Serpentine Drive, which you can follow to the summit, where the romantic Cave of the Winds is open daily with guided tours every 15 minutes.

Cheyenne Mountain

The toll road up the slopes of Cheyenne Mountain, Colorado Springs's other peak, is full of attractions. The Cheyenne Mountain Zoo is the first of these, with an excellent collection of animals. The Will Rogers Memorial nearby is full of memorabilia on the life and times of one of America's favorite humorists. Before heading on to the summit, stop at Seven Falls, a 300-yard chasm with picturesque rapids and cataracts.

U.S. Air Force Academy

The United States Air Force Academy is located north of town on I–25 and Academy Boulevard. The 18,000-acre grounds are open to visitors during daylight hours and offer scenic overlooks, nature trails, a B-52 bomber display, free planetarium, and a unique chapel. Call 472–2555 for information. During the academic year, the noontime parade of cadets on their way to mess is well worth a look.

Garden of the Gods

Just west of town, the Garden of the Gods is a series of natural sandstone formations cut by two roads and numerous hiking trails. The formations are Paleozoic and Mesozoic rocks bent by uplifting and faulting into towers, pinnacles, and mushrooms.

Thirty-five miles west of Colorado Springs on Route 24, the Florisant Fossil Beds National Monument preserves an ancient lake bed whose layers of shale have yielded extraordinary fossils.

Manitou Springs

Tucked at the foot of Pikes Peak near Ute Pass on Route 24, this lovely Victorian spa no longer attracts consumptives as it did 100 years ago, but you can still sample naturally carbonated waters from its 26 natural springs.

Many local artists and craftsmen have set up shop on Manitou's busier streets. A trolley will take you to Miramont Castle Museum or to the Pikes Peak Cog Railroad Depot, for a ride to the top of the mountain. Just outside of town are the Colorado Car Museum and the Manitou Cliff Dwellings Museum, with its fine collection of Pueblo Indian artifacts.

Cripple Creek and Royal Gorge

An hour's drive southwest of Colorado Springs is one of the most legendary of mining camps. Cripple Creek, named for the cow that stumbled and kicked up a fortune, still sees sporadic mining activity, but today the economy relies on the summer tourist trade. Travelers flock to the many fascinating ghost towns in the area, including Altman, Elleton, and Goldfield.

The Cripple Creek Mining District Museum tells the story of the overnight millionaires and the violent labor struggles that characterized these frontier mining towns. The Cripple Creek and Victor Railroad gives riders a four-mile ride through mining country, and the Imperial Hotel, one of Colorado's proud relics of the mining era, draws visitors to the downtown area. The district has a combination of scenery and history that makes it irresistible.

Tucked along the Arkansas River on Route 50 is Canon City, home of Colorado's State Prison, but equally famous as the entry to Colorado's Royal Gorge. The Gorge, southwest of Canon City, is one of the deepest canyons in Colorado—1,200 feet, with the canyon narrowing to 30 feet at some points. Famous as the site of Colorado's railroad wars and as one of Colorado's premier scenic attractions, it is today spanned by one of the world's highest suspension bridges. An incline railway leads to the bottom of the chasm.

PRACTICAL INFORMATION FOR PIKES PEAK COUNTRY

HOW TO GET THERE AND HOW TO GET AROUND. By air. Colorado's southern half is served by several commuter airlines and has airports capable of handling jets in Colorado Springs, Pueblo, Gunnison, Montrose, and Durango, all served by regularly scheduled service. The major carriers are *American West, Continental Express, Delta,* and *United Express.*

By car. Auto travel in Colorado is as varied as the Interstates and jeep trails that cross the state. In general, Colorado roads are excellent, but passes can be frightening for the first-time driver. Hint: To make time in the summer's tourist crunch, travel after sundown. For *car rentals,* the following is a sample of what's available in Colorado Springs: *Budget,* 473–6357; *Holiday Payless,* 471–4444; *National,* 596–1519; and *Thrifty,* 574–2472.

WHEN TO GO. Sightseeing and outdoor activities come into their own from spring to fall, when the magnificent wilderness can be enjoyed in full. Hunting season opens in fall. Cross-country skiing is popular from Thanksgiving to mid-April.

TOURIST INFORMATION. Pikes Peak Country Attractions Association, 354 Manitou Avenue, Manitou Springs 80829 (685–5894), publishes a yearly visitors guide chock-full of local Pikes Peak area events and attractions. *Canon City* **Chamber of Commerce,** Box 366, Canon City 81212 (275–2331), can send you specific information about their area, as can the *Colorado Springs* **Convention & Visitors Bureau,** 104 S. Cascade, Colorado Springs 80903 (635–1632). They also have an up-to-date event line called FUN FONE (635–1723).

Pikes Peak Country Passport is a coupon book that offers discounts at over 25 local attractions. Call 685–5894 for information.

ACCOMMODATIONS. There are two high seasons in the Pikes Peak Country—June through Labor Day and, for those areas near the ski slopes, December through March. Rates are based on double occupancy and average as follows: *Deluxe,* $100–$185; *Expensive,* $80–$100; *Moderate,* $50–$80; and *Inexpensive,* under $50.

Canon City

Royal Gorge Best Western. *Expensive.* 1925 Fremont (275–3377). Heated pool, restaurant, lounge.

Super 8 Motel. *Inexpensive.* 209 N. 19th St. (275–8680 or 800–843–1991). Economy hotel. Color TV.

Colorado Springs

The Antlers Hotel. *Deluxe.* In Chase Stone Center, Pikes Peak and Cascade (473–5600). Elegant downtown hotel with rooftop pool, several restaurants. Managed by the Broadmoor.

The Broadmoor Hotel. *Deluxe.* On Route 122; I–25 Exit 140B (634–7711). A world-class resort with all of the service and amenities the phrase implies. Tennis courts, pools, three outstanding 18-hole golf courses, all athletic facilities, bicycle and boat rentals, ice rinks; many restaurants, live entertainment, and dancing.

The Clarion Hotel. *Expensive.* 2886 South Circle Dr. (576–5900). Full resort and conference center with spa and athletic facilities, pool, restaurants.

Colorado Springs Hilton Inn. *Expensive.* 505 Pope's Bluff Trail (598–7656 or 800–HILTONS). Outdoor pool, restaurant.

Motel 7. *Moderate.* 3402 Sinton Rd., off I–25, Exit 145 (635–5486). This is a popular local motel with free HBO and Continental breakfast.

Motel 6. *Inexpensive.* N. Chestnut at Exit 64 from I–25 (471–2340). Clean, minimal housing.

Cripple Creek

Imperial Hotel. *Expensive.* 123 N. Third St. (689–2713). Restored mining camp with antique furnishings. Restaurant, lounge.

Manitou Springs

LaFon Motel. *Inexpensive.* 123 Manitou (685–5488). Pool. No dining facilities.

Red Wing Motel. *Inexpensive.* Beckers Lane and El Paso Blvd. (685–9547). Pool. No restaurant.

BED AND BREAKFASTS. *Bed-and-Breakfast Rocky Mountains,* Box 804, Colorado Springs 80901 (630–3433), has listings for the entire Rocky Mountain region. A sample of local accommodations:

Griffin's Hospitality House. *Moderate.* 4222 N. Chestnut, Colorado Springs 80907 (599–3035). Four rooms, one private bath. Picnic table, TV, washer and dryer, large breakfast. Open all year. No credit cards.

Hearthstone Inn. *Moderate.* 506 N. Cascade, Colorado Springs 80903 (473–4413). This restored Victorian mansion has 25 rooms, most with private bath, fireplaces, porches, and lovely antiques. Excellent breakfast.

GUEST RANCHES. For information on the guest ranches in Colorado, write *Colorado Guest and Dude Ranch Association,* Box 300, Tabernash, CO 80478 (887–3128). Or try:

Lost Valley Ranch. *Expensive.* Route 2, Box 70, Sedalia 80135 (647–2311). This working ranch in a wooded area is two hours from Colorado Springs. It has cabins with fireplaces, pool, riding, entertainment, day care, and semimar rooms. Good home cooking.

RESTAURANTS. A full range of cuisine can be found in the Pikes Peak area, from gourmet steak and seafood to Chinese cooking and family-style restaurants. Restaurant categories are: *Super Deluxe,* $80 and up; *Deluxe,* $50–$75; *Expensive,* $25–$50; *Moderate,* $15–$25; and *Inexpensive,* under $15. These prices are for two meals, including appetizer, soup, or salad, exclusive of drinks and tips. All restaurants listed take major credit cards unless otherwise noted.

Canon City

Salis. *Expensive.* 1431 S. Ninth St. (275–7221). Nouvelle cuisine; patio dining.

Mr. Ed's Family Restaurant. *Moderate.* 1201 Royal Gorge Blvd. (275–5833). Standard fare in a relaxed atmosphere.

Colorado Springs

Broadmoor Hotel Dining Rooms. *Deluxe.* In the Broadmoor Hotel (634–7711). There are a number of fine restaurants in this complex: the *Broadmoor Tavern,* the *Main Dining Room,* the elegant *Charles Court,* the *Penrose Dining Room,* and the *Golden Bee,* an English pub of the 19th century that was imported and rebuilt. In particular, the Penrose Room is a superbly managed gourmet restaurant with elegant appointments, view of the Cheyenne Mountain. International cuisine: noisettes of veal with chanterelles, osso bucco milanese, Wiener schnitzel, filet mignon, fresh poached salmon, rack of lamb. Delicious appetizers and desserts. Nightly dancing to old-fashioned music.

King's Table Buffet. *Inexpensive.* 3015 N. Nevada (473–8471) and 3020 E. Platte (634–5182). All-you-can-eat meals include entree, salad, dessert, and beverage. This place is an outstanding value but noisy because it is popular with tour-bus groups.

The London Grill. *Expensive.* Pikes Peak and Cascade at the Antlers Hotel (473–5600). Well-known cuisine. Excellent meats and fresh fish. Tableside cooking.

The Unicorn Chinese Restaurant. *Inexpensive.* 3408 N. Academy Blvd. (591–6222). Lots of selections. Polynesian drinks.

SPECIAL-INTEREST TOURS AND SIGHTSEEING. The Gray Line, 322 N. Nevada, Colorado Springs 80903 (633–1747 or 800–423–9515), runs daily bus tours to the major attractions in the area and can pick you up at your hotel or campground. **Pikes Peak Tours,** 3704 W. Colorado Ave., Colorado Springs 80904 (633–1181 or 800–345–8197), makes three trips daily up Pikes Peak in minibuses.

Colorado Springs

Cave of the Winds. Six miles west on Route 24 (685–5444). A 40-minute guided tour through ancient underground caverns filled with beautiful natural formations. Photography allowed. Bring a jacket and wear sturdy shoes.

Flying W Ranch, 3330 Chuckwagon Rd. (598–4000). Restored Old West town with lots of memorabilia and a working cattle ranch. Barbecue and authentic western stage show, May–Sept.; Flying W Winter Steakhouse Oct.–April. Reservations required.

Florisant Fossil Beds National Monument, 35 miles west of Colorado Springs on Route 24 (748–3253), is a 6,000-acre site once covered by a prehistoric lake. A museum and interpretive center are on the grounds—some fine fossils have been found here. Open daily.

North Pole, 10 miles west on Route 24 (684–9432). Children's attraction, with Santa and his elves, train ride, Ferris wheel, magic shows.

Pikes Peak Toll Road, on Pikes Peak (684–9383). A four-hour drive will take you to the top of this 14,110-foot peak. Breathtaking views of Sangre de Cristo range and the Continental Divide. Deer, elk, and Rocky Mountain bighorn sheep roam the Pike National Forest here, and the natural vegetation of the area shelters many small animals and birds. Open May–Oct.

Cripple Creek Area

The Cripple Creek and Victor Railroad (689–2640) gives riders a four-mile trip through the mining country of the area. Catch the narrow-gauge train at the Cripple Creek depot. Open Memorial Day-Labor Day.

Manitou Springs

Mt. Manitou Incline, Ruxton Ave. (685–9086). Cable car ride up Mt. Manitou climbs from 6,400 feet to 9,000 feet in 1¼ miles. Great view. Picnic area and hiking. Open May–Sept. For information write Mt. Manitou Incline, 508 Ruxton Ave., Manitou Springs 80829.

SPECTATOR SPORTS. Colorado is **rodeo** country, and every month of the summer offers a good one. For **football** fans, the *United States Air Force Academy* plays a major-college slate as a member of the Western Athletic Conference. *Rocky Mountain Greyhound Park,* 3701 North Nevada, Colorado Springs (632–1391) offers **greyhound racing** and pari-mutuel betting. Sept.–Nov.

OUTDOOR ACTIVITIES. Cross-country skiing is increasingly popular; a favorite spot among local enthusiasts is *Florissant National Monument,* 35 miles west of Colorado Springs on Route 24.

Backpackers should carry both warm and cool clothing, crepe- or Vibram-soled shoes, a frame pack, and a first-aid kit. When trekking through government-supervised areas, you are required to sign in and out and let rangers know the general direction you're heading and roughly when you expect to return. **Bicycling** is an old Colorado favorite, and it's not unusual to see a loaded-up bike whizzing down one of the mountain passes. For routes and rules write to *Colorado Department of Highways,* 4201 E. Arkansas, Denver 80222.

Rafting. For springtime thrills whitewater rafting can't be beat. River adventures vary in intensity, depending on whether you go along for the ride or grab an oar and wrestle the current yourself. Reservations are often essential during the summer months. More than 100 outfitters run the Browns Canyon and the Arkansas River in the Pikes Peak area, offering guided river trips that last from a half day to three weeks. Make sure that the outfitter is licensed as required by the State Department of Parks and Outdoor Recreation. For furthur information contact: *Western River Guides Assn.,* Colorado Chapter, 7600 E. Arapahoe, Suite 114, Englewood, CO 80112 (771–0389). A few guides in the area include:

Echo Canyon River Expeditions, Inc., Box 1002, Colorado Springs 80901 (275–3145, 632–3684, or 800–367–2167). Based near Royal Gorge. Group rates available.

Rocky Mountain Tours, Inc., Box 38353, Colorado Springs 80937. Half- and full-day Arkansas River trips, with steak lunch.

Arkansas Adventures Recreation Ranch, Box 1359, Canon City 81212 (269–3700 or 800–892–8929 in CO), offers scenic raft trips, from two hours to two days. Canoe and raft rentals. Gold panning, horseback riding, pack trips, and rock hounding. Wilderness access.

Golf. Although Colorado has been known more for rodeo than golf in the past, it's becoming a top locale for championship-class golf courses, as winter resorts find that summer tourists bring their clubs and want to tee off into the alpine sunset.

Leading the pack are the fabulous resort courses of the *Broadmoor* in Colorado Springs (634–7711). Open to guests of the Broadmoor and the Antlers Hotel, the three courses include the 1918 Donald Ross course and the new challenge of the Arnold Palmer Organization south course. Not to be forgotten are the municipals of the area, such as Colorado Springs's *Patty Jewett* (578–6825), the oldest surviving golf course in Colorado.

Hang Gliding. Black Forest Gliderport, 9990 Gliderport Rd., Colorado Springs 80908 (495–2436 or 495–4144).

Hot Air Ballooning. Pikes Peak Country is perfect for ballooning. Labor Day weekend marks the annual *Balloon Classic.* Call 473–2120 for details.

Horseback Riding. *Academy Riding Stables,* 4 El Paso Blvd., (633–

5667) near the Garden of the Gods, has riding with or without guides, April–Labor Day, weather permitting.

CAMPING. The great outdoors lures the visitor to camp out, and the national forests are the place to do it. Each of the forests in the region has numerous camping facilities, usually consisting of around 20 camping sites, with a picnic table, firepit, pump water, and outhouses at each site. No electricity. All on a first-come, first-serve basis.

Local private campgrounds include:

Royal Gorge KOA Campground, Route 50, west of Canon City (275–6116). Laundry, groceries, pool, game room. Pets allowed. 190 sites. Open April–Oct.

Golden Lane Campground, Route 24 Exit 31st St., west of Colorado Springs (633–2192). 120 sites, with pads, laundry, propane, game room. Pets allowed. Open May–Oct.

For complete listings of summer campsites, contact the *American Camping Association,* 400 S. Broadway, Denver, CO 80211 (778–8774).

HUNTING. Colorado is one of America's most popular hunting regions. Big-game animals include deer (mule and whitetail), elk, bear, mountain lion, bighorn sheep, and Rocky Mountain goat.

Regular elk and deer seasons open in October. The antelope season starts in September, and bighorn sheep and mountain goat seasons begin in late August. Special archery, muzzle-loading, and high-country deer and elk periods usually start prior to the regular deer and elk rifle seasons. Black bear may be hunted during the spring and summer and again during the state's regular big-game seasons. The period for hunting mountain lion runs concurrently with the regular big-game dates.

Residents and non-residents may bag all species of big-game animals except bighorn sheep and Rocky Mountain goat—only Colorado residents may hunt those two species.

All regular big-game licenses may be bought from authorized license agents, i.e., most of the state's hardware and sporting-goods stores. However, the Colorado Wildlife Commission may insist that you get your deer and elk licenses at Division of Wildlife offices after the opening of the regular rifle seasons. Licenses for some areas, for antlerless deer and elk hunting, for bighorn sheep, mountain goat, and antelope hunting are issued by application and drawing. The latter are usually available after May 1 each year. The passage of a hunter safety course or proof of completion of such a course is required for hunting. A license from another state is not be sufficient.

Printed regulations on deer, elk, bear, and mountain lion seasons may be obtained after August 1 each year. Contact the division for information on waterfowl, pheasant, quail, partridge, and grouse seasons. Archery regulations are available in late May.

Guides are not required by law for big game hunting, but hunters unfamiliar with Colorado's more rugged mountains would be wise to use guide services, especially for elk hunting. A list of licensed guides and outfitters is published in July of each year by the division, 6060 Broadway, Denver, CO 80216 (303–297–1192).

SEASONAL EVENTS. March. *U.S. National Men's Curling Championships* at the World Arena, Colorado Springs. **May.** *Blossom Festival,* Canon City. **June.** *Melodramas* begin in Cripple Creek. **July.** *Pikes Peak Hill Climb. Broadmoor International Theater* season begins at the Broadmoor Hotel in Colorado Springs; name entertainers appear. The *Annual Ice Revue* at the Broadmoor World Ice Arena. **November.** *Festival of Lights Christmas Parade,* Colorado Springs. **December.** *Hockey season* opens at the World Arena, Colorado Springs. *Pikes Peak Climb* with fireworks rings in the New Year.

MUSEUMS. The museums in Colorado Springs are numerous: The **Wildlife World Art Museum,** I–15 Exit 161 (488–2460), has an extensive collection of taxidermy, sculpture, and paintings of rare and trophy wildlife. Open Mon.–Fri., 8 A.M.–5 P.M.; Sat.–Sun., 10 A.M.–5 P.M.

The **Colorado Springs Fine Arts Center,** 30 W. Dale St. (634–5581), shows contemporary painting and special exhibits. Open Tues.–Sat., 10 A.M.–5 P.M.; Sun., 1:30–5 P.M.

The **Western Museum of Mining and Industry,** I–25 Exit 156A (598–8850), is dedicated to the hard rock miners. Ore samples, demonstrations. Open daily 9 A.M.–4:30 P.M.

THE CONTINENTAL DIVIDE AND SUMMIT COUNTY

Study the Colorado map: You'll find Summit County at the foot of the 11,992-foot-high Continental Divide. The area is made up of lovely meadows, forests, hiking trails, and serpentine alpine highways. The centerpiece of the county is 3,300-acre Lake Dillon. On summer days, its waters are deep blue, dotted by white triangles of sails, and alive with small motorboats, cabin cruisers, and canoes skimming the surface. Now and then, a fisherman angles for rainbow trout in privacy.

Georgetown

Georgetown, just over 50 miles west of Denver along I–70, was named for George Griffith, who discovered gold in 1860 at the confluence of two streams near the present-day Tenth and Rose streets.

The discovery of silver after the gold played out gave Georgetown a continuing stability that other boomtowns lacked. Many miners built opulent Victorian mansions that have been preserved and added to the National Historic Register.

Unlike other old Colorado mining communities, Georgetown was never leveled by a major fire, thanks to the efficiency of its volunteer fire companies. Three of the antique fire houses still stand: the Alpine Hose Company on Fifth Street, the Star Hook and Ladder (now the Georgetown municipal offices) on Sixth Street, and Old Missouri on Taos Street, across from Georgetown City Park.

You can also take a giant step backward in time and board the old Colorado and Southern narrow-gauge train that runs the four miles between

Georgetown and Silver Plume. The line was a main supply route 100 years ago. Now, visitors can make the 45-minute "loop"—so called because the track crosses over and under itself repeatedly—on great bridges rising 600 feet above the valley floor.

Granby and Grand Lake

Granby, elevation 7,939 feet, sits on the western side of the divide. Allow yourself three hours for a leisurely drive along Trail Ridge Road, more if you can afford it. Three sizable lakes—Grand Lake, Shadow Mountain, and Granby Reservoir—make the Granby area a recreation center. The Colorado River and its tributaries provide trout fishing. The lakes have been stocked with kokanee salmon, among other species, and they provide fair angling as well as a unique sport—snagging with treble hooks—during the early winter spawning season (September–January). Since the kokanee die anyway after they spawn, snagging is permitted to avoid wasting a food resource. Granby is also in the center of the Middle Park area, famed for its guest ranches.

The sleepy village of Grand Lake is a popular area for summer homes. The namesake lake, Colorado's largest natural body of water, and nearby Shadow Mountain Recreation Area have the nation's highest chartered yacht club, at two miles above sea level. Each summer, the group sponsors regattas and other boating events.

The 20-mile drive east on Route 34 through Big Thompson Canyon is among the most scenic mountain passages in the state, passing craggy rock cliffs as it parallels the Big Thompson River.

Leadville

Leadville is the historical center of this central Rockies area. The community of 4,000 people owes its existence to a gold boom in the 1860s and 1870s. By 1880, Leadville counted 30,000 citizens and had become "the richest and roughest town in the world." Oscar Wilde visited Leadville on his 1882 American tour. "I read the miners passages from the *Autobiography of Benvenuto Cellini,*" Wilde recalled, "and they seemed much delighted. I was reproved by my hearers for not having brought him with me. I explained that he had been dead for some little time, which elicited the inquiry, 'Who shot him?' "

The story of Leadville is largely the story of Horace Tabor. He came to the gold fields as a shopkeeper and put up a $17 grubstake for two miners in return for a one-third interest in whatever they found. The two men quickly stumbled onto the Matchless Mine, one of the richest silver veins ever uncovered. Tabor lavished his income from the mine—as much as $100,000 a month—on Leadville and Denver, building opera houses, grand homes, and other projects. He created Colorado's greatest scandal after he divorced his prim wife, Augusta, and married Elizabeth "Baby" Doe, a working-class woman 30 years his junior. Tabor was ruined when the value of silver plummeted in 1893, and died penniless in 1896. His last words to Baby Doe were "hang onto the Matchless." She did, in the vain hope it would again make millions. She died in Leadville during the cold winter of 1935.

The Matchless Cabin, one mile out of town on E. Seventh St., contains a small museum that tells the Tabor story to summer visitors. Tabor's original frame home at 116 E. Fifth Street has been preserved. Some of the rooms can be entered. Tabor's Opera House on Harrison Ave. has also been restored.

Several hundred lakes are close by, including Turquoise Lake on the western edge of town, rimmed by hiking and bicycle trails.

Breckenridge

The ski town of Breckenridge is typically Coloradan; it has all the right traces of mining (gold began in 1858, silver in 1878), and all the right Old West bars and cafes. Accommodations are generally town houses and forest-surrounded condominiums.

Breckenridge appeals to families, especially those from the East and Midwest. Nonskiers will find many shops to browse in. It is a lively vacation spot, both summer and winter.

PRACTICAL INFORMATION FOR THE CONTINENTAL DIVIDE AND SUMMIT COUNTY

HOW TO GET THERE AND HOW TO GET AROUND. By bus. *Greyhound* (292–6111 or 800–531–5332) has daily service from Denver's Stapleton Airport and downtown Denver. *Resort Express* (468–0330 or 800–334–7433) operates chauffeured vans to Breckenridge and Keystone.

By car. To reach Georgetown from Denver, travel west on I–70. Breckenridge is two hours west of Denver via I–70. Go through the Eisenhower Tunnel to Exit 203 (Route 9), about nine miles from Frisco. Breckenridge is 120 miles from Colorado Springs via I–25, I–70 and Route 9.

Keystone is 75 miles west of Denver. Take I–70 through the Eisenhower Tunnel to Exit 205, then follow Route 6 six miles east. In good weather take the spectacular Loveland Pass by exiting from I–70 onto Route 6 just before the tunnel.

To get to Loveland, Grand Lake, and Granby, take I–25 north from Denver, then Route 36 from Boulder toward Estes Park, where you can follow Route 34 east to Loveland, or—in summer—west over Trail Ridge Rd. toward Grand Lake and Granby.

To reach Leadville, take I–70 west from Denver and exit just after the town of Dillon.

WHEN TO GO. From Thanksgiving to mid-April the Continental Divide has some of the best skiing in the country. As the weather warms up, many of these ski resorts become summer playgrounds, with summer sports readily available.

TOURIST INFORMATION. For **Summit County:** *Summit County Chamber,* Box 446, Dillon 80435 (468–6205).

For **Grand Lake** and **Granby:** *Chamber of Commerce,* 114 E. Fifth Ave., Loveland 80537 (667–6311).

For **Leadville:** *Chamber of Commerce,* 809 Harrison, Leadville 80461 (468–3900).

The *Colorado Visitors Bureau,* 225 W. Colfax, Denver 80202 (892–1112), will have information on **Georgetown.**

ACCOMMODATIONS. Rates are based on double occupancy and average as follows: *Deluxe,* \$100–\$180; *Expensive,* \$80–\$100; *Moderate,* \$50–\$80; and *Inexpensive,* under \$50.

Breckenridge

Reservations can be booked through the *Breckenridge Resort Chamber,* 111 S. Main, Breckenridge 80424 (800–221–1091; in Colorado 453–2918; from Denver 453–6018).

Beaver Run. *Deluxe.* 649 Village Rd., Breckenridge 80424 (453–6000). Pool, hot tubs, saunas, steam and exercise rooms, day care.

Breckenridge Hilton Lodge. *Expensive.* 550 Village Rd., 80424 (453–4500 or 800–321–8444). Plush rooms with refrigerators are offered here, along with a ski shop and heated parking. Popular for meetings.

Georgetown

Georgetown Motor Inn. *Moderate.* I-70 Exit 228, 80444 (569–3201). Alpine-style inn in a scenic, historic location. Restaurant, cocktail lounge.

Granby

El Monte Lodge. *Expensive.* Box 105, Route 40, 80446 (887–3348). Heated pool, playground, pets limited. Cafe and cocktail lounge. A Best Western chain member.

Inn at Silver Creek. *Moderate.* Box 4001, 80446 (887–2131). There are over 300 units available here with ski packages. There are also shopping and tennis.

Broken Arrow Motel. *Inexpensive.* Box 143, Route 40, 80446 (887–3532). Small establishment. No phones in rooms. Playground, outdoor picnic tables.

Keystone

The main reservations service is Keystone Central Reservations, Box 38, Keystone 80435 (468–4242 or 800–222–0188).

Keystone Lodge. *Expensive.* Box 38 (468–2316). Keystone's full-service hotel, with 152 rooms. Condos available, too. Sauna and hot therapy baths.

Comfort Inn. *Moderate.* 560 Silverthorne La., 80498 (468–6200 or 800–228–5150). 158 rooms, some suites, are featured here, with handicapped facilities and nonsmoking floors. Free Continental breakfast.

Leadville

Best Western Silver King Motor Inn. *Expensive.* 2020 N. Poplar, 80461 (486–2610 or 800–528–1234). Large, modern hotel with sauna, restaurant, and cocktail lounge, dancing. Pets allowed. Rates are moderate in summer.

Super 8 Motel. *Moderate.* 1126 Elm St., 80461 (486–3637 or 800–842–1991). Located in the downtown area. Ski and tour packages are available here. Nearby restaurant.

Timberline Motel. *Inexpensive.* 216 Harrison Ave., 80461 (486–1876). Small but comfortable.

BED AND BREAKFASTS AND GUEST RANCHES. Brass Bed Inn. *Inexpensive.* 229 S. Main St., Breckenridge 80424 (453–0843). Restored Victorian bed-and-breakfast inn.

C Lazy U Ranch. *Deluxe.* Box 378A, Granby 80446 (887–3344). Off routes 40 and 125. The state's most versatile vacation center. American plan; horses, riding instruction, tennis, fishing, guided hiking, racquetball, whirlpool-sauna, cross-country skiing, Western evening entertainment. Scenic location.

The Hardy House Bed & Breakfast Inn. *Moderate.* 605 Brownell St., Georgetown 80444 (569–3388). Three quiet guest rooms are offered in this 1877 home. Comfortable parlor has potbellied stove. Feather comforters, full breakfast and cable TV are added features.

Hilltop House. *Moderate.* 100 W. 9th St., Leadville 80461 (486–2362). This quaint Victorian home has cheerful rooms. Full breakfast and optional sack lunch are offered. No smoking.

Riverside Guesthouses. *Expensive.* Box R Central, Grand Lake (627–3619). Fully carpeted log homes. Friendly owners.

Tumbling River Dude Ranch. *Expensive.* Grant 80448 (838–5981). 20 miles south of Georgetown, surrounded by the Pike National Forest. Cabins with fireplaces, at an altitude of 9,200 feet. Pack and raft trips, horseback riding, fishing, heated pool, hayrides, square dancing, jeep tours, cross-country skiing, sauna. Supervised program for children.

RESTAURANTS. For a full meal for two, exclusive of drinks, tax, and tip, the price categories are as follows: *Super Deluxe,* $75 and up; *Deluxe,* $50–$75; *Expensive,* $30–$50; *Moderate,* $15–$30, and *Inexpensive* under $15. All restaurants listed accept major credit cards unless noted otherwise.

Breckenridge

Briar Rose. *Expensive.* 109 E. Lincoln St. (453–9948). Prime rib, seafood, and steaks. Reservations.

St. Bernard. *Expensive.* 103 S. Main St. (453–2572). Italian food.

Stein Eriksen's. *Expensive.* Main St. and South Park Rd. (453–2000). Continental elegance is featured in this place, serving beef, veal, poultry. There are a good wine selection and a view of Maggie Pond.

Georgetown

Silver Queen Restaurant. *Expensive.* 500 Sixth St. (569–2961). Victorian atmosphere, complete with cherry paneling and stained glass. Varied menu.

The Renaissance. *Moderate.* 1025 Rose St. (569–3336). Northern Italian cuisine. Cocktails, wines. Good value.

Happy Cooker. *Inexpensive.* 507 Taos Square (569–3166). Quiches, stews, waffles, sandwiches for tourists and skiers. Cozy.

Granby

Windy Gap Inn. *Moderate–Expensive.* 15 East Agate Ave. (887–3693). This cheerful, friendly local spot has hearty home cooking, a dessert bar, and daily specials.

Grand Lake

The Rapids Restaurant. *Expensive.* 201 Rapid La. (627–3707). Italian specialties are offered in this log building on the riverbank.

Chuck Hole Café. *Inexpensive.* 1119 Grand Ave. (627–3509). Home cooking. Locally popular.

Keystone

Garden Room. *Deluxe.* In the Keystone Lodge (468–2316). Continental meals prepared tableside. Reservations recommended.

Bighorn Steakhouse. *Expensive.* In the Keystone Lodge (468–2316). Serves steaks and offers a large salad bar.

Old Dillon Inn. *Moderate.* 305 Dillon Lane, Silverthorn (468–2791). Mexican food, loud music, and weekend entertainment make this the most popular hangout for locals.

Leadville

The Golden Burro Cafe. *Moderate.* 710 Harrison Ave. (486–1239). Family dining. Large breakfasts, chicken-fried steak, homemade soup, and baked goods.

The Pizzeria. *Inexpensive.* 603 Harrison Ave. (486–0873). Pizza, calzone, spaghetti, sandwiches, salads, beer.

SPECIAL-INTEREST TOURS AND SIGHTSEEING. *Best Mountain Tours* by The Mountain Men, 3003 S. Macon Circle, Aurora 80014 (750–5200), conducts a variety of four-wheel-drive tours year-round. The Georgetown tour focuses on Guanella Pass and does not stop in town.

In the fall a number of "*Aspencades*" depart from various towns to view the spectacular foliage. *Jeep tours* are popular in various parts of the state as a way to enjoy the mountains and get into little-traveled areas more comfortably than on the back of a horse or by foot. Local chambers of commerce can help in arranging both trips.

Georgetown

The historic **Georgetown Loop Railroad,** 1207 Argentine St. 80444 (670–1686, in Denver 279–9670) is a narrow-gauge train running along its original century-old route. Board either at Georgetown, I–70 exit 228, or Silver Plume, I–70 exit 226, for the roundtrip, which includes a stop at the Lebanon Mine and an adjoining museum. Open Memorial Day-Sept.

A brochure describing a self-guided walking tour can be picked up at businesses around town or from the Georgetown Society, Box 667, Georgetown 80444 (569–2840; in Denver 674–2625).

It's difficult to top the nation's highest auto road—paved all the way—to the 14,260-foot summit of Mount Evans. Follow the signs from town. The road is closed in winter.

Leadville

Tours of the **U.S. Fish Hatchery** (486–0189), four miles south of town, are held daily, 7:30 A.M.–4 P.M. Hiking and cross country ski trails nearby.

OUTDOOR ACTIVITIES. See also *Boating* and *Fishing* below. For **golf,** try the *Grand Lake Metropolitan Recreation District Golf Course* (627–8008). *Mt. Massive Golf Course,* 259 County Rd. 5, Leadville (486–2176) is the highest in the world. Also, try *Breckenridge Municipal Golf Course* (453–9104).

Rafting is popular in spring and early summer. *Mad River Rafting, Inc.,* Box 650, Winter Park 80482 (726–5290) conducts trips on the Colorado and Arkansas rivers. Make reservations early.

Mountain climbing isn't for experts only. Two Leadville area peaks above 14,000 feet, Mt. Elbert and Mt. Massive, are accessible to people with little experience. Visit the Forest Service for maps.

Summer **hiking** in the Continental Divide is unsurpassed for wildlife, wildflowers, and spectacular views. Hiking maps are available through the *U.S. Forest Service,* 130 W. Fifth St., Leadville 80461. The U.S. Geological Survey maps are ideal for hikers and can be found in most large backpacking stores. There are **bicycling** trails around Turquoise Lake, near Leadville. Contact the Chamber of Commerce (see *Tourist Information* above) for details. **Windsurfing** and **swimming** are popular summertime activities at *Green Mountain Reservoir,* southwest of Granby. Groomed **cross-country skiing** trails are available at the *Nordic Center,* Box 207, Frisco 80443 (668–0866), and at the *Breckenridge Nordic Center* (453–6855).

BOATING. Grand Lake. In the three large lakes surrounding this charming town, boating and sailing are the most popular activities. The *Grand Lake Yacht Club* is the highest registered yacht club in the world. Races are held most summer weekends. Boats may be rented at the *Trail Ridge Marina,* Route 34 (627–3586); *Sunrise Harbor,* on Shadow Mountain Lake (627–3668); *Lake Kove Marina,* also on Shadow Mountain Lake (627–3605); and at the *Gala Marina,* on the north shore of Lake Granby (627–3220).

Leadville. *Turquoise Lake Recreation Area* is operated by U.S. Forest Service. Eight miles west of Leadville at Sixth St. stoplight. Elevation 9,800 ft. 49 sites, drinking water, boat ramp, access for large trailers.

FISHING. The Summit County Divide area is dotted with mountain lakes and reservoirs full of rainbow, Mackinaw, cutthroat, and German brown trout; catfish; kokanee salmon; crappie, and perch. Licenses are required, and most sporting goods stores carry them. Non-resident licenses are available for two-day and 10-day periods, at a reasonable fee. Colorado's fishing season runs almost year-round, with a few exceptions. You might want to try **ice-fishing** in the winter.

Some of the more popular fishing spots are *Grand Lake* at the town of Grand Lake; *Granby* and *Shadow Mountain* reservoirs, near Granby;

Twin Lakes and *Turquoise Lake,* near Leadville; lakes of the Grand Mesa, near Grand Junction; and *Lon Hagler Reservoir,* near Loveland.

CAMPING. Rustic accommodations of all types abound. For general camping information in the state, and for directories, write **KOA (Kampgrounds of America),** Box 30558, Billings, Montana 59114; **Mistix** (671–4500) makes reservations for state parks. A fee is charged. **National Park Service,** 655 Parfet, Box 25287, Denver 80225 (969–2000); **U.S. Forest Service,** 11177 W. Eighth Ave., Lakewood 80225 (236–9431); and *Colorado Division of Parks and Outdoor Recreation,* 1313 Sherman St., Rm. 618, Denver 80203 (866–3437).

Here is a sampling of campgrounds: **Camp Hale Memorial.** From Leadville go 17 miles north of Route 24. 21 sites, picnic area. Hiking trails, boat dock, and fishing. **Timber Creek Campground.** Nine miles north of Grand Lake on Route 34. Picnic area with grills, 100 sites. **Big Rock Campground.** Six miles north from Granby on Route 34, then 7 ¾ miles east on Route 150, a dirt road. Picnic area, boating, waterskiing, fishing. 20 sites.

DOWNHILL SKIING. The ski resorts of the Continental Divide are incredibly convenient to Denver on major highways. While they can't match the resort areas in western Colorado for vertical elevation, the skiing here is top-notch. Rates range $20–$30 for lift tickets. Check locally for discounts and ski packages.

Breckenridge. Box 1058, Breckenridge 80424 (453–2368). Take I-70 to Route 9 (Exit 203); 85 miles from Denver. An old mining town with short ski runs. 14 lifts; 107 trails (23% beginner, 28% intermediate, 49% expert). Vertical drop of 2,583 feet.

Copper Mountain. Box 3001, Copper Mountain 80443 (968–2882 or 800–458–8386). Take I-70; 75 miles from Denver. Truly diverse terrain. 20 lifts; 75 trails (25% beginner, 40% intermediate, 35% expert). Vertical drop of 2,760 feet.

Keystone. Box 38, Keystone 80435 (468–2316 or 800–222–0188). Take I-70 to Exit 205 at Dillon and head east on Route 6; 75 miles from Denver. Elegant resort with excellent accommodations. 14 lifts; 71 trails (18% beginner, 50% intermediate, 32% expert). Vertical drop of 2,360 feet at Keystone Mountain, 1,670 feet at Arapahoe Basin.

Loveland. Box 899, Georgetown 80444 (569–2288). Take I-70 to Exit 216; 56 miles from Denver. No accommodations at area. Eight lifts; 28 trails (25% beginner, 50% intermediate, 25% expert). Vertical drop of 1,340 feet.

Silvercreek. Box 4222, Silver Creek 80446 (887–3384 or 800–526–0590). Take I-70 and Route 40; 78 miles from Denver. Small ski area with good motel. Five lifts; 22 trails (30% beginner, 50% intermediate, 20% expert). Vertical drop of 970 feet.

SEASONAL EVENTS. In **January,** Grand Lake holds its *Winter Carnival,* with ice skating, snowmobiling, and parades. In **February,** Leadville's *Winter Carnival* is held each weekend. In **June,** *rodeos* are scheduled all over. *Keystone Summer Music Festival,* through Labor Day. In **July,** Grand Lake hosts *Western Week* and a *buffalo barbecue,* and begins its summer with *sailing regattas.* Look for fall *harvest festivals.* **December.** *Georgetown Christmas Market* with food, crafts.

MUSEUMS AND HISTORIC BUILDINGS. As one of the first areas of the American West to be transformed by the discovery of gold, Colorado is full of institutions devoted to 19th-century life. Most are well-attended and well kept up.

Georgetown

The Hamill House, 305 Argentine St. (569–2840). Mining czar William Hamill built this edifice in the late 1870s; it is now almost completely restored and open for public tours. Two stone buildings on the back of the property—Hamill's office and counting house—today house the Georgetown Historical Society. Open daily 9:30 A.M.–6 P.M. in summer, noon–4 P.M. in winter. Small fee.

The **Hotel de Paris,** 409 Sixth St. (569–2311), dating to 1875, became famous throughout the West for its gourmet cuisine. Proprietor Louis DuPuy, a Frenchman, took 15 years to complete the inn. When DuPuy died in 1900, it was revealed that he was actually a French army deserter named Adolphe Gerard and had lived in Georgetown for 30 years under a false identity. Open Tues.-Sun. 9:30 A.M.–6 P.M. in summer; noon–4 P.M. in winter.

Leadville

Memories of this mining town's early days are preserved in the **Heritage Museum and Gallery,** Ninth St. and Harrison Ave. (486–1878). Small fee. The **Healy House,** 912 Harrison Ave. (486–0487), built in 1878, is restored and serves as a museum of the bonanza mining period. On the same grounds is the **Dexter Cabin,** a finely made log cabin, open June–Oct. **Tabor House,** 308 Harrison (486–1147), is now an elegant museum.

ROCKY MOUNTAIN NATIONAL PARK

More than 100 years ago, an English woman named Isabella Bird fell in love with the area that would become the Rocky Mountain National Park. She visited the Longs Peak region on horseback and found "exquisite stretches of flowery pastures dotted with trees sloping down to bright streams full of red waist-coated trout." She described the soft glades of Colorado's dark forests and marveled at the snow peaks.

Established by the federal government in 1915, the 414 square-mile span of Rocky Mountain National Park now encompasses 84 peaks of more than 11,000 feet. Longs Peak is the highest, at 14,256 feet.

Nature studies, lectures, and tours are conducted by Park Rangers, and a number of short self-guiding nature paths are ideal for families. A bustle of activity during summer makes the region especially attractive to tourists. A Colorado fishing license entitles you to angle for trout in the Park's many lakes, while nearby resort hotels invite you to rest and absorb the scenery.

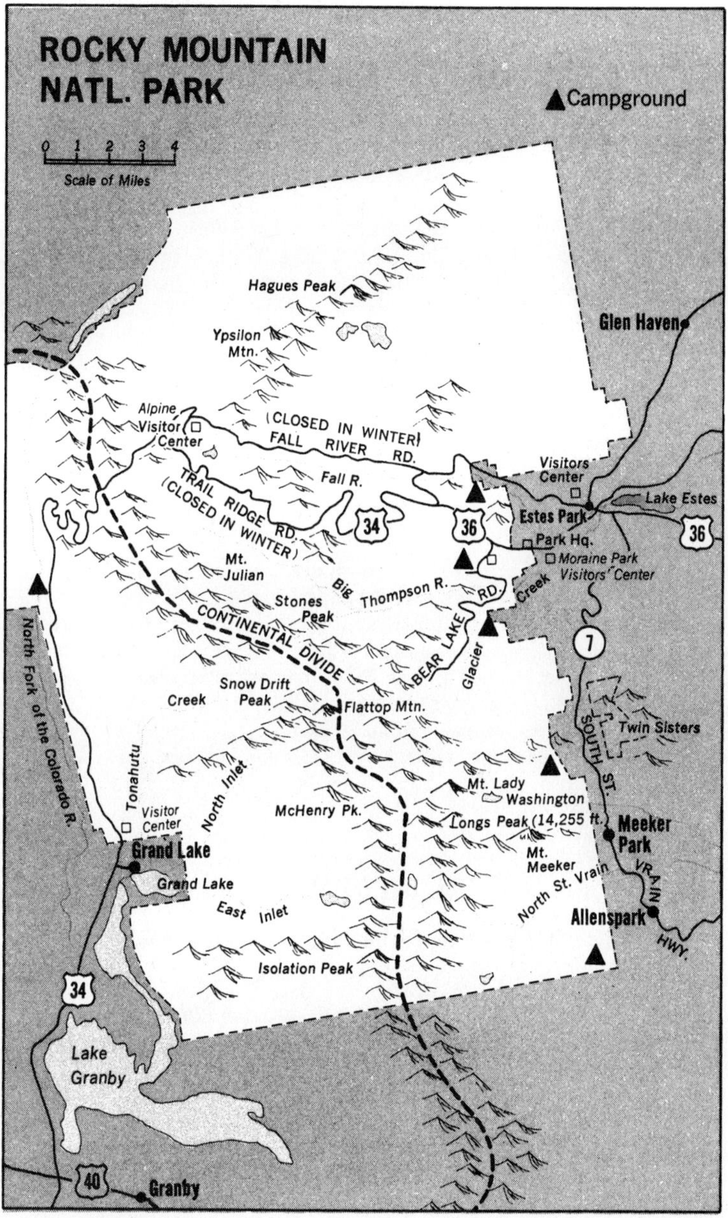
ROCKY MOUNTAIN
NATL. PARK
Campground
0 1 2 3 4
Scale of Miles
Hagues Peak
Ypsilon Mtn.
Glen Haven
Alpine Visitor Center
(CLOSED IN WINTER)
FALL RIVER RD.
Fall R.
TRAIL RIDGE RD. (CLOSED IN WINTER)
Visitors Center
Lake Estes
Estes Park
34
36
36
Park Hq.
Moraine Park Visitors' Center
Mt. Julian
Big Thompson R.
Stones Peak
CONTINENTAL DIVIDE
BEAR LAKE RD.
Glacier Creek
7
North Fork of the Colorado R.
Snow Drift Peak
Creek
Flattop Mtn.
SOUTH ST.
Twin Sisters
Tonahutu
North Inlet
Mt. Lady Washington
Visitor Center
McHenry Pk.
Longs Peak (14,255 ft.)
Meeker Park
Grand Lake
Grand Lake
Mt. Meeker
VRAIN
North St. Vrain
East Inlet
Allenspark
HWY.
Isolation Peak
34
Lake Granby
40
Granby

At the National Park headquarters in Estes Park, you can obtain maps to lead you to some of the park's outstanding features. Some 300 miles of trails lead to Dream and Odessa lakes, Tyndall and Andrews glaciers, Ouzel Falls, and Lulu City, an old mining camp. There are more than 750 kinds of plants and trees in the Rocky Mountain National Park, including quaking aspen, Douglas fir, narrowleaf cottonwood, thinleaf alder, Rocky Mountain juniper, blue spruce, and ponderosa and lodgepole pines. During autumn, the aspen leaves explode in color. Visitors will see plenty of chipmunks and squirrels and—if lucky—even elk, bighorn sheep, bears, martens, or coyotes.

Headquarters of the park is at the town of Estes Park; there is also an entrance at Grand Lake. The 50-mile-long Trail Ridge Road (open June–Labor Day) connects the two towns and is considered one of the great "high roads" of the world, crossing the Continental Divide at 12,000 feet along the route of an old Indian trail. At Rock Cut you'll see one of the park's most awe-inspiring views. Nearby is Tundra Trail, which can give visitors the chance to learn about the unusual plants of the alpine tundra. Other roads in the park include Fall River Road, with steep grades and many switchbacks, and Bear Lake Road, nine miles from the Moraine Park Visitors Center.

Estes Park

Estes Park isn't a park but a city—indeed, among the most popular tourist cities in the state. Located 61 miles northwest of Denver in the heart of the Rockies, Estes is an attractive site and tourist town *par excellence,* annually receiving three million visitors to Rocky Mountain National Park. In summer, Estes Park's 2,700 permanent residents are joined by 80,000 summer folk and 30,000 tourists daily.

After a flood some years ago, Main Street (Elhorn Avenue) was rebuilt; it is now a handsome thoroughfare with trees and benches, flanked by all kinds of shops.

PRACTICAL INFORMATION FOR ROCKY MOUNTAIN NATIONAL PARK

HOW TO GET THERE. By bus. *Greyhound* (292–6111 or 800–531–5332) serves all of northwestern Colorado. Daily buses run between Estes Park and Denver, year-round.

By car. Both Rocky Mountain National Park and Estes Park are easily reached from Denver on good paved roads. Travel times may be longer in winter, when snow and ice sometimes accumulate on the highways.

Route 36 from Boulder leads directly to Estes Park, where you can pick up Route 34, the only major road running through Rocky Mountain National Park.

TOURIST INFORMATION. Contact the *Chamber of Commerce* in Estes Park, 500 Big Thompson Ave., Box 3050, Estes Park 80517

(585–4431 or 800–621–5888), for information on Estes Park and environs. For more detailed information on Rocky Mountain National Park, call or write the *National Park Service,* Rocky Mountain Region, Box 25287, DFC, Denver 80225 (969–2000).

For forest maps, write to the *U.S. Forest Service,* Rocky Mountain Regional Office, 11177 W. 8th Ave., Box 25127, Lakewood 80225 (236–9431). This office has maps of all Colorado's forests.

ACCOMMODATIONS. Rates for double occupancy average as follows: *Deluxe,* $100–$150; *Expensive,* $80–$100; *Moderate,* $50–$80; and *Inexpensive,* under $50.

Estes Park

Because of the influx of people in the summer, Estes Park has 8,000 beds. During July and August, however, few rooms are to be found without reservations of up to three months in advance.

Longs Peak Inn and Guest Ranch. *Deluxe.* Longs Peak, Route 3A, 80517 (586–2110 or 800–262–2034). Summer ranch with stunning scenery, horses. Swimming pool, children's games, fishing. Evening entertainment includes square dancing.

Stanley Hotel. *Deluxe.* 333 Wonderview Ave. (586–3371). Elegant, historic hotel with Victorian rooms, fine ambience. Large solar-heated outdoor pool and whirlpool. Tennis court, children's playground, restaurants, theater.

Holiday Inn. *Expensive.* 101 S. Vrain Hwy. (586–2332 or 800–465–4329). At routes 36 and 7. Large rooms, Olympic-size indoor pool, game area. Cafe and bar on premises. Favored by conventions.

Ponderosa Lodge. *Moderate.* 1820 Fall River Rd. (586–4233). Overlooking the river, this lodge has comfortable, year-round accommodations. Playground.

RESTAURANTS. For a full meal for two, exclusive of drinks, tax, and tip the price categories are as follows: *Expensive,* $25–$65; *Moderate,* $15–$25; and *Inexpensive,* under $15.

Estes Park

Aspen's Restaurant. *Expensive.* At Holiday Inn, 101 S. Vrain Hwy. (586–2332). Variety of dishes; outstanding salad bar.

Stanley Hotel MacGregor Room. *Expensive.* 333 Wonderview Ave. (586–3371). Charming and elegant. Good management. Pretheater restaurant. Sunday brunch. Wine list.

Sundeck Restaurant. *Moderate.* 915 Moraine (586–9832). This homey, family-operated restaurant has fantastic mountain views. It is famous for fresh poached trout, Viennese goulash, and chili rellenos. A great value. Closed in winter.

Coffee Bar Cafe. *Inexpensive.* 167 E. Elkhorn Ave. (586–3626). Well-established cafe on main street. Good value. Long summer hours. No liquor.

La Casa. *Inexpensive.* 222 E. Elkhorn (586–2807). Outstanding Mexican and Cajun food are offered here, either indoors or in a summer outdoor garden. Congenial. Open all year.

Mountain Man Family Restaurant. *Inexpensive.* Routes 34 and 36 (586–8646). Good ham, beef, chicken. Drinks.

SIGHTSEEING AND TOURS. In the fall a number of *"Aspencades"* depart from the area to view the spectacular colors of the changing leaves. Check with the local chambers of commerce for exact dates and times (see *Tourist Information* above).

Estes Park

American Wilderness Tours, (586–4237) offers excursions to the backcountry, 9:30 A.M. daily.

Estes Park Aerial Tramway 420 E. Riverside Dr. (586–3675), carries passengers to the 8,896-foot summit of Prospect Mountain for an unmatched look at the community and surrounding mountains. Open mid-May-mid-Sept.

The rangers at Rocky Mountain National Park offer free guided hikes, lectures, and other programs. Inquire at the park's Visitors Center.

OUTDOOR ACTIVITIES. The Visitors Centers in the park provide all kinds of information—maps, details on programs and camping, backcountry permits, and more. Visitors Centers are located at Estes Park, Grand Lake, at the beginning of Trail Ridge Road, and Deer Ridge Junction (the *Moraine Park Visitors Center*).

A favorite way to see Estes Park and the surrounding country is on **horseback.** Estes Park calls itself the "horse capital of Colorado." Some stables offer breakfast rides, fishing trips, and other outings. Full details at the Estes Park Visitors Center, or try *Village Stables* (586–5269) or *Cowpoke Corner Corral* (586–5890).

For **cross-country skiing,** try the Estes Park Center/YMCA, 2515 Tunnel Rd. (586–3341), which has rental equipment available.

Some of the best **fishing** in the state is at Grand Lake, Shadow Mountain Lake, and Lake Granby, all in the Shadow Mountain Recreation Area. Kokanee salmon (snagging season is Oct.–Dec.) and Mackinaw, rainbow, German brown, and cutthroat trout are plentiful in the lakes and mountain streams. A particularly popular area is Trout Haven, one mile west of Estes Park on Route 36. Fishing is permitted within park boundaries, except at Bear Lake and where otherwise posted, and you will need a Colorado license. No live bait or hunting is allowed in the park, although once outside park boundaries, you can hunt in the Shadow Mountain Recreation Area, west of Shadow Mountain Lake.

Estes Park Adventures, Ltd., Box 2924, Estes Park 80517 (586–2303 or 800–762–5968), has **rafting** trips down the Poudre, Colorado, and Arkansas rivers.

Estes Park has two **golf** courses, both challenging. The 18-hole *Estes Park Golf and Country Club,* Route 7 (586–4431), has a pro shop, snack shop, driving range, rental bags, clubs, pull and electric carts, and all other equipment. The nine-hole *Lake Estes Golf Course,* east of the Visitors Center on Route 34 (586–9871), is next to the Big Thompson River and Lake Estes.

At Lake Estes you will find rental **boats,** boat docks, a tackle shop, snack shop, and other boating and fishing needs.

The district-owned **tennis** courts are available free both day and night. Two of the courts are lit at night for a small charge. Other courts are located in Stanley Park on Community Drive.

CAMPING. Rustic accommodations of all types abound. For general camping information in the state and for directories, write **KOA (Kampgrounds of America),** Box 30558, Billings, Montana 59114; **Mistix** (671–4500) makes reservations for state parks. A fee is charged. **National Park Service,** 655 Parfet, Box 25287, Denver 80225 (969–2000); and **U.S. Forest Service,** 11177 W. Eighth Ave., Lakewood 80225 (236–9431). The following list contains some of the best campgrounds in the region:

Estes Park

Estes Park Campground, Route 66, Box 3517, 80517 (586–4188). Wooded area ideal for tents and camping trailers. Reservations accepted.

Mary's Lake Campground, 1½ miles south of town on Hwy. 7, Box 2514, 80517 (586–4411). Mountain setting with tent sites and 90 RV hookups. Heated pool, modern rest rooms, fishing.

Olive Ridge Campground is on Route 7, about 15 miles south of Estes Park. Operated by the Forest Service.

Rocky Mountain National Park

Campgrounds are available on a first-come, first-serve basis, except for two: **Glacier Basin,** eight miles west of Estes Park on Bear Lake Rd., and **Moraine Park,** one mile west of the Moraine Park Visitors Center. Reservations may be made in person at the park or at the National Park Service in Denver (see above). No telephone reservations. Mail reservations are handled through Ticketron, Dept. R, 401 Hackensack Ave., Hackensack, NJ 07601.

You can get complete listings of campsites in the park, with maps and regulations, at any ranger station.

MUSEUMS AND HISTORIC SITES. When you're not absorbing the scenery or involved in your favorite sport, spend some time learning about the history and culture of this area.

Estes Park

Estes Park Area Historical Museum, 200 Fourth St. (586–6256). On Route 36, next to rodeo grounds, it relates the history of the region through photos, artifacts, and documents. Open daily, June–Sept; Tues.–Sat. in winter. Free.

The modest **MacGregor Ranch Museum,** (586–3749), a half-mile north of downtown on Devil's Gulch Road, preserves a 100-year-old working cattle ranch. MacGregor's first cabin and the 1896 farmhouse display tools, clothes, and other memorabilia of the owners and their times. Open Memorial Day–Labor Day; closed Mon.

SEASONAL EVENTS. January. *Dog Sled Weight Pull,* Estes Park. **February.** *Estes Park Mardi Gras.* **March.** *Ski Estes Park Spring Snow Festival.* **April.** *Estes Park Hobby Show.* **May.** *Invitational Loveland to Estes*

Park Stanley Steamer Run. **June.** Trail Ridge Road opens. *Alpine Marathon* and *Westernaires Horse Show,* Estes Park. **July.** Annual *4th of July Celebration* with barbecue, Sousa concert, fireworks over Lake Estes. *Arabian Horse Show* and *Rooftop Rodeo* in Estes Park. The YMCA of the Rockies hosts their annual *Festival of the Arts.* **August.** *Christian Artists Music Seminar* and International Coors Bicycle Classic. **September.** *Americade Rockies Tour Expo* motorcycle rally and *Scottish Highland Festival.* The aspens begin to turn. On Labor Day, *Aspenfest,* Estes Park. **October.** *Estes Park Invitational Jazz Festival* at the Stanley Hotel. **November.** Goose season opens. **December.** *Holiday Season Festival* in Estes Park. Opening of *Ski Estes Park* at Rocky Mountain National Park.

THE SANGRE DE CRISTO MOUNTAINS

The Spanish padres first saw this lone southern chain at sunset, when its peaks were glowing orange and purple, and named it *Sangre de Cristo,* or "Blood of Christ." Years later, a prominent English visitor wrote: "The scenery here bankrupts the English language." And no wonder: The Sangre de Cristo range, extending from horizon to horizon, is the largest continuous mountain chain in North America, with 42 peaks exceeding 13,000 feet. In the valleys, the Arkansas River appeals to river-rafters, especially between the communities of Salida and Canon City; anglers favor the river for trout fishing.

Salida, the major population center in the area, is blessed with scenic views, excellent air, and friendly inhabitants. The high mountains visible from Salida are part of the Collegiate Range—Mt. Harvard and Mt. Princeton, among others. At the southwestern foot of the Sangre de Cristos is the old railroad town of Alamosa, now an important Colorado farming community.

The Great Sand Dunes National Monument

Some 31 miles northeast of Alamosa via Route 150, Great Sand Dunes National Monument offers the highest naturally formed sand mountains in the United States, some towering 800 feet above the valley floor. The constant pressure of the wind sculpts the finely pulverized sand into a wonderland of hills, valleys, and plains. During the day the dunes can be visible for 70 miles, radiating a rosy warmth of sun on hot sand. The color and mood shift with the angle of the sun, as lengthening shadows change the dunes to violet and mauve. The dunes also produce some of the greatest lightning displays in America: The combination of wind and heat rising from the 55 square miles of sand creates titanic thunderstorms accompanied by extraordinary lightning bolts. The Visitors Center contains history and information on the area (call 378–2312). Campsites (no reservations; open April–Nov.) and picnic grounds wait at the end of well-marked hiking trails.

PRACTICAL INFORMATION FOR THE SANGRE DE CRISTO MOUNTAINS

HOW TO GET THERE AND HOW TO GET AROUND. By air. *Continental Express* has regularly scheduled service to Alamosa via *Rocky Mountain Airways.*

By bus. *Greyhound* serves the Sangre de Cristo range along I–25 and routes 285 and 160. Routes converge in Denver.

To get to Alamosa from Denver or Colorado Springs, take I–25 South, exit to Walsenberg at the junction with Route 160 West, and continue on approximately 62 miles. To reach Salida from Denver, take I–25 South to Pueblo, then head west on Route 50. The old Route 285 also connects Denver and Salida.

Road information is available from the Colorado State Patrol (east of I–25: 639–1234; west: 639–1111).

TOURIST INFORMATION. In **Alamosa:** Chamber of Commerce, Cole Park 81101 (589–3681). In **Salida:** Heart of the Rockies Chamber of Commerce, 406 W. Rainbow Blvd. 81201 (539–2068).

ACCOMMODATIONS. The Sangre de Cristo range has two high seasons—June–Labor Day and, for areas near ski slopes, Dec.–March. Our price categories for double occupancy are: *Expensive,* $80–$100; *Moderate,* $50–$80; and *Inexpensive,* under $50.

Alamosa

Best Western Alamosa. *Moderate.* 1919 Main St. (589–2567 or 800–528–1234). With restaurant, indoor pool on western edge of town. Golf, airport shuttle.

Holiday Inn. *Moderate.* Route 160, 333 Santa Fe Ave. (589–5833 or 800–465–4329). On eastern edge of town. Restaurant and indoor recreation center. Lounge.

Econo Lodge. *Inexpensive.* Route 160, 425 Main St. 81101 (589–6636 or 800–446–6900). In downtown Alamosa. Pool, restaurant, lounge, free cable TV.

Walsh Hotel. *Inexpensive.* 617 6th St. (589–6641). Small, friendly hotel.

Salida

Redwood Lodge. *Moderate.* 7310 U.S. 50 (539–2528). This is a small motel with some cottages. Sundeck, pool, nearby hot spring pool.

Best Western Colorado Lodge. *Inexpensive.* 352 W. Rainbow Blvd. 81201 (539–2514 or 800–528–1234). Heated pool, cafe, color TV, free local airport and bus station transportation.

BED AND BREAKFASTS. Poor Farm Country Inn. *Moderate.* 8495 County Rd. 160, Salida 81201 (539–3818). Five rooms furnished with antiques, two private baths. Full breakfast, free tea and wine. Library, piano; bicycles available. In a rural setting near the Arkansas River. Summer rafting trips, winter skiing.

DUDE AND GUEST RANCHES. The Pines Ranch. *Moderate.* Box 311, Westcliffe 81252 (783–9261). Approximately 50 miles south of Salida. Carpeted guest cabins, hot tub, recreation area, and dining room. Horseback riding and alpine skiing in season.

RESTAURANTS. With a long Spanish heritage, southern Colorado is home to the state's finest Mexican food, and good restaurants abound.

Alamosa

Lara's Soft-Spoken Restaurant. *Moderate.* 801 State Ave. (589–6769). Family-run restaurant with varied menu.

Salida

Salida Inn. *Expensive.* Route 50 and Hunt St. (539–4561). American and Italian food. Locally popular. Sun. brunch. Salad bar, home-baked goods. Bar.

Country Bounty. *Moderate.* 413 W. Rainbow Blvd. (539–3546). This family spot features Mexican specialties. A children's menu is available.

Windmill Restaurant. *Inexpensive.* 720 E. Hwy. 50 (539–3594). This unpretentious place serves hearty dinners and a lunch buffet. Good value.

SPECIAL-INTEREST TOURS AND SIGHTSEEING. This part of the Rockies is particularly well situated for tourists who wish to take time out to explore an area in depth. Old mining centers are filled with interesting touring opportunities, offering a break from nature watching.

Alamosa

Alamosa Wildlife Refuge. 9388 El Rancho Lane (589–4021). Just the place for bird-watching, five miles from routes 160 and 17E. Open daily.

Cole Park. 425 4th St. This old train station houses the Chamber of Commerce and has a narrow-gauge train display. Picnic grounds. Free.

Cumbres & Toltec Scenic Railroad. Box 668, Antonito 81120 (376–5483). Narrow-gauge trip through spectacular mountains and forests, 21 miles south of Alamosa. Open mid-June to mid-Oct. Reservations necessary.

Salida

Mount Shavano Fish Hatchery. Route 291 (539–6877). State-run. Open daily, 8 A.M.–4 P.M. Free.

Ghost Town Scenic Jeep Tours, 11150 Route 50, 81201 (539–2144 locally; 800–332–9100 in Colorado; 800–525–2081 elsewhere) offers half- and all-day tours through deserted mining towns, where you can actually pan for gold.

Monarch Aerial Tramway, 21 miles west of Salida on Route 50 at Monarch Ski Resort (539–3573). Trip goes from Monarch Pass to the top of the Continental Divide.

CAMPING. The great outdoors lures the visitor to camp out, and the national forests are the place to do it. Each of the forests in the region has numerous camping facilities, usually consisting of around 20 camping sites, with a picnic table and firepit at each site. Each area has pump water and outhouses, but no electricity. All on a first-come, first-serve basis.

Rio Grande National Forest. 1.8 million acres, with campsites available. Information from 1803 W. Hwy. 160, Monte Vista, CO 81144.

San Isabel National Forest. 1,107,000 acres. Information from 3417 N. Elizabeth St., Pueblo, CO 81002.

Many private sites with facilities are available, including:

Great Sand Dunes Oasis. Sand Dunes Rd., Mosca 81146 (378–2222). At entrance to Great Sand Dunes Monument. Wooded site. Jeep tours, trout pond, hiking trail. All amenities.

Heart of the Rockies KOA. 16105 Hwy. 50, Salida 81201 (539–2025). Laundry, pool, hiking trails, grocery store. Pets allowed. 20 tent sites, 45 RV hookups on 32 acres. Open May–Oct.

OUTDOOR ACTIVITIES. Hikers and **climbers** are blessed with thousands of square miles of national forest and park to choose from. Inquire locally and consult the U.S. Geologic Survey topographic series maps for trails and conditions.

River-rafting is an ever-popular spring activity in Colorado. *River Runners Ltd.,* Dept. W 11150, Route 50, Salida 81201 (800–332–9100 in Colorado; 800–525–2081 outside the state), has white-water raft trips lasting from several hours to three days on the river. They also have a campground and offer jeep tours of ghost towns. *Independent Whitewater,* Box T, Garfield 81227 (539–4634), guides high- and low-water raft trips through Brown's Canyon on the Arkansas River. Float fishing trips on the Arkansas, Taylor, and Gunnison rivers are also offered.

Alamosa has a beautiful nine-hole **golf** course (589–2260), and there is a municipal course in Salida (539–6373).

Alamosa also has a **skating** rink and tennis courts at Cole Park, 425 4th St. (589–6531).

HUNTING. Colorado's big-game herds draw nimrods from around the West for the annual harvest of deer, elk, and antelope. All big-game hunting in Colorado, whether on private land or national forest, is governed by the Colorado Wildlife Commission, and all hunting seasons and other regulations are set by that body.

Season starts in late August with special limited seasons for archery and black powder. Late October sees "separate" seasons for elk and deer, usually separated by a few days. The season finishes off with a "combined season" in early November. Exact dates vary from year-to-year and are usually set by the Wildlife Commission at its June meeting.

FISHING. Colorado's streams and lakes are open to fishing year-round, with only some local closures for spawning purposes. Year-round fishing can be inexpensively enjoyed by visitors who obtain one of several types of fishing licenses available to out-of-state residents. Fishing on private property requires no license, and many resorts maintain lakes and streams for their guests. Colorado is primarily known for its high mountain trout fishing. Popular spots are North Fork and Cottonwood lakes, and the Arkansas River.

SEASONAL EVENTS. June. *Arkansas River International White Water Boat Race,* Salida. *Sunshine Festival, Roundup Rodeo,* Alamosa. **July.** *Chaffee County Fair* and *Antique Alley Show and Sale,* both in Salida.

August. *Early Iron Festival,* a custom car show, begins in Alamosa. *Continental Divide Auto Hill Climb,* Salida. **September.** *Valley Rally* balloon races and *Fall Fire Festival,* Alamosa. **November.** Hunting season opens.

THE SAN JUAN RANGE

This is without a doubt Colorado's most rugged and spectacular mountain range, with some of its highest peaks and steepest valleys. This sea of pinnacles in the state's southwest reminds one of the Swiss Alps, complete with villages at high elevations, serpentine switchback roads, and thundering waterfalls. Summer travelers enjoy Ouray and Silverton. Skiers favor the quiet and remoteness of Telluride.

Telluride

This Victorian town lies at the end of a box canyon in a truly remote southwestern Colorado valley. Typically, Telluride sprang to life as a bustling mining camp's gold and silver miners thronged the streets, and the exuberant red-light district became famous for miles around. The name Telluride comes from the rare, lustrous crystalline element tellurium, found in a compound with either gold or silver.

Following the gold rush, Telluride slumbered for over half a century. Hippies migrated to this unconventional town in the 1960s, and renovated the elegant Victorian buildings. Today Telluride is registered as a National Historic District; it is a self-contained, dramatic mountain hideaway with one main street, a two-block walk from the backcountry.

In the past few years, with the opening of its new airport, Telluride has become more accessible but it is still a good value. Due to the numerous summer music festivals, summer business is as good as it is in winter.

Ouray, 37 miles south of Montrose on Route 550, is a Victorian mining town that has been made a National Historic District.

Of special interest here is a superb collection of artworks in the County Courthouse. Across the street from the courthouse is the County Museum, located in what was once the local hospital. The turn-of-the-century Elks Home on Main Street is a historic site that Brother Elks should not miss.

Durango

Over a million tourists pass through Durango every year to enjoy the surrounding mesa and butte country. This former pioneer town is now the headquarters for the San Juan National Forest and the home of Fort

Lewis College, as well as the main source of entertainment and recreation for the entire San Juan area. The mountain country around it offers excellent camping, fishing, and hunting, as well as winter sports.

Durango was named after the city in Mexico; its past is rich with Spanish associations. Spanish prospectors came through in 1765 and 1776; at that time the river upon which Durango is located was already named *Río de las Animas,* River of Souls. Its present prosperity dates from 1880, when the Denver and Rio Grande Railway chose Durango as the site for one of its depots. By the end of that year, the town could boast 500 buildings and 3,000 souls.

A National Historic Landmark, Durango retains many traces of its Spanish and Indian heritage. Of its 16,000 permanent residents, many are ranchers, college faculty, artists, and small-business owners. Durango is the terminus of Colorado's most famous remaining narrow-gauge railroad line. The trip from Durango to Silverton is a highlight of any visit to the area.

Mesa Verde National Park

The ruins of the cliff dwellings at Mesa Verde tell of a civilization that flourished nearly 1,000 years before the American Revolution. Archeologists and national park experts speculate that Mesa Verde's early inhabitants—now known as the Anasazi—were pueblo people. There are three general types of ruins open for inspection. The *pithouses* are shallow holes in the ground, usually covered with straw or grass roofs, that were inhabited by one family. The *pueblos* form a village around the *kiva,* which was used for religious ceremonies. The *cliff dwellings* were built much later and offered excellent protection to their inhabitants. The *cliff palace* was built 200 feet above the canyon floor and contains some 200 rooms. The *Spruce Tree House* is relatively easy to enter and is well preserved. It has 114 rooms and eight kivas and is not unlike today's apartment houses. No one may enter the fragile cliff dwellings unless accompanied by a park ranger.

The museum at Park Headquarters (529–4465) will add to your understanding of Mesa Verde and its people. The park is on Route 160, 10 miles east of Cortez. Bus service from Spruce Tree Lodge is available for those who do not wish to drive their cars into the park. The park includes a restaurant, service station, AAA road service, tire agency, and some campsites. Evening campfire talks are given by park rangers and archeologists. The Park Service has done everything it can to provide easy access to several of the sites, particularly Cliff House and Balcony House, where the ruins are open for inspection and guided tours. Call 529–4421 for lodging information.

The park is open daily, although the Wetherill Ruins, a separate group, and Far View Visitor Center are open only in summer.

Black Canyon of the Gunnison

The Black Canyon of the Gunnison National Monument is probably the deepest, darkest, wildest, and rockiest piece of real estate you will ever see. The Gunnison River has cut a narrow gorge, at times only 40 feet wide, through nearly solid granite, to depths ranging from 1,730 feet to

2,725 feet. From higher elevations it is possible to see the frothing white water below against a background of sunlight reflected from pink mica in the otherwise black walls. Legend has it that the canyon is so dark and narrow at the bottom that it is possible in broad daylight to see the stars by looking straight up. Well-organized boat trips down the river and descents on Indian trails may be taken, but only experienced climbers should attempt any other route down the ravine. Some of the best fishing in Colorado is to be found on the Gunnison.

The North Rim of the canyon is reached by a 14-mile gravel road east of Crawford on Route 92. The South Rim is reached by Route 50 to Montrose and then Route 347 six miles east. Park rangers have nightly programs during the summer at the Visitors Center here. Campsites and picnic areas are available. South Rim is open daily; North Rim is closed in winter by snow. Campsites are on a first-come, first-serve basis. For information call 249–7036.

PRACTICAL INFORMATION FOR THE SAN JUAN RANGE

HOW TO GET THERE AND HOW TO GET AROUND. By air. The Telluride Regional Airport is served by *Mesa Airlines* from New Mexico and Arizona, and from Colorado via *Continental Express.* Durango can be reached directly via *United Express, American West,* and *Continental Express.*

By bus. *Telluride Transit* (728–3856) provides ground transportation to Telluride from Montrose and Durango with 24-hour advance reservations. *Telluride Taxi* (728–3275) changes $4.50 per person for a ride into town from the airport. *Greyhound* has regular bus service to Montrose and Durango; Telluride Transit will connect with bus or flight arrivals if called in advance.

By car. Denver to Durango is a long ride on routes 285, 50, and 550. To get to Telluride by car, take routes 285, 50, 550, 62, and 145. Ouray is on Route 550, about 75 miles north of Durango. Mesa Verde National Park is on Route 160, about 36 miles west of Durango. The Black Canyon of the Gunnison can be reached by taking Route 50 to Route 92, or Route 347 from Montrose.

The "Million Dollar Highway" between Montrose and Durango offers some of the state's most dramatic mountain views in summer. In winter, however, expect blowing snow, and rocks on the highway.

For car rentals, here is a sample of what's available:

Durango: *Avis* (800–331–1212), *National* (259–0064 or 800–328–4567).

Gunnison: *Budget* (641–4403 or 800–527–0700), *Hertz* (800–654–3131).

Montrose: *Budget* (249–6083), *Dollar* (249–3810).

Pueblo: *Budget* (948–3363), *Hertz* (800–654–3131).

Road information is available from the *Colorado State Patrol* (east of I-25: 639–1234; west: 639–1111).

TOURIST INFORMATION. The following chambers of commerce can be very helpful: In **Durango:** 2301 Main Ave. 81303 (247–0312). In **Cortez:**

(Mesa Verde area) Box 968, 81321 (565–3414). In **Ouray:** Box 145, 81427. The *Telluride Ski Resort Association* is at Box 653, 81435 (728–3041 or 800–525–3455). For road conditions, call 728–3931; for weather, call 728–3856.

ACCOMMODATIONS. With tourism one of the biggest industries in the area, accommodations are available from the most luxurious to the most modest. Rates are for double occupancy: *Deluxe,* over $125; *Expensive,* $80–$125; *Moderate,* $50–$79; and *Inexpensive,* under $50.

Black Canyon of the Gunnison Area

Harmel's Ranch Resort. *Moderate–Deluxe.* Taylor River Rd., Gunnison, Box 944A (641–1740). This ranch is on a scenic spot on the Gunnison River, with lodge, cabins, and recreation.

Comfort Inn Water Wheel. *Moderate.* Box 882 (641–1650). One-and-a-half miles west of Gunnison. Adjacent to Gunnison River, Dos Rios Golf Course, tennis court. Rooms and town houses with cooking facilities, cable TV.

Red Arrow Inn. *Moderate.* 1702 E. Main, Montrose (249–9641 or 800–528–1234). Best Western. Heated pool, pleasant rooms.

San Juan Inn. *Moderate.* 1480 Route 550 S., Montrose (249–6644). Newer motel, pleasant rooms, next to restaurant. Indoor pool, hot tub.

Tomichi Village Inn Motel. *Moderate.* Route 50 (641–1131 or 800–528–1234). One mile east of Gunnison. Restaurant, lounge, heated pool, color TV.

ABC Motel. *Inexpensive.* 212 E. Tomichi, Gunnison (641–2400 or 800–341–8000). This place has modest rooms, cable TV, and whirlpool; nearby restaurant.

Durango

Tamarron. *Deluxe.* Drawer 3131 (247–8801 or 800–525–5420). One of Colorado's leading four-season resorts. Elegant lodge accommodations and condos. Tennis, 18-hole golf. Theme restaurants, coffee shop, indoor pool, health club, stables, cross-country skiing, conference facilities. Outstanding management and service.

Angelhaus. *Expensive.* Box 666 (247–8090). At base of Purgatory ski area. Reasonably priced condominiums.

Best Western General Palmer Hotel. *Expensive.* 567 Main St. (247–4747). Historic 19th-century house, Victorian decor. Restaurant and bar.

Strater Hotel. *Expensive.* 699 Main St. (247–4431 or 800–247–4431). Restored historic hotel. Honeymoon suite. Restaurant and saloon. Charming atmosphere.

Iron Horse Inn. *Moderate.* U.S. 550, four miles north of town, Drawer J (259–1010). Full convention facilities and cable TV are offered here.

Alpine North Motel. *Inexpensive.* 3515 N. Main Ave. (247–4042). Modest accommodations.

Chalet Lodge. *Inexpensive.* 20280 Route 160W (247–1350). Studios with kitchens, ski shuttle service.

Mesa Verde National Park Area

Cortez Inn. *Moderate.* 2121 E. Main, Cortez 81321 (565–6000). 100 units and conference rooms are available here, with pool and sauna. Airport transportation. Nearby restaurant.

Ramada Inn. *Moderate.* 666 S. Broadway (565–3773 or 800–2–RAMADA). Besides this chain's standard rooms, there are a pool, restaurant, and bar.

Turquoise Motor Inn. *Moderate.* 535 East Main St., Cortez. West on Route 160 (565–3778). Full-service restaurant, heated pool.

Ouray

St. Elmo Hotel. *Moderate.* 426 Main, 81427 (325–4951). Restored 1898 hotel furnished in antiques. Complimentary breakfast. Sauna and hot tub.

Telluride

Telluride Central Reservations, Box 1009, Telluride 81435 (800–525–3455; in Colorado 728–4431), handles lodging information and reservations for all properties in town. With only 10 lodges and accommodations for 3,300, the area fills quickly during holiday periods. The base of the ski area is four blocks from town, six blocks from Main Street condos.

Resort Rentals. *Deluxe.* 673 W. Pacific, Box 1278, 81435 (728–4405 or 800–538–7754). Some of Telluride's finest condo apartments. Good maid service, various locations.

LuLu City Condos. *Expensive.* 182½ S. Mahoney Dr., Box 1278 (728–4387). Phones, TVs, hot tubs in all units. Close to lifts.

The Dahl House. *Moderate.* 403 W. Colorado, Box 695 (728–3316). Former boarding house, with antiques. Breakfast included.

Manitou Hotel. *Moderate.* 333 S. Fir (728–4311 or 800–852–0015). On San Miguel River, this hotel is close to ski lifts. Decorated with antiques. Après-ski wine and cheese is served.

Telluride Lodge. *Moderate.* 666 W. Colorado Ave., at the base area (728–4446). Oldest ski lodge in Telluride Valley, four blocks from historic downtown. Common hot tub.

New Sheridan Hotel. *Inexpensive.* Box 980, 231 W. Colorado Ave. (728–4351). Victorian beauty, built in 1895 and renovated in 1977. Free ski shuttle to take you to mountain six blocks away. Lots of cafes in neighborhood.

BED AND BREAKFASTS. B&Bs are increasingly popular in Colorado, and the southwestern part of the state has more than its share. All offer a comfortable bed and a full breakfast in a local home. Many offer other amenities. The majority of B&Bs fall in the *Inexpensive* and *Moderate* hotel categories.

Durango

Blue Lake Ranch. 16919 Hwy. 140, Hesperus 81326 (385–4537). Five rooms, four private baths are available in this beautiful Victorian farmhouse. Lake, gardens, hot tub. Open May–Sept. only.

Victorian Inn. 2117 W. Second Ave. 81301 (247–2223). Six rooms, four baths. Breakfast and complimentary wine and chocolate. Bicycles, barbeque, airport pick-up. Some kitchenettes.

Ouray

Baker's Manor Guest House. 317 Second St. 81427 (325–4574). Shared bath. Continental breakfast. Near shops, restaurants, and municipal hot springs pool.

The House of Yesteryear. 516 Oak St., Box 440, 81427 (325–4277). Eight rooms, two private baths. Continental breakfast. Beautiful view overlooking Ouray.

Telluride

Johnstone Inn. 403 W. Colorado Ave. (728–3316). Three blocks from Coonskin Lift. Victorian-style bed and breakfast.

GUEST RANCHES. The San Juan Mountains are prime Colorado guest-ranch territory. Following is a selection of these truly Western accommodations.

Ah, Wilderness Guest Ranch and Winter Resort, Box 977, Durango 81301 (347–4121), is accessible only from the Durango-Silverton Narrow-Gauge Railroad. Activities include ice-skating, cross-country skiing, sleigh rides, pack trips, and fishing.

Colorado Trails Ranch. Box 848G, Durango 81302 (247–5055). Tennis, swimming, shooting, rafting, horses in the San Juan mountains. Modern cabins, large staff.

Lake Mancos Ranch, 42688 A County Road N, Box 218, Mancos 81328 (533–7900), offers riding, hiking, jeeping, and fishing in a relaxed atmosphere. Mesa Verde National Park area.

Mac Tiernan's San Juan Guest Ranch, 2882 Hwy. 23, Ridgeway 81432 (626–5360), is four miles south of Ouray.

Skyline Ranch. *Deluxe.* Box 67, Telluride 81435 (728–3757). Horseback riding, fishing, jeeps. Open June-Oct.

Wilderness Trails Ranch, 23486 County Road 501, Bayfield 81122 (247–0722), is a real horse ranch that breeds and trains Morgans, and offers pack trips, cookouts, sailboating, trap shooting, staff shows.

YOUTH HOSTELS. Durango Hostel. *Inexpensive.* 543 E. 2nd Ave., Durango (247–9905). Dorm rooms and cooking facilities. Near the train depot.

Oak Street Inn & Youth Hostel. *Inexpensive.* 134 N. Oak, Telluride (728–3383). This inn is housed in a former church, now on the National Historic Register. Color TV, fireplace.

RESTAURANTS. Our price categories are for two full meals with appetizer: *Deluxe,* $60 and up; *Expensive,* $30–$60; *Moderate,* $15–$30; and *Inexpensive,* under $15.

Black Canyon of the Gunnison Area

Glenn Eyrie. *Expensive.* Route 50S, Montrose (249–9263). Noted restaurant with superb staff and menu. Chef's choice always a winner.

Tomichi Village Restaurant. *Moderate.* In Best Western, on U.S. 50 (641–5032). Good food, German specialties.

Trough Restaurant. *Moderate.* Route 50 (641–0019). Steak, seafood, and libations a mile and a half west of Gunnison.

Durango

Canyon Restaurant-Tamarron. *Deluxe.* Box 3131 (247–8801). International cuisine in the grand manner, 18 miles from town. Excellent wild game, long wine list. Tuxedoed waiters. Obligatory 15% service charge. Lovely view of National Forest.

Palace Grill. *Expensive.* 1 Depot Pl. (247–2018). This well-known Western restaurant has a Victorian decor with a wide variety of entrees and mesquite grill. Live music weekdays, 4–7 P.M.

The Red Snapper. *Expensive.* 144 E. 9th St. (259–3417). Rick Langhart's well-respected, cheery seafood restaurant. Fresh snapper, salmon, marlin, king crab. Attentive service, pleasant atmosphere.

Francisco's. *Moderate.* 6th and Main (247–4098). Good Mexican-American food, steaks, and seafood are served here. Children's menu.

Bar D Chuckwagon Suppers. *Inexpensive.* 8080 County Rd. 250 (247–5753). Cowboy-style diner in outdoor setting. 7 days a week, summers only. Western entertainment. Good for large families. Reservations needed.

Mesa Verde Area

Far View Cafeteria. *Moderate.* In Far View Lodge, Mesa Verde National Park (524–4421). Family cafeteria with cocktail service available.

Ouray

Bon Ton. *Expensive.* 426 Main, Ouray (325–4951). Italian-style seafood and steaks in a cellar. Closed Tues.-Wed. in winter.

Telluride

Julian's. *Deluxe.* In the Sheridan Hotel, 231 W. Colorado Ave. (728–4351). Italian dinners in Victorian setting.

Cimarron Restaurant. *Expensive.* 150 W. San Juan Ave. (728–3377). Hand-cut steaks, seafood, and a salad buffet.

The Senate. *Expensive.* 123 S. Spruce (728–3201). A historic bar with intimate dining from a Continental menu. Scrumptious desserts, live entertainment.

Silverglade. *Expensive.* 115 W. Colorado Ave. (728–4943). The specialty is mesquite-broiled fresh fish, quail, shrimp, all with garlic bread. Dinner only.

Excelsior Cafe. *Moderate.* 200 W. Colorado (728–4250). Upscale breakfasts and lunches; soups, fondues, expresso, and wine by the glass are featured here.

Sofio's. *Moderate.* 110 E. Colorado (728–4882). Elaborate Mexican meals. Bar.

SPECIAL-INTEREST TOURS AND SIGHTSEEING. San Juan Tours, 567 Main Ave., Durango 81301 (247–9190), has sightseeing tours of Mesa Verde National Park, Ouray, the Durango-Silverton narrow-gauge train, and more.

One of the most scenic tours in the region is the guide-driven **San Juan Jeep Tour** (325–4444) out of Ouray. Leaving from the center of town, these all-day or half-day summer tours take passengers up the legendary jeep roads and around the mines of the high San Juans. At Bear Creek Falls, three miles south of Ouray on US 550, bridge crosses over 227-foot falls. Observation area nearby.

In Ouray, the **Bachelor Syracuse Mine** (325–4500 or 325–4122) offers tours 3,350 feet into Gold Hill.

The **Cumbres and Toltec Scenic Railway,** 64 miles of narrow-gauge line at the south end of the San Luis Valley, once designed to reach Mexico. It takes riders on a spectacular trip to the summit of Cumbres Pass. Catch it at the Antonito depot, one mile south of town, Route 285. Call 376–5483 for reservations. Open June–Oct.

The Durango-Silverton Narrow-Gauge Railroad, 479 Main Ave., Durango 81301 (247–2733), offers memorable views of the San Juan Range. The journeys please photographers. Don't dress your best for these railroad trips. Advance reservations necessary; open May–Oct.

NATIONAL PARKLANDS AND MONUMENTS. If you follow the Gunnison River for about 30 miles east of Montrose, you will reach the **Curecanti National Recreation Area,** consisting of three reservoirs—Blue Mesa, Morrow Point, and Crystal. Blue Mesa Lake, 20 miles long, offers three campgrounds (no reservations), boat ramps, and water sports. A marina has rental boats and equipment for fishing and waterskiing. Shore fishing for rainbow trout is best in early spring and late fall. The best salmon fishing usually starts in late June and continues through August. Fishing is regulated by state laws. Be sure you have a current license. Call 641–0707 for information. The National Park Service offers boat tours of Gunnison Gorge; see *Special-Interest Tours and Sightseeing* above.

In 1.7-million-acre **Gunnison National Forest** facilities are rare, though there are around 60 campsites. Hunting, fishing, and hiking are all popular. Write to headquarters at 2250 Hwy. 50, Delta, CO 81416.

Hovenweep National Monument is reached by a 20-mile gravel park road west of Pleasant View, off Route 666. The monument is a series of long-abandoned Pueblo settlements that punctuate the barren land and extend into southern Utah. The prehistoric buildings, evidently built by a people similar to those who built Mesa Verde, are open for inspection. A ranger is on duty at Square Tower. Campsites and picnic areas are available first-come, first-serve. In rainy or snowy weather, check in Cortez before attempting the dirt road. Call 529–4461.

Other national forests:

Rio Grande National Forest. 1.8 million acres with campsites available. Write headquarters at 1803 W. Route 160, Monte Vista, CO 81144. Within is the Wheeler Geologic Area, soon to be a national monument. Unique geologic formations nestled in the San Juans; accessible by four-wheel drive or on foot.

San Miguel National Forest. For information write Box 210, Dolores, CO 81323 (882–7296).

Uncompahgre National Forest. One million acres. Headquarters at Gunnison (see above).

San Isabel National Forest. 1.1 million acres. 1920 Valley Dr., Pueblo 81108 (545–8737).

San Juan National Forest. Contact Supervisor, Federal Bldg., 701 Camino del Rio, Durango, CO 81301 (247–4879).

CAMPING. The San Juan Range's National Forests are a great place to camp, with around 20 sites, each with numerous camping facilities, including picnic table and firepit. Each area has a water pump and outhouses, but no electricity. All are available on a first-come, first-serve basis.

The **Gunnison National Forest** has nearly 60 campsites. Write the Supervisor, 2250 Route 50, Delta, CO 81416. For information on **San Miguel National Forest,** write Box 210, Dolores, CO 81323 (882–7296). Camping is also popular in the **San Juan National Forest.** Contact the Supervisor, Federal Bldg., 701 Camino del Rio, Durango, CO 81301 (247–4879). Camping opportunities are numerous in the Telluride area.

Two blocks east of town by the San Miguel River is the **Telluride Town Park and Public Campground;** shady, pleasant, can walk to town; fee. **Cayton Campground** is 20 miles south of Telluride on Route 145; stream nearby for fishing, good hiking; U.S. Forest Service, 14-day limit, fee. Sunshine (327–4261) is eight miles southwest on Route 145; fishing, no showers. 14-day limit, with fee.

For Forest Service campgrounds in the Durango area, no reservations are necessary, but call district ranger, 259–0195, for information. Some popular spots are: **Purgatory Campground.** Drinking water, 14-day limit, fee; U.S. Forest Service. **Junction Creek** is six miles north of Durango on Junction Creek Road; U.S. Forest Service, restrooms, water, 14-day limit; fee. **Hermosa Meadows Camper Park** (247–3055) is ten miles north of town; full trailer and tent facilities, laundry, groceries, propane; commercial and fee-charging. **Cottonwood Camper Park,** (247–1977), within walking distance of town to the west, is also commercial; showers, restrooms, tent spaces, daily or weekly fees. For more developed sites, the **KOA** chain has campgrounds in Cortez, Gunnison, Pagosa, Ouray, Montrose and Durango. Write them at Box 30558, Billings, MT 59114.

Try also **Mesa Oasis Campground,** (565–8716), 4 miles south of Cortez on Routes 160 and 666. Open all year. 48 sites with water, electricity, flush toilets, showers, pay phone, laundry room. **Sunnyside Campground,** 12 miles west of Gunnison, U.S. 50 (641–0477), on Blue Mesa Lake. Fishing, boat launch nearby, laundry, store, 73 hookups.

OUTDOOR ACTIVITIES. Mountain climbing courses and guide services are available from *Beyond the Abyss* (728–3705) June–Sept., and *Fantasy Ridge Mountain Guides* (728–3456) for winter ice climbing.

Telluride Academy, 666 W. Colorado Ave., Box 2255, 81435 (728–5311), conducts one- and two-week classes on outdoor sports, mushrooming, French, local history, and other eclectic subjects.

Raft the San Miguel or Dolores rivers, or learn to **kayak** with *Far Flung Adventures* (728–3895) in Telluride. **Oar** and **paddle** trips on the Animas, Dolores, and San Juan rivers and Rio Grande can be booked through *Colorado River Tours,* 339 E. 13th St., Durango 81301 (259–0708 or 800–451–0708), April–Sept., or *Peregrine River Outfitters,* Box 808, Mancos 81328 (533–7235). *Rocky Mountain Outpost,* 288 County Rd., 203, #115, Durango 81301 (259–4783), has guided rafting, kayaking, and canoeing tours and river-skills clinics. Half-day, full-day, and overnight trips on the San Juan River. Professional photography service available.

Rope-guided **rock climbing** is taught in the summer by *Antoine Savelli Guides,* Box 952, Telluride 81435 (728–3705).

The *Curecanti Recreation Area,* located in the Black Canyon area, has a full-service marina, with boat tours on Morrow Point Lake, Visitors Center, and many other activities. An outdoor **hot springs pool** in Ouray City Park, off U.S. 550N, is fed by natural mineral waters. Small fee.

For **horseback rides,** contact the *Ouray Chamber of Commerce,* Box 145, Ouray 81427 (325–4746). *Bear Creek Horses,* southwest of Telluride (728–4431), offers chuck-wagon dinners, hayrides, trail rides, and pack trips (reserve two weeks in advance). *Telluride Sports* (728–3501) rents sturdy **mountain bikes** for exploring back roads of the area.

San Juan Outfitting, Inc., 120 Beaver Meadows Rd., Bayfield 81122 (884–2731 or 247–9063), offers hunting and fishing trips, pack trips, bowhunts, nine-day horseback rides, and wildlife photography trips in the San Juan National Forest and the Weminuche Wilderness areas.

The High Mountain Fitness Club, 1600 Florida St., Durango (259–2579), is open year-round with racquetball, handball, basketball, weight training, steam, sauna, pool, restaurant, and juice bar.

Tennis and **golf** are available everywhere, with two resort centers with professional instruction at Tamarron and Pagosa-Fairfield. Municipal courts abound; there are two in Ouray and Cortez has six. Check local phone books.

Tamarron, 18 miles north of Durango, is a manicured haven surrounded by the mountainous San Juans. The 6,400-yard golf course has a bit of everything in an almost-wild setting. Open to guests of the Tamarron Resort (247–8801 or 800–525–5420). Some of the municipal golf courses are little gems. Try Gunnison's *Dos Rios* (641–1482), and courses in Cortez (565–9208), Durango (247–1499), and Montrose (249–2167).

In winter, **cross-country skiing** equipment can be rented at the *Nordic Center,* Box 307, Telluride (728–3404), the place to learn or practice cross-country skiing. **Ice skating parties,** are held Wednesday evenings, at the town pond.

Downhill skiing in Telluride, Box 307, Telluride 81435 (728–3856). Take I–70 and routes 50, 550, 62, and 145; 335 miles from Denver. Historic and remote town. Nine lifts; 45 trails (14% beginner, 54% intermediate, 32% expert). Vertical drop of 3,155 feet.

FISHING. Colorado is known mostly for its high mountain trout fishing, but the lakes in the southern part of the state have many warm-water fish as well, notably bass and catfish at Navajo Reservoir.

In the winter, the Blue Mesa Reservoir is the mecca of ice fishermen, with the Pinnacles and Iola Basin areas the most popular spots for the cold-footers. This is Colorado's largest body of water and one of its best-known fisheries, with good supplies of lake trout and kokanee salmon, which spawn in the fall up the Gunnison.

Trout fishing on the Las Animas, Gunnison, and other rivers is famous worldwide; and the popularity of fishing has led to a "Gold Medal" waters concept for several streams. The Wildlife Commission sets bags and size limits, or restricts fishing on these waters to lures and artificial flies only, to encourage growth of the trophy-fish that is the goal of most fishermen.

Also well known to avid fishing enthusiasts is the Black Canyon of the Gunnison. The action starts below the series of Bureau of Land Management dams and continues on to the junction with the North Fork. Because of the cold discharge from the bottom of the reservoir, the Canyon is now prime trout water, and no fisherman should ever pass up a chance to try his or her luck here.

Vallecito Lake, 20 miles northwest of Durango, is known for its kokanee salmon and pike, as well as several species of trout. In the Durango area, fishing is also good on Vallecito, Temon, Navajo, and Piedra lakes and streams in the wilderness areas. Check with local sporting-goods stores for details and licenses. Local Colorado newspapers publish the Division of Wildlife "Fishing Report" in the Wednesday or Thursday editions, which runs down the current conditions on every stream and lake in the region.

SEASONAL EVENTS. January. *Governor's Cup* in mid-month, Telluride; great for politician-watchers. *Snowdown,* with many Winter Carnival events, Durango.

May. *Mountainfilm Festival,* Telluride. Durango celebrates *Narrow-Gauge Days* and an *Iron Horse Bike Race.*

June. *Bluegrass Festival* and *RM Photography Workshop,* Telluride.

July. *Independence Day Parade,* Silverton; *Jazz Festival,* Telluride.

August. *Great Western Brass Band Festival,* Silverton; *International Film Festival,* and *Wild Mushroom Fair,* Telluride; *Fiesta Days,* Durango.

September. *Imogene Pass Run,* Ouray to Telluride; *Hang Gliding Festival,* Telluride.

October. *Hunting season* begins in the Ouray area; *River Rendezvous,* Telluride; *Colorfest,* Durango.

WEST-CENTRAL COLORADO

Colorado's resorts are not what the first mountainmen came looking for, but they're enjoyable to the modern traveler nonetheless. Modern and full of flashy clubs, rides, and resort facilities, they'll thrill the excitement-seeker more than the hermit. Yet nearby are some of the finest climbing, fishing, skiing, and rafting opportunities the Rockies can offer.

Winter Park

In 1928, enthusiastic Denverites began riding the train to West Portal Station to hike up the mountain and ski down. Winter Park ski area was born. The little mountain town of Winter Park, two miles north of the ski area on Route 40, grew in the following years. Today minimalls, lodges, and motels are scattered along the highway.

Winter Park is a four-season resort, attracting people to ski in winter and golf, hike, raft, fish, bicycle, and enjoy the splendid scenery the rest of the year. Winter Park prides itself on being a "people's resort." Rates are consistently less than those at other Colorado resorts.

Steamboat Springs

The Ute Indians considered the Yampa Valley a summer playground, with numerous hot mineral springs and abundant hunting and fishing. Trappers came upon the area in the mid-1800's, naming it Steamboat for the chugging sound made by the mineral springs bubbling through the rock formations.

Mining had its turn in the valley, but farming and ranching have been the mainstay of this town of 5,000 inhabitants. Today, the area bustles with skiers in winter. The mood here is friendly, the dress casual; if you don't own a cowboy hat when you arrive, you probably will before you leave.

Steamboat is geared to families, and its prices are quite affordable.

Vail

What is now known as Gore Creek Valley was once a high mountain pasture, cradled by the Gore and Sawatch mountain ranges, that provided a rich summer hunting ground for the Ute Indians. Sir St. George Gore, a baronet from Ireland known as Lord Gore, spent the summers of 1854–56 with famous mountain man Jim Bridger on the east side of the Gore Range. Gore killed every animal he could raise his rifle to before he was "requested" to return home. Five years later, Bridger returned to the area and he named the mountain range and valley after him, though Lord Gore never set foot as far west as the range and valley that now bear his name.

The intrusion of the white man searching for gold and silver in the 1870s and 1880s was the last straw for the Utes. Leaving the mountains, they set "spite fires" that burned thousands of acres of timber. Years later, the deforested terrain serves skiers as Vail's famous back bowls.

With the exception of a few sheep ranchers, the Gore Creek Valley slept until 1940 when Route 6 followed the passes from Denver through the valley. Charlie Vail was in charge of construction for the state department of highways, hence the name Vail Pass. The Tenth Mountain Division trained 20 miles away near Leadville during World War II, drawing many of the men back to these mountain valleys after the war. It was one of these veterans who saw the skiing possibilities of the Vail Pass area.

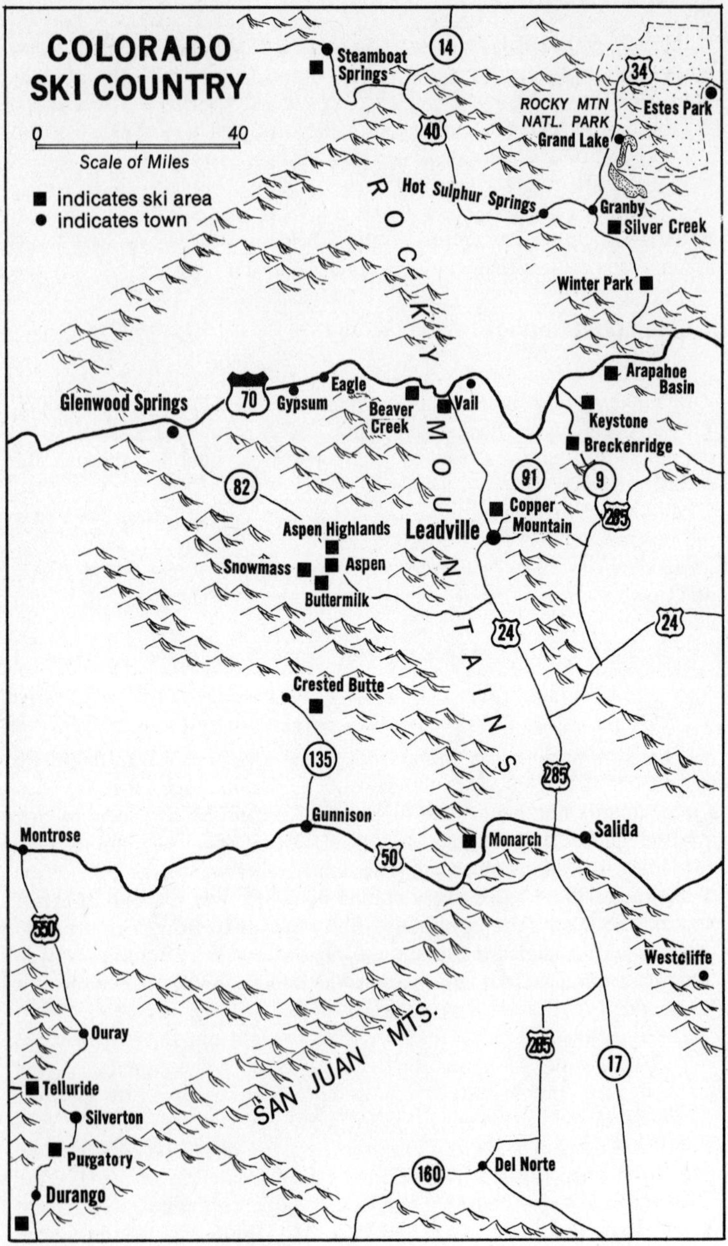
COLORADO SKI COUNTRY
0 40
Scale of Miles
■ indicates ski area
● indicates town
Steamboat Springs
14
34
40
ROCKY MTN NATL. PARK
Estes Park
Grand Lake
Hot Sulphur Springs
Granby
Silver Creek
Winter Park
ROCKY MOUNTAINS
Arapahoe Basin
Keystone
Breckenridge
Glenwood Springs
70
Gypsum
Eagle
Beaver Creek
Vail
82
91
9
285
Copper Mountain
Leadville
Aspen Highlands
Snowmass
Aspen
Buttermilk
24
24
Crested Butte
135
285
Gunnison
Montrose
50
Monarch
Salida
550
Westcliffe
Ouray
SAN JUAN MTS.
285
17
Telluride
Silverton
Purgatory
Durango
160
Del Norte

Glenwood Springs

Glenwood, as residents call it, sits in the White River National Forest, whose two million acres are renowned for all manner of open-air sport. The forest includes the Flat Tops Wilderness, a 117,800-acre plateau north of Glenwood Springs and Rifle, which extends across three counties. Allow a few hours for a hike to Hanging Lake and Spouting Rock, 10 miles east of Glenwood Springs.

Glenwood Springs's location at the confluence of the Roaring Fork, Crystal, and Colorado rivers makes it one of the state's most popular river-rafting centers. Local guides are available for trips of all lengths and difficulties.

Glenwood's original attraction, the acclaimed hot springs mineral baths, are always open to the public. In the 1880s, silver baron Walter Devereaux decided to convert the springs used by the Utes into a health resort for the rich. He built the two-block-long swimming pool, intended for use only by guests of the posh Hotel Colorado adjacent. By the early 1900s, so many wealthy and famous people were coming to the spa that a rail siding was installed beside the hotel to hold their private railroad cars. Teddy Roosevelt made the hotel his summer White House in 1901 while bear hunting in the nearby hills.

Aspen

As a winter playground, Aspen needs no introduction. Dozens of well-groomed trails await the skier, and a slew of winter sports and social activities distract the visitor. Yet Aspen is a fine summer town as well, with activities running the gamut of mountain climbing, hiking, horseback riding, indoor and outdoor tennis, jeeps, massages, ballooning, gymnastics, and whatever else you could think of. The turn-of-the-century Victorian mining town atmosphere has been preserved and updated, and the town has become a haven for celebrities.

Aspen's summer mainstay is its Summer Music Festival, held from late June to late August, when a number of locales come alive with concerts several times a week. Numerous special events are held each summer including opera performances and various classes. In addition to the concerts, the Aspen Music School conducts a session for students.

Crested Butte

Unlike the other Colorado mining towns, Crested Butte never really died. Amax Mining Company extracts molybdenum from the area, sparking classic confrontations between mining officials and environmentalists. This rather remote town in the Gunnison Valley has been listed as a National Historic District. Crested Butte's weatherbeaten buildings reflect the price of survival in the harsh mountain winters. Behind the 1880s facades are trendy gourmet restaurants, shops, and art galleries. Nevertheless, the ambience remains Victorian.

Grand Junction

The town of Grand Junction takes its name from the nearby meeting point of the Colorado and Gunnison rivers. Summer events range from horse shows and rodeos to drag racing and balloon rallies. Local points of interest include the downtown Museum of Western Colorado, an exhibit of the region's geological and social history.

Uranium, lead, zinc, and other minerals have been mined here for years. The Book Cliff Mountains and Piceance Basin to the north hold much of the nation's recoverable shale oil—perhaps some three billion barrels, or enough to power the entire nation for almost a century. The rich soil of the area produces especially good peaches and pears.

PRACTICAL INFORMATION FOR THE COLORADO RESORTS

HOW TO GET THERE. Colorado's resort towns are far-flung, yet all can be reached via the interstate highways, and some even have airports of their own.

Aspen

Aspen is 205 miles west of Denver in the White River National Forest.

By air. *Continental Express* has regular service to Aspen. For private planes, the Aspen Airport tower is open from 7 A.M. until 30 minutes after sunset.

By bus. *Greyhound* offers daily bus service between the Denver airport and bus terminal and the Aspen airport, as well as service from Grand Junction.

By train. *Amtrak* serves Glenwood Springs (40 miles from Aspen) daily. For full details call toll-free 800–872–7245. Amtrak or your travel agent can book you a *Mellow Yellow Taxi* (925–2282) or *High Mountain Taxi* (925–8294) for a special rate between Glenwood Springs and the Aspen area.

By car. Aspen can be reached from Denver by taking I-70 to Glenwood Springs and Route 82 from Glenwood to Aspen, 40 miles southeast. It is a 4½-hour drive under normal conditions. Rental cars are also available in Denver, Aspen, and Grand Junction.

Crested Butte

Crested Butte is in the Gunnison National Forest, 235 miles southwest of Denver.

By air. *American* flies from Dallas to Gunnison, 28 miles away. *Continental Express* arrives from Denver, *Delta* from Salt Lake City, and *United* from Chicago. *Crested Butte Aviator* (349–7334) and *Monarch* (243–7559) connect Crested Butte with Aspen. Crested Butte operates a free shuttle from the town to Mt. Crested Butte.

From Gunnison Airport, taxis (349–5749) and limousines (349–5874) operate daily schedules to Crested Butte; rental cars are also available at the airport from *Budget* (641–4403), *Great American Rental* (641–1391), or *Hertz* (641–2881).

By bus. *Greyhound* runs from Denver, Colorado Springs, and Grand Junction to Gunnison, 30 miles from the area.

Glenwood Springs

Glenwood Springs is in the White River National Forest, 170 miles west of Denver.

By air. Grand Junction is the closest gateway, served by *Continental Express* and *United Express.*

By bus. *Greyhound* (800–531–5332) services Glenwood Springs daily.

By train. *Amtrak* serves Glenwood Springs from Denver.

By car. To reach Glenwood Springs from Denver, take I-70 west. For rental-car information see *Practical Information for Denver.*

Grand Junction

Grand Junction is 253 miles west of Denver.

By air. *Continental Express* and *United Express* fly into Grand Junction from Denver.

By bus. *Greyhound* (800–531–5332) has daily service to Grand Junction from Denver.

By train. *Amtrak* serves Grand Junction from Denver.

By car. Take I-70 west from Denver.

Steamboat Springs

Steamboat is in the Routt National Forest, 157 miles northwest of Denver.

By air. *Continental Express* has connecting flights between Stapleton Airport in Denver and Bob Adams Field/Routt County Stolport, two miles west of town. *American Airlines* has daily flights to Steamboat from Chicago and Dallas/Ft. Worth. Taxis and limos are available from the airport to the lodges; try *Alpine Taxi/Limo* (879–2800) or *Ultimate Limousine* (879–7417). There are also rental cars at the airport; *Budget* (800–527–0700) and *National* (800–328–4567).

By bus. *Steamboat Express Bus* runs between Denver's Stapleton Airport and Steamboat Springs mid-Dec.-early April. Advance reservations during Feb. and March recommended; call 879–0740 or in Colorado 800–332–3204; write Box 774408, Steamboat Springs, CO 80477. Regularly scheduled *Greyhound* buses come from Denver and from Salt Lake City (340 miles west of Steamboat).

By car. From Denver, Steamboat is 157 miles west via I-70 through the Eisenhower Tunnel to Exit 205; follow CO 9 to U.S. 40, over Rabbit Ears Pass and into the Yampa Valley. From Grand Junction, drive east on I-70 to Route 131 at Wolcott, then onto U.S. 40 in the valley, a total of 200 miles. From Laramie, Wyoming, it is 122 miles via routes 230, 127, 14, and 40.

Vail

Vail is in the White River National Forest, 100 miles west of Denver.

By air. All major airlines serve Denver's Stapleton Airport (see also *Practical Information for Denver*). The following companies provide ground transportation between Stapleton and Vail: *Airport Transportation* Service (800–247–7074), *Colorado Ground Transportation* (398–5669 or 800–824–1104), *Colorado Mountain Transporter* (398–2177 or 800–722–2177), *TCG Limousines* (790–4004), *Vail Transportation, Inc.* (800–992–TAXI), and *Van to Vail* (476–4467 or 800–222–2112).

Continental Express makes connections between Denver and the Avon Stolport, 10 miles west of Vail at Beaver Creek. There is a general aviation airport at Eagle, 30 miles west of Vail; no connecting ground transportation except taxi or rental car.

By bus. *Greyhound* serves the Vail Transportation Center from downtown Denver, Stapleton Airport and Grand Junction.

By car. From Denver, Vail lies 100 miles west on I-70. From Grand Junction it is 150 miles east on I-70; Colorado Springs is 145 miles away via I-25 and I-70. *American International* (800–527–0202), *Hertz* (800–654–3131), and *Thrifty* (949–7787) have rental agencies in Vail; all the major rental car companies are at the Denver airport (see *Practical Information for Denver*).

HOTELS AND ACCOMMODATIONS. Hotels in the west of Colorado can be surprisingly upscale, considering their distance from major cities. Our categories for a one-night stay, double occupancy, are: *Deluxe,* over $110; *Expensive,* $80–$100; *Moderate,* $50–$80; and *Inexpensive,* under $50.

Aspen

For lodging information, contact: *Aspen Central Reservations,* 700 S. Aspen St., Aspen 81611 (925–9000).

Aspen Square. *Deluxe.* 617 East Cooper (925–1000). Condos with all amenities. Adjacent to Aspen Mountain.

Independence Square Hotel. *Deluxe.* 404 S. Galena (920–2313). Restored Victorian rooming house. Close to Aspen shuttles and restaurants.

Ullr Lodge. *Expensive.* 520 West Main (925–7696). Good for skiers and summer travelers.

Brass Bed Inn. *Moderate.* 926 E. Durant St. (925–3622). This friendly inn features brass beds, puffy down comforters, full breakfasts, and a Jacuzzi.

St. Moritz Lodge. *Moderate.* 334 West Hyman (925–3220). This 1930s lodge with European flavor is near the center of Aspen. Apartments, rooms with bath, and dorm rooms are available. Fireplace lobby, TV lounge, library and game rooms, après-ski refreshments, pool, sauna and Jacuzzi complete the list of attractions at this lodge. There is no restaurant.

Heatherbed Ski Lodge. *Inexpensive.* Maroon Creek Rd. (925–7077). This spic-and-span place, with Early American decor, has outdoor pool and spectacular views. Excellent Continental breakfast.

Crested Butte

Grand Butte Hotel. *Deluxe.* Box 5006, Mt. Crested Butte (349–7561 or 800–341–5437). Region's most elegant hotel, with marbled gourmet dining room, comfortable coffee shops, bars, evening entertainment. Convention facilities, underground parking.

Nordic Inn. *Moderate–Expensive.* Treasury Rd., Box 939 (349–5542). This is a cozy two-story, 28-unit inn; some rooms have kitchenettes. Continental breakfast included.

Glenwood Springs

Best Western Antlers Motel. *Expensive.* 305 Laurel St. (945–8535 or 800–528–1234). 80-unit motel. Clean.

Holiday Inn. *Expensive.* I-70 Glenwood (945–8551). Heated pool, saunas. Restaurant, bar, entertainment, dancing. Two miles west of town at I-70 exit; car needed.

Hot Springs Lodge and Pool. *Expensive.* Box 308 (945–6571). Bright 107-room lodge overlooking Glenwood's famous thermal pool.

Super 8 Motel. *Inexpensive.* 51823 Hwy. 6 and 24, between Exits 114 and 116 on I–70 (945–8888 or 800–843–1991). This budget motel has many amenities and is convenient to hot springs pool, ski areas, golf. Nearby restaurant. Airport and train station shuttle.

Grand Junction

Grand Junction Hilton. *Deluxe.* 743 Horizon Dr. (241–8888). Golf, tennis, health spa, restaurant, lounge.

Holiday Inn. *Expensive.* 755 Horizon Dr. (243–6790). Massive convention hotel. Two cafes, free airport shuttle.

Howard Johnson Motor Lodge. *Expensive.* 752 Horizon Dr. (243–5150). Cafe, cocktail lounge, tennis, laundry, heated pool.

American Family Lodge. *Inexpensive–Moderate.* 721 Horizon Dr. (243–6050). North, near I-70 airport exit. Attractive rooms. Heated pool, playground, pets allowed. Cafe opposite.

Steamboat Springs

Sheraton Steamboat Resort & Conference Center. *Deluxe.* Box 773419 (879–2220 or 800–325–3535). Luxury hotel at the base area. Tennis, golf, pool, several bars and restaurants.

Scandinavian Lodge. *Moderate.* 2883 Burgess Creek Rd. (879–0517). This famous Swedish ski lodge is located above the ski area. Ski to the lifts and ski out the back door. Cross-country lessons by expert instructors. Gym.

Harbor Hotel. *Moderate.* 703 Lincoln Ave. (879–1522). Renovated Victorian rooms in downtown Steamboat. Some kitchens.

Vail

For information on lodgings: *Vail Resort Association,* 241 E. Meadow Dr., Vail 81657 (476–1000 or 800–525–3875).

Antlers Lodge at Vail. *Deluxe.* 680 West Lionshead Pl. (476–2471). Condo complex overlooking Gore Creek, with fireplaces, balconies, saunas, heated outdoor pool, and Jacuzzi. Close to gondola.

Charter at Beaver Creek. *Deluxe.* Box 5310, Avon 81620 (949–6660 or 800–824–3064). One of Colorado's most gracious condo complexes, with 172 luxurious units. Free ski shuttle.

The Lodge at Vail. *Deluxe.* 174 East Gore Dr. (476–5011). One- to three-bedroom apartments with balconies. Central location. Restaurant, lounge, swimming pool, saunas.

Westin Hotel Vail. *Deluxe.* 1300 Westhaven Dr. (476–7111). Sleek European-style mountain hotel with elegant lobby, gourmet restaurants, health club, shuttle to Vail. Two heated pools, golf, tennis, raquetball. Important convention hotel. Open year-round.

BED AND BREAKFASTS. *Bed & Breakfast Vail Valley,* Box 491, Vail 81658 (949–1212), arranges fairly pricey accommodations throughout Vail Valley. Among the choices in Vail and elsewhere:

Claim Jumper. *Moderate.* 704 Whiterock, Crested Butte (348–6471). Brass beds, antique furnishings.

Roost Lodge. *Moderate.* 1783 N. Frontage Rd., Vail (476–5451). Longtime favorite of those on a budget. Bus or drive to the village.

GUEST RANCHES. The resorts of Colorado thrive on tourists seeking modern amenities, yet the outdoors life can be lived comfortably nearby. Here are two selections from around the state.

T Lazy 7 Guest & Horse Ranch. *Expensive.* Maroon Creek Rd., Box 240, Aspen 81612 (925–7254). Located at the Maroon-Snowmass Primitive Area. Sleigh rides and stables. Snowmobiles are available in winter.

The Vista Verde Ranch. *Expensive.* Steamboat Springs 80477 (879–3858). Cozy log cabins, family-style meals. Horses, fishing, cross-country skiing in wilderness area.

RESTAURANTS. Colorado's resorts have in recent years grown worthier of their culinary pretensions, particularly in Aspen, which now boasts a number of topflight restaurants.

Our categories are based on full dinner for two, including appetizer, exclusive of tax and tip: *Deluxe,* $60 and over; *Expensive,* $25–$60; *Moderate,* $15–$25; and *Inexpensive,* under $15.

Aspen

Andre's. *Deluxe.* 312 S. Galena (925–6200). International menu, well-known for breakfast and lunch.

Crystal Palace. *Deluxe.* Hyman and Monarch (925–1455). Steak dinners accompanied by cabaret shows. Victorian decor. Reservations hard to get in winter.

Guido's Swiss Inn. *Expensive.* 403 S. Galena (925–7222). Swiss chefs, Swiss ambience under Aspen Mountain.

Home Plate. *Moderate.* 333 E. Durant (925–1986). Fresh trout, chicken, spaghetti. Home cooking. Busy in winter.

Takah Sushi. *Inexpensive.* 420 E. Hyman (925–8588). Complete sushi bar and Japanese menu are featured here. Dinners only. Takeout; reservations suggested.

Crested Butte

Artichoke. *Expensive.* 433 Emmons Rd. (349–5400). Specializes in steaks, chops, with side orders of mushrooms and, of course, artichokes. Salad bar.

Penelope's. *Expensive.* 120 Elk Ave. (349–5178). A longtime favorite, this is a cheery restaurant, with plenty of ferns and antiques. Outdoor summer dining.

Skyland Resort and Country Club. *Expensive.* 385 Country Club (349–6129). Basic American food.

Slogar's Bar & Restaurant. *Expensive.* 517 2nd Ave. (349–5765). Home cooking. Chicken, served family-style, in generous helpings. Victorian atmosphere.

Spaghetti Slope. *Moderate.* 500 Gothic Country Rd. (349–7561). Italian cuisine.

Donita's Cantina. *Inexpensive.* 332 Elk Ave. (349–6674). Good Mexican food.

The Tin Cup Cafe and Bakery. *Inexpensive.* Crested Mountain Village (349–7555). Chopped steaks, chicken, hearty breakfasts. Slopeside.

Glenwood Springs

Sopris. *Expensive.* Seven miles south on Hwy. 82 (945–7771). European cuisine.

Buffalo Valley Inn. *Moderate.* Route 82 (945–5297). In rustic Western setting. Steaks and ribs.

Fireside Inn. *Moderate.* 51701 Routes 6 and 24 (945–6613). Bright family restaurant. Sizzlers. Salad bar.

Grand Junction

The Winery. *Expensive.* 642 Main (242–4100). Full-service restaurant, with steak and seafood specialties. Dinner only.

Mom's. *Moderate.* 1610 Hwy. 50 (241–8062). Barbecue specialties.

Furr's Cafeteria. *Inexpensive.* 2817 North Ave. (293–4415). Excellent value. No credit cards.

Steamboat Springs

Cipriani's. *Expensive.* Thunderhead Lodge, 35215 Mt. Werner Way (879–8876). Northern Italian cuisine. Wine list. Reservations recommended.

Remington's, *Expensive.* 2200 Village Inn Court (879–2220). Overlooking the slopes of the ski area. Reservations are essential.

Dos Amigos. *Moderate.* 1910 Mount Werner Rd. (879–4270). An old-time hangout in Steamboat. Good Mexican food and lots of activity. Dinner only. Margaritas.

Vail

Alfredo's. *Deluxe.* Westin Hotel, 1300 Westhaven Dr. (476–7111). Northern Italian and nouveau American cuisine. Fine wines.

Gasthof Gramshammer. *Deluxe.* E. Gore Creek (476–5626). Cozy Austrian restaurant. Wild game. Cocktails.

Chart House. *Expensive.* At Lionshead (476–1525). Steaks, fowl, fish, salad bar.

Red Lion. *Moderate–Expensive.* Bridge St. (476–7676). Hearty Mexican and Italian food, steaks. Popular with skiers.

SPECIAL-INTEREST TOURS AND SIGHTSEEING. This is ski country, but the west of Colorado is not lacking in other types of diversion. From tours of old mining towns to impromptu walks through modern resorts, there's plenty here to satisfy any traveler's demand for diversity.

Aspen

Aspen Club (925–8900) offers **snowcat tours** in season. *T Lazy 7 Ranch* (925–4614 or 925–7040) has snowmobile lunch tours of the ghost town of Independence and the Gold Hill mine. The *Aspen Center for Environmental Studies* (925–5756) at Hallam Lake has guided naturalist outings on foot and snowshoes in a beautiful 22-acre wildlife sanctuary.

In summer, drive to Aspen over 12,000-foot-high **Independence Pass.** It is not for the faint-hearted but it is one of the most spectacular drives anywhere in the state. Also in summer, visit the **Maroon Bells,** famous landmark of the area, seen in nearly every poster shot of the Aspen area. There are trails around the lake. Catch the bus at Aspen Highlands parking lot, since no cars are allowed. Closed in winter.

An hour's drive to the ghost town of Redstone and the historic **Redstone Inn** is a step back in time. Go to **Marble** over rough roads to see the marble quarries (the Lincoln Memorial in Washington, D.C. is made from Marble marble). The long, rough drive over **Kebler Pass** to Crested Butte takes you through the largest stand of aspen trees in the world.

The **Smuggler's Mine** (925–7159), on the northeast side of Aspen, is open for tours year-round. It was from this mine that the largest silver nugget ever mined was found—it weighed over a ton, but had to be cut down to 1,800 pounds to be excavated.

Ashcroft Mining Camp (925–3721), 12 miles south of town on Castle Creek Rd., is a ghost town of nine structures in the midst of restoration.

Glenwood Springs

The *Chamber of Commerce,* 1102 Grand Ave. (945–6589), arranges summer bus tours of the Maroon Bells Wilderness.

Grand Junction

Colorado National Monument is southwest of Grand Junction; follow Rim Rock Drive. Five-hundred-foot-high Independence Rock, Window Rock, and Red Canyon may be seen from lookouts along the 22-mile drive. Meadows of wildflowers and forests of juniper and pine surround the mountains. Wildlife, protected by the National Park Service, roams the area. Dinosaur beds have been excavated here during the past decade. Stratified ramparts carved by time create a gallery of strangely beautiful natural sculptures.

The Visitors Center at park headquarters (off Route 340, about four miles west of Grand Junction) will assist the traveler in the area. Nightly programs are given by rangers during the summer. Campsites with excellent facilities and picnic areas are available; no reservations. Well-marked trails beckon to hikers. For information write: Colorado National Monument, Fruita, CO 81521 (858–3617).

Dinosaur National Monument, in the northwest corner of the state, contains one of the world's most outstanding collections of dinosaur bones. Displayed in the quarry as they were found, there are over 2,000 bones on view. Visitors can watch as archeologists expose the fossils; the setup permits an unusual chance to see these scientists at work.

Among the exceptional features of the monument are deep, narrow gorges with sheer, strangely carved, and delicately tinted sandstone cliffs. Lodore Canyon, cut by the meandering Green River, varies in depth from 1,000 to 3,300 feet.

A 31-mile paved road from the town of Dinosaur leads north into the heart of the canyon country. Scenic overlooks and the two-mile-long trail at Harpers Corner provide spectacular views of the Green and Yampa rivers and their confluences at Steamboat Rock—over 2,500 feet below. Rather primitive camping sites are available; no reservations. For information write Box 210, Dinosaur, CO 81601 (374–2216).

Steamboat Springs Area

Steamboat Powder Cats, Box 2468, Steamboat 80477 (879–5188), offers powder **snowcat tours.** Run by Jupiter and Barbara Jones. The *Home Ranch* (879–1780) outside Steamboat operates day and overnight **treks** with llamas doing the work. They also have *horse-packing trips.*

Year-round early morning **balloon rides** are available through *Balloons Over Steamboat* (879–3298), and *Pegasus Balloon Tours* (879–7529).

Blackmer Drive is a scenic road trip from town up Emerald Mountain. **Buffalo Pass,** 15 miles northeast of town, tops the Continental Divide.

Vail

Piney River Ranch and *Indian Creek Ranch,* 884 Spruce Ct., Vail 81657 (476–4820 or 476–3941), offer **snowmobile tours** in winter, and horseback riding, boating, cookouts and camping in summer.

CAMPING. Rustic accommodations of all types abound. For general camping information in the state, and for directories, write **KOA (Kampgrounds of America),** Box 30558, Billings, Montana 59114; **Mistix** (671–4500) makes reservations for state parks. A fee is charged. **National Park Service,** 655 Parfet, Box 25287, Denver 80225 (969–2000); and **U.S. Forest Service,** 11177 W. Eighth Ave., Lakewood 80225 (236–9431).

Aspen

While overnight RV parking is forbidden on the streets of Aspen, there are several campgrounds nearby, all on a first-come, first-serve basis.

Difficult Campground is four miles southeast of Aspen at the base of Independence Pass. Water, toilets, hiking trails. Five-day limit, fee.

Lincoln Gulch is 10 miles southeast of Aspen, part way up Independence Pass. Water, toilets, good fishing in Roaring Fork River, rock climbing, sandy beaches. Five-day limit. Free. **Weller,** in the same area, has water, toilets, and five-day limit. Near Roaring Fork River. Free.

Lost Man is 16 miles from Aspen, nearly atop Independence Pass. Water, toilets, fishing in nearby reservoir. Five-day limit, no fee. It gets cold at 12,000 feet, even on summer nights, so come prepared.

Maroon Lake is 11 miles southwest of Aspen on Maroon Creek Road, near Aspen Highlands. Water, toilets, picnic tables, fishing, hiking trails. Two-day limit, fee. **Silver Bar, Silver Bell,** and **Silver Queen** are all along Maroon Creek Road and have woodsy settings, good fishing, water, and toilets. One- or two-day limits. Free. **KOA Aspen** (927–3532) is two miles west of Basalt, off Hwy. 82.

Crested Butte

Seven miles north of Crested Butte is **Avery Peak Campground,** off County Rd. 317 at 9,600 feet. Piped and stream water, pit toilets, tables. No trailers over 16 feet. 14-day limit. **Gothic Campground** is nearby, no trailers; 14-day limit. Southeast of Crested Butte about eight miles is **Cement Creek** at 9,000 feet. Tank and stream water, no trailers over 32 feet; 14-day limit with fee. **Lake Irwin Campground** is 9 ¾ miles northwest of town at 10,200 feet. Pit toilets, piped and lake water, fishing, and boating. No trailers over 32 feet; 14-day limit.

Glenwood Springs

Ami's Acres Camping, I–70, Exit 114, Box 1239, 81601 (945–5340). Primitive camping and facilities for trailers.

The Hideout, 1293 Road 117, 81601 (945–5621). Campgrounds, quiet in wooded area. Picnic tables, playground, restrooms, and showers. Cabins available.

Rock Gardens, 1308 County Rd. 129, 81601 (945–6737). Camper park on the Colorado River two miles east of Hot Springs Pool. River rafting.

Grand Junction

Highline Lake. 14 miles west, then six miles north of town. State recreation area with 25 campsites on 824 acres. Swimming, boating, waterskiing. (858–7208.)

Island Acres. 15 miles east of town, near Palisades. State recreation area on the Colorado River. Buffalo herd. 32 campsites. (464–7297.)

Steamboat Springs

The U.S. Forest Service maintains many campgrounds within a 30-mile radius of Steamboat. First-come, first-serve. Most popular are on Rabbit Ears Pass, off Route 40, and in Steamboat Lake State Park, 25 miles north of town off County Rd. 129.

Dumont Lake Campground is near the top of Rabbit Ears Pass, 24 miles southeast of Steamboat at 9,500 ft. Piped and lake water, no trailers over 22 feet. Only 12 sites. Good hiking; 14-day limit, fee.

Just east of town off Route 40 is **Fish Creek Campground;** bathhouse, nearby restaurant, close to town; commercial, with fee (879–5476). *Meadows* is 15 miles southeast of town at 9,300 feet up Rabbit Ears Pass; no trailers over 22 feet; piped drinking water; 14-day limit, fee.

Walton Creek is in the same area, with good stream fishing and hiking; 14-day limit. Fee.

Vail

All the campgrounds in the Vail area are operated by the U.S. Forest Service, with nightly fees and 10-day limit on stay. For information, call 945–3297.

Five miles east of Vail, just off I–70, is **Gore Creek Campground;** trailers up to 16 feet, drinking water. Ten miles southeast is **Black Lakes,** just off I–70 at 10,500 feet; drinking water, trailers up to 16 feet. **Blodgett** is three miles south of Redcliff on Route 24, with trailers up to 16 feet; no drinking water, nearby stream. **Hornsilver Campground** is a mile-and-a-half south of Redcliff with drinking water and a nearby stream; trailers under 15 feet. **Halfmoon Campground** is six miles from Minturn off Highway 24, near a stream, with drinking water, campers and trailers up to 16 feet. Nearby **Tigiwon** at 9,000 feet, is along the same stream, with drinking water.

Winter Park

Follow the Experimental Forest Road past Fraser to **St. Louis Creek Campground:** well water, small trailers, good hiking; free.

Byers Creek is at an elevation of about 9,700 feet, beyond St. Louis Creek on the Experimental Forest Road; from here a steep, difficult trail goes up to Byers Peak for an incredible view. Free. **Willow Creek** is west of Route 34 five miles, on Willow Creek Reservoir; piped water, fire grates, picnic tables.

Robber's Roost is near the base of Berthoud Pass, five miles south of Winter Park at a wide spot in the road. No facilities. Free.

OUTDOOR ACTIVITIES. Aside from mining, it is sports and outdoor activities that made this region what it is. Tops on the list are skiing and hiking, of course, but local chambers of commerce will be helpful in suggesting other possibilities.

Aspen

There are guided **cross-country skiing** tours on the Tenth Mountain Trail, a hut-to-hut European-type experience. Moonlight dinner tours and cross-country lessons are available. Check *Aspen Touring Center,* Box 2432, Aspen 81612 (925–7625), or the *Tenth Mountain Trail Hut System* (925–5775). A system of well-equipped shelters on the *Alfred A. Braun Hut System* (925–7162) connects Aspen with Crested Butte. Ski and snowshoe rentals are available from *Ute Mountaineer* (925–2849).

Helicopter **downhill skiing** is available Feb.–March through *Colorado First Tracks* (925–7735). *Aspen Mountain Adventure Tours* (925–1220) conducts powder-skiing excursions that include trained guides, lunch, and a round-trip ride on the Silver Queen gondola.

River rafting and **kayaking** are available on the Colorado, Roaring Fork, and Arkansas rivers from *Blazing Paddles* (925–5651) and *River Rats* (925–7648).

In summer there is **backpacking** and **hiking.** Trailheads are at Maroon Lake, Silver Queen, Difficulty Creek, Lincoln Gulch, and Lost Man campgrounds (see *Camping* above), and along Hunter Creek. Book and sport shops have guidebooks and maps, or go to the Forest Service, 315 N. 7th.

Bicycling is enjoyable along the paved bike paths; rentals at *Aspen Sports,* 408 E. Cooper Ave. (925–6331).

Biplane rides are from the *Aspen Barnstorming Co.* (925–3331).

Horseback riding is available from *Heatherbed Stables* (925–6987), and *T Lazy 7* (925–7040).

Soar with *Gliders of Aspen* (925–3418).

Public **tennis** courts are at *Iselin Park* (925–9220), *Aspen Club* (925–8900), and *Owl Creek* (925–7794).

Golf can be played at *Aspen Golf Course* (925–2145), which offers a 7,125-yard championship 18-hole course; pro shop, carts, driving range, PGA instruction.

Crested Butte

For information on guided **cross-country skiing** tours, call the *Ski Touring Center* (349–2250).

In winter, the *Crested Butte Mountain Resort,* Box A, Mt. Crested Butte 81225 (349–2211 or 800–525–4220) offers an outstanding **cross-country ski** program, for beginners, intermediates, and experts.

Summer finds the typical mountain activities of **rafting, kayaking, hiking, windsurfing** and, of course, **fat-tire bicycling.** Call Chamber of Commerce (349–6438) for information.

Outdoor **tennis** is available at the public courts in *Crested Butte Town Park,* on the south side of Route 135—free; no reservations; More courts are at Mt. Crested Butte Town Park, at the Town Hall north end of town—free; no reservations. The *Plaza at Woodcreek* (349–2130) has two courts for their guests. Indoor tennis is available at *Skyland Resort* (349–6131).

Also at Skyland is the sprawling 18-hole Robert Trent Jones II golf course. Clinics are available all inclusive (lessons, meals, lodging, greens and cart fees); contact John Jacobs/Shelby Futch Practical Golf School (349–6129).

Glenwood Springs

For daylong **rafting** trips on the Colorado and Roaring Fork rivers, contact *Rock Gardens Rafting,* 1308 County Rd. 129, Glenwood Springs 81601 (945–6737), or *Wet, Inc.,* Box 277, Glenwood Springs 81602 (945–9417).

Steamboat Springs

Cross-country skiing is avidly pursued in Steamboat. Besides ski touring from the *Scandinavian Lodge,* the *Ski Touring Center* (879–6111) maintains 12 miles of trails; guided tours on Rabbit Ears Pass, moonlight tours by appointment; lessons. Other lodges that offer cross-country skiing are

Bear Pole Ranch, Dutch Creek Guest Ranch, Elk River Guest Ranch, Glen Eden, Home Ranch, Post Ranch, Red Barn Ranch, and *Vista Verde Guest Ranch.* Anyone can ski here—it's open forest land.

Dog sledding is nearby at *Dog Sled Adventures* (879–5280). **Ice fishing** is from Steamboat and Dumont lakes, license required; call 879–1870 for information. **Ice skating** is at Howelsen Hill, open to the public at no charge. Rent skates at *Ski Haus,* 1450 Lincoln (879–0385). **Sledding** is also popular at Howelsen Hill. Young children only; call 879–4300.

Sleigh rides go from *All Seasons Ranch* (879–2606); *El Rancho* (879–9988); *Red Barn Ranch* (879–4580); and *Vista Verde Guest Ranch* (879–3858). In summer, the teams take hayrides out. **Snowshoeing** expeditions head out from *Elk River, Red Barn, Vista Verde,* and *Post* ranches. **Snowmobiles** can be rented at *Dutch Creek, Elk River, Post,* and *Red Barn* ranches.

Ski powder by Sno-Cat, contact the *Steamboat Powder Cats* (879–5188).

Mike's Marina at Steamboat Lake (879–7019) has **fishing,** and **sailing** rentals.

Tennis courts are available for guests at *Glen Eden Ranch, Lodge at Sky Valley, Overlook Hotel, Scandinavian Lodge,* the *Sheraton,* and in the town parks; **volleyball** buffs should head for the *Lodge at Sky Valley,* and the town park at Howelsen Hill.

Golfers can play at the 9-hole *Steamboat Golf Club* (879–4295) five miles west of town; or the 18-hole course at the *Sheraton Hotel and Resort* (879–2220). Open to the public on a non-reservation basis, greens fees are $32 including required carts.

The *Routt National Forest* surrounding the town of Steamboat has many **hiking** trails; stop by the *Chamber Resort Office,* 625 S. Lincoln St., or the *Forest Service Supervisor's Office,* 57 10th St., for maps and information.

Half-day to five-day **rafting** trips are available from *Adventure Bound,* 2392 H Rd., Grand Junction 81505 (241–5633) and *Buggywhips Float Service,* 903 Lincoln St., Steamboat Springs 80477 (897–8033). Nearby rivers include the Arkansas, North Platte, Colorado, and Dolores.

Vail

The *Cross-Country Skiing Center* (476–5750) teaches basic to advanced track **skiing** and use of touring skis; full- or half-day tours available. Gourmet lunches (Thursdays only) and a Vail-to-Red Cliff tour for six or more people can be planned by advance registration; call 476–3239, ext. 4380. Experienced cross-country skiers can head out from the top of China Bowl or from the top of Vail Pass for back-country skiing. The *U.S. Forest Service* (827–5715) has trail information.

Sleigh rides start from the golf course every night; call 476–1330.

Ice skating is available at *Dobson Ice Arena,* 321 E. Lionshead Circle (476–1560). $2.50 admission, $1 skate rental.

Aerobic workouts, swimming, racquetball are available at the *Vail Racquet Club* (476–4840) and *Vail Athletic Club* (476–0700).

Summer is **golf** time. Five courses are within a 20-mile radius, with play generally possible late May–Oct. *Eagle-Vail* (949–5267) is a par-72 course located off Route 6 at Eagle-Vail.

Vail Golf Club (476–1330) is home of the Jerry Ford Invitational: 18 holes, par 71.

Singletree Golf Club (926–3533) is just west of Beaver Creek. Facilities include sun deck, swimming pool, tennis courts, pro shop.

Beaver Creek Golf Course and *Arrowhead at Vail* (476–1972) are open only to guests.

The town of Vail has 24 **tennis** courts for public use at a modest hourly charge; call 476–5823 for details. *Eagle-Vail* (949–5356) has eight tennis courts, ball machines, rentals, lounge, grill at the same fee. *Vail Run Resort* (476–1500) also offers tennis.

Horseback riding is available at *Spraddle Creek Ranch,* 476–6941, and *Piney River Ranch,* 476–3941.

Bicycle paths head in all directions from town; the energetic can bike over Vail Pass. Rentals from most sport shops.

Take a gondola ride halfway up the mountain for miles of **hiking** trails; guided hikes from Eagle's Nest three days a week at 1 P.M. Call 476–5601. *Vail Nature* (476–7000, ext. 227 weekdays, 476–7005 weekends) has guided nature walks and recreational programs in summer; some require advance registration.

Backpacking trails fan out from the top of Vail Pass; from Gore Creek Campground into Eagle's Nest Primitive Area; from Red Sandstone Creek; and from Tigiwon Campgrounds. Maps and information are available from most sport shops in Vail and from the U.S.

Snowshoe walks and backcountry **hikes** are offered through *Vail Nature Center* (476–7000, ext. 227 weekdays, 476–7005 weekends); *Vail Mountaineering* (476–1414); and *Eagle River Mountain Guides* (476–3296).

There are a number of **rafting** companies that lead guided trips on the White, Colorado, Arkansas, Crystal, and Roaring Fork rivers; contact *Raftmeister* (476–7238), or call 476–2266 for a current list of outfitters. **Float fishing** and **alpine lake fishing** trips are available; check at a Vail Information Booth.

HUNTING AND FISHING. Colorado's Rockies boast some of the best hunting and fishing in the country. The area is dotted with hundreds of lakes and streams in thousands of acres of forest lands. Deer, elk, and antelope are all abundant, and bighorn sheep, Rocky Mountain goats, and black bear are also present.

For anglers, there are rainbow, mackinaw, cutthroat, and German brown trout, as well as catfish, kokanee salmon, cappies, and perch. As in the rest of the state, licenses are required for both sports. License fees vary; most large sporting-goods stores sell them.

Stream fishing is superb in the Fraser Valley. President Eisenhower's favorite fishing haunts were right here; contact *Nelson's Fly and Tackle Shop,* Tabernash (726–8558) for licenses and information. Fine fishing is also found in Irwin, Emerald, Meridian, and Taylor lakes and Spring Creek Reservoir, near Crested Butte.

Near Glenwood Springs, the White River National Forest is excellent elk and deer country. Sweetwater Lake, east of Glenwood, is a prime spot for kokanee, and both the Colorado and Roaring Fork rivers are popular for trout. Glenwood also serves as a good base for exploring the well-known Frying Pan River and the Reudi Dam area, which can be reached from the town of Basalt southeast of Glenwood on Route 82. The dam offers both shore fishing and trolling.

West of Glenwood Springs, Rifle is a popular center for elk and deer hunting. Farther along Route 82, near Leadville, are the Twin Lakes. Also good for fishing are Turquoise, Crystal, and Emerald lakes near Leadville. Leadville's *U.S. Forest Service Office,* 130 W. 5th St., has maps and information.

Grand Mesa National Forest is a first-rate elk locale, and also offers excellent fishing and waterfowl hunting. Bear also roam the wilderness areas along Grand Mesa.

For forest maps, write to the *U.S. Forest Service,* Rocky Mountain Regional Office, 11177 W. 8th Ave., Box 25127, Lakewood, CO 80225 (236–9431). The office has maps of all Colorado's forests.

DOWNHILL SKIING. Central Colorado's ski areas and resorts are known throughout the world for sensational snow, sophisticated hostelries, fine ski restaurants, and first-rate management. A network of feeder airlines, rapid buses, and car-rental depots allows quick access. Here is a representative list. Lift ticket prices can vary greatly; check local discounts and ski packages.

Aspen Highlands. Box T, Aspen 81612 (925–5300 or 800–262–7736). Just west of Aspen. Well-established ski area. 11 lifts; 55 trails (25% beginner, 50% intermediate, 25% expert). Vertical drop of 3,800 feet.

Aspen Mountain. Box 1248, Aspen 81612 (925–1220). Take I–70 to Glenwood Springs and Route 82; 204 miles from Denver. One of the oldest and most famous mountains. Eight lifts; 70 trails (35% intermediate, 65% expert). Vertical drop of 3,300 feet.

Beaver Creek. Box 915, Beaver Creek 81620 (949–5750 or 800–525–2257). Take I–70 to Avon/Beaver Creek Exit; 110 miles from Denver. Relatively recent addition to Colorado ski scene. No lift lines. 10 lifts; 49 trails (23% beginner, 43% intermediate, 34% expert). Vertical drop of 3,340 feet.

Crested Butte. Box A, Crested Butte 81225 (349–2333). Take routes 285, 50, and 135; 230 miles from Denver. A gem in south-central Colorado. Ten lifts; 51 trails (27% beginner, 53% intermediate, 20% expert). Vertical drop of 2,150 feet.

Snowmass. Box 1248, Snowmass Village 81612 (925–1220). Take I–70 to Route 82; 210 miles from Denver. Reminds one of the Alps; excellent for average skiers. 15 lifts; 84 trails (10% beginner, 62% intermediate, 21% difficult, 7% expert). Vertical drop of 3,555 feet.

Vail. Box 7, Vail 81658 (476–5601 or 800–525–2257). Take I–70; 100 miles from Denver. Colorado's answer to St. Moritz. 17 lifts; 92 trails (32% beginner, 36% intermediate, 32% expert). Vertical drop of 3,150 feet.

SEASONAL EVENTS. January. *Winterfaire,* Vail; *Winterskol,* Aspen. *Cowboy Downhill,* Steamboat, with real rodeo cowboys doing the racing.

February. Steamboat has the oldest continuous *Winter Carnival* in the West, complete with hot-air balloons. *Butte Cup/North American Ski Trophy Series,* Crested Butte. *Mountain Man Triathlon,* Beaver Creek. *Mardi Gras* celebration, Snowmass. *Snowfest,* Crested Butte.

March. *Al Johnson Uphill-Downhill Nordic Race,* Crested Butte. *National Masters Championships* and *Subaru Aspen Winternationals* amateur races, Steamboat.

April. *Spring Stampede,* Crested Butte. *Aspen Music Festival,* Aspen.

June. *10K Run for the Arts,* Steamboat Springs. *Food and Wine Classic,* Aspen. A three-day *Colorado Stampede rodeo,* Grand Junction. *Strawberry Days Festival,* Glenwood Springs.

July. *Tennis Classic,* Vail. *Jazz Festival,* Winter Park. *The Aspen Writers Conference,* Aspen. *Gothic/Crested Butte Marathon,* Crested Butte. The *Gold Creek Klunker Klassic,* Crested Butte, features bicycles with fat heavy-duty tires made to withstand mountain roads. *Aerial Weekend,* Crested Butte, finds the sky filled with hot-air balloons, hang gliders, sky divers, and stunt planes. *Cowboy Roundup Rodeo,* Steamboat. *Ballet/Aspen Summer Dance Festival* begins summer season, Aspen.

August. *House and Gardens Tour,* Aspen. *Jerry Ford Invitational Golf Tournament* and *Eagle County Rodeo,* Vail. *Intermountain Market Days,* stock car races, and *Rocky Mountain Open Golf Tournament,* Grand Junction. *Festival of the Arts,* Grand Junction. *Rabbit Ears Bicycle Hillclimb Classic,* Steamboat.

September. Labor Day sees the *Vintage Auto Race* at Eagle Ridge, Steamboat Springs, and a mountaintop dinner at Lionshead, Vail. *Art Festivals,* Glenwood Springs and Grand Junction. *Vail Symposium,* where national issues are discussed, and *Vailfest* (similar to Oktoberfest), Vail, and *Octoberfest,* Aspen. There are many rodeos and harvest festivals throughout the month.

October. *Potato Days,* Glenwood Springs.

November. *Hunting season* opens.

December. *Tree Lighting Ceremony,* Vail. Mountainside *torchlight parades* throughout the month, Steamboat Springs and Winter Park.

THE UTAH ROCKIES

by
CURTIS W. CASEWIT

Though never exceeding 13,000 feet, Utah's Rockies are spectacular. In winter, the mountains—and celebrated ski areas—receive dizzying snowstorms and snow masses; in summer, rock climbers and hikers move above the timberline in the brightest sunshine.

Utah is colorful, scenic, unforgettable. The dramatic Wasatch Range runs south from the Idaho border past such scenic communities as Logan and Salt Lake City; turn east in the direction of Vernal and you'll see the colorful Uintas and Kings Peak. The cliffs of Moab, the dazzling stone walls of Natural Bridges National Monument, the colossi of Monument Valley and Arches National Park, and the Zion Gorges are long remembered by the visitor. Finally, there is Salt Lake City—the Mormon metropolis.

Religion has placed an unmistakable stamp on Utah. The Mormons have always displayed a love of growing things, and a devotion to both industry and God. The Salt Lake City Tabernacle Choir is world-famous. The state capital is carefully laid out with spacious, tree-lined streets. And more Utah roads are constantly being built, with circular routes that allow you to see much without retracing your steps.

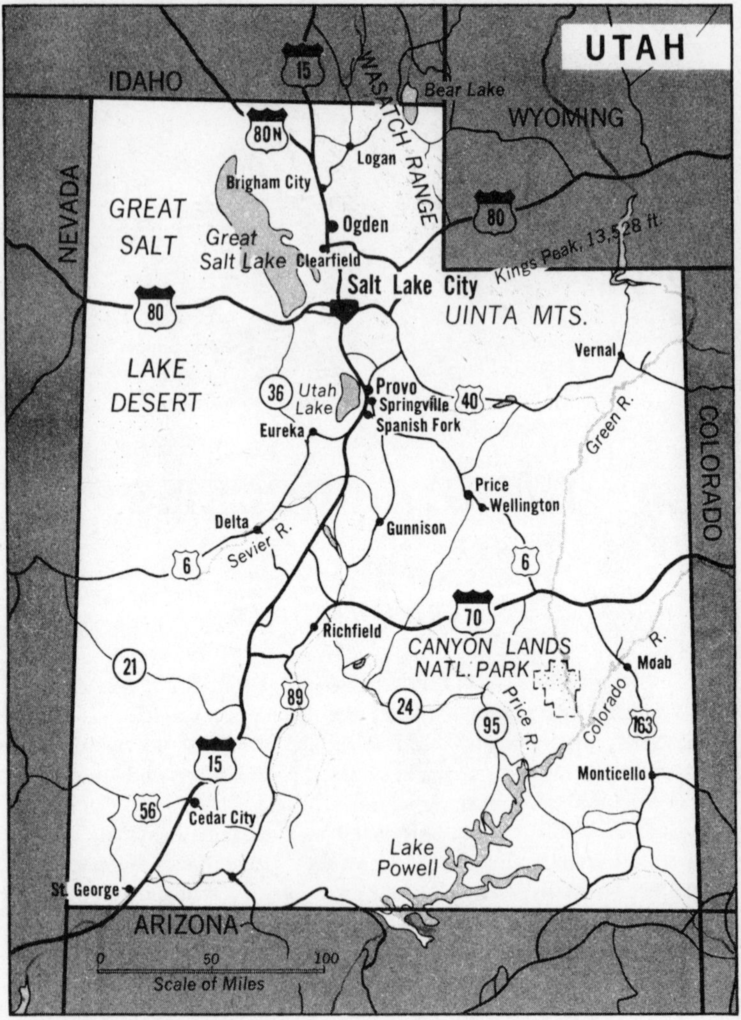
UTAH
IDAHO
WYOMING
NEVADA
COLORADO
ARIZONA
Bear Lake
WASATCH RANGE
Logan
Brigham City
Ogden
Clearfield
GREAT SALT LAKE DESERT
Great Salt Lake
Salt Lake City
Kings Peak, 13,528 ft.
UINTA MTS.
Vernal
Utah Lake
Provo
Springville
Spanish Fork
Eureka
Green R.
Price
Wellington
Delta
Sevier R.
Gunnison
Richfield
CANYON LANDS NATL. PARK
Moab
Colorado R.
Price R.
Monticello
Cedar City
St. George
Lake Powell
15
80N
80
36
40
6
70
21
89
24
95
163
56
0 50 100
Scale of Miles

Salt Lake City

Salt Lake City's greatest single attraction for visitors is the Temple Square area in the middle of town. Here, on two 10-acre blocks flanking Main Street are the central religious shrines of Latter-Day Saint worship. The Temple block on the west is surrounded by a 15-foot-high masonry wall. On the grounds stand the Temple, Museum, Tabernacle, Assembly Hall, and Visitors Center.

Guided tours are offered on the Temple grounds every half hour. On the itinerary is the Tabernacle, which houses the famous Temple Square pipe organ.

South Temple is a good street to follow east from downtown. It leads to the University of Utah, laid out on a fine vantage point from which to view the city below. The 482-acre rejuvenated campus includes structures and landscaping that create a particularly engaging combination at the institution's southern half, which embraces pleasant walkways and fountains. The older northern half is well-cared-for and a portal to nostalgia. It contains a highly regarded Museum of Natural History, housed in the university's former library. Guided tours are available. The school of architecture maintains a Fine Arts Museum. The school's various theaters and auditoriums produce drama, ballet, popular music festivals, and classical recitals.

On the campus edge, the Art Barn provides new showings of contemporary paintings, drawings, photography, sculptures, and industrial art about every three weeks. Researchers at the university's teaching hospital have excelled in bone, blood, and organ transplant work. World attention focused here in 1982 when Barney Clark became the first recipient of an artificial heart.

Salt Lake City is surrounded by mountainous terrain, making skiing at nearby Snowbird and Alta a popular winter pastime. Park City, on the east side of the mountains, a onetime mining town now revived as a recreation area, still retains much of its Victorian character.

Ogden

Ogden, 33 miles north of Salt Lake City, is, with 64,400 residents, Utah's fourth largest city. It was planned by Brigham Young, but became a rowdy railroad town for a while in the late 1800s. The city is now a quiet commercial and industrial center and the home of Weber State College.

Provo

Provo, south of Salt Lake City on Route 15, is located at the foot of 11,000-foot Provo Peak and is typically Mormon, with clean, wide streets and pleasant landscaping. The city thrives on farming and industry, and is the home of Brigham Young University. Nearby Utah Lake, the largest body of fresh water in the state, is a popular spot for boating, swimming, fishing, and water-skiing.

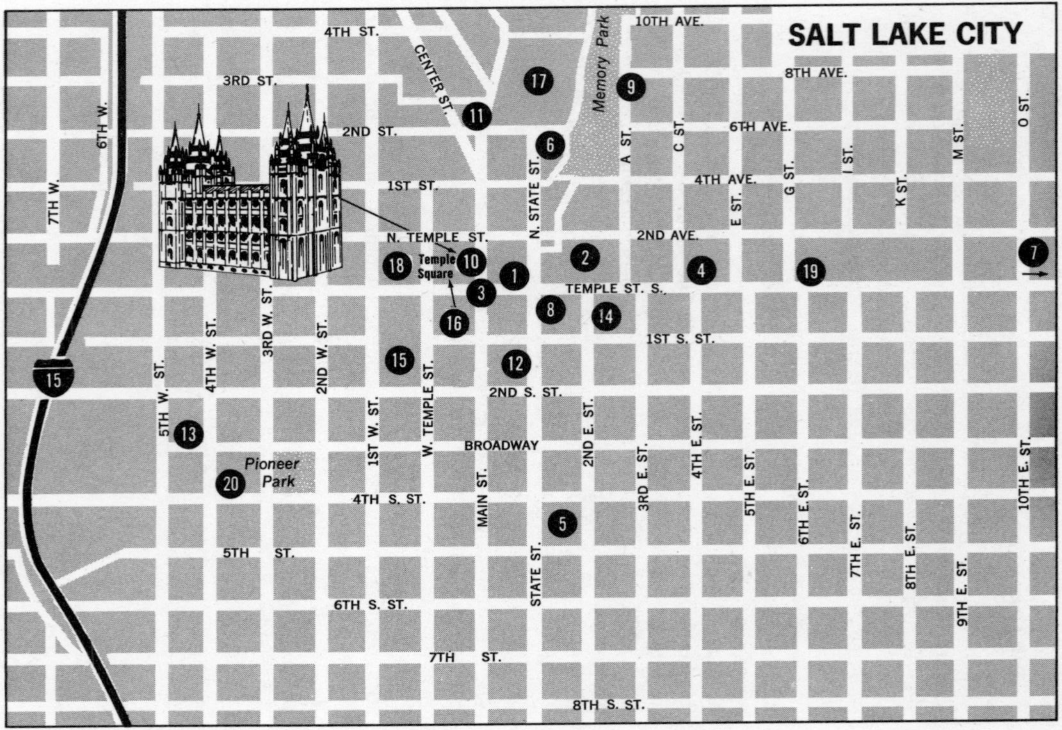

Points of Interest

1) Beehive House
2) Brigham Young's Grave
3) Brigham Young Statue
4) Cathedral of the Madeleine
5) City County Building
6) Council Hall
7) University of Utah and Museum of Natural History
8) Hansen Planetarium
9) Memory Grove
10) Mormon Temple
11) Pioneer Museum
12) Promised Valley Theater
13) Rio Grand Railroad Station
14) Saint Mark's Cathedral
15) Salt Palace and Concert Hall
16) Seagull Monument
17) State Capitol
18) Tabernacle & Assembly Hall
19) Utah Governor's Mansion
20) Utah State Historical Society

PRACTICAL INFORMATION FOR THE UTAH ROCKIES

HOW TO GET THERE. By air. Salt Lake City is the major terminal. Among the long-distance carriers serving it are *American, America West, Continental, Delta, Northwest, TWA,* and *United.*

By train. *Amtrak's California Zephyr* runs from Denver to Salt Lake City, on the route previously used by the *Denver and Rio Grande Zephyr.* Amtrak's *Desert Wind* connects Salt Lake City and Los Angeles. The *Pioneer* connects Salt Lake City and Seattle, through Ogden and Boise.

By bus. *Trailways* and *Greyhound* are the major carriers to Utah. The region is also served by numerous other lines, including *Crown Transit, Linea Azul, Sun Valley,* and *Bremerton-Tacoma.*

By car. I–80, probably the most heavily traveled transcontinental highway, passes through Salt Lake City. From the north I–80N runs southeast through Salt Lake from Portland, Oregon. I–15 comes from the Los Angeles area through Cedar City, Utah.

TOURIST INFORMATION. Detailed information may be obtained from the *Utah Travel Council,* Council Hall, Capitol Hill, Salt Lake City 84114 (538–1030).

TELEPHONES. The area code for all Utah numbers is 801.

ACCOMMODATIONS in Utah are relatively inexpensive. Rates are highest during ski time (Nov.–April) and the summer months that bring tourists to the national parks and forest lands.

Based on double occupancy, the rate categories for Utah are: *Deluxe,* over $75; *Expensive,* $55–$75; *Moderate,* $40–$55; and *Inexpensive,* under $40.

Alta

Alta Lodge. *Expensive.* On Rte. 210 84092 (742–3500). Fireplace, library.

Rustler Lodge. *Expensive.* On Rte. 210 84092 (532–4061). Family rates, cafe, bar, sauna, rec room.

Ogden

Hilton Hotel. *Expensive.* 247 24th St., 84401 (627–1190 or 800–HILTONS). Ogden's finest hotel. Three restaurants, indoor swimming pool.

Best Western High Country Inn. *Moderate.* 1335 W. 12th, 84401 (394–9474 or 800–528–1234). King- and queen-size beds, waterbeds, in-room movies, bridal suite.

Holiday Inn. *Moderate.* 3306 Washington Blvd. 84401 (399–5671).

TraveLodge. *Inexpensive.* 2110 Washington Blvd. 84401 (394–4563 or 800–255–3030).

Park City

Park City Reservations, 1790 Bonanza Dr. 84060 (649–9598), will arrange for condo and motel rentals for skiiers. *Park City Resort Lodging,* 1515 Park Ave. 84060 (649–6368), can arrange for condos and motels near the slopes.

Stein Eriksen Lodge. *Deluxe.* Box 3177, Royal St., off Rte. 224, 84060 (649–3700 or 800–453–1302). Scenic setting, full breakfast. Health club.

Omni Yarrow. *Expensive–Deluxe.* 1800 Park Ave. 84060 (649–7000 or 800–THE–OMNI). Offered here are ski packages, golf privileges, and tennis. Restaurant and bar.

Provo

Best Western Rome Inn. *Moderate.* 1200 W. University Ave. 84601 (373–0060 or 800–528–1234). Free Continental breakfast, family units, king- and queen-size beds.

Chez Fontaine Bed & Breakfast. *Moderate.* 45 N. 300 E. 84601 (375–8484). A turn-of-the-century inn filled with pioneer furniture.

Colony Inn. *Moderate.* 1380 S. University Ave. 84601 (374–6800). Saunas, cable TV.

Holiday Inn. *Moderate.* 1460 S. University Ave. 84601 (374–9750). Across from golf course. Restaurant. Jacuzzis.

The Pullman Bed & Breakfast. *Moderate.* 415 S. University Ave. 84601 (374–8141). In a lovely old home, close to Brigham Young University.

TraveLodge. *Inexpensive.* 124 S. University Ave. 84601 (373–1974 or 800–255–3050). Near the university, restaurant.

Salt Lake City

Hilton Hotel and Inn. *Deluxe.* 150 W. 500 S. 84101 (523–3344 or 800–HILTONS); and 5151 Wiley Post Dr., Wylie (539–1515), at the airport. Restaurant, lounge, 24-hour coffee shop.

Westin Hotel Utah. *Deluxe.* Main at S. Temple 84111 (531–1000). Barber shop and beauty salon. Shuttle bus to airport.

Brigham Street Inn. *Expensive.* 1135 South Temple 84102 (364–4461). This historic 1898 inn is near downtown. Free breakfast and private baths are added features.

Embassy Suites. *Expensive.* 600 S. West Temple 84104 (359–7800 or 800–EMBASSY). All two-room suites. Wet bars, microwaves, complimentary breakfast, indoor pool, sauna, restaurant.

Little America Motel. *Expensive.* 500 S. Main St. 84111 (363–6781). Combination motel/high rise, with different rates for each. Indoor pool, sauna, exercise room, entertainment. 24-hour coffee shop.

Sheraton Triad Hotel and Towers. *Expensive.* 255 S. West Temple 84102 (328–2000 or 800–325–3535).

Orleans Inn. *Moderate.* 325 S. 300 E. 84111 (521–3790). Kitchens, restaurant, cable TV.

Peery Hotel. *Moderate.* 110 W. 300 South 84101 (521–4300 or 800–331–0073). This historic building offers a health club, two restaurants, and a Continental breakfast.

Shilo Inn. *Moderate.* 206 S. West Temple 84101 (521–9500 or 800–222–2244). Free Continental breakfast is available here, along with airport shuttle and a shopping arcade.

TraveLodge Salt Palace. *Moderate.* 215 W. North Temple 84166 (532–1000). Restaurant, sauna, 24-hour movies, bridal suite.

Deseret Inn Motel. *Inexpensive.* 50 W. 500 S. 84101 (532–2900). Pool, extra-large beds, room service.

Imperial 400 Motel. *Inexpensive.* 476 S. State St. 84101 (533–9300). Next to the Salt Palace and opposite a park.

Snowbird

The Lodge at Snowbird. *Expensive.* Snowbird 84092 (742–2222). Skiing, tennis, hiking, kitchens, fireplaces, balconies, saunas. Restaurant nearby.

RESTAURANTS. There is nothing different or unique about Mormon cooking. Statewide restaurant quality has improved considerably, and it's possible to discover tasty cuisine in out-of-the-way locations, but don't count on it. Salt Lake City, however, is beginning to acquire a kitchen. The going is slow because liquor laws discourage heavy investment in grand cafes or four-star restaurants. But specialty places, offering French, Spanish, and German dishes, are increasing. Seafood, believe it or not, is found fresh and well-prepared in several Salt Lake City dining rooms. Some of the best menus will be found up nearby canyons or south of the city.

Restaurant price categories are as follows, for two meals with appetizer, exclusive of tax and tip: *Deluxe,* $55 and up; *Expensive* $30–$54, *Moderate,* $20–$30; and *Inexpensive,* under $20.

Park City

Car 19. *Expensive.* 438 Main St. (649–9338). Mostly steaks served in an old railroad car.

Glitretind Room. *Expensive.* In the Stein Eriksen Lodge (649–3700). Continental dining is featured here in a romantic setting.

Janeaux's. *Expensive.* 306 Main St. (649–6800). Gourmet fare, duck, cordon bleu.

Grub Steak. *Moderate.* Prospector Sq. (649–8060). Steaks, seafood, prime rib, large salad bar.

Baja Cantina. *Inexpensive.* 1284 Empire Ave. (649–2252). A wild Mexican restaurant.

Salt Lake City

Deluxe

La Caille at Quail Run. 9565 Wasatch Blvd., Sandy (942–1751). Local residents regularly make the drive out of the city to enjoy the home baking, fresh flowers, and candlelit atmosphere. Call for reservations.

Devereaux. Devereaux Plaza Triad Center (575–2000). In a restored 19th-century mansion, restaurant is centerpiece of a multimillion-dollar office, apartment, and shopping-center development. Varied menu, from chicken and beef to pork and pastas. Well worth a visit.

La Fleur de Lys. 165 S. West Temple (359–5753). Sweetbreads, roast pheasant, and live lobsters cooked to order. Posh atmosphere and fine service.

Expensive

Diamond Lil's. 1528 W. North Temple (533–0547). In restored 100-year-old building. Prime rib and steak specialties graced by generous portions of homemade bread. The period saloon is worth a visit.

Log Haven. 3800 S. Mill Creek Canyon (272–8255). Varied menu in mountain setting overlooking a lake. Home baking. Reservations required.

Mikado. 67 W. 100 South (328–0929). Japanese cuisine and sushi bar are offered here. Private dining rooms.

The New Orleans Cafe. 200 S. 307 W. (363–6573). This downtown restaurant conveys an authentic Louisiana atmosphere, with superbly prepared Creole and Cajun entrees. Live Dixiel and melodies on Friday and Saturday nights and at Sunday brunch. The menu changes daily but usually features shrimp creole, oyster stew, fried catfish, creole gumbo, and redfish pecan.

The Roof. Westin Hotel, S. Temple and Main (531–1000). Magnificent view of Temple Square. Live piano accompaniment completes the setting for superb dining.

Thirteenth Floor. 161 W. 600 S. (364–7013). Soup is served in individual tureens, and loaves of hot bread accompany every meal. Great views of the entire Salt Lake Valley. Steaks are the staples.

Moderate

The Cedars. 154 E. 200 S. (364–4096). Authentic Armenian, Lebanese, and Moroccan fare. From falafel with sesame-seed sauce to stuffed grape leaves.

Ho Ho Gourmet. 1504 S. State St. (487–7709). A pleasant dining experience of Cantonese and Mandarin favorites, prepared as they would be in Hong Kong.

Ristorante Fontana Della. 336 S. 400 E. (328–4243). In addition to Italian food, there are representative dishes from many Mediterranean countries, with a dinner normally running a full seven courses. The dining room is an old church, complete with fountain and ornately carved interior.

Inexpensive

The Hawaiian. 2920 Highland Dr. (486–5076). Chinese and Polynesian food to the accompaniment of a Hawaiian thunderstorm.

Sophia Garcia's. 154 W. 6th S. (521–2930). Traditional Mexican food is served here in a festive manner.

Spaghetti Factory. Trolley Sq. (521–0424). Great family dining in a fun setting.

LIQUOR LAWS. Utah's liquor laws try the visitor's patience. Beer is the only alcoholic beverage served in all public bars, and it is the 3.2 variety. Certain licensed restaurants also serve two-ounce "mini-bottles" of the most common liquors, but these can only be ordered with food. That applies to wine as well.

"Private clubs" can serve mini-bottle mixed drinks whether food is also served or not. Some private clubs aren't overly careful in verifying the membership of their customers and all have liberal guest privileges. The difficulty is finding these oases without a local resident as guide. Almost all public eating and drinking establishments permit customers to carry their own liquor to the table or bar. This has earned collective state restrictions on the subject the title of "brown bag laws."

In public restaurants, waiters and waitresses aren't permitted to fetch, open or mix mini-bottles; that must be done by the customer. Mix will be served, however, and most good restaurants will chill wine brought to the establishment. Retail liquor is sold in state stores, or package agencies, including restaurants, clubs, and hotels. Grocery stores sell beer with 3.2% alcohol content. The legal age is 21 and strictly enforced.

HOW TO GET AROUND. By air. From Salt Lake City, *Skywest* flies to Vernal, Cedar City, and St. George. There is charter service from Salt Lake City to local airports near the national parks of Zion, Bryce, and Canyonlands.

By train. Ogden and Salt Lake City are on the *Amtrak* line.

By bus. All the major cities and towns in Utah have good bus service. *Greyhound, Wilkins, Sun Valley,* and *Cook.* are some of the carriers.

By car. The interstates (I–70 and I–80 east-west, and I–15 north-south) are the primary means of communication where there are long distances between towns. State roads crisscross the rest of the state, except in truly desolate areas like the Great Salt Lake Desert.

STATE PARKS. There are 48 state parks in Utah. One of the largest, **Wasatch Mountain** (22,000 acres), near Heber City, has trailer hookups, tent spaces, fishing, and hunting. There is a golf course nearby. In Heber City is the Wasatch Mountain Railway, which makes a three-hour trip through Heber Valley, Provo Canyon, and Bridal Veil Falls.

FISHING. Generally, Utah's fishing season starts the Saturday closest to June 1 and runs through November. Some 200 waters are open year-round. The state's most popular and regularly caught fish is rainbow trout. Frequently taken from many waters are brook, native cutthroat, German brown, Kokanee salmon, Mackinaw, and lake trout; grayling, largemouth, and white bass; channel catfish; and walleyed pike.

The state has many reservoirs and several streams, running through high mountain country and down along valley floors, joining sizable rivers. All are good sport for fishermen. These include the Provo, Weber, and Logan rivers; and streams in Big Cottonwood Canyon, the High Uinta Mountains, and most of the state's national forests. Non-resident licenses good for a year cost $40. A five-day adult tourist license is $15, a one-day tourist license, $5. Non-residents under 12 may fish without a license provided they are accompanied by a licensed angler and their catch is counted in the adult's daily limit.

Limits are: *trout* or *salmon,* eight fish, with a bonus of six *cutthroat* or *brook trout* in some counties; *grayling,* eight; *Bonneville cisco,* 30 (in Bear Lake only); *largemouth* or *smallmouth bass,* six total; *white bass,* no limit; *crappie,* 50 fish (no limit in Lake Powell); *northern pike,* six (two in Provo River); *whitefish,* 10; *channel cat,* eight.

HUNTING. Hunting is popular in Utah, whether for deer, elk, antelope, jack rabbits, badgers, woodchucks and gophers or quail, pheasant, chukar partridge, ducks, and geese. The large mule deer has been stocked around the state wherever the range allows. For years the annual harvest, attracting hunters from throughout the west, has averaged 100,000 deer. A non-resident big-game license costs $120 for one deer, either sex.

Quail is best hunted in Washington County and the Uintah Basin while ring-necked pheasants can be found throughout central Utah during a short season in early November. Marshes along lakes and rivers are usual ambush sites for ducks and geese. Non-resident waterfowl and game bird licenses cost $40. Contact Division of Wildlife Resources, 1596 W. North Temple, Salt Lake City 84116 (533–9333), for further hunting and fishing information.

SUMMER SPORTS. Utah is a wonderland for outdoor recreation, a land of wide-open spaces, magnificent scenic variety, and matchless natural wonders. **Tennis** is everywhere. There are 45 public **golf** courses in operation around Utah. Many are nestled in unique mountain or desert settings. The state maintains one at Wasatch Mountain State Park, near Midway in Wasatch County.

For hardy individualists, possibilities for **fishing, hunting, camping, horseback riding, swimming, water-skiing,** and **boating, rafting,** and **bicycle tours** abound. Water slides are appearing along the Wasatch Front, between Ogden and Provo. Trails are excellent for **hiking** in Utah's national forests for short trips or several weeks of **backpacking.**

DOWNHILL SKIING. Utah does not have the most ski resorts of any Rocky Mountain state, but many skiers claim it has the best. The major ones combine large vertical drops, gorgeous and unusual scenery, and proximity to Salt Lake City. Individual lift-ticket prices can range from $15 to $30, but many discounts are offered locally or through tour packages.

Alta. Alta Ski Lifts, Alta 84092 (742–3333). Take Route 210 southeast to Little Cottonwood Canyon; 33 miles from Salt Lake City. Famous for alpine runs and consistent snow conditions. 8 lifts. Vertical drop of 8,500 feet.

Deer Valley. Box 1525, Park City 04060 (649–1000). Take I–80 35 miles southeast from Salt Lake City. Utah's most elegant and expensive resort. 8 lifts. Vertical drop of 2,200 feet.

Park City. Box 39–UP86, Park City 84060 (649–8111). Take I–80 to Route 224; 27 miles east of Salt Lake City. Utah's largest ski area. 17 lifts. Vertical drop of 3,100 feet.

Snowbird. Snowbird 84092 (742–2222 or 800–453–3000). Take I–80 to routes 215 and 210; 25 miles southeast of Salt Lake City. A scenic resort with tramway and seven other lifts. Vertical drop of 3,100 feet.

Solitude. Box 17557, Salt Lake City 84117 (534–1400). Take Route 152. 6 lifts. Vertical drop of 2,000 feet. Longest run: 2 ½ miles.

THE WYOMING ROCKIES

by
CURTIS W. CASEWIT

Wyoming boasts two of the country's great mountain chains—the mighty Grand Tetons, by general consensus among the most awesome peaks in America; and the isolated Wind River Range in the center of the state. Nothing matches these peaks for sheer drama except perhaps Eiger, Mönch, or Jungfrau in the Alps, or Pikes Peak in Colorado.

The state's mountain flora and fauna are various and unusual. In some parts of the backcountry and the national parks you might see trumpeter swans, sandhill cranes, ducks, geese, grouse, hawks of several species, and golden and bald eagles. Animals include coyote, ground squirrels, black bears, beavers, marten, bobcat, otter, and mink. Thousands of elk are scattered throughout the forests. Occasionally bighorn sheep wander along the Gros Ventre River around Red Hills, at the lower end of Crystal Creek.

Wyoming offers views of timber, waterfalls, wide meadows, lakes, streams—with excellent fishing—and broad valleys. All are made oddly beautiful by the changing seasons. In steep canyons and barren alpine country along the Continental Divide, snowfall is not uncommon in July.

The Wyoming Rockies have always intrigued geologists. Some of the complex pyramidal rock structures for which the range is known are visible to the lay person. Mt. Moran, for instance, one of the Grand Tetons, features a streak of black on its face. This is of volcanic origin, formed

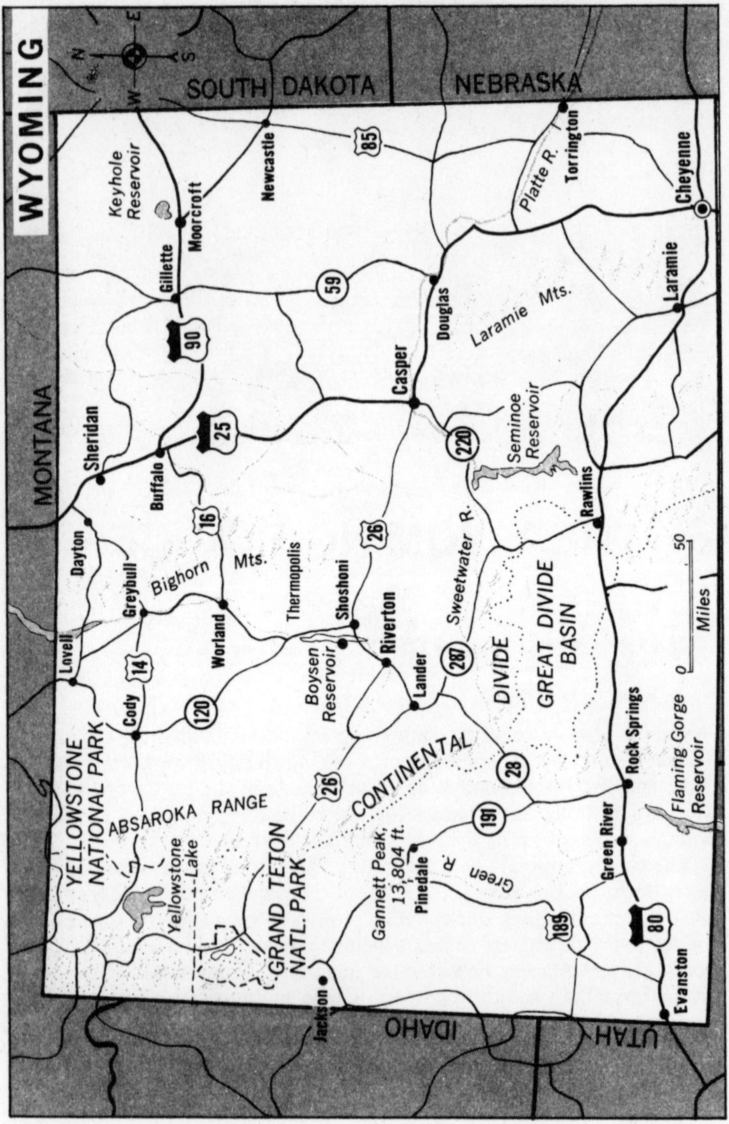
WYOMING
MONTANA
SOUTH DAKOTA
NEBRASKA
IDAHO
UTAH
N
E
S
W
Keyhole Reservoir
Moorcroft
Gillette
Newcastle
Sheridan
Buffalo
Casper
Douglas
Torrington
Platte R.
Cheyenne
Laramie
Laramie Mts.
Seminoe Reservoir
Rawlins
Sweetwater R.
Dayton
Greybull
Bighorn Mts.
Thermopolis
Shoshoni
Riverton
Worland
Lovell
Cody
Boysen Reservoir
Lander
DIVIDE
GREAT DIVIDE BASIN
CONTINENTAL
YELLOWSTONE NATIONAL PARK
ABSAROKA RANGE
Yellowstone Lake
GRAND TETON NATL. PARK
Gannett Peak, 13,804 ft.
Pinedale
Green R.
Jackson
Green River
Rock Springs
Flaming Gorge Reservoir
Evanston
0
50
Miles
90
25
16
26
59
85
14
120
220
287
28
191
189
80

by hot lava that boiled its way into a long, cold crack. If you see the imprint of marine fossils on your hikes, you'll learn that an ocean once covered these land masses. Traces of ancient water ripples are as common as the shells found in large boulders.

Wagon trains crossed Wyoming, as did cattle drives to the summer ranges in Montana and Canada. Wyoming has oil, mining, and missile bases. But first and foremost it's a cowboy state. During the last week in July for almost a century Cheyenne Frontier Days have brought the cowboy lifestyle to life, culminating each year in the greatest of all rodeos.

GRAND TETON NATIONAL PARK

Grand Teton National Park, 485 square miles of some of this country's best mountain, valley, and lake scenery, is easily reached by Route 287. Scattered throughout the park are a variety of facilities and campgrounds. You can spread your bedroll on the ground, pitch your tent, find a simple tent village with the tents already pitched for you, use the marina on 26,000-acre Jackson Lake, or enjoy the more comfortable surroundings at one of the lodges.

One of the most interesting and varied ways of touring the park is to hop from one accommodation to another. After Colter Bay Village it is a short move to Jackson Lake Lodge. Here you have a choice of 385 luxurious rooms in the lodge itself and adjacent cottages. In the lodge's main lounge, a ceiling-to-floor picture window frames the lake and the Grand Teton Range. Dining facilities include a coffee shop, dining room, and room service. A few steps from the main lodge and cabins is the Olympic-size pool.

From Jackson Lake Lodge be sure to take the Teton Park Road to Jenny Lake Lodge, one of the most luxurious accommodations in the park. It has campgrounds and excellent fishing sites; most of the trails through the mountains start here.

Motor through the park first to familiarize yourself with the various areas so you can revisit and spend more time at those you find especially appealing. Then park your car and take to the trails, either on foot or horseback, for intimate and uninterrupted views of the natural beauty of the region.

Park Service personnel can direct you to many short and long trails, all of which take you away from masses of tourists who stick close to their trailers in the luxurious campgrounds. Guides can be hired at Jenny Lake, headquarters for an excellent mountaineering school. One of the most spectacular trips, along the Glacier Trail, begins at Lupine Meadows, hits a series of steep switchbacks after about a mile, and shoots up to a thundering stream in Garnet Canyon. More difficult and far longer trails with fantastic views lead all the way from Jenny Lake to Lake Solitude, across the 13,766-foot Grand Teton itself.

Each of the six major routes across the park offers an entirely different set of attractions. You might find that some trails are too long and arduous to be followed on foot, so rent one of the docile, sure-footed horses and settle back for a relaxing ride through the dramatic scenery. Other trails,

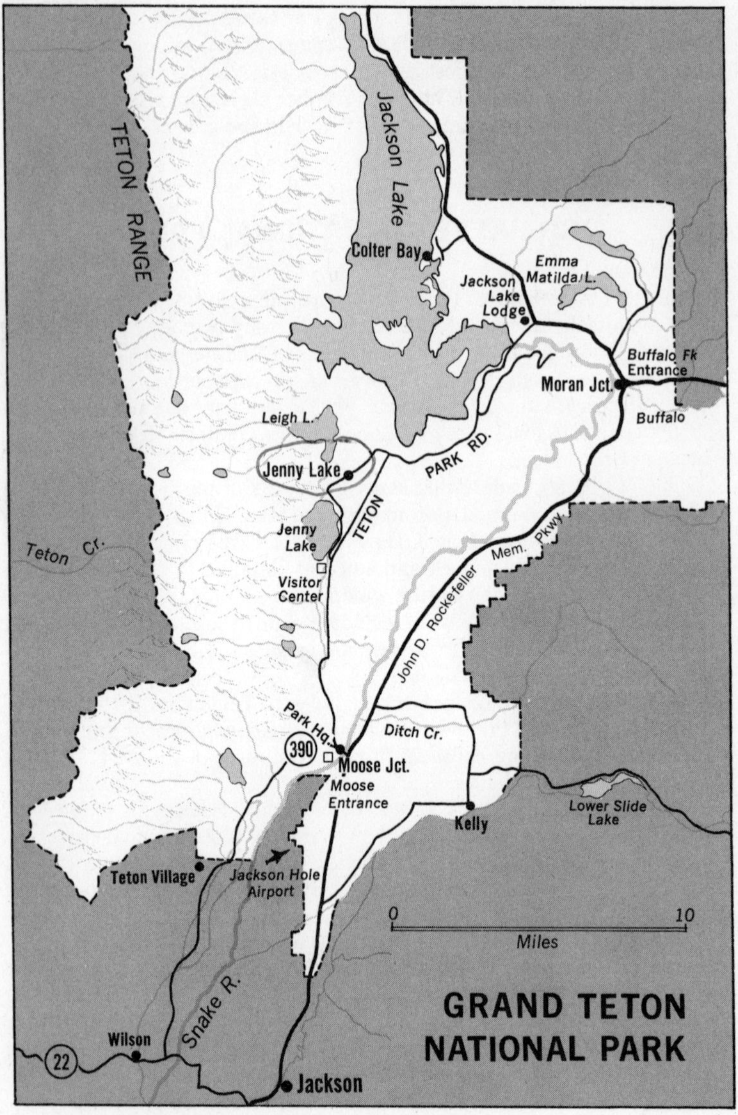
TETON RANGE
Jackson Lake
Colter Bay
Emma Matilda L.
Jackson Lake Lodge
Buffalo Fk Entrance
Moran Jct.
Buffalo
Leigh L.
Jenny Lake
PARK RD.
TETON
Jenny Lake
Visitor Center
Teton Cr.
John D. Rockefeller Mem. Pkwy.
Park Hq.
390
Ditch Cr.
Moose Jct.
Moose Entrance
Kelly
Lower Slide Lake
Teton Village
Jackson Hole Airport
0
10
Miles
Snake R.
Wilson
22
Jackson
GRAND TETON NATIONAL PARK

shorter and less rugged, can be appreciated on foot. For the truly adventurous, horseback and foot trails end at the dizzying height of 11,000 feet on the Static Peak Divide. Many a mountain climber has been lured to the summit.

If the lowlands are your ticket, try the Lakes Trail, which hugs the lakes at the bottom of the Teton Range. Branching out from this point, three other routes cut deeply into the canyon territory. Death Canyon, Cascade Canyon, and Indian Paintbrush Canyon, with their incredibly steep walls and myriad wildflowers, are thrilling to behold. If you are lucky, you may catch a glimpse of an elk, coyote, or any of the other wild animals that inhabit the region.

Skyline Trail and Teton Glacier Trail are unforgettable visual experiences, but never attempt them alone or before mid-June or after mid-September. Before starting out, check in with officials. Mountain climbing is taught in the park at a fee for those who lack experience but would like to try it.

If water is your element, float trips down the Snake River are available at the lake or at Jackson. These exciting trips take either a half or a full day. Along the route the majestic bald eagles may be seen high in the trees in one of their few remaining natural habitats. Tours also pass the historic Menor's Ferry at Moose. The Grand Teton National Park is open all year long, but its lodges close in winter. But there are year-round accommodations in nearby Teton Village.

Jackson

Gateway to the Tetons and the national parks is Jackson, at the southern edge of the park. Fourteen miles from Moose, Jackson is headquarters for the Bridger-Teton National Forest, an area of 1,701,000 acres of wilderness land bordering on both Grand Teton and Yellowstone national parks. The town and nearby countryside abound with dude ranches, motels, entertainment centers, and good fishing and hunting. There are three exceptional ski slopes—Snow King, Teton, and Targhee—and a Robert Trent Jones championship 18-hole golf course.

For those with cultural and historical interests, Jackson remains entirely Western, while boasting many art galleries, fine shops, a summer Fine Arts Festival, summer symphony, and summer-stock theater.

Arts Festival in the Mountains

With camera in tow, summer or winter, board the chair lift at Jackson and ride to the crest of Snow King Mountain some 2,000 feet above. Or look out the 50-foot-high lobby windows of the Snow King Inn and watch the skiers slaloming down Kelley's Alley.

Jackson Hole is Wyoming's premier ski area. A scenic aerial tramway leaves from Teton Village, part of the area 12 miles west of Jackson on the Wilson-Moose Road. Teton Village consists of hotels, chalets, lodges, and condominiums. The Ski Tram here rises 4,139 feet in 10 minutes, in an almost vertical ascent to Rendezvous Peak, offering a panoramic view of the Teton Range.

PRACTICAL INFORMATION FOR THE GRAND TETON NATIONAL PARK

HOW TO GET THERE. By air. *Delta* and *Continental* fly into Jackson. **By bus.** *Greyhound, Jackson/Rock Springs Stages,* and *Zenetti Bus Lines* provide transportation within the state.

TOURIST INFORMATION. For park information, call 307–733–2880 or 307–543–2851. Alternatively, contact the *Wyoming Travel Commission,* I–25 at College Dr., Cheyenne 82002 (777–7777 or 800–225–5996).

ACCOMMODATIONS. The central reservations and information number for the Jackson Hole area is 800–443–6931.

Jenny Lake Lodge. *Super Deluxe.* Box 240, Moran 83013 (733–4647). Rustic lodge and log cabins nestled under the Tetons at Jenny Lake. Fishing, horseback riding, hiking, and more.

Alpenhof. *Deluxe.* Box 288, Teton Village 83025 (733–3242 or 800–528–1234). Full-service resort lodge at base of Rendezvous Mountain. Skiing, horseback riding. Excellent restaurant. Heated pool, sauna.

Teton Pines. *Deluxe.* Box 362A, Star Route, Jackson 83001 (800–328–2223). Large, complex, with Gardiner Tennis Ranch. All sports amenities.

Wort Hotel. *Deluxe.* 50 N. Glenwood, Jackson 83001 (733–2190 or 800–322–2727). This refurbished hotel in the downtown area has a restaurant, cafe, and entertainment. Convention facilities, parking.

Jackson Lake Lodge. *Expensive.* Box 240, Moran 83013 (543–2855). In Grand Teton National Park. Landscaped grounds with pleasing views of the lake and Tetons. Hiking, rafting, horseback riding.

Trapper Motel. *Moderate–Expensive.* 235 N. Cache Dr., Jackson 83001 (733–2648). There are 28 well-kept rooms in this motel near the center of town. Cable TV, handicapped facilities, laundry room are available. Restaurants and shops are nearby.

Colter Bay Village. *Moderate.* Box 240, Moran 83013 (543–2855). In Grand Teton National Park. Log cabins with attractive view of Grand Tetons. Hiking, rafting, horseback riding.

BED AND BREAKFASTS. B and B's have been introduced to Wyoming and are beginning to catch on. Here are some typically homey establishments offering full breakfast to guests at moderate prices.

Jackson Hole. Teton Tree House. Box 550, Wilson 83014 (733–3233). This lovely home on mountainside has six rooms with private baths.

Moose. The Bunkhouse. Box 384, 83012 (733–7283). At foot of Tetons.

Moran. Fir Creek Ranch. Box 190, 83013 (543–2416) Seven rooms, each with private bath are available here. All meals available.

RESTAURANTS. For a full meal for two, exclusive of drinks, tax, and tip, the price categories are as follows: *Deluxe,* $55 and up; *Expensive,* $30–$55; *Moderate,* $15–$30; and *Inexpensive,* under $15. All restaurants listed accept major credit cards unless otherwise noted.

Jackson

Alpenhof. *Deluxe.* (733–3462). European restaurant at Teton Village. Seafood, veal. Reservations advised.

Stiegler's. *Deluxe.* Box 508 (733–1071). Teton Village Road. Austrian food.

Jenny Lake Lodge. *Expensive.* Box 250 (733–2811). Awards for international cuisine. Summer only.

Strutting Grouse. *Moderate–Expensive.* Jackson Hole Golf Course, U.S. 89 (733–7788). Gourmet food and a great view are featured at this pleasant place.

The Bunnery. *Inexpensive.* 130 N. Cache (733–5475). Sandwiches, baked goods, and light dinners are featured here.

Lame Duck. *Inexpensive.* 680 E. Broadway (733–4311). Oriental roast duck a specialty. Seafood and sushi offerings, too.

Moran

Aspens Restaurant. *Moderate.* (733–5470). At Signal Mountain, Lodge on the shore of Jackson Lake in Teton National Park. Full view of Grand Tetons. Offers excellent food in dining room. Housekeeping rooms available.

LIQUOR LAWS. Wyoming bars are open 6 A.M.–2 A.M.; noon–10 P.M. on Sunday. Minimum drinking age is 21. Liquor may be sold in bars either by the drink or the bottle, in cocktail lounges and in dining rooms by the drink, and in liquor stores by the bottle.

CAMPGROUNDS. Colter Bay Campground. Park Headquarters, Moose 83012 (733–2880). Disposal station, coin laundry, groceries, and propane. Swimming, riding. North of Moose on routes 89 and 287.

Colter Bay Tent Village. Box 240, Moran 83013 (543–2855). Coin laundry, groceries, propane, and restaurant. Beach, rental boats, canoes, fishing. Northwest of Moran Junction on routes 89 and 287.

Snake River Park KOA. Box 14A, Jackson 83001 (733–7078). Ten miles south of Jackson on Hwy. 191. Grassy sites, hiking trails.

RAFTING. Ranging from exciting white-water adventures to leisurely down-river excursions, rafting trips are among the best ways to see the part of the Tetons cars don't reach.

Barker-Ewing Float Trips, Box 3032-A, Jackson 83001 (733–1000).

Charles Sands' Wild Water River Trips, 110 W. Broadway, Box 696A, Wilson 83014 (733–4410 or 800–338–4600 in WY).

Dave Hansen Float Trips, Box 328-A, Jackson 83001 (733–6295).

Fort Jackson Float Trips, Box 1176, Jackson 83001 (733–2583).

Mad River Boat Trips, Inc., Box 2222, Jackson 83001 (733–6203 or 800–458–RAFT).

Triangle X Float Trips, Box 120A, Jackson 83001 (733–6445 or 5500).

MUSIC. In mid-July, Teton Village in Jackson Hole hosts the six-week *Grand Teton Music Festival.* In past years concerts have included symphonic and chamber pieces. *The Watermelon Concerts,* so-called because after the concert the audience and musicians sit down to discuss the performance over large slices of watermelon, have been very popular.

YELLOWSTONE NATIONAL PARK

Yellowstone National Park is 53 miles from the city of Cody via routes 14, 16, and 20, known collectively as the "Buffalo Bill Scenic Hiway to Yellowstone." Open from May through September, this paved road snakes west through the Shoshone Canyon, tunnels its way beneath Rattlesnake Mountain, and affords sweeping panoramic views of the Buffalo Bill Dam and Canyon. There are spacious parking places for picture-taking stops.

The highway passes lush ranch country through the Shoshone Valley, plunges into the Shoshone National Forest, then twists through the Absaroka Mountains. Here such strange and colorful rock formations as the Chinese Wall, Laughing Pig Rock, Devil's Elbow, the Camel, the Palisades, Chimney Rock, and Holy City are found in the area known as the Playgrounds of the Gods. Finally, the road enters Yellowstone Park and continues past Lake Eleanor and Sylvan Lake, to reach Yellowstone Lake, the largest high-altitude lake in the United States.

Yellowstone National Park

So vast is Yellowstone National Park—about 3,472 square miles—that weeks on end would be needed to explore all of its scenic and varied attractions. No other national park embraces so many of nature's masterpieces. Most outstanding are the world's largest geyser basins and the thundering falls and canyon of the Yellowstone River.

Nowhere else in the West will you find so large a wildlife sanctuary. Bear, elk, buffalo, moose, deer, and antelope may be seen in their natural habitat. It is strictly against park regulations to feed or approach the bears.

The park is alive and well after the 1988 fires. There are still wide sweeps of green forest, and all the lodges and attractions are intact. The burn area itself has become a site of interest.

An excellent highway system swings close to many of the prominent sights, but accommodations within the park, including campgrounds, are limited. Early reservations are advised.

Yellowstone National Park has five entrances: from the north, by way of Livingston and Gardiner, Montana—I-90 and routes 10 and 89; from the northeast, by way of Billings and Cooke City, Montana—I-90 and routes 10 and 212; from the east, by way of Cody, Wyoming—routes 14, 16, and 20; from the south, by way of Jackson, Wyoming, and Grand Teton National Park—routes 26, 89, 191, 189, and 287; and from the west by way of West Yellowstone, Montana—routes 20 and 191.

From the east entrance the highway passes Yellowstone Lake, whose sparkling blue waters invite a tour of its 110-mile shoreline. Scenic cruisers operate daily during the summer. From their decks the wildlife and waterfowl can be observed in a setting unchanged since fur trappers discovered the lake more than a hundred years ago.

On past the lake, the road leads to Fishing Bridge Junction, where anglers attempt to lure the large trout that abound there (free permits available at visitor centers or ranger stations). Cabin accommodations are available two miles south of the lake.

Treasures of Yellowstone

Go north from Fishing Bridge, on the road to Canyon Village at Canyon Junction. This circle tour offers some of the park's outstanding scenery and passes near good accommodations.

At Canyon Junction is the magnificent Grand Canyon of the Yellowstone. This 24-mile-long, 1,200-foot-deep gorge is a visual delight. Countless shades of red and ochre within the canyon are enhanced by the emerald green of the surrounding forest. There are two waterfalls, one twice as high as Niagara, that will thrill you. While the canyon and the falls may be viewed and photographed from several angles, Inspiration Point on the north rim and Artist Point across the gorge are popular vantage points.

Mt. Washburn, rising 10,317 feet, is on your right as you drive the 19 miles from Canyon Village to Tower Junction. The road slips through Dunraven Pass at an elevation of 8,859 feet before dropping a couple of thousand feet to Tower Falls, where the Roosevelt Lodge provides excellent rustic accommodations. Pause here to enjoy steak cookouts and to allow the children the fun of riding on a stagecoach.

Mammoth Hot Springs, at the north entrance, is 18 miles west of Tower Junction. The impressive travertine terraces of these fabled springs are sometimes vividly colored, sometimes snow-white. There are accommodations at the Mammoth Hot Springs Hotel Motor Inn and Cabins.

Having reached the top of the loop at Mammoth Hot Springs, the route swings down 21 miles to Norris Junction, then 14 miles to Madison Junction, and finally 16 miles to Old Faithful.

Old Faithful

Nowhere in the world can match Yellowstone's variety of geysers. Some erupt in rage and fury, spewing thousands of gallons of water over 100 feet in the air, others merely splash up a few inches. And most beloved of them all is Old Faithful.

Old Faithful is one of the gathering points for all visitors to the park, and no one leaves until he has seen this geyser shoot its thousands of gallons of steaming water high into the air. It "blows" on the average of every 66 minutes and has not missed a performance in over 80 years. In the Old Faithful Visitor Center is a geyser diagram which explains in detail just what goes on beneath the ground to cause this phenomenon. Old Faithful Inn is hard pressed to take care of demands for accommodations, and reservations must be made in advance.

If you have an appetite for more geysers, you can walk around the Old Faithful area and see others, like "Grotto." Leaving Old Faithful southbound, take the 17-mile drive from Old Faithful to West Thumb Junction,

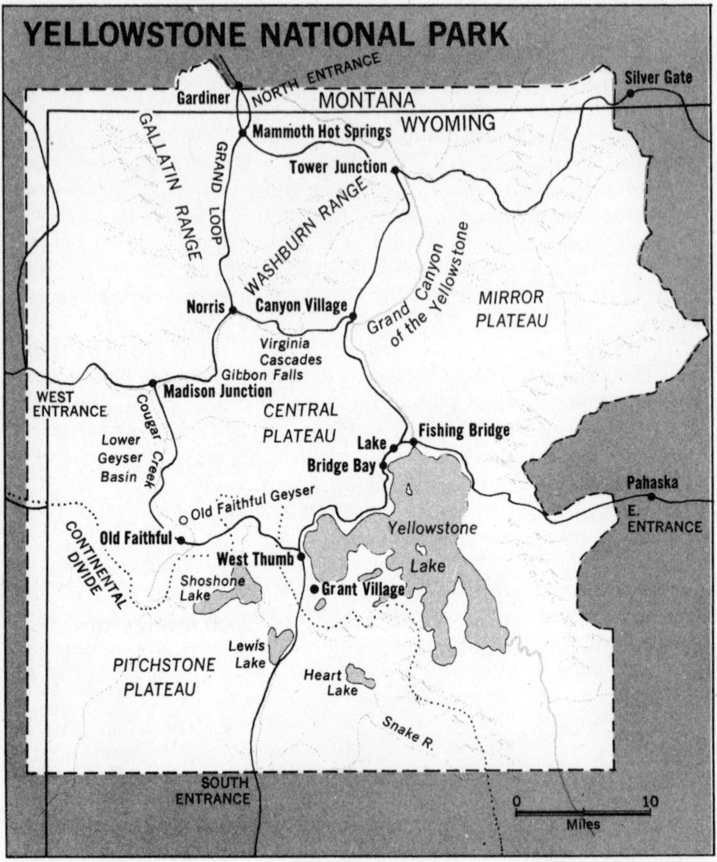
YELLOWSTONE NATIONAL PARK
NORTH ENTRANCE
Gardiner
MONTANA
WYOMING
Silver Gate
Mammoth Hot Springs
GALLATIN RANGE
GRAND LOOP
Tower Junction
WASHBURN RANGE
Grand Canyon of the Yellowstone
MIRROR PLATEAU
Norris
Canyon Village
Virginia Cascades
Gibbon Falls
Madison Junction
WEST ENTRANCE
CENTRAL PLATEAU
Cougar Creek
Lower Geyser Basin
Fishing Bridge
Lake
Bridge Bay
Pahaska
E. ENTRANCE
Old Faithful Geyser
Old Faithful
CONTINENTAL DIVIDE
West Thumb
Yellowstone Lake
Shoshone Lake
Grant Village
Lewis Lake
PITCHSTONE PLATEAU
Heart Lake
Snake R.
SOUTH ENTRANCE
0 10
Miles

where the Grant Village on Yellowstone Lake offers campgrounds and lodging.

From West Thumb to Bridge Lake and the start of this loop is a distance of 21 miles. In Bridge Lake are two worthwhile points of interest: the Bridge Bay Marina, capable of handling 200 boats; and the Lake Hotel, with every facility, including a hospital.

There are some 1,000 miles of trails in the park, including some short ones. You will need a pair of sturdy, comfortable hiking boots, and it's best to break them in before arriving at the park.

For the experienced horseback rider, there are more than 900 miles of paths. Horses may be rented, but all horseback trips into the wilderness areas must be accompanied by a guide.

You can visit Yellowstone from May through October and from mid-December to mid-March. There are always accommodations open in the communities that surround the park. In winter, all wheeled vehicles are prohibited. Access is possible by snow coach or snowmobile, into the spectacular snowy wilderness.

PRACTICAL INFORMATION FOR YELLOWSTONE NATIONAL PARK

Two-million-acre Yellowstone is the nation's first and largest national park. Located in the northwestern corner of Wyoming, it is a scenic wonderland of spouting geysers, steaming hot springs, magnificent waterfalls, beautiful lakes, towering mountains, big game, wildlife, birds, fishing and, of course, the inevitable bear (don't pet him, he's not tame). Yellowstone is open part of the winter, too. Take a "Snow Coach" trip through the south entrance to Old Faithful Lodge. Old Faithful geyser spouting on a frosty day, the most famous of Yellowstone's 10,000 hydrothermal features, is unsurpassed. Both excursions leave Bridge Bay. For conditions in the park, year-round, call 344–7381 or 543–2559.

ACCOMMODATIONS AND RESTAURANTS. You're a captive audience at Yellowstone, and lodging prices reflect this. All the establishments listed below fall into our *Expensive* category of $30–$60 per person per night, double occupancy. This is nonetheless cheaper than what you'd pay for equivalent rooms in a major city.

Canyon Village. TW Services, Yellowstone National Park 82190 (344–7311). Rustic cabins, with cafeteria. Horseback riding and park touring possible.

Lake Yellowstone Hotel and Cabins. TW Services, Yellowstone National Park 82190 (344–7311). This 1891 hotel was remodeled in 1903 and 1929. Wood frame cabins available. Lake-view dining room.

Mammoth Hot Springs Hotel. TW Services, Yellowstone National Park 82190 (344–7311). Park headquarters. Near major geothermal activity. Comfortable rooms in older lodge. Attractive restaurant.

Old Faithful Inn. TW Services, Yellowstone National Park 82190 (344–7311). Across from the famous geyser. Attractive restaurant. Open all year, with reservations only.

CAMPGROUNDS. Bridge Bay. Lake Station. (347–2329). Disposal station, coin laundry, and propane. Rental boats, fishing. South of Lake Village at the Natural Bridge.

Fishing Bridge. Lake Station. (344–7381). Disposal station, coin laundry, groceries, and propane. Boating, fishing, museum. East of junction at Fishing Bridge.

Grant Village Camp. Grant Village. (344–7381). Disposal station, coin laundry, and propane. Boating. South of West Thumb Junction.

WYOMING MOUNTAIN TOWNS

Apart from the Grand Tetons and Yellowstone, Wyoming's Rockies also offer lots more Old West history and diversion. During mid-July the Sheridan-Wyoming Rodeo, one of the oldest in the country, takes place. Sheridan is the headquarters for the Bighorn National Forest, covering 1,107,670 acres. There are at least 38 campgrounds and many picnic spots in the forest. Fishing and hunting expeditions can be arranged, as can saddle and pack pleasure trips deep into the wilderness. The area saw many Indian battles, and several battle sites remain.

From Sheridan, drive on to Dayton, via I–90 and Route 14, and take a look at one of the finest cattle and horse regions of the West. Genuine western hospitality reigns in Dayton, where the locals use first names as soon as you're introduced and like you to reciprocate. Here in Dayton is America's oldest guest ranch, and the Fourth of July celebration features a barbecue, with all visitors welcome.

From Dayton, drive over the summit of the Big Horn Mountains, along Route 14 to Greybull, where routes 20 and 16 join for the journey to Yellowstone National Park. But don't miss the town of Cody on the way. Here you can check in at a working guest ranch for a few days of rest and unhurried sightseeing amid awesome scenery. An equestrian statue of the great scout "Buffalo Bill" Cody looks down the main street of the town that has taken his name. Mementos of the famed Westerner are on exhibit in the Buffalo Bill Historical Center, which includes Cody's boyhood home and a replica of the old Cody ranch. The Center features four museums. Cody was born in LeClaire, Iowa, but his house was taken apart and re-erected here. In early July, visitors flock to the area for the Cody Stampede rodeo. The Whitney Gallery contains one of America's greatest collections of western art.

Two Tribes with One Reservation

To the east of the Grand Tetons are Wyoming's highest and most massive mountains, the Wind River Range. If you like fishing and big-game hunting, settle in here for a while and it won't be long before you'll have your limit. This somewhat remote region boasts more than a thousand lakes and streams, and six of the larger lakes are accessible by road. In the quiet retreats of the Bridger-Teton National Forest, there are many choice campsites. Pinedale has modern motels, guest-ranch accommodations, and restaurants.

The Dubois area, surrounded on three sides by Shoshone National Forest on the Upper Big Wind River, is one of the richest places in the nation for prospectors and rockhounds. Found in the region are gem-quality agatized opalized woods, pine and fir cone replacements, amethyst-lined trees and limb casts, and all types of high-grade agate.

Bordering the Dubois area is the big Shoshone and Arapahoe Indian Reservation. In July, first the Shoshone and then the Arapahoe Indians hold their sun dances. Dressed in full costume, they dance continuously for three days and nights without taking food or water. Routes 287 and 26 pass through the reservation, where the Indians tend their horses and cattle or irrigate their haylands. On your way to Dubois note Crowheart Butte, a State Monument commemorating the scene of the great battle between the Shoshone and the Crow tribes.

Further along on routes 26 and 287 from Dubois, the town of Lander, one of Wyoming's oldest communities, is worth a stopover. Known as the place where the rails end and the trails begin, Lander is a great place to fish, hunt, and climb. Sinks Canyon State Park is nearby.

Follow Route 26 into Riverton, where the Riverton Museum has Indian displays. There are three Indian missions in this vicinity: St. Stephens on Route 789; St. Michael's Mission at Ethete; and Fort Washakie, the Indian headquarters in Fort Washakie.

Laramie and Cheyenne

Laramie, at an altitude of more than 7,000 feet, offers an invigorating climate and clean, clear air. Nearly a century old, the town has flourished since its inception as a station on the Union Pacific Railroad line. A short jaunt from Laramie is historic Fort Sanders, a stopping place for Western pioneers and Mormons.

From Laramie to Cheyenne, the state capital, I–80 swings past one of the highest points along the entire Lincoln Highway. A good photo stop is the Ames Monument, located about two miles off Route 30 on a marked road. This 65-foot pyramid was erected in honor of the Ames Brothers who helped finance the Union Pacific.

Cheyenne, now a peaceful, prosperous community of 47,000, was known as "Hell on Wheels" in the days of the Old West. This spirit is revived once a year, usually during the last full week of July, at Cheyenne Frontier Days. At Frontier Park, the nation's top cowboys muster all their skill, strength, and sheer nerve to try to stay astride the backs of bucking Brahmans and broncos. For tickets, write: Cheyenne Frontier Days Committee, Box 2666, Dept 881, Cheyenne, WY 82003.

While in Cheyenne, visit the Capitol Building. Guided tours of the Gold Dome are available June to August, but the panoramic view is worth a visit anytime. The State Museum, located on Central Avenue at 23rd Street, exhibits archeological and historical treasures of Wyoming and the Old West. The Frontier Days Old West Museum boasts a large collection of horse-drawn vehicles and old sleighs.

PRACTICAL INFORMATION FOR WYOMING MOUNTAIN TOWNS

HOW TO GET THERE AND AROUND. By air. *Continental Express* flies into Jackson Hole, Casper, Cheyenne, Rock Springs, and Riverton; *Delta* into Casper and Jackson; *United* into Casper, Cody, Gillet, Sheridan, and Cheyenne.

By car. I-80 crosses southern Wyoming, entering from Nebraska in the east and leaving into Utah in the west. I-25 passes into the state from Colorado in the south. I-90, from Montana in the north and South Dakota in the east, serves the northern part of Wyoming.

By bus. *Greyhound* offers transportation to and within Wyoming. *Zenetti Bus Lines* connects Rock Springs, Lander, and Riverton. *Jackson-Rock Springs Stages* also provides intrastate service.

TOURIST INFORMATION. For all Wyoming travel, vacation, resort, and camping information, write for brochures from *Wyoming Travel Commission,* Cheyenne, WY 82002 (800–225–5996).

ACCOMMODATIONS. The larger towns in Wyoming have excellent hotel and motel accommodations; most have parking facilities, restaurants, and bars. Rates are usually higher in summer, though some have special family rates. Cost figures are generally for the minimum- or moderate-priced rooms, unless a range is indicated. Listings are in order of price category.

The price categories, based on the cost of a double room, will average as follows: *Super Deluxe,* over $115; *Deluxe,* $65–$115; *Expensive,* $45–$65; *Moderate,* $35–$45; and *Inexpensive,* $25–$35. No meals are included in these prices. All area codes are 307 unless otherwise noted.

Afton. Mountain Inn. *Deluxe.* Route 1, 83110 (886–3156). Pool. Golf nearby.

The Corral. *Expensive.* 161 Washington 38110 (886–5424). Group of rustic cabins in the heart of the Star Valley cheese country. Children's playground. Has an AAA listing.

Alta. Grand Targhee Resort. *Deluxe.* Near Driggs, Idaho (353–2304 or 800–443–8146). One of Wyoming's leading ski resorts. Early and late snow. Open summers. Swimming pool. One-, one-and-a-half, and two-level condominiums.

Buffalo. Best Western Cross Roads Inn. *Expensive.* Box 639, 82834 (684–2256 or 800–528–1234). A 60-unit motel just off the interstate. Dining room, cocktail lounge, swimming pool. Meeting rooms. Pets allowed.

Canyon Motel. *Moderate.* 997 Fort St., 82834 (684–2957). Pool. Some kitchens. Free coffee and cable TV.

Keahey's Motel. *Moderate.* 350 N. Main, 82834 (684–2225). Old-time hospitality in historic downtown area. Some cooking units.

Z-Bar Motel. *Inexpensive.* 626 Fort St. 82834 (684–5535). This well-kept place features weekly rates in winter.

Casper. Casper Hilton Inn. *Deluxe.* I-25 & Rancho Rd., North Poplar 82601 (266–6000 or 800–HILTONS). One of Wyoming's plushest hostelries. All services. Two restaurants.

Holiday Inn. *Deluxe.* 300 W. F St., Box 3500, 82601 (235–2531 or 800–HOLIDAY). Plush accommodations.

Best Western East. *Expensive.* Box 3249, 82601 (234–3541). Heated pool. Parking. Restaurant next door.

Showboat Motel. *Expensive.* 100 W. F St., 82601 (235–2711).

La Quinta Inn. *Moderate.* 301 East E. St. 82601 (234–1159 or 800–531–5900). Pool, cable TV, and free coffee are offered in this chain. Nearby cafe.

Cheyenne. Hitching Post Inn. *Deluxe.* 1700 W. Lincolnway, 82001 (638–3301). Long a Wyoming landmark near the downtown area. Large, attractive rooms; indoor and outdoor pools, sauna, gourmet "Carriage Court" dining room, coffee shop, cocktail lounge, beauty salon, gift shop, outdoor tennis.

Holding's Little America. *Moderate–Expensive.* 2800 W. Lincolnway, 82001 (634–2771). At junction of I-80 and I-20, just west of the city limits, this motor hotel conforms to other "Little America" establishments in Wyoming, Arizona, and Utah. Almost 200 elaborate rooms and suites. Wyoming Best Western establishment. Heated pool, coffee shop, dining room, and cocktail lounge. Antiques and curios.

Rodeway Inn. *Moderate.* 3839 E. Lincolnway, 82001 (634–2171 or 800–228–2000). Besides the comfortable rooms there are pool, bar, entertainment, and dancing; discount for senior citizens.

Sapp Bros. Friendship Inn. *Inexpensive.* 3350 E. I–80 Service Rd., Exit 370. 82001 (778–8878). 40 rooms are available here, with laundry, and a restaurant.

Stage Coach Motel. *Moderate.* 1515 W. Lincolnway, 82001 (634–4495). I-80 Business & Route 30. Cable TV; pets allowed.

Super 8 Motel. *Inexpensive.* 1900 W. Lincolnway, 82001 (635–8741 or 800–255–3050). On Route 30 West. Popular with truckers.

Cody. Holiday Inn Convention Center. *Deluxe.* 1701 Sheridan Ave., 82414 (587–5555 or 800–HOLIDAY). This place is located downtown, in the historic Buffalo Bill Village. Dining room, cocktail lounge, swimming pool, meeting rooms. Gift shop.

Bill Cody's Ranch Inn. *Expensive.* Box 1390, 82414 (587–2097). Outdoor recreation nearby. Fishing, skiing.

Buffalo Bill Village. *Expensive.* 1603 Sheridan Ave., 82414 (587–5544). Large group of Western cabins, a trailer parking area, playground, heated pool, and western entertainment. Famous for chuckwagon dinners.

Absaroka Mountain Lodge. *Moderate.* Box 168, Wapiti 82450 (587–3963). Rustic motel on a rushing mountain stream in the Wapiti Valley. Dining room and large Western lobby with stone fireplace.

Rainbow Park. *Moderate.* 1136 17th St. (587–6251). TV, playground.

The Irma. *Inexpensive–Moderate.* 1192 Sheridan Ave., 82414 (587–4221). This Victorian home was built by Buffalo Bill. Restaurant and Bar.

Douglas. Holiday Inn. *Expensive.* 1450 Riverbend Dr. 82633 (800–HOLIDAY). Pool, restaurant, and many amenities are offered at this popular chain.

Best Western Prairie Winds Motel. *Moderate.* 311 Center St. 82633 (358–4780 or 800–528–1234). Close to all town services.

Dubois. Branding Iron Motel. *Inexpensive.* 401 W. Ramshorn St., 82513 (455–2893). West on routes 26 and 287, in the heart of a western town. Nearby cafe and cocktail lounge. Western charm.

Stagecoach Motor Inn. *Moderate.* Box 216, 82513 (455–2303). West side on main highway. In the best tourist tradition. Family atmosphere.

Evanston. Best Western Dunmar. *Expensive.* Box 768, 82930 (789–3770). At west entrance of Route 30 and I-80. Free transportation to airport, bus and train stations. Complimentary breakfast; pool. Restaurant and lounge nearby.

Friendship Classic Lodge. *Moderate.* 202 Route 30E, 82930 (789–6830). Restaurant nearby. Whirlpool and laundry on premises.

Super 8. *Moderate.* 70 Route 30E, 82930 (800–843–1991). Restaurant and minimart next door.

Triangle Motor Inn. *Moderate.* 261 U.S. 30 E., 82930 (789–0790). Pool, hot tub, and Continental breakfast are offered at this modest place. Pets permitted.

Greybull. K-Bar Motel. *Inexpensive.* 300 Greybull Ave., 82426 (765–4426). Open all year.

Lander. Holiday Lodge. *Moderate.* 210 McFarlane Dr., 82520 (332–2511). At intersection of routes 26 and 287 on south edge of Lander. Miniature golf.

Maverick Motel. *Moderate.* 808 Main St., 82520 (332–2821). Small, well-appointed motel with coffee shop.

Pronghorn Lodge. *Moderate.* 150 E. Main St., 82520 (332–3940). Clean rooms, TV.

Laramie. Laramie Inn. *Expensive.* 1503 S. 3rd St., 82070 (742–3721). Dining room, cocktail lounge, meeting and banquet room.

Circle S Motel. *Moderate.* 2440 Grand, 82070 (745–4811). On the east edge of town, with attractively landscaped ground and pleasant rooms. Heated pool.

Friendship Inn Downtown Motel. *Moderate.* 165 N. 3rd St., 82070 (742–6671). 30 clean units. Central.

Little America. *Moderate.* I–80, exit 68. Box 1, 82929 (875–2400). This is a large oasis in the middle of the desert, with large, warm guest rooms, dining room, coffee shop, and cocktail lounge.

Wyoming Motel. *Moderate.* 1720 Grand, 82070 (742–6633). Friendly motel across the street from the University.

Super 8. *Inexpensive.* I-80 and Curtis St., 82070 (745–8901 or 800–843–1991). Popular with tourists.

Medicine Bow. Virginian Hotel/Motel. *Inexpensive.* 404 Lincoln Hwy., 82329 (379–2377). Wyoming landmark. Dining room, coffee shop, and cocktail lounge.

Rawlins. Bel Air Inn. *Expensive.* 23d at Spruce, 82301 (324–2737 or 800–528–1234). A sleek 122-unit motel. Heated pool. Good restaurant and bar. Popular with airline personnel.

Holiday Inn. *Expensive.* 1801 E. Cedar, 82301 (324–2783). New, large, and reliable. All amenities.

Bridger Inn. *Inexpensive.* 1904 E. Cedar, 82301 (328–1401). TV, near cafe.

Jade Lodge. *Inexpensive.* 5th at Spruce, Box 958, 82301 (324–2791). 26 rooms with cable TV are available in this lodge in town center.

Riverton. Sundowner II. *Expensive.* 1616 N. Federal, 82501 (856–6503). Many amenities. Restaurant on premises.

Holiday Inn. *Moderate.* N. Federal Blvd. at Sunset, Dept. A3, 82501 (856–8100 or 800–HOLIDAY). Besides this chain's standard rooms, there are a pool, coin laundry, and airport shuttle.

Tomahawk Motor Lodge. *Moderate.* 208 E. Main, 82501 (856–9205). Downtown motel. Sauna, hot tub, free coffee.

Saratoga. Saratoga Inn. *Expensive.* Box 869, 82331 (326–5261). Located on the North Platte River, with golf course, tennis. Dining room, cocktail lounge.

Cary's Sage & Sand Motel. *Moderate.* 311 S. First St., 82331 (326–8339). Small, clean.

Sheridan. Sheridan Center Motor Inn. *Expensive.* 612 N. Main St., 82801 (800–528–1234). Large Best Western establishment. Dining room, cocktail lounge. Banquet and meeting rooms. Swimming pool. Two blocks from business district.

Trails End Motel. *Moderate.* 2125 N. Main St. (672–2477). Small, attractive motel with an indoor pool.

The Mill Inn Motel. *Inexpensive.* 2161 Coffeen Ave., 82801 (672–6401). This is a former historic flour mill turned into charming motel.

Thermopolis. Best Western Moonlighter Motel. *Expensive.* 600 Broadway 82443 (864–2321). Pool, tennis; hunting, fishing; restaurant and lounge nearby.

Holiday Inn of the Waters. *Expensive.* In Hot Springs State Park, 82443 (800–HOLIDAY). Pool, dining room, coffee shop, cocktail lounge, banquet and convention center. Mineral baths. Fishing.

Wheatland. Motel West Winds. *Moderate.* 1765 South Rd., 82201 (322–2705). 30 pleasant rooms with cable TV. Nearby cafe.

Vimbo's Motel. *Inexpensive.* South of town (322–3843). A free shuttle to airport.

AND BREAKFASTS. Wyoming's B&Bs are a human touch ıis larger-than-life scenery. Most fall in price ranges that for ho- d be *moderate.* All offer a large breakfast in the morning, and many serve an afternoon snack.

Cody. Lockhart B & B Inn. 109 W. Yellowstone, 82414 (587–6074). Historic home of western author Caroline Lockhart.

Shoshone Lodge Resort. Box 790T, 82414 (587–4044). Horseback riding, fishing, pack trips in summer.

Evanston. Pine Gables B & B Inn. 1049 Center St. 82930 (789–2069). Located in historic district. Five rooms, furnished with antiques.

Lander. Black Mountain Ranch. 548 North Fork Rd., 82520 (332–6442). This is the original bunkhouse of the former Boeseke ranch with eight rooms, two with private bath. A "Ranch Recreation" package includes all meals as well as trout fishing, horseback riding, a llama picnic, and guided tours.

Rawlins. Ferris Mansion. 607 W. Maple, 82301 (324–3961). Onetime prison, with museums, hot pool nearby.

FARM VACATIONS AND GUEST RANCHES. Wyoming is famous for its great variety of guest ranches. A selection of those available is included here; complete information is available from the **Wyoming Travel Commission,** Cheyenne, WY 82002.

Buffalo. Horton's Ranch. Saddle String 82840 (684–2487).

Paradise Guest Ranch. Box 790, 83824 (684–7876).

Pines Lodge. Box 100, 83824.

South Fork Inn. Box 854, 82834.

Cody. Absaroka Mountain Lodge. Box 168, Wapiti 82450 (587–3963).

Hunter Peak Ranch. Box 1931, 82414 (587–3711 summer, 754–5878 winter).

Pahaska Tepee Resort. Box 2370, 82414 (527–7701).

Rimrock Dude Ranch. 2728 North Fork Route, 82414 (587–3970).

Shoshone Lodge. Box 790WT, 82414 (587–4044).

Valley Ranch. Valley Ranch Road, West Cody, 82414. Since 1892. Fishing, pack trips, wrangler school, hayrides.

Crowheart. Cross Mill Iron Ranch. 82512 (486–2279). On Big Wind River.

Douglas. Deer Forks Ranch. Route 6, 1200 Poison Lake Rd., 82633 (358–2033).

Dubois. Absaroka Ranch. 82513 (455–2275).

Bitterroot Ranch. 82513 (455–2778).

CM Ranch. 82513 (455–2331). In Wind River Mountains. Favored by hunters and families since 1927.

Double Bar J Ranch. Box 695, 82513 (455–2725).

Timberline Ranch. Box 308, 82513 (455–2513).
Triangle C Ranch. 82513 (455–2225).
Wind River Ranch. 82513 (455–2500 or 455–2721).

Greybull. Paintrock Outfitters, Inc. Box 509, 82426 (765–2556).

Sheridan. Spear-O-Wigwam Ranch. Box 1081, 82801; (674–4496).

Wapiti. Crossed Sabres. Box WTC 82450 (587–3760). Summer pack trips, cabins, horses four miles from Yellowstone.

CAMPGROUNDS. Wyoming has hundreds of campgrounds, ranging from dirt spaces to complete trailer facilities. Yellowstone Park and adjacent Teton and Shoshone counties offer many campsites on a first-come, first-serve basis. Reservations are accepted only for large organized groups, such as the Boy Scouts.

Special regulations governing food storage apply at most Wyoming campsites to avoid trouble with bears. All food or similar organic material must be kept completely sealed in a vehicle or camping unit that is constructed of solid, non-pliable material; or, may be suspended at least 10 feet above the ground, and 4 feet horizontally from any post or tree trunk. The cleaner the camp, the less chance there is of being bothered by bears.

For complete information about the location and facilities of campgrounds in Wyoming, contact the *Wyoming Travel Commission,* Cheyenne, WY 82002 (777–7777 or 800–225–5996).

Buffalo. Deer Park Campground. Box 568, 82834, (684–5722). Disposal station, coin laundry, groceries, pool, playground. West of I-90 Exit 58; ¾ mile east of I-25 Exit 299 on Route 16.

Indian Campground. Clearmont Route, Box 13, 82834 (684–9601). Disposal station, coin laundry, groceries, propane. Pool, playground. Just west of I-25 Exit 299 on Route 16; 1¼ miles west of I-90 Exit 58.

Cheyenne. AB Campground. 1503 W. College Dr. 82007 (634–7035). Disposal station, coin laundry. South of junction of I-80 and I-25.

Karl's Cheyenne KOA. 4510 Charles St. 82001 (638–6371). Disposal station, coin laundry, groceries, propane, playground. From I-80, take E. Lincolnway Exit 364, 1½ miles north on College Drive, then ¼ mile east on Charles Street.

Restway Travel Park. 4212 Whitney Rd., Box 3343, 82001 (634–3811). Disposal station, coin laundry, pool, playground. From I-80, take E. Lincolnway exit to Route 30 East.

Cody. Cody KOA Campground. 5561 Greybull Hwy., 82414 (587–2369). Disposal station, coin laundry, groceries, propane. Pool, playground. 2½ miles east on Hwys. 14, 16, and 20.

Hitching Post Campground. North Fork Star Route 82414 (587–4149). Disposal station, coin laundry, groceries, propane, restaurant. Pool, fishing, miniature golf, playground. 20 miles west on routes 14, 16, and 20.

Newton Creek. U.S. Forest Service campground, 37.3 miles west of Cody on U.S. 16 (14 miles from Yellowstone). Tents and trailers, 14-day limit; fee.

Douglas. Jackalope Campground. Box 1190, 82633 (358–2164). Disposal station, coin laundry, groceries, propane, pool. Take I-25W Douglas Exit 140E to routes 94 and 91S, then ½ mile west to route 92, then 1½ miles west.

Dubois. Pinnacles. U.S. Forest Service campground, 23 miles west of Dubois on U.S. 287, five miles north on forest service road. Tents and trailers, toilets, no drinking water. Boating and fishing.

Greybull. The Green Oasis. 540 12th Ave. N, 82426 (765–2524). Coin laundry and groceries. Recreation room. North on routes 14, 16, and 20.

Lander. Triangle C Ranch. Box 691, 82513 (455–2225). Tents and trailer sites, 14-day limit, all facilities. Horses, fishing, hunting, restaurant. 18 miles northwest of Dubois.

Laramie. Laramie KOA. 1271 Baker St., 82070 (742–6553). Disposal station, coin laundry, groceries, propane, playground. Just southeast of I-80 Curtis St. Exit.

Rawlins. R.V. World Campground. 2401 Wagon Circle Dr., 82301 (324–2011). Disposal station, coin laundry. Pool, whirlpool, playground, miniature golf. West on Wagon Circle Rd.

Riverton. Owl Creek Kampground. 11124 Route 26, 82501 (856–2869). Disposal station, coin laundry, groceries, propane, playground. 6½ miles northeast on routes 26 and 789.

Sheridan. Big Horn Mountain KOA. 63 Decker Rd., Box 35A, 82801 (674–8766). Disposal station, coin laundry, groceries, propane, pool, fishing, playground. I-90 Exit 20 south to Main St. Right to Route 338, then north.

Thermopolis. Fountain of Youth RV Park. Box 711, 82443 (864–9977). Disposal station, propane. Hot mineral pool. 2½ miles north on routes 20 and 789.

Grandview Trailer Court. Star Route 3, 82443 (864–3463). Disposal station, coin laundry, propane, playground. 1½ miles south on routes 20 and 789.

Wapiti. Wapiti Valley Inn Camper Village. Wapiti 82450 (587–3961). Disposal station, coin laundry, groceries, propane, restaurant, lounge. Pool, fishing, playground. 18 miles west on routes 14, 16, and 20.

RESTAURANTS. People in Wyoming are not particularly interested in exotic cuisine, so steak and potatoes is often the best fare to be found. Beef is somewhat cheaper here than in some other states, and the cuts are quite good. Native trout is excellent and unusually well-prepared. The following list is just a selection; for other worthwhile restaurants, check the accommodations list. Restaurants are listed alphabetically by town. The price categories, based on the cost of a full meal for two without beverage, tax, or tip included, are: *Deluxe,* $55 and up; *Expensive,* $35–$55; *Moderate,* $20–$35; and *Inexpensive,* under $20.

Buffalo. Steve's. *Moderate–Expensive.* 820 N. Main (684–5111). This friendly restaurant boasts well-prepared food and home-baked goods.

Casper. Armor's. *Expensive.* 3422 S. Energy La. (235–3000). Continental cuisine, long wine list, and fresh seafood are offered here. Children's menu is available.

Benham's. *Expensive.* 739 North Center (234–4531). Businessman's lunches and charcoal-broiled steaks.

Goose Egg Inn. *Moderate.* West of Casper (473–8838). A tradition for family dining.

Wyatt Cafeteria. *Inexpensive.* 601 Wyoming Blvd. (266–2257). This is a good-value place for family dining.

Cheyenne. Hitching Post Restaurant. *Expensive.* 1600 W. Lincolnway (638–3301). An excellent gourmet restaurant at the Hitching Post Inn. Specialties: veal dishes, flambée entrees. Fine wine list.

Owl Inn. *Moderate.* 3919 Central Ave. (638–8578). Good American cooking, from fried chicken to chicken-fried steak.

Poor Richard's. *Moderate.* 2233 E. Lincolnway (635–5114). Beef and seafood.

King's Table Buffet. *Inexpensive.* 3451 E. Lincolnway (635–2083). Nice variety of food. Large seating area.

Los Amigos. *Inexpensive.* 620 Central Ave. (638–8591). Traditional Mexican dishes are served here in a lively atmosphere. Closed Sundays.

Cody. Green Gables. *Expensive.* 937 Sheridan Ave., routes 14, 16, 20 (587–4640). Dinner smorgasbord; pancakes a specialty.

Irma Grill. *Moderate.* 1192 Sheridan Ave. (587–4221). This restaurant, located in the hotel "Buffalo Bill" Cody built, has Old West atmosphere. Specialties are steak, prime rib, and trout.

La Comida. *Moderate.* 1385 Sheridan Ave. (587–9556). American and Mexican food are featured at this place, which is popular with locals.

Lander. Miner's Delight. *Deluxe.* (332–3513). A ghost town out of Lander off Route 28. A local tradition. Continental cuisine includes crepes, escargot, coq au vin. Atmosphere of the Old West. By reservation only.

Hitching Rack. *Expensive.* ½ mile south on Route 287 (332–4322). Supper club. Good steaks.

Husky Cafe. *Inexpensive.* Route 287S (332–4628). Opens at 5:30 A.M. for early risers. Home-style meals.

Laramie. Cavalryman Supper Club. *Moderate.* 4425 S. 3rd St., (745–5551). Formal dining with Western ambience is featured here. Steak, prime rib, and seafood. Dinners include salad bar and dessert.

Rawlins. Bel-Air Inn. *Moderate.* 2301 W. Spruce, Route 30, I-80 Business (324–2737). Large portions. Western fare. Handsome decor.

Riverton. The Broker Restaurant. *Expensive.* 203 E. Main St. (856–0555). Great atmosphere in an old hotel. Roast duck and prime rib are featured. Reservations advised.

Saratoga. Wolf Hotel Restaurant. *Expensive.* 101 E. Bridge (326–5525). Excellent corn-fed prime rib.

Sheridan. Golden Steer. *Expensive.* 2071 N. Main (674–9334). Known for good char-broiled steaks.

Historic Sheridan Inn. *Expensive.* 856 Broadway (672–5861). Dining in an old, historic inn. Well-known for prime rib and steak. Worth a detour.

JB's. *Inexpensive.* 1294 Coffeen Ave. (672–7050). Family chain restaurant. Salad bar, breakfast bar.

SPECIAL-INTEREST TOURS. Many dude ranches and outfitters offer pack trips, float trips, and guided hikes, particularly in Wyoming's mountain regions. For a list of guides, write the state travel commission.

GARDENS. From mid-May to mid-September, the University of Wyoming campus in Laramie is a blaze of flowers. Visitors welcome. Free.

INDIANS. Arapahoe and Shoshone Indians preserve many of their native customs on one of the nation's largest reservations, the Wind River Agency in Fremont County. Two Indian missions still operate on the reservation—St. Stephen's Jesuit Mission near Riverton and St. Michael's Mission near Ethete in the heart of the reservation. Chief Washakie, the famous Shoshone, is buried in St. Michael's, and so is Sacajawea, the Shoshone girl Indian scout for the Lewis and Clark expedition. It is now the Indian Agency headquarters. Tours of the reservation can be arranged there, or at the chambers of commerce in Riverton or Lander. More than 5,000 Indians live on the reservation. A favorite spot to start a tour is at Paul Hines General Store on Route 287, 15 miles northwest of Lander. During Frontier Days, the Southern Plains Indians perform their traditional dances. During summer many traditional sun dances and pow-wows are held.

The Arapahoe, fierce and fearless warriors, were among the last Indians to submit to a reservation. The Shoshone are famed for horsemanship; many are cattle ranchers. Both tribes provide sterling bronco busters and race horses for rodeos in Wyoming. A visit to the reservation is a must for Wyoming tourists.

Shoshone and Arapahoe Indian craft may be found at Fort Washakie on the reservation, at Riverton and Lander. Museums in Lander and Riverton offer exhibits on Indian history and folklore. And Indian pictographs and petroglyphs survive on sandstone cliffs.

NATIONAL PARKS. In addition to Yellowstone and Grand Teton national parks (see separate sections) there are other parks and monuments worth mentioning:

John D. Rockefeller, Jr. Parkway, fills the gap between Yellowstone and Teton national parks. Beautiful forested land, hot springs, and wilderness horseback riding.

Fossil Butte National Monument, located near Kemmerer in southwest Wyoming, contains a rich concentration of fossils, which illustrate the evolution of freshwater fishes—reminders of the great oceans that once covered this portion of the state. Hike through the colorful fossil beds and stop at the visitor center. Call 877–3450 or 877–4898 for information.

Wyoming has seven national forests, among them **Black Hills** in northeastern Wyoming, **Medicine Bow** in the southeast, **Bridger, Shoshone,** and **Teton** in northwestern Wyoming, and the **Big Horn** in north-central Wyoming. Each forest has wilderness and primitive areas, hundreds of campsites, all the wonders of the mountain West. Fishing streams abound, as do snowcapped mountains and wildlife. If you plan to utilize the national forest, be sure and obtain a recreation sticker. Write to *Shoshone National Forest,* Cody, Wyoming; *Bridger-Teton National Forest,* Jackson, Wyoming; *Big Horn National Forest,* Sheridan; *Medicine Bow National Forest,* Laramie.

STATE PARKS. Wyoming also has 10 state parks. **Buffalo Bill State Park** is an hour's drive from the east gate of Yellowstone on the north shore of Buffalo Bill Reservoir. It offers complete picnicking and minimal camping facilities. The adjacent dam, a prototype for world arch dam construction, features excellent trout fishing, as do the north and south forks of the Shoshone River that feed it. A commercial concession, campground, trailer park, and marina are also available.

Boysen State Park is located in central Wyoming and can be reached by driving either north or west of Shoshone on route 20 or 26. The park is surrounded by the Wind River Indian Reservation, home grounds for the Shoshone and Arapahoe tribes. Day-use and overnight camping facilities are offered, and the reservoir and the river provide trout and walleye fishing.

Sinks Canyon State Park, in a spectacular mountain canyon 10 miles southwest of Lander, is one of the newest additions to the Wyoming park system, with hiking trails, nature walks, scenic overlooks, and countless glacier-fed pools and swirling eddies. Fishing is excellent. The river disappears into a gaping canyon wall cave and reappears in a crystal-clear trout-filled spring pool. Camping facilities are limited.

Seminoe State Park is surrounded by giant dunes of white sand and miles of sagebrush, and is home to thousands of pronghorn antelope and sage grouse. Located near Seminoe Reservoir 28 miles north of Sinclair, the area offers excellent beaches, fishing and camping; the nearby "Miracle Mile" of the North Platte River got the name for its reputation for trout fishing.

Keyhole State Park is four miles north of I–90 between Sundance and Moorcroft, along the southeastern shore of Keyhold Reservoir and within sight of Devil's Tower. Antelope, deer, and wild turkey are common in this area, and the reservoir offers excellent fishing for trout, walleye, catfish, and perch. The water is warm, and camping and picnic sites are readily available.

Glendo State Park, four miles east of the town of Glendo, off U.S. 87, is the best developed area in Wyoming's park system. There are excellent day-use facilities, a complete commercial concession, cabin, trailer court, and marina operation, and some of the finest boating and trout fishing in the state. Arrive early on weekends to be assured of getting picnic and campsites.

Guernsey Lake State Park, three miles west of Guernsey on Route 26, is located on the shores of one of Wyoming's most attractive reservoirs. High bluffs surround the park and block the wind so the water is always warm for the swimmer and water-skier. Historically, this is the country of the Oregon Trail, and the State Park Museum has full information. Complete day-use facilities are available, but camping space is limited, and fishing is poor due to the lake's annual draining.

Curt Gowdy State Park is located in the foothills of a mountain range separating Cheyenne and Laramie amid massive granite towers, rocky soils, and timbered slopes. Granite Reservoir and Crystal Lake offer fishing opportunities, and a variety of winter sports. The hills around the lakes invite the hiker, rockhound and, in winter, the snowmobiler.

Hot Springs State Park, on the edge of Thermopolis, features hot springs, pools and waterfalls, a buffalo herd, lodgings, and excellent health and recreation activities.

HOT SPRINGS. Fort Washakie Hot Springs, south of Fort Washakie on the road to Ethete, on the Wind River Indian Reservation. **Saratoga Hot Springs,** near Saratoga on Route 130. **Hot Springs State Park,** Thermopolis.

SUMMER SPORTS. Boating. The numerous lakes and reservoirs provide ample opportunity for boating recreation. The Bridger National Forest, Flaming Gorge National Recreation Area, Grand Teton National Park, and all the Wyoming state parks offer particularly good boating waters. Raft and canoe trips down the rivers are popular, but care should be taken to explore the waters thoroughly before heading out.

Float trips. Wyoming offers a great number of outfitters and firms that specialize in river trips. Among the more prominent firms are *Triangle X,* Box 120A, Moose 83012, and *River Runners,* Box 211, Cody 82414.

Fishing. Wyoming's 20,000 miles of streams and 264,000 acres of lakes provide unlimited fishing possibilities. Trout is king, but there are many other species of game fish. A five-day fishing license costs $15. The highly detailed *Wyoming Fishing Guide* is available from the *Wyoming Game and Fish Department,* Cheyenne 82002 (777–7735).

Hunting. There are seasons for pronghorn antelope, moose, elk, whitetail and mule deer, and bighorn sheep. For complete hunting and fishing information, contact the Wyoming Game and Fish Commission, Cheyenne 82002. Write to the same address for a copy of the fishing regulations.

Horseback riding and pack trips. Available throughout the state, particularly at guest ranches and in the Bighorn National Forest, Grand Teton and Yellowstone national parks.

SEASONAL EVENTS. Almost every Wyoming community holds a pageant, rodeo, or western event during the summer. The Wyoming Travel Commission (see above) can tell you what events will coincide with your visit.

January. *Wyoming State Winter Fair,* Lander.

June. *Plains Indian Powwow,* Cody.

July. *Cheyenne Frontier Days,* world's largest rodeo with top-name entertainers, Cheyenne. *Lander Pioneer Days,* Lander. *Cody Stampede,* Cody. *Jubilee Days,* Laramie. *Green River Rendezvous Pageant,* Pinedale, a re-creation of the "mountain man" era. *Hot Air Balloon Rally,* Riverton.

August. *Gift of the Waters Pageant,* Thermopolis. *Wyoming State Fair,* Douglas.

September. *Mountain Man Rendezvous and Powder Shoot,* Fort Bridger.

October. *Oktoberfest,* a two-day Bavarian festival, Worland.

MUSEUMS AND GALLERIES. Wyoming boasts more than 70 museums. Among them: The **Buffalo Bill Historical Center** at Cody features several excellent museums of western lore including **Plains Indian Museum.** The **Buffalo Bill Museum** contains the guns, saddles, paintings, furniture, letters, personal effects, and a valuable trophy collection of the famed William F. "Buffalo Bill" Cody. The **Whitney Gallery** features original art of such figures as Frederic Remington, George Catlin, Alfred Jacob Miller, and Charles M. Russell. The *Winchester Arms Museum* has a collection of historic firearms.

Bradford Brinton Memorial Museum is a working ranch near Big Horn with a fine collection of pioneer western art, Indian relics, and sculpture. Guided tours begin in the main ranch house and nearby buildings, the horse and carriage barns, and a "trophy" lodge near the main entrance. Frank Tenney Johnson and Charles M. Russell, among others, are featured.

The **University of Wyoming Geological Museum** in Laramie has many exhibits, including restored dinosaurs, fossil fish, and prehistoric mammoth. **Coe Library** contains a western lore museum, a contemporary art museum, and many valuable archives.

Other Western and pioneer museums can be found at Buffalo, Casper, Fort Bridger, Greybull (rock collection), Kemmerer, Rawlins, and Thermopolis. And Lander has its **Fremont County Pioneer Museum.**

In Cheyenne, the **Wyoming State Museum** offers displays of mountain men, railroad memorabilia, a cowboy cabin, saddles, minerals and gems, Indian and early-day western relics, and a military uniform and button collection. The **National First Day Cover Museum** was opened in 1979. Unique and valuable stamps and first-edition covers, original art. The **Nicolaysen Art Museum and Children's Center** in Casper exhibits regional artists and offers imaginative activities for youngsters. Cheyenne's **Old West Museum** should not be missed, with its massive array of horsedrawn carriages and sleighs.

In Jackson, the centrally located **Jackson Hole Museum** displays many guns of the area, contains a large collection of hand-forged knives, mounted deer antlers, and pioneer and trapper relics. The museum also has dioramas. In the nearby Grand Teton National Park, the *Indian Arts Museum* can be found at the Colter Bay Visitor Center. The museum offers an insight into Indian bead-making and other arts. Lectures and films and other activities.

HISTORIC FORTS AND SETTLEMENTS. **Fort Laramie.** One of Wyoming's most famous historical sites is on Route 26, an interesting "first stop" in the state when entering from the east. Trappers built the original fort in 1834 and named it after Jacques LaRamie, a French fur trapper killed by the Indians in 1820. Later they sold it to the American Fur Company, who then sold it in 1849 to the U.S. Government. For many years it was headquarters for U.S. Cavalry units and protected the pioneers from marauding Indians. A number of peace treaties with the Indians were signed at Fort Laramie. Abandoned in 1890, it was declared a National Monument by President Roosevelt in 1938. Much of Fort Laramie has been restored, and there are more than 20 historical structures. "Old Bedlam," which served as the bachelor officers' quarters, is now completely restored and open to the public.

South Pass City State Historical Site. Gold discoveries were first reported in 1842 in the South Pass area some 30 miles southeast of Lander. Of course, Lander wasn't there at the time. Nobody came to the district, except a few trappers, until 1867 and 1868, mainly because the Indians of that region fought fiercely against encroachment on their lands. This was the scene of Wyoming's only major gold strike. For a few years mining boomed, but gradually died out after 1870. An authentic western gold ghost town remains much as it was nearly 100 years ago. The Carissa and Duncan mines, as well as a museum, may be seen. Neighboring Atlantic City also contains many historical sites, including old Carpenter Hotel. The Oregon Trail, the Mormon Trail, and the original Pony Express Route pass near South Pass City.

Fort Bridger, built in 1842–43 by the trapper and guide Jim Bridger, is located in Fort Bridger State Park in southwestern Wyoming and has been largely restored. **Fort Casper,** on the outskirts of Casper, has many pioneer and Indian relics preserved in a museum, and part of the old fort has been restored. **Fort Fetterman** is near Douglas; **Fort Sanders** near Laramie; **Fort Bonneville** near Pinedale; **Fort Mackenzie** near Sheridan; **Fort Phil Kearny** near Story in the Sheridan area; **Fort Stanbaugh** near Atlantic City; **Fort McKinney** near Buffalo; **Fort D. A. Russell** near Cheyenne; **Fort Steele** near Sinclair. Travelers should inquire about directions at the chambers of commerce in cities located nearest these famous forts of the West.

PIONEER SITES. St. Mary's Stage Station, near South Pass City, was the site of a disaster in which 90 Mormons perished in a blizzard and were ravaged by wolves.

The first cabin built by a white man in Wyoming is at **Bessemer Bend,** near Casper. A **Buffalo Bill statue** is near Cody. There are charcoal kilns near Evanston. **Register Cliff,** near Guernsey, has early graves with names and inscriptions of pioneers. The Crowheart Battle, where Chief Washakie cut out the heart of the Crow chief and saved his people, occurred near **Riverton.** The first oil well in Wyoming was dug at **Dallas,** near Lander. At **Pinedale,** Father DeSmet celebrated the first Catholic mass in Wyoming. Nearby are **Independence Rock,** which Father DeSmet called "the register of the desert"; **Sweetwater Stage Station,** near Casper; **Oregon Trail Ruts,** Guernsey; and **Fetterman Massacre Monument,** Buffalo.

Trapper's Rendezvous is near Riverton. Kemmerer and Rock Springs give access to early ghost coal-mine camps. **Teapot Dome** is near Casper. Inquire at Shoshone about the **Big Teepee ranch home.**

MUSIC. The concert hall in the **Fine Arts Center** of the University of Wyoming at Laramie hosts numerous concerts and music festivals throughout the year. Their Walcker pipe organ, designed in Germany especially for the college, is one of the largest tracker organs in the United States.

In Casper, the **Civic Symphony Orchestra** performances are worth a combined symphony-skiing trip during the winter months. Casper's new Events Center, with 10,000 seats, hosts everything from concerts to rodeos and wrestling.

Sheridan holds a **Bluegrass Festival** in August.

STAGE AND REVUES. Wyoming, once considered culturally deprived, boasts an ever-increasing variety of theatrical entertainment. The University of Wyoming at Laramie has a **Fine Arts Center** whose theatrical section provides space not only for the legitimate theater but also for a teaching center. In Jackson, the **Jackson Hole Opera House** and **Dirty Jack's** offer theatrical and melodrama productions throughout the summer, as do the **Pink Garter Theatre** and the **Playhouse Theatre.** Casper, Cody, Sheridan, and Lander all have **Little Theaters.** In Cheyenne, the seasonal "Old Fashioned Drama" at the **Atlas Theatre** presents melodramas from June to mid-August.

THE MONTANA ROCKIES

by
STEPHEN ALLEN

It is the Rockies that earned Montana the nickname "Big Sky Country." This is an immense, wide-open place. At every turn, the traveler is confronted with fantastic landscapes receding to immense and infinitely varied horizons. Montana is the fourth-largest state in the Union, and even the westernmost third of it—the Rocky Mountain portion, with which we are concerned—would take years to explore. For Montana is new to the traveler in a way that more-developed Rocky Mountain areas are not. The state seems to have preserved many of the aspects of America that the rest of the country has forgotten it possesses: not just wide-open spaces, but a lifestyle based on hard work and closeness to the land. Montanans are a patriotic bunch.

France and Spain bickered over sovereignty in the region, until it passed to the United States with the Louisiana Purchase in 1803. Lewis and Clark opened up the area with their early explorations, and John Jacob Astor's Missouri Trading Company started a profitable trapping concern in the 1820s. When gold was struck near Grasshopper Creek in 1862, Montana came into its own. Millions of dollars worth of ore was taken out of the hillsides and riverbeds, the major towns were established, and entrepreneurs and vagabonds flocked to the territory, ushering in an era of lawlessness and excess. As if the region were not already violent enough, a series

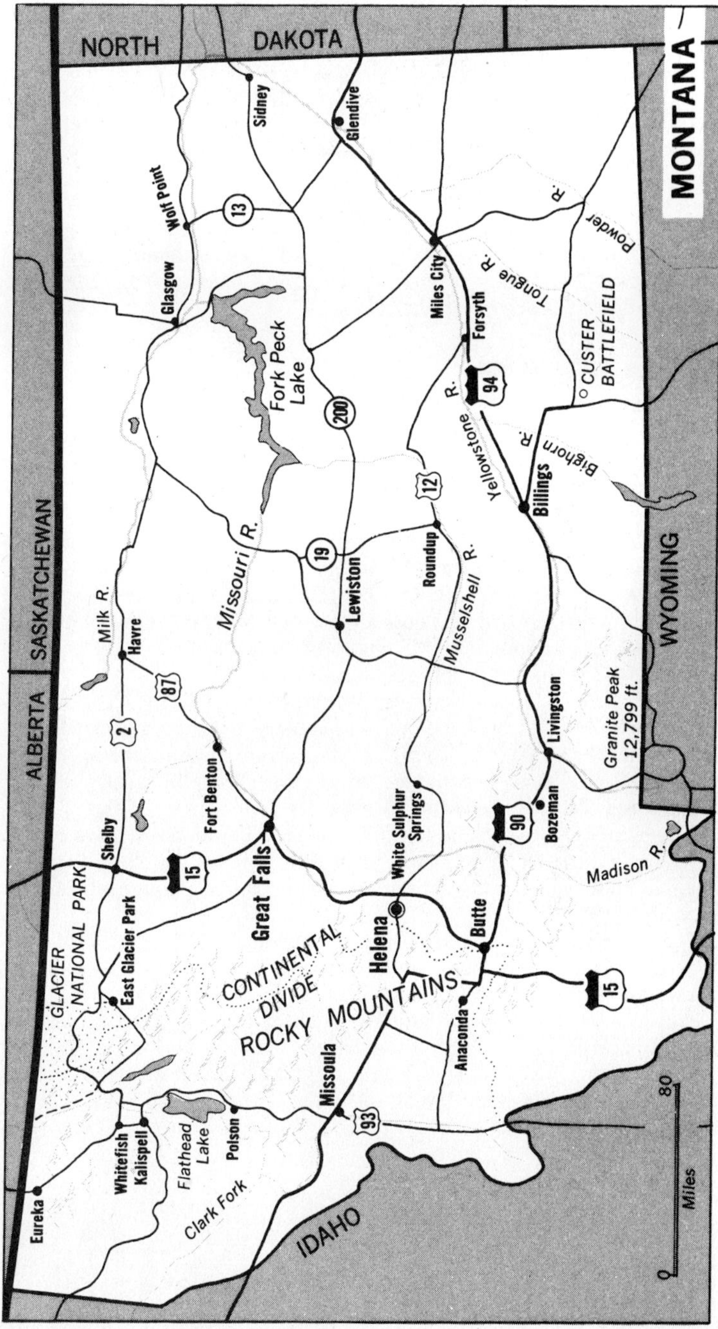
MONTANA
NORTH DAKOTA
SASKATCHEWAN
ALBERTA
WYOMING
IDAHO
Sidney
Glendive
Wolf Point
Glasgow
Miles City
Forsyth
Fork Peck Lake
Missouri R.
Milk R.
Havre
Lewiston
Roundup
Musselshell R.
Yellowstone R.
Billings
Bighorn R.
Tongue R.
Powder R.
CUSTER BATTLEFIELD
Livingston
Granite Peak 12,799 ft.
Bozeman
Madison R.
Fort Benton
Great Falls
Shelby
GLACIER NATIONAL PARK
East Glacier Park
White Sulphur Springs
Helena
Butte
Anaconda
CONTINENTAL DIVIDE
ROCKY MOUNTAINS
Missoula
Flathead Lake
Polson
Whitefish
Kalispell
Eureka
Clark Fork
13
200
19
12
94
87
2
15
90
93
0
80
Miles

of bloody Indian battles took place in the decades following the Civil War, culminating in the defeat and death of General Custer at Little Big Horn.

Today, Montana is a more peaceful place to visit. Many tourists enter at the tranquil northern edge of Yellowstone National Park, which runs along Montana's border with Wyoming. The Continental Divide, with its many majestic peaks, follows the border with Idaho before veering back into the state's Gold Country, where it beautifies the pleasant cities of Helena and Butte.

In the northwest corner of the state is Glacier Country, where a wealth of treasures may be found. They range from cowboys to Indians, and from waterfalls to mountains. They range from wild rivers to shimmering lakes, from forests to abundant wildlife, from historic sights to dude ranches. And finally—to Glacier National Park.

Glacier National Park

Located 175 miles north of Great Falls, Glacier National Park lies at the heart of the Montana Rockies and remains Montana's greatest natural attraction. The 1,600 square miles of jagged mountain scenery have drawn visitors since 1910. The park contains 50 living glaciers and 200 sparkling lakes. Brilliant mountain wildflowers dot the fields, cascading waterfalls roar in the forests, and the wildlife inspires the shutterbug. The season in Glacier Park runs from June 15 to September 10. The main roads may stay clear, however, until mid-October, depending on the weather.

There is only one road that goes all the way through Glacier National Park—but what a road it is! "Going-to-the-Sun Road" is open June to October, and the name is appropriately chosen.

Going-to-the-Sun is a spectacular 50-mile jaunt across the Continental Divide, with some of the most dramatic scenery in America. The road is not for the faint of heart at any time of year, and during the winter, buried under 20 feet of snow, it is not for *anyone.* In July and August, vehicles over 30 feet are forbidden; after August the limit rises to 35 feet.

To reach Going-to-the-Sun from Browning or East Glacier, drive north on routes 49 and 89 to St. Mary. Then turn west for the 50-mile drive; you will know you are at the Continental Divide when you reach Logan Pass.

Garden Wall, one of America's greatest mountain road sights, descends west from Logan Pass. Forests and streams give just a hint of what the park must be like on the inside, and hikes to the interior are highly recommended for those who are adventurous and in good shape. Most of Glacier Park is accessible only by its 700 miles of horse and foot trails.

The Glacier Park Lodge on Route 2 at East Glacier is typical of the huge log hotels that were developed by the Great Northern Railway at the turn of the century to handle wealthy railroad travelers. The Many Glacier Hotel on Swiftcurrent Lake is another such structure, and well worth a look.

Ranger stations can provide information on the many campgrounds in the park; many parts are accessible by car, and camping is definitely encouraged. Trails lead deep into the park and are recommended to serious hikers and backpackers. Whether you are camping or hiking, be sure to heed the rangers' warnings regarding the bears, which are not at all like those you may have seen on television.

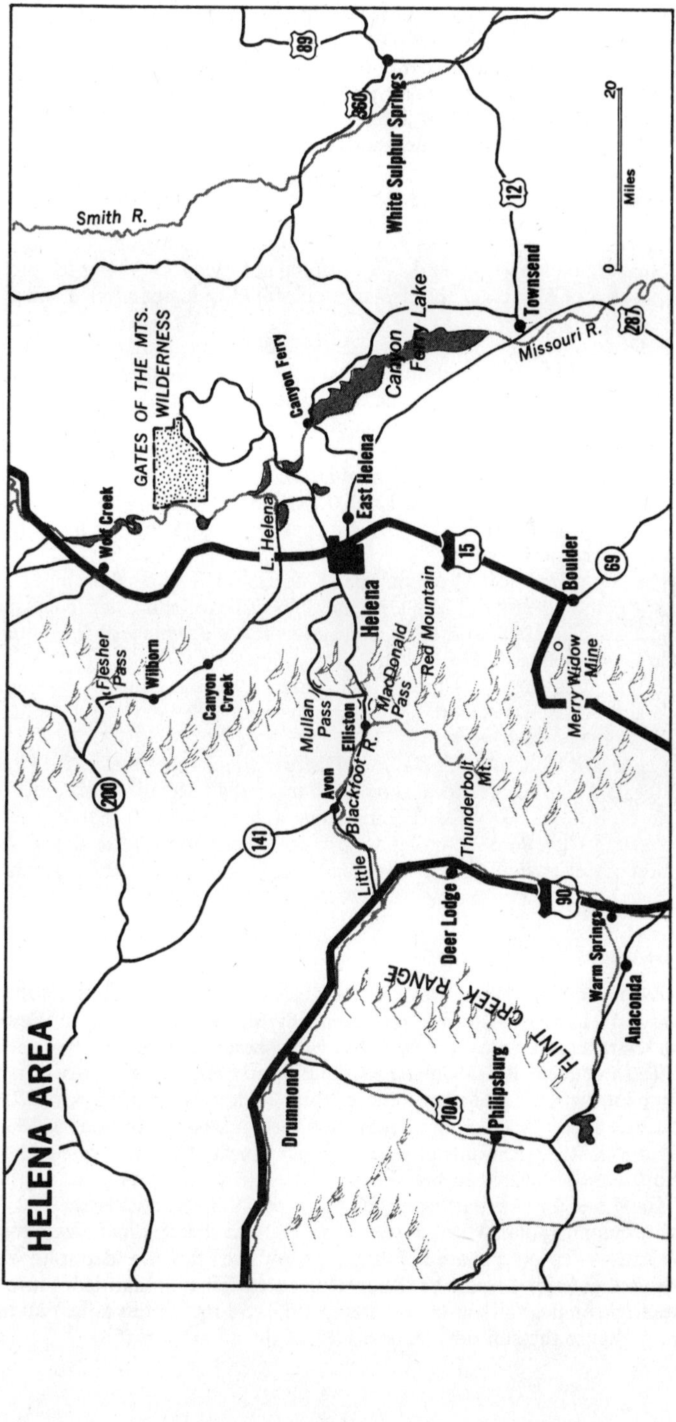
HELENA AREA
Smith R.
GATES OF THE MTS. WILDERNESS
Canyon Ferry
Canyon Ferry Lake
White Sulphur Springs
Townsend
Missouri R.
0
20
Miles
89
360
12
287
Wolf Creek
L. Helena
East Helena
Helena
15
Boulder
69
Flesher Pass
Wilborn
Canyon Creek
MacDonald Pass
Red Mountain
Mullan Pass
Elliston
Merry Widow Mine
200
Avon
Blackfoot R.
Little
Thunderbolt Mt.
141
Deer Lodge
90
Warm Springs
Anaconda
FLINT CREEK RANGE
Drummond
10A
Philipsburg

For maps and other information, contact the Superintendent, Glacier National Park, West Glacier, MT 59936 (888–5441).

The National Bison Range, off Route 93 at Moiese, protects one of the most important remaining herds of American bison.

Flathead Lake, the largest natural freshwater lake in the western United States, occupies nearly 200 square miles. The fishing is renowned, and the 35-mile East Shore Drive offers unexcelled lakeside beauty.

Helena and Environs

Immediately below Glacier Country is a mineral-rich, mountain-studded region centering on the state capital at Helena. Gold was the prize in this area of Montana, and its history is still alive in abandoned and restored mining camps.

Helena got its start in 1864, when some discouraged miners took their last chance and struck gold on what is now the main street of the city. Before the rush was over, Helena had 50 millionaires and was reportedly the richest city per capita in the country.

The main business of Helena is now government. The third floor of the capitol building is decorated with what is considered to be a masterpiece by American artist Charlie Russell, *Lewis and Clark Meeting the Flatheads.* "Flatheads" refers to the 19th-century Indians, not to the politicians who came later.

The State Historical Museum, east of the capitol, features dioramas telling the complete story of Montana, as well as an excellent Charlie Russell collection. The Cathedral of St. Helena, which is a replica of the Votive Church of Vienna, is also worth seeing.

As a political base, Helena has been home to Jannette Rankin, the country's first Congresswoman. Other famous people from Helena include Gary Cooper and Myrna Loy.

The Grant Kohrs Ranch National Historic Site, on the outskirts of Deer Lodge, is a step backward in time, with more than 30 buildings, some of them more than 100 years old, including a 23-room ranch house.

Virginia City, some 67 miles southwest of Bozeman, is the site of the richest placer gold discovery ever made—and also is the former state capital.

Gates of the Mountains

Sixteen miles north of Helena, the Gates of the Mountains is a 2,000-foot gorge in the Missouri River, named by Meriwether Lewis, (of Lewis and Clark fame), who thought it the most spectacular he had ever seen.

North of Helena is Montana's second-largest city, Great Falls, which also happens to be one of the windiest and coldest cities in America. The area was first mapped out by Lewis and Clark in their expeditions of 1805. Great Falls was the home of western artist Charlie Russell; a fine gallery of his work is located in his old studio at 1201 Fourth Avenue North.

The Chief Joseph Battleground, south of Chinook, recalls the last of the Montana Indian Wars in this area. The Nez Perce Chief Joseph led the U.S. Army on a chase across the breadth of Montana before he was captured emerging from the Yellowstone area. Chief Joseph lost the last round in the Bear's Paw Mountains in 1877 and then uttered the famous line, "Where the sun now stands, I will fight no more forever."

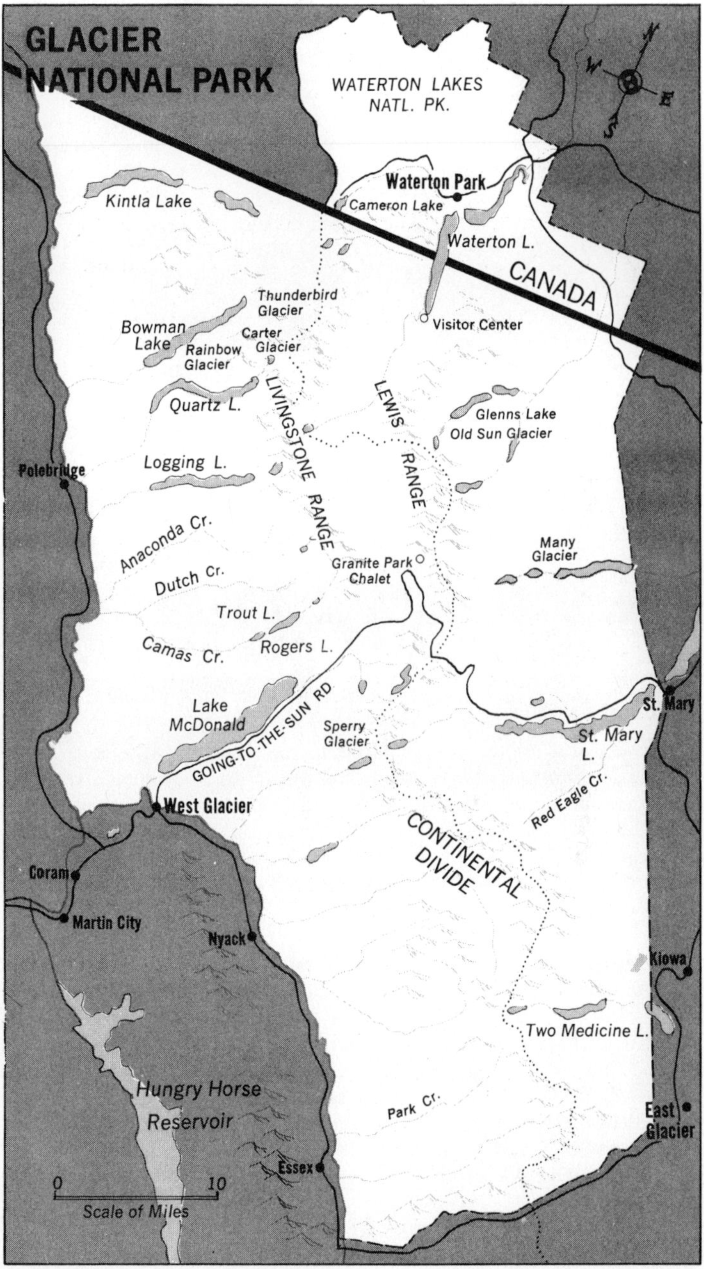
GLACIER NATIONAL PARK
WATERTON LAKES NATL. PK.
Waterton Park
Cameron Lake
Waterton L.
CANADA
Kintla Lake
Thunderbird Glacier
Visitor Center
Bowman Lake
Carter Glacier
Rainbow Glacier
Quartz L.
LIVINGSTONE RANGE
LEWIS RANGE
Glenns Lake
Old Sun Glacier
Polebridge
Logging L.
Anaconda Cr.
Many Glacier
Granite Park Chalet
Dutch Cr.
Trout L.
Camas Cr.
Rogers L.
Lake McDonald
GOING-TO-THE-SUN RD
Sperry Glacier
St. Mary
St. Mary L.
Red Eagle Cr.
West Glacier
CONTINENTAL DIVIDE
Coram
Martin City
Nyack
Kiowa
Two Medicine L.
Hungry Horse Reservoir
Park Cr.
East Glacier
Essex
0 10
Scale of Miles
N
E
S
W

From Fort Benton, the Missouri River moves eastward 180 miles through the primitive Missouri Breaks, which provides a wonderful opportunity for canoeists to view this rugged land in the way it should be seen.

Blackfoot Country

The Blackfoot Country begins around Browning, the gateway to Glacier National Park. Browning is headquarters to the 2,400-acre Blackfoot Indian Reservation. In the summer months, the town is alive with colorful tribesmen, who celebrate North American Indian Days, in the second week of July with traditional dances. The Museum of the Plains Indian, on routes 2 and 89, is worth a look and open year-round.

PRACTICAL INFORMATION FOR THE MONTANA ROCKIES

HOW TO GET THERE. Since much of Montana is wild, it is not the most accessible state in the Union, but that is a considerable part of its appeal.

By air. The major cities in the Montana Rockies—Kalispell, Butte, Helena, Missoula, and Bozeman—are served by five airlines: *Continental, Delta, Horizon, Northwest,* and *United.* Montana's own *Northwest AirLink* makes connections to all that the Big Sky Country has to offer. Canada's *Time Air* provides regular service between Great Falls, Calgary, and Edmonton in Alberta.

By bus. Most major cities of Montana are served by *Greyhound.*

By train. *Amtrak* parallels Route 2 across northern Montana with one of the most beautiful train rides in America. This train also serves Glacier National Park. For information, call Amtrak toll-free at 800–872–7245.

By car. Major interstates that go through the Rocky Mountain section of Montana are I–90 and I–15. The major U.S. highways are routes 2, 93, 10A, and 287.

TOURIST INFORMATION. General information about Montana can be obtained from *Travel Montana,* Department of Commerce, Helena MT 59620 (800–541–1447). If you also want information about wilderness exploration, ask for the Montana Travel Planner.

TELEPHONES. The area code for Montana is 406. The Montana Highway Patrol can be reached at 800–472–8765. Other emergency telephone numbers can be found at the front of the telephone directory. Dialing 411 will connect you to local directory information. Local pay-phone calls cost 25¢.

ACCOMMODATIONS. Montana has some of the most unusual accommodations to be found anywhere. They range from palatial hotels at the national parks to cozy log cabins complete with fireplaces. You will need to book accommodations at the lodge in Glacier National Park or West Yellowstone, and it is best to do so as much as a year in advance.

Our categories for double occupancy are: *Deluxe,* $100–$125; *Expensive,* $80–$100; *Moderate,* $50–$80; and *Inexpensive,* under $50.

Anaconda. Fairmount Hot Springs Resort. *Deluxe.* Mountain Village 59711 (797–3241). Indoor-outdoor swimming and hot springs.

Vagabond Lodge. *Moderate.* 1421 E. Park Ave. 59711 (563–5251). Family rates, 24-hour cafe, tennis, racquetball.

Big Fork. Flathead Lake Lodge. *Expensive.* Big Fork 59911 (837–4391). Beach parties, barbecues, tennis, boating, canoeing, sailing, raft and pack trips, lake cruises, white-water rafting, private patios, 2,000-acre ranch. Open mid-May-mid-Sept.

Big Sky. Big Sky Resort. *Deluxe.* Mountain Village 59716 (995–4211 or 800–548–4486). Located in the heart of Gallatin Canyon, 40 miles south of Bozeman on Route 191, this resort includes the ski lodge of the famed late newscaster Chet Huntley. Large, bright rooms, condominiums, lofts, outdoor pool, health club, golf course, horseback riding.

Best Western Buck's 4-T Lodge. *Moderate.* Box 229, 59716 (995–4111 or 800–528–1234). Cafe, lounge, tennis, golf, whirlpool, oversized beds. Free coffee in rooms.

Big Timber. C.M. Russell Lodge. *Moderate.* Box 670, 59011 (932–5244). Named for the famed Montana western artist. Cable TV, cafe, room service.

Bozeman. Best Western City Center. *Expensive.* 507 W. Main St., 59715 (587–3158 or 800–528–1234). Indoor heated pool, sauna, free coffee, 24-hour cafe nearby.

Holiday Inn. *Expensive.* 5 Baxter Lane 59715 (587–4561 or 800–HOLIDAY). Near the interstate.

The Vose Inn. *Expensive.* 319 S. Wilson St. 59715 (587–0982). Bed and breakfast in a 100-year-old mansion.

Grantree Inn. *Moderate.* 1325 N. 7th St., 59715 (800–624–5865). Cafe, room service, entertainment, game room, steam bath, ski plan.

Imperial 400. *Moderate.* 122 W. Main St. 59715 (587–4481). Near the university. Heated pool.

Western Heritage Inn. *Moderate.* 1200 E. Main St. 59715 (586–8534) Cable TV, ski plan, in-room movies, free coffee, cafe nearby, whirlpool in suites.

Super 8. *Inexpensive.* 800 Wheat Drive 59715 (586–1521). Cable TV, 24-hour cafe nearby.

Butte. Best Western Copper King Inn. *Expensive.* 4655 Harrison Ave. 59701 (494–6666 or 800–528–1234). Near the airport. Sauna.

Best Western War Bonnet Inn. *Expensive.* 2400 Cornell Ave. 59701 (494–7800 or 800–528–1234).

Filen Hotel. *Moderate.* Broadway 59701 (723–5461). Bar, beauty shop.

Townhouse Inn. *Moderate.* 2777 Harrison Ave., 59701 (494–8850). Free coffee, Continental breakfast, cafe nearby.

Super 8. *Inexpensive.* 2929 Harrison Ave. 59701 (494–6000). Cable TV, free coffee, Continental breakfast.

Cooke City. All Seasons Inn. *Expensive.* Cooke City (838–2251). On Route 212 overlooking the mountains, four miles from Yellowstone Park. Restaurant, bar, skiing, snowmobiling, hunting, and fishing.

Deer Lodge. Downtowner. *Moderate.* 506 4th St. 59722 (846–1021). Cable TV, cafe nearby.

Super 8. *Moderate.* 1150 Main St. 59722 (846–2370). Cable TV, indoor pool, 24-hour cafe nearby.

Dillon. Best Western Royal Inn. *Moderate.* 650 N. Montana Ave. 59725 (683–4214 or 800–528–1234). Heated pool, cafe.

Creston Motor Inn. *Moderate.* 335 S. Atlantic Ave. 59725 (683–2341). 24-hour cafe nearby.

Townhouse Inn. *Moderate.* 450 N. Interchange 59725 (683–4364). Cable TV, indoor pool, cafe nearby.

Sundowner. *Inexpensive.* 500 N. Montana St. 59725 (683–2375). Cable TV, free Continental breakfast.

Ennis. Best Western Royal Inn. *Expensive.* Box 487, 59729 (683–4217 or 800–528–1234). On the Madison River. Hunting, fishing, float trips.

Gardiner. Best Western By Mammoth Hot Springs. *Expensive.* Box 646, 59030 (848–7557 or 800–528–1234). Cable TV, sauna, whirlpool, balconies. On the Yellowstone River. Cafe nearby.

Westernaire. *Moderate.* Box 20 (848–7397). Cable TV, cafe nearby.

Glacier National Park. Glacier Park Lodge. *Expensive.* West Glacier 59936 (226–9311). Heated indoor pool, restaurant, bar, beauty shop, golf course, volleyball, riding, fishing. Open June-Labor Day. Reserve early.

Many Glacier Hotel. *Expensive.* West Glacier 59936 (226–9311). On the lake 12 miles west of Babb via Route 89. Restaurant, bar, beauty shop, fishing, boating, riding, pack trips. Reserve early.

Rising Sun Motor Inn. *Moderate.* West Glacier 59936 (226–5551). Six miles west of St. Mary Park on Going-to-the-Sun Road. Restaurant. Open June 15-Sept. 3.

Swift Current Motor Inn. *Moderate.* West Glacier 59936 (732–4411). West of Babb via Route 89.

Hamilton. Best Western Hamilton Inn. *Moderate.* 409 S. First St. 59840 (363–2142 or 800–528–1234). Cable TV, cafe nearby.

Helena. Aladdin Coach House Downtown Motor Inn. *Expensive.* 910 N. Last Chance Gulch 59601 (442–6080). Heated pool, saunas, steam baths, fireplaces, 24-hour cafe nearby.

Best Western Colonial Inn. *Expensive.* 2301 Colonial Dr. 59601 (443–2100 or 800–528–1234). Heated pool, sauna, cafe, bar, beauty shop, entertainment.

Park Plaza Hotel. *Expensive.* 22 N. Last Chance Gulch 59601 (443–2200).

Aladdin Coach House East Hotel. *Moderate.* 2101 11th Ave. 59601 (443–2300). Indoor pool, whirlpool, cafe, health club, fireplaces in some rooms.

Imperial 400 Motor Inn. *Moderate.* 524 Last Chance Gulch 59601 (442–0600). Centrally located.

Shilo Inn. *Moderate.* 2020 Prospect Ave. 59601 (442–0320). In-room movies, indoor pool, whirlpool, sauna, steam room.

Kalispell. Best Western Outlaw Inn. *Expensive.* 1701 Route 93, 59901 (755–6100 or 800–528–1234). Pool, tennis.

Red Lion Motor Inn. *Expensive.* 1330 Route 2W, 59901 (755–6700). Some suites.

Diamond Lil's Inn. *Moderate.* 1680 Route 93, 59901 (752–3467). Cable TV, in-room movies, heated pool, hot tubs, cafe.

Four Seasons Motor Inn. *Moderate.* 350 N. Main St. 59901 (755–6123). Highly rated.

Vacationer. *Inexpensive.* 285 7th Ave. 59901 (755–7144). Cable TV, heated pool, 24-hour cafe.

Libby. Sandman. *Moderate.* Box 1272, 59923 (293–8831). In-room movies, coffee in rooms, cafe nearby.

Venture Motor Inn. *Moderate.* Box AN, 59923 (293–7711). Heated pool, whirlpool, sauna, cafe.

Caboose Motel. *Inexpensive.* Box 792, 59923 (293–6201). Free morning coffee, cafe nearby.

Livingston. Yellowstone Motor Inn. *Expensive.* 1515 W. Park Ave., 59047 (222–6110). A three-story motel with all the amenities.

Mountain Sky Guest Ranch. *Expensive.* Box 317, 59027 (333–4911). Heated pool, whirlpool, sauna, cafe, grocery, laundry, tennis, float trips, pack trips, hunting. Open June-mid-Oct.

Paradise Inn. *Moderate.* Box 3053A, 59047 (222–6320). A half-mile south at I-90 exit. Cable TV, indoor pool, cafe.

Missoula. Best Western Executive Motor Inn. *Expensive.* 201 E. Main St. 59801 (543–7221 or 800–528–1234). Heated pool, cafe; recommended.

Holiday Inn Parkside. *Expensive.* 200 S. Pattee St. 59801 (721–8550 or 800–HOLIDAY). Indoor pool, game area, lounge, gift shop.

Village Red Lion Motor Inn. *Expensive.* 100 Madison St. 59801 (728–3100). Satellite TV, heated pool, whirlpool, cafe, entertainment, dancing, shopping arcade, beauty and barber shops, airport bus.

Best Western Southgate Inn. *Moderate.* 3530 Brooks St. 59801 (251–2250 or 800–528–1234). Cable TV, heated pool, sauna, 24-hour cafe.

Comfort Inn. *Moderate.* 744 E. Broadway 59801 (549–5134). Cable TV, heated pool, cafe.

Red Lion Inn. *Moderate.* 700 W. Broadway 59802 (728–3300). Satellite TV, heated pool, cafe.

TraveLodge. *Moderate.* 420 W. Broadway 59801 (728–4500). Cable TV, in-room movies, cafe.

Quality Inn. *Inexpensive.* 1609 W. Broadway 59802 (543–7231). Cable TV, in-room movies, heated pool, cafe.

on. Best Western Queen's Court. *Moderate.* Route 93, 59860 85 or 800–528–1234). On Flathead Lake. Continental breakfast, ooating, fishing, water skiing. Cafe nearby.

Red Lodge. Best Western Lupine Inn. *Expensive.* Route 212, 59068 (446–1321 or 800–528–1234). In Beartooth Wilderness, 50 miles from Yellowstone. Indoor pool, skiing, snowmobiling.

Eagle's Nest Motel. *Inexpensive.* 702 S. Broadway 59068 (446–2312). Pets accepted.

Virginia City. Fairweather Inn. *Moderate.* Box 338, 59755 (843–5377). Cafe nearby.

Virginia Terrace Motel. *Inexpensive.* Wallace St. 59766 (843–5368). Cafe and music hall nearby.

West Yellowstone. Stage Coach Inn. *Expensive.* West Yellowstone 59758 (646–7381). Sauna, hot tubs, indoor pool, lounge with entertainment, restaurant, tennis, skiing, snowmobiling. At west entrance to Yellowstone.

Best Western Desert Inn. *Moderate.* 133 Canyon St. 58758 (646–7376 or 800–528–1234). Cable TV, pool, cafe nearby.

Best Western Executive Inn. *Moderate.* Box 1280, 59758 (646–7681 or 800–528–1234). Cable TV, heated pool, whirlpool, cafe, airport bus.

Best Western Pine. *Moderate.* 234 Firehold Ave. 59758 (646–7622 or 800–528–1234). Heated pool, tennis.

Best Western Weston Inn. *Moderate.* 103 Gibbon Ave. 59758 (646–7373 or 800–528–1234). Cable TV, heated pool, cafe nearby.

Teepee Motor Lodge. *Moderate.* 205 Yellowstone Ave. 59798 (646–7391). Near west entrance to Yellowstone.

Three Bears Lodge. *Moderate.* 217 Yellowstone Ave. 59758 (646–7353).

Whitefish. Alpinglow Inn. *Deluxe.* Box 1670, 59937 (862–6966). Next to Big Mountain. Skiing, sauna, restaurant, lounge. Highly rated.

Grouse Mountain Lodge. *Expensive.* 1205 Route 93W, 59937 (862–3000). Skiing, golfing, rafting, cable TV, sauna, entertainment, indoor pool, tennis, airport bus, hot tubs, game room.

Whitefish Motel. *Inexpensive.* 620 8th St. (862–3507) Units with kitchens, including utensils, are offered at this home away from home.

Wolf Point. Sherman Motor Inn. *Moderate.* 200 E. Main St. 59201 (653–1300). Pleasant three-story inn.

GUEST RANCHES. Formerly known as "dude ranches," these are places where an urban or suburban person can sample a little of what it means to be called a "cowboy." Montana has many of the best ranches in the world, some of them working, some of them just for show. Most of the ranches will arrange to meet you at your plane or train and will furnish everything you need to "rough it" in comfort. Most guest ranches are open June to Sept.

Bear Creek Ranch. East Glacier Park 59434 (226–4489). Trail rides into the park and into Flathead National Forest. Open all year.

JJJ Wilderness Ranch. August 59410 (562–3653). Wilderness pack trips.

Mountain Sky Guest Ranch. Emigrant 59027 (800–548–3392). Near Yellowstone.

Parade Rest Ranch. West Yellowstone 59758 (646–7217). Enjoy horseback riding in the wild areas of Yellowstone Park.

HUNTING LODGES AND COUNTRY INNS. Holland Lake Lodge. *Expensive.* Condon 59826 (754–2282). On Holland Lake in the spectacular Swan Valley between two wilderness areas. Just off Route 83 in the Flathead National Forest. Skiing, snowmobiling, log lodge, winterized cabins, restaurant, lounge, ski rentals. Best way to get there in the winter is to fly to Missoula or Kalispell and rent a car.

Izaak Walton Inn. *Expensive.* Box 653, Essex 59916 (888–5700). On Route 2 between the east and west sides of Glacier Park. Skiing from the front door. Trails in and out of the park, lodge rooms in a historic railroad inn, restaurant, lounge, sauna. Closest city is Great Falls, but Amtrak makes a flag stop right outside the front door.

Lone Mountain Ranch. *Expensive.* Box 69, Big Sky 59716 (995–4644). Skiing, ranch-style accommodations, log cabins with fireplaces, restaurant, nature ski tours, horse-drawn sleighs, entertainment, ski lessons. Forty miles south of Bozeman, 20 miles northwest of Yellowstone.

HOT-SPRING RESORTS. There are hot springs in the Bitterroot National Forest near Hamilton; in the Beaverhead National Forest near Dillon and around such towns as White Sulphur Springs, Hot Springs, and Camas. Some resorts follow.

Chico Hot Springs Resort. Pray 59065 (333–4933). Twenty-six miles south of Livingston and 29 miles north of Yellowstone on Route 89; turn at Emigrant. Ski trips, famous dining room, mineral hot springs, condominiums, old inn. Bozeman is the nearest large city.

Elkhorn Hot Springs Resort. *Moderate.* Box 514, Polaris 59746 (834–3434). About 26 miles from Dillon on Route 278. Skiing, mountaineering, restaurant, hot springs, Grecian sauna. Butte is the nearest city.

Lost Trail Hot Springs Resort. Box 37, Sula 59871 (821–3574). Six miles north of Lost Trail Pass on Route 93. Skiing, pool, sauna, hot springs, restaurant, lounge.

RESTAURANTS. The Rocky Mountain section of Montana is logger country, where men are men. This is the home of steak 'n' potatoes; don't order a white wine at a logger bar unless you are with hefty friends. Sometimes local game, especially trout, elk, deer, and buffalo finds its way onto the menus and is definitely worth trying. Look especially for buffalo stew, but stay away from the variety known as jackalope (a rabbit with antlers; don't believe a word of it.)

Our price categories are for two meals, including appetizer, exclusive of tax and tip. *Deluxe,* $50 and up; *Expensive,* $25–$50; *Moderate,* $15–$25; and *Inexpensive,* under $15.

Anaconda. Barclay. *Moderate.* 1300 E. Commercial St. (563–5541). Steak and seafood.

Big Fork. Big Fork Inn. *Moderate.* 604 Electric Ave. (837–6680). Seafood, chicken, and home-baked goods.

Bozeman. Avellino. *Moderate.* In the Bozeman Inn, 1235 N. 7th St. (587–1535). Seafood and home-baked goods are featured.

Black Angus Steak House. *Moderate.* 507 W. Main St. (587–0652). Popular with locals.

The Overland Express. *Moderate.* 15 N. Rouse (587–7982). Steak and lobster. Open late.

Bacchus Pub. *Inexpensive.* 105 Main St. (586–1314). In what was one of Bozeman's best hotels, this is an unpretentious place, serving three hearty meals daily. Outstanding are the homemade soups and baked goods.

4 B's Cafe. *Inexpensive.* 421 W. Main St. (587–4661). Popular with locals. Open 24 hours.

Butte. Lydia's. *Expensive.* Two miles south of I–90 on Route 10 (494–2000). Excellent steak and Italian fare; pleasant atmosphere.

Apache Dining Room. *Moderate.* In Best Western War Bonnet Inn, 2100 Cornell Ave. (494–7800). Prime rib, veal, tournedos of beef, and chicken Kiev.

Copper King Dining Room. *Moderate.* In Best Western Copper King Motel, 4655 Harrison Ave. (494–6666). Meals cooked right at your table, home-baking.

4 B's Cafe. *Inexpensive.* Montana and Front sts. (782–5311). Popular with locals, specializes in chicken.

Dillon. The Bannack House. *Moderate.* 35 E. Bannack St. (683–5088). Italian and American menu.

Ennis. Continental Divide. *Inexpensive.* Main St. (682–7600). French and Creole menu, barbecued shrimp.

Gardiner. Yellowstone Mine. *Inexpensive.* On Route 89 near the park entrance (848–7336). Beef Oscar, buffalo, salmon.

Glacier National Park. Many Glacier. *Expensive.* Many Glacier Hotel, West Glacier (226–9311). Prime rib, trout, steak, home-baked goods.

Hamilton. Western Cafe. *Inexpensive.* 443 E. Main St. (587–0436). This cafe is great for burgers and other fast food.

Helena. Chapter 7. *Moderate.* 920 Lyndale Ave. (449–7937). Shrimp and prime rib. Rustic decor.

4 B's Cafe. *Moderate.* In the Coach House, 910 N. Last Chance Gulch (442–5275). Steak and chicken.

Jorgenson's. *Moderate.* In Jorgenson's Holiday Motel, 1714 11th Ave. (442–6380). Family-style menu.

On Broadway. *Inexpensive.* 106 Broadway (443–1929). Northern Italian dishes.

Overland Express. *Inexpensive.* 21 Last Chance Gulch (442–1410). Rack of lamb and prime rib.

Kalispell. Best Western Outlaw Inn. *Moderate.* Route 93 (755–6100). In the inn of the same name. Good food.

Diamond Lil's. *Inexpensive.* In Diamond Lil's Motel, 1680 Route 93 (752–3463). Seafood and home-baked goods.

1st Avenue West. *Inexpensive.* 139 1st Ave. (752–5757). Fresh seafood, prime rib, home baking, with a menu in Braille.

Libby. Todd's. *Inexpensive.* In the Venture Motor Inn, Route 2 (293–7711). Steak, seafood, salad bar.

Livingston. Chico Inn. *Moderate.* In Chico Hot Springs Lodge, 26 miles south on Route 89 (333–4936). Prime rib, lamb, seafood, weekend buffet.

Missoula. Mansion Overland Express. *Expensive.* 102 Ben Hogan Dr. (728–5132). American food in a Victorian setting.

Depot. *Moderate.* 201 W. Railroad St. (728–7007). Seafood, prime rib, steak, salad bar, home baking.

Edgewater. *Moderate.* In Village Red Lion Motor Inn, 100 Madison St. (728–3100). Steak Diane, seafood.

Encore. *Moderate.* In Holiday Inn., 200 S. Pattee St. (721–8550). Maine lobster, fresh seafood, outdoor dining.

Heidelhaus. *Moderate.* 2620 Brooks St. (543–3200). Bavarian menu, sauerbraten.

The Lily. *Moderate.* 515 S. Higgins St. (542–0002). Continental menu, veal Oscar, seafood, home baking.

Montana Mining Co. *Moderate.* 1210 W. Broadway (543–6192). Relaxing atmosphere, good beef, children's menu, entertainment.

King's Table Buffet. *Inexpensive.* 3611 Brook St. (728–6040). All-you-can-eat buffet.

Red Lodge. Pius International Room. *Moderate.* 117 S. Broadway (446–3333). Steak David, pepper steak, seafood.

Red Lodge Cafe. *Inexpensive.* 16 S. Broadway (446–2808). Buffalo when available, barbecued ribs, salad bar.

West Glacier. Lake McDonald Lodge. *Expensive.* Going-to-the-Sun Rd., on Lake McDonald (226–5551). Trout, barbecued ribs, roast duck, and famous Sunday brunch.

West Yellowstone. Rustler's Roost. *Moderate.* In the Best Western Pine Motel (646–7622). Buffalo barbecue and chuckwagon stew.

Strozzi's Dude Lounge. *Moderate.* In the Dude Motel, 4 Madison Ave. (646–7316). Prime rib.

Whitefish. Alpinglow Inn. *Expensive.* Box 1670 (862–6966). Steak, lobster, crab. Beautiful view.

La Dump. *Moderate.* Route 93 (752–3000). Seven miles south on Route 93. Popular with locals. Serves regional specialties; spectacular view of Flathead Valley.

LIQUOR LAWS. The legal drinking age in Montana is 21. Most bars are open Mon.–Sat. until 2 A.M. You can buy liquor by the bottle at the state liquor store in each town, as well as in bars until 2 A.M. You may order liquor by the drink in bars.

HOW TO GET AROUND. Since Montana is a wilderness state, the best way to get around and to see everything is by car. Cars can be rented at all the major Montana Rockies cities, such as Helena, Butte, and Missoula, and at the airports.

By bus. Most areas of Montana are served by *Greyhound.*

TOURS AND SPECIAL-INTEREST SIGHTSEEING. *Glacier Park Inc.,* East Glacier 59434 (226–5551), offers four-, five-, and six-day tours of the park. The tours include lodging, meals, launch cruises, and transportation via scenic coaches.

Montana Wilderness Assn., Helena (442–7350), organizes wilderness walks into the many remote areas of Montana for visitors without the equipment or stamina to do more.

Off The Beaten Path, 109 E. Main St., Bozeman 59715 (586–1311), offers personal itineraries through the Northern Rockies.

Missouri River boat cruises are held each June. They usually take three or more days, and the companies will furnish everything you need to feel like a modern-day Lewis or Clark. Contact the *State Travel Promotion Unit,* Helena 59620 (444–2654).

West Yellowstone Park Winter Tour. One of the best ways to see West Yellowstone National Park is on a winter snowmobiling tour. You can rent a snowmobile and take off for Old Faithful, Mammoth Hot Springs, or other scenic areas. Packages vary in length from four to seven days and include accommodations, snowmobile use, guide services, and proper clothing. All machines feature handlebar warmers and luggage racks. Write Box 369, West Yellowstone, MT 59758 (800–221–1151).

INDIANS. Montana has the largest Indian population of the Rocky Mountain states, with close to 25,000 Blackfoot, Sioux, Crow, Assiniboine, and Cheyenne Indians living on or near its seven reservations. At various times of the year, these tribes hold powwows, dances, celebrations, fairs, and rodeos.

NATIONAL PARKS. The most famous of these, of course, is **Glacier National Park,** covering 1,600 square miles, in the northwest corner of the state. The east and west sides of the park are connected by the spectacular Going-to-the-Sun Road, one of the most beautiful drives in the world. For information, contact the Superintendent, Glacier National Park, West Glacier 59936 (888–5441).

Kootenai National Forest, in the northwest corner of the state, offers wilderness, hunting, fishing, and winter sports. Write Kootenai National Forest, 506 Route 2 W., Libby 59923 (293–6211).

Flathead National Forest, southwest of Glacier, is heavily timbered with rugged mountains. There are wilderness and primitive areas, hunting, fishing, boating, swimming, winter sports, and scenic drives. Write Flathead National Forest, 1935 Third Ave., Kalispell 59901 (755–5401).

Bitterroot National Forest, west of the Continental Divide in southwestern Montana, contains the 1,000,000-acre Selway-Bitterroot Wilderness, the largest and the most impressive wilderness in the United States, with mountain lakes, hot springs, scenic drives, hunting, fishing, and winter sports. Write Bitterroot National Forest, Hamilton 59840 (363–3131).

Helena National Forest, straddling the Continental Divide in the west-central portion of the state, offers almost 1,000,000 acres of hunting and fishing and wilderness areas. The Missouri River begins here, at the Gates of the Mountains. Write Helena National Forest, Federal Bldg., 301 S. Park St., Helena 59601 (449–5201).

Beaverhead National Forest, east of the Continental Divide, is a great hunting and fishing area, with alpine lakes, hot springs, and winter sports. Write Beaverhead National Forest, Skihi St., Box 1258, Dillon 59725 (683–3900).

Yellowstone National Park. The very top edge of Yellowstone is in the state of Montana, so a visit may be the next logical step. See the *Wyoming* chapter.

STATE PARKS. For information on the state parks, contact *Montana Fish, Wildlife and Parks,* 1420 E. 6th St., Helena 59620 (444–2535).

Giant Springs State Park. Four miles northeast of Great Falls on the Missouri River, this is home to one of the world's largest freshwater springs.

West Shore State Park. Twenty miles south of Kalispell on Flathead Lake.

Missouri River/Wolf Creek Canyon Area. Twenty-five miles north of Helena. Fishing, picnicking, and hiking.

CAMPING AND HIKING. Most state parks and recreation areas are open May–Sept. Camping is limited to 14 consecutive days. Fees are charged per night per vehicle. For complete information on camping facilities, write the Montana Department of Fish, Wildlife and Parks (see *State Parks,* above). Camping is also available in the national forests. Some campgrounds:

Bitterroot Lake. Twenty-three miles west of Kalispell. Complete facilities.

Logan. Forty-five miles west of Kalispell. Complete facilities.

Those with trailers can use the following facilities:

West Yellowstone Beaver Creek National Forest has 65 sites. Open June–Sept. 15.

Bitterroot State Park, near Kalispell, has 20 sites, with boating, swimming, and fishing. Open May–Oct.

Two Medicine National Park, near East Glacier Park, has 100 sites with swimming, boating, fishing, and a store.

Fish Creek National Park, near West Glacier Park, has 180 sites, with swimming and fishing.

HUNTING. Hunting regulations vary according to the game and residence status; licenses can be expensive for nonresidents. Seasons vary from year to year depending on the conditions, but there is usually a September **elk** and **deer** season in the wilder areas of the state. The regular deer and elk season begins in late October and generally runs until late November. **Antelope** hunting is on a "drawing-quota" basis, which means that the size of the herd is determined by the Fish and Game Department, which awards only enough hunting permits to thin the herd out. The season begins one week earlier than deer season and ends around the middle of November. **Goat, sheep,** and **moose** seasons, also on the quota system, begin in mid-September and run until mid-November. Black and brown bear season opens in mid-March and runs until mid-November. **Duck** and **geese** can be hunted from early September until the end of the year. For further information, write to *Montana Department of Fish, Wildlife and Parks,* 1420 E. 6th St., Helena 59601 (444–2535).

FISHING. Montana offers some of the finest fishing in America. There are more than 15,000 miles of excellent fishing waters, including 1,500 lakes and 452 miles of nationally famous trout streams. These include portions of the Big Hole, Flathead, Madison, Missouri, West Gallatin, Kootenai, Clark's Fork, and Yellowstone rivers.

Montana is the land of the rainbow trout. Other trout varieties found in Montana are cutthroat, eastern brook, Dolly Varden, bull, and lake. Nonresident fishermen can obtain season licenses for $35 or two-day licenses for $8. A permit (no fee) is required for fishing in either Glacier National Park or Yellowstone. For more information, contact *Travel Montana,* Department of Commerce, Helena 59620 (444–2654).

Some of the best spots:

Flathead River, six miles east of Somers at New Holt Bridge.
Clark Fork River, at Rock Creek, south of the Missoula turnoff on I–90.
Skyles Lake, near Whitefish.
Big Blackfoot River, near Bonner.
Bitterroot River, a few miles south of Missoula.
Clark Fork River, west of Missoula.
Flathead Lake (good Dolly Varden).
Gallatin River, near Bozeman.
Kootenai River, near Libby and Troy.
Milk River, Glascow to Havre.
Yellowstone River, from Yellowstone Park headwaters south.

CROSS-COUNTRY SKIING. Montana has become a leader in the growth of cross-country skiing in America. The U.S. Cross Country and Biathlon Ski Teams train in Montana every year. For more detailed information, contact *Montana Promotional Division,* Department of Commerce, Helena 59620 (800–548–3390).

Crosscut Ranch. 12065 Bridger Canyon Rd., Bozeman 59715 (586–9070). Fifteen miles north of Bozeman at the base of Bridger Bowl.

Izaak Walton Inn. Box 653, Essea 59916 (888–5700). Nestled along the south boundary of Glacier National Park, this is one of the most unique cross-country ski resorts in America, with 18 miles of groomed and ungroomed ski trails through the park.

Lone Mountain Ranch. Box 69, Big Sky 59716 (995–4644). Fifty miles south of Bozeman, near Yellowstone, with 35 miles of groomed ski trails and lodging.

Sundance Lodge. Wise River 59762 (689–3611). Fifteen miles of groomed trails and accommodations.

Tobacco Root Ranch. Mill Creek Rd., Sheridan 59749 (842–5443). In Mill Creek Canyon, with both cross-country and downhill skiing.

West Yellowstone. Yellowstone National Park, West Yellowstone Chamber of Commerce, West Yellowstone 59758 (646–7701). At the west entrance to the park. Miles of beautifully groomed trails, on which the U.S. Cross Country Ski Team trains. The main Yellowstone number is 307–344–7311.

DOWNHILL SKIING. Montana rolls out the "white carpet" from mid-November through the spring season. The state's average snowfall is 260 inches—more than 20 feet! There is every kind of terrain to ski in Montana's Rocky Mountains, from long, steep drops to user-friendly runs for novices. For detailed information on skiing in the state, write *Travel Montana,* Department of Commerce, Helena, MT 59620 (444–2654).

The Big Mountain. Box 1400, Whitefish 59937 (862–3511). Eight miles north of Whitefish. Four triple chairs, two double chairs, one t-bar, ski school, rentals, lodging.

Big Sky of Montana. Box 1, Big Sky 59716 (995–4211). 45 miles south of Bozeman and 18 miles north of Yellowstone. Only area in Montana offering gondola lifts. One triple chair, three doubles, one rope tow, ski rentals, lodging.

Bridger Bowl. 15795 Bridger Canyon Rd., Bozeman 59715 (587–2111). Sixteen miles northeast of Bozeman. Five double chairs, one rope tow, one t-bar, rentals, lessons, lodging.

Lost Trail Powder Mountain. Box 191, Darby 59829 (821–3211). Ninety miles south of Missoula, near the Idaho border. Two double chairs, two rope tows. In the heart of the Bitterroot National Forest.

Maverick Mountain. 101 N. Montana St., Dillon 59725 (683–4521). Thirty-eight miles northeast of Dillon in southwest Montana. One double chair and a pony lift. Lodging and nearby hot springs.

Red Lodge Mountain. Drawer R, Red Lodge 59068 (446–2610). Sixty miles south of Billings, in the Beartooth Mountains and near the entrance to Yellowstone Park. Four double chairs, one triple chair, ski school, rentals, accommodations.

Snow Bowl. 1700 Snow Bowl Rd., Missoula 59802 (549–9777). Twelve miles northeast of Missoula. Two double chairs, one t-bar, one rope tow, lessons, rentals.

Marshall Ski Area. 5250 Marshall Canyon Rd., Missoula 59802 (258–6619). Montana's "Biggest Little Ski Area," just seven miles from Missoula. One triple chair, one t-bar, two rope tows, lessons, rentals.

Ski the Great Divide. Box SKI, Marysville 59640 (449–3746). Twenty-five miles northeast of Helena. One chair lift.

SEASONAL EVENTS. January. *Montana Winter Fair,* Bozeman.

February. *Winter Carnival,* Whitefish.

May. *Fishing season* opens.

June. *Glacier National Park* and main roads into Yellowstone open. *Big Sky Logging Championships,* Kalispell. *Viking Boat Regatta,* Whitefish. *Logger Days,* Missoula.

July. *Whitefish Lake Regatta,* Whitefish. *Indian Powwows* throughout the state. *North American Indian Days,* Browning. *North Montana State Fair and Rodeo,* Great Falls.

August. *Rodeo Roundup,* Bozeman.. *Western Montana Fair,* Missoula.

October. *Hunting season* opens.

November. *Ski season* begins.

December. *Snowmobile Roundup,* West Yellowstone Park.

MUSEUMS. Montana Historical Society. 225 N. Roberts St., Helena 50601 (444–2694). A capsule history of Montana is presented in dramatic dioramas. The museum also houses a permanent collection of western artist Charlie Russell's work.

Museum of the Rockies. Montana State University, Bozeman 59715 (994–2251). Indian and pioneer relics.

Museum of the Plains Indians. Routes 2 and 89, west of Browning (338–2230). Comprehensive collection of Blackfoot Indian artifacts, as well as a history of the Northern Great Plains tribes. The museum also sells native American arts and crafts.

Fort Missoula Historical Museum. Building 322, South Ave., Missoula 59801 (728–3476). Exhibits on Montana timber industry, military, commerce, and agriculture.

HISTORIC SIGHTS. Bannack. Route 278, west of Dillon. Site of Montana's first major gold discovery in 1862. A walking tour of this ghost town includes an old gallows that was once well-used.

Big Hole Battlefield National Monument. Twelve miles west of Wisdom on Route 43. This was the site of the 1877 battle between the Nez Perce Indians, led by Chief Joseph, and the U.S. Army. Visitor center and walking tour.

Conrad Mansion. Woodland Ave., Kalispell. Built in 1895 and restored to Victorian elegance, this was the home of C.E. Conrad, Montana pioneer, Missouri River trader, and founder of Kalispell.

Governor's Mansion. Helena. Built in 1885.

Grant Kohrs Ranch National Historic Site. Near Deer Lodge. A step back in time, with more than 30 structures and some of them more than 100 years old. Be sure to visit the 23-room ranch house.

Missouri River Headquarters Monument. I–90, near Three Forks. It was here that Lewis and Clark discovered the Jefferson, Madison, and Gallatin rivers, all tributaries of the mighty Missouri.

Montana Historical Prison. 1106 Main St., Deer Lodge. This was the Montana State Prison from 1871 until 1979. Tours offer a view of early western prison life. Daily tours during the summer months. (846–3111). Cost $2 per person.

Nevada City. Some 67 miles southwest of Bozeman. A restored town showing how Montanans lived during the boom days.

St. Ignatius Mission. St. Ignatius. Constructed in the early 1890s, this unique Catholic church contains 58 original murals on its walls and ceilings.

Towne Antique Ford Collection. 1106 Main St., Deer Lodge. A collection of 140 antique Fords.

Virginia City. Southwest of Bozeman on Route 287. Restored mining boom-town and political capital.

ARTS AND ENTERTAINMENT. Check out the activities at **Montana State University**, Bozeman.

The Grand Street Theatre, Helena, offers summer productions every weekend. Helena also offers municipal band concerts during the summer.

In West Yellowstone, the **Playmill Theatre** gives nightly musical comedy and melodrama performances May–Sept.

CHILDREN'S ACTIVITIES. Frontier Town, on Route 2 west of Helena (442–4560), is an authentic frontier village built of hand-hewn logs atop the Continental Divide.

THE IDAHO ROCKIES

by
STEPHEN ALLEN

The name Idaho is thought to have originated from the Indian *Ee da How,* which meant "gem of the mountains" or "light shining down from the mountains." If so, the name was well-chosen, for Idaho is a state of dramatic mountains, wild rivers, and impressive canyons. Within its 83,000 square miles are 200 mountain peaks of 8,000 feet or more and America's deepest gorge. There are 16,000 miles of rivers and streams in the state and more than 2,000 natural lakes. With 40 percent of its 53 million acres covered by trees, Idaho is the most heavily forested of the Rocky Mountain states.

History and Highlights

The first white men to visit Idaho came with Lewis and Clark, who broke up their 1805 trek to the Pacific to winter with the Nez Perce Indians. The era of the mountain men, which began three years later and lasted for three decades, was one of the most colorful periods in the history of the American West. Settlers in search of land came next, but, finding the land inhospitable to farming, most moved on to the green valleys of the Pacific Northwest.

When gold was discovered in Orofino Creek in North Idaho in 1860, a frenzied rush of miners and prospectors began. In 1864 the Territory

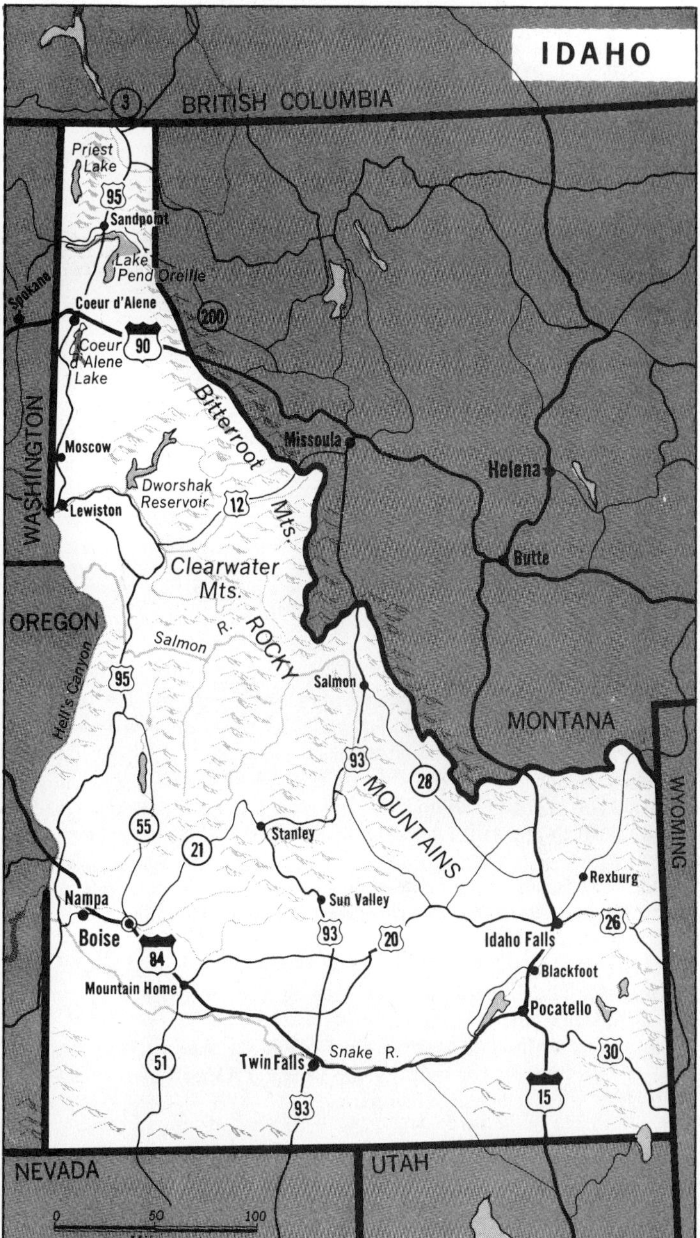
IDAHO
BRITISH COLUMBIA
3
Priest Lake
95
Sandpoint
Lake Pend Oreille
Spokane
Coeur d'Alene
200
90
Coeur d'Alene Lake
Bitterroot
Missoula
Helena
WASHINGTON
Moscow
Dworshak Reservoir
12
Mts.
Lewiston
Butte
Clearwater Mts.
OREGON
Salmon R.
ROCKY
Hell's Canyon
95
Salmon
MONTANA
93
28
MOUNTAINS
WYOMING
55
21
Stanley
Rexburg
Nampa
Sun Valley
Boise
93
20
26
Idaho Falls
84
Blackfoot
Mountain Home
Pocatello
51
Twin Falls
Snake R.
30
93
15
NEVADA
UTAH
0 50 100
Miles

of Idaho was established, with its capital at Lewiston. The capital had moved to its present location at Boise by the time President Harrison signed the Idaho Admissions Act on July 3, 1890, to make Idaho the 43d state.

The irony is that throughout much of the United States and even the world, Idaho is known primarily for its "famous potatoes"—which are even invoked on the state license plates. But potato fields make up only a small portion of the state; outside of its small towns and farms, Idaho is as wild and scenic as any state in the Lower 48.

EXPLORING IDAHO

Idaho owes its natural beauty to water as well as mountains. From Bear Lake in the south to Priest Lake in the north, Idaho has more lakes, more rivers, and more reservoirs than any other state. Its lakes come in all shapes and sizes. Many of them are so wild and primitive you can enjoy everything from meditation to skinny-dipping. The spirit of Idaho rests in places like the Sawtooth Wilderness area, the largest wilderness area in the contiguous states. No road will take you in here, for no road may enter. To experience the Sawtooth Wilderness, you must hike, backpack, ride, or float in. But if you do, you will find a world that you thought was long gone in America.

The Idaho Panhandle

This is the northernmost region of Idaho, where the glaciers of the last great Ice Age have carved a wonderland of lakes, big and small, including Pend Oreille, Coeur d'Alene, and Priest.

Located on the west side of Priest Lake, the Grove of Ancient Cedars is a virgin forest with trees up to 12 feet across and 150 feet high. A short trail leads from the grove to Granite Falls, which cascades over moss-covered rocks.

One of the most spectacular waterfalls in Idaho is the Moyie Falls, which can be seen on the Moyie River, about a half mile upriver from the bridge on Route 2.

The Coeur d'Alene mining district was once the largest silver producer in the world. The Sierra Mine near Wallace offers underground tours for visitors throughout the summer.

The Cataldo Mission, overlooking I–90 at Cataldo, is Idaho's oldest standing building. It was built by the Coeur d'Alene Indians under the direction of the European missionaries.

Lewis and Clark Country/Hell's Canyon

The Bitterroot Range on the Idaho/Montana border proved such difficult going for Lewis and Clark that when they first reached this less rugged part of north-central Idaho it seemed like a paradise. The native Nez Perce Indians were gracious hosts and provided them with needed provisions and guides. Even today, Route 12 runs along the Lewis and Clark Trail, allowing you to retrace their steps between the Continental Divide and the Snake River.

Even the Indians were afraid of Hell's Canyon and warned Lewis and Clark to stay away from the area, now the border between Idaho and Oregon. Also known as the Grand Canyon of the Snake River, it is the deepest gorge in North America, dropping 9,300 feet to the river in some places. Although the wilderness portions of Hell's Canyon are closed to all motor vehicles, there are a few roadways leading to strategic viewpoints. Check with the Hell's Gate State Park Information Center in Lewiston.

The most accessible viewpoint is from the Buckhorn Lookout Tower, on the Oregon side of the river. The river itself is best seen from Imnaha on the Idaho side. From there, it's a 24-mile drive to Hat Point Lookout, and you should not even think of doing it if the weather looks bad or if your car is not in excellent shape. The road winds its way down into the canyon from Route 95 just north of White Bird. The end of the line is Pittsburgh's Landing.

Some miles north, Dworshak Lake is almost 53 miles long and was created by the Dworshak Dam. The largest Steelhead Trout fish hatchery in the world is four miles west of Orofino on Route 7.

Seven Devils, near Riggins, is the area's highest mountain range. Heaven's Gate Lookout offers a spectacular view of four states.

Continental Divide Country

This area, in the northeastern notch of the state, offers a choice of spectacular mountains and wild rivers. Ranges include the Tetons, Sawtooths, Lost River Range, among many others. Two of the most famous rivers in America, the Snake and the Salmon, wind through the region.

The Salmon River Valley is the white-water capital of the world. You can even float the famed River of No Return, and here also you will find Steelhead Trout fishing at its best.

The Sawtooth National Recreation Area, near Stanley, is Idaho's oldest scenic outdoor recreation area.

Not many people realize that you can see the Tetons, normally thought of in connection with Wyoming, on their western side from Idaho. Teton Valley is a sightseer's dream for those on their way to Yellowstone via Jackson Hole, Wyoming. The Henderson and Patterson canyons are the gateways for exploration of the Big Hole Range on the west side of the Teton Valley.

Mt. Borah, north of Mackay, is Idaho's tallest peak at 12,662 feet.

The Yankee Fork Gold Dredge was built in 1870 on the Yankee Fork of the Salmon River. The mining camps that surround it are now ghost towns, offering reminders of that period of the American past.

Ketchum/Sun Valley

The little town of Ketchum is an excellent starting point for tourists who want to take in the splendor of the Idaho Rockies by car. Near the famous winter resort of Sun Valley, Ketchum was the last home of Ernest Hemingway. He lived on the Wood River and, on the night before his death, dined at the nearby Christiana Inn. He is buried in Ketchum's rustic cemetery.

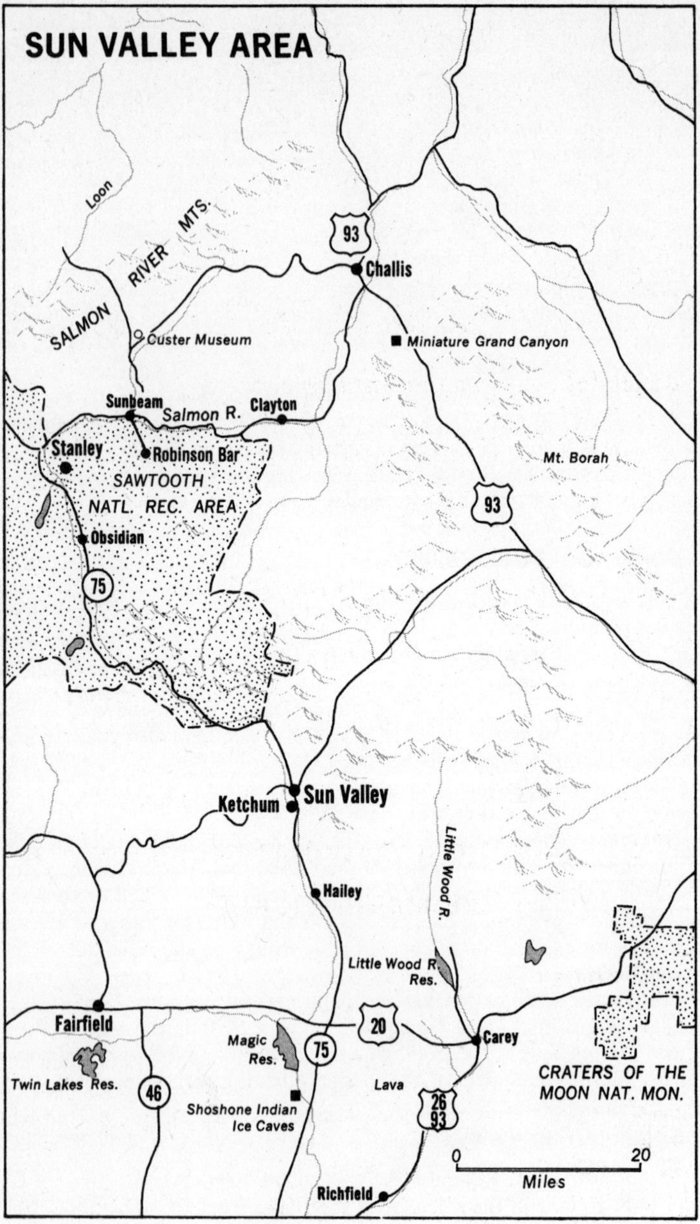
SUN VALLEY AREA
Loon
SALMON RIVER MTS.
93
Challis
Custer Museum
Miniature Grand Canyon
Sunbeam
Salmon R.
Clayton
Stanley
Robinson Bar
SAWTOOTH
NATL. REC. AREA
Mt. Borah
93
Obsidian
75
Sun Valley
Ketchum
Little Wood R.
Hailey
Little Wood R.
Res.
Fairfield
20
Carey
Magic
Res.
75
Twin Lakes Res.
46
Lava
CRATERS OF THE
MOON NAT. MON.
Shoshone Indian
Ice Caves
26
93
0
20
Miles
Richfield

The Trail Creek Road leads from Ketchum up to the spectacular vista at the 7,894-foot summit of Trail Creek, for views of Mount Borah, at 12,655 feet, Idaho's highest peak. If time permits, continue on to Craters of the Moon National Monument. You'll think you've landed on another planet when you experience the eerie ambience of this immense sea of lava left by an ancient volcano. And children will love scrambling around on the black hillocks. Though the road is fairly well-maintained, it is wise to check in at the Forest Service Ranger Station in Ketchum (see below) before starting out. This drive is not advisable in winter.

One of the most scenic trips in all of the Rockies is the drive from Ketchum to Stanley on Route 75. This road runs along the Big Wood River past Redfish and Stanley lakes. It affords glorious, photogenic views of the Sawtooth Mountain Range, before dropping into the Stanley Basin. Be on the lookout for deer, particularly in the early evening hours.

Craters of the Moon National Monument

If you'd like to know what the moon looks like, this is the closest you can come on Earth. The similarity between this area to the pockmarked surface of the moon is so great that NASA has actually brought some of the astronauts here for training. Craters of the Moon is just about in the very center of Idaho, on Route 93 near Arco, 70 miles west of Sun Valley.

The Craters of the Moon is essentially a lava bed. A series of volcanic explosions thousands of years ago formed the black ash and lava cones visible today, some of them as high as 800 feet. A seven-mile loop drive will take you past the most interesting sights. But you also should not miss the Indian Tunnel, an 830-foot-long lava tube that was used as a cave by the Indians of that area. For more information, write Superintendent, Craters of the Moon National Monument, Box 29, Arco, ID 83213 (527–3257).

PRACTICAL INFORMATION FOR THE IDAHO ROCKIES

HOW TO GET THERE. There are not many major cities in Idaho, and even the capital, Boise, is one of the smallest in the U.S. Boise and Pocatello have the major airports.

By air. *Delta Airlines* flies to Boise from Salt Lake City, Utah, and Pasco, Washington. *America West* flies there from Las Vegas, Nevada. Service to Boise, as with many small American cities, has declined through the years. For more information, call the Boise Airport, 208–383–3110.

By train. *Empire Builder* stops at beautiful Sandpoint on its Chicago-to-Seattle run. A couple of years ago, the *Wall Street Journal* conducted a survey on what was the most desirable city in America in which to live—and Sandpoint was the winner.

By car. The major interstate highways that run through a portion of Idaho's Rocky Mountains are Interstate 90, through the top Panhandle portion, and Interstate 15, through the eastern portion of the state. The

S. highways going through the same area are routes 95, 93, and

By bus. Nearly all major cities in the Idaho Rockies are served by *Greyhound.*

TOURIST INFORMATION. You can get general information on Idaho by writing to the *Idaho Travel Council,* Statehouse, Boise, ID 83720 (800–635–7820). You can get information on the Panhandle by contacting *Big Water Mountain Land,* Box 928, Sandpoint, ID 84864 (263–2161). Information on Lewis and Clark Country can be obtained from *Lewis and Clark Country,* Box 8936, Moscow, ID 83843 (882–3581). Information on eastern Idaho is obtainable from *Mountain River Country,* Box 50498, Idaho Falls ID 83405 (523–1010).

TELEPHONES. The area code for all of Idaho is 208. The cost of a pay call is 25¢.

ACCOMMODATIONS. Lodging in Idaho ranges from the small hotel that looks as if it was built for prospectors during the gold rush—and probably was—to the modern chain motel. But there's really not much between the two extremes. Alternative lodgings, like bed-and-breakfasts, have not really caught on here yet, and Boise is about the only city in which you will find larger hotels.

Price categories for double occupancy are: *Deluxe,* over $60; *Expensive,* $50–$60; *Moderate* $40–$50; and *Inexpensive,* under $40.

Boise. Allison Ranch. *Expensive.* 7259 Cascade Dr. (376–5270). Lodge, hunting, fishing, backpacking, horseback riding.

Mackay Bar. *Expensive.* 3190 Airport Way 83705 (344–1881). Idaho's Wilderness Company, at South Fork and Main. Lodge, cabins, hunting, fishing, rafting, mountain climbing, backpacking, horseback riding, family-style dining.

Shepp Ranch. *Expensive.* c/o Box 5466, 83705 (343–7729). 45 miles east of Riggins on the Salmon River. Access by plane or jetboat. Cabins, hunting, fishing, horseback riding, jet boating.

City Center Motel. *Inexpensive.* 108 E. Kootenai St. 83805 (267–2133). Rustic hospitality; cafe nearby.

Bonners Ferry. Best Western Connie's Motor Inn. *Expensive.* Kootenai River Plaza 83805 (267–8511). In downtown Bonners Ferry. All rooms with river view. Sauna, Jacuzzi, exercise room, cable TV, docks.

Deep Creek Inn. *Moderate.* Route 1, 83805 (267–7578). Playground, RV spaces, restaurant.

Lantern Motel and KOA. *Moderate.* Route 4, Box 4700, 83805 (267–2422). One mile south of town. Swimming pool.

Challis. Challis Lodge. *Moderate.* Box 6, 83226 (879–2251). Cozy motel, near shopping.

Village Inn. *Moderate.* Box 8, 83226 (879–2239). Cable TV, cafe, pets allowed.

Coeur D'Alene. Coeur d'Alene Resort Hotel. *Deluxe.* On the lake, 83814 (765–4000). Four restaurants, four lounges, health club and spa, views of the lake, North America's longest floating boardwalk, fishing charters, and boat cruises.

Flamingo Motel. *Expensive.* 718 Sherman Ave. 83815 (664–2159). Small and homelike.

Greenbriar Bed 'n' Breakfast Inn. *Expensive.* 315 Wallace St. 83814 (667–9660). Coeur d'Alene's only nationally registered Historic Home. Seven bedrooms, gourmet-style breakfast, four blocks from downtown and beach.

Holiday Inn of Coeur d'Alene. *Expensive.* 414 Appleway 83814 (765–3200 or 800–HOLIDAY). Private spas, closed-circuit movies, cable TV, water beds, honeymoon suites.

Cedar Motel. *Moderate.* 319 S. 24th St. 83814 (664–2278). Heated pool, game room, kitchenettes, RV park.

Garden Motel. *Moderate.* 1808 Northwest Blvd. 83814 (664–2743). Cable TV, indoor pool, spa.

Kingsport Inn. *Moderate.* 2100 Sherman Ave., 83814 (664–8191) There are cooking units available here; pets are permitted.

Pines Resort. *Moderate.* 1422 Northwest Blvd. 83814 (664–8244). Rooms with a view, cable TV.

Star Motel. *Inexpensive.* 1516 Sherman Ave. 83814 (664–5035). Mini kitchens, cable TV; cafe nearby; small pets allowed.

Driggs. Best Western Teton West. *Moderate.* 476 N. Main St. 83422 (354–2363 or 800–528–1234). Whirlpool, game room; near Jackson Hole and Yellowstone Park.

Pines Motel. *Inexpensive.* 105 S. Main St. 83422 (354–2774). Restaurant and shops nearby.

Hayden Lake. Affordable Inn. *Inexpensive.* 9986 N. Government Way 83835 (772–4414). Tavern, outdoor barbecue, golf course nearby.

Island Park. Pond's Lodge. *Moderate.* Island Park 83429 (558–7221). Open year-round, ski shop, horseback riding, snowmobile rentals.

Jerome. Salmon River Lodge. *Expensive.* Box 348, 83338 (324–3553). West of Shoup. Guest ranch with family-style meals, hunting, fishing, horseback riding, jet-boat rides.

Mackay. Wagon Wheel Motel. *Inexpensive.* 809 W. Custer St. 83251 (588–3331). Scenic views, restaurants and shops nearby, cable TV.

Montpelier. Best Western Crest Motel. *Expensive.* 243 N. 4th St. 83254 (847–1782 or 800–528–1234). Pleasant, comfortable rooms; restaurant and golf nearby.

Budget Motel. *Inexpensive.* 240 N. 4th St., 83254 (847–1273).

Michelle Motel. *Inexpensive.* 402 Boise St., 83254 (847–1772). Ten ground-level rooms, outdoor pool, restaurant nearby. Pets permitted.

Priest Lake. Grandview Lodge. *Expensive.* Star Route, Box 48, Nordman 83848 (443–2433). Lodge and cottages, snowmobiling, boat rentals, cross-country skiing.

Hill's Resort. *Expensive.* Route 5, Box 162A, Priest Lake 83856 (443–2551). Cabins and condos, boat rentals, tennis, golf.

Elkins on Priest Lake. *Moderate.* Star Route, Box 40, Nordman 83848 (443–2432). Beautifully appointed log cabins, restaurant and bar, beach, boat moorage, snowmobile trails.

Priest River. Priest River Motel. *Inexpensive.* 1221 W. Albeni St. 83856 (448–2853). Scenic view, close to shopping.

Rexburg. Best Western Cottontree Inn. *Moderate.* 450 W. 14th St. 83440 (356–4646 or 800–528–1234). Indoor pool, hunting, fishing, snowmobiling.

Viking Motel. *Inexpensive.* 271 S. 2d St. 83440 (356–9222). Hunting, fishing, snowmobiling.

Riggins. The Lodge. *Expensive.* Box 498, 83549 (842–2343). A bed and breakfast on the Little Salmon River, just south of town. Family-style dining, hot tub, sauna, hunting, fishing, rafting, backpacking, scenic tours, right on the river.

Half Way Inn. *Inexpensive.* 83549 (628–3259). Cabins, scenic location on the river, fishing.

Riggins Motel. *Inexpensive.* Box 1157, 83549 (628–3456). Located right in Riggins. Cable TV; cafe nearby.

Salmon River Motel. *Inexpensive.* Box 348, 83549 (628–3231). Cable TV.

St. Anthony. Best Western Weston Inn. *Moderate.* 115 S. Bridge St. 83445. (624–3711). Located on Henry's Fork River. Skiing, snowmobiling.

Salmon. Best Western Wagons West Motel. *Moderate.* Route 83 N. 83467 (756–4281 or 800–528–1234). Pets allowed, but no cats.

Stagecoach Inn Motel. *Moderate.* 201 Route 93 N., 83467 (756–4251). Right on the Salmon River.

Motel Deluxe. *Inexpensive.* 112 S. Church St. 83467 (756–2231). Restaurants and lounge nearby.

Suncrest Motel. *Inexpensive.* 705 Challis St. 83467 (756–2294). Barbecue area, quiet setting.

Sandpoint. Lakeside Motel. *Expensive.* 106 Bridge St. 83864 (263–3717). Large, comfortable rooms; easy access to beach, tennis courts; cafe nearby; seasonal rates.

The Overniter Lodge. *Expensive.* Box 1468, 83864 (263–9564). In the Schweitzer ski area. Managed by Four Seasons Resorts.

Schweitzer Condominium Rentals. *Expensive.* Box 815, 83864. In the Schweitzer ski area. Fireplaces, sauna, whirlpool, ski rentals.

Whitaker House. *Expensive.* 410 Railroad Ave. 83864 (263–0816). A bed and breakfast. Four guest rooms in an 1895 home on the lake.

Best Western Connie's Motor Inn. *Moderate.* 323 Cedar St. 83864 (263–9581 or 800–528–1234). Whirlpool, cable TV, water beds, nine miles from the Schweitzer Ski Basin, but only two blocks from Lake Pend Oreille.

Edgewater Lodge. *Moderate.* 56 Bridge St. 83864 (263–3194). All units have lake views; tennis and park nearby.

Monarch Inn. *Moderate.* Bonner Mall Station 83864 (263–1222). Jacuzzi, sauna.

Quality Inn. *Inexpensive.* 807 N. 5th St. 83864 (263–2111 or 800–228–5151). Cable TV, Jacuzzi, whirlpool.

Stanley. Idaho Rocky Mountain Ranch. *Moderate.* 83278 (774–3544). Fifty miles north of Sun Valley. Lodge, cabins, fireplaces, dining room, fishing, backpacking.

Mountain Village Lodge. *Moderate.* Box 150, 83278 (774–3661). At the junction of routes 75 and 21. Snowmobiling, cross-country skiing, restaurant.

Redfish Lake Lodge. *Moderate.* Box 9, 83278 (774–3536). Five miles south of Stanley on Route 75, then two miles west. Fishing, boating, and horseback riding.

Sawtooth Hotel. *Inexpensive.* Main St. 83278 (774–9947). Bed and breakfast. Home cooking; view of the Sawtooth Mountains.

Sun Valley. Christiana Lodge. *Deluxe.* 651 Sun Valley Rd., Ketchum 83340 (726–3351). Fine motel, fireplaces, restaurant; was a favorite of Ernest Hemingway.

Elkhorn at Sun Valley. *Deluxe.* Box 1067, 83353 (622–4511). The ultimate in winter luxury.

Heidelberg Inn. *Deluxe.* Warm Springs Rd. 83353 (726–5361). Attractive motel in Bavarian style. Heated pool, golf course.

Sun Valley Lodge. *Deluxe.* Sun Valley Rd. 83353 (622–4111). One mile north of Ketchum. Huge facility with apartments, suites, kitchens; indoor and outdoor pool, fishing, skiing, golf, tennis, entertainment.

Tamarack Lodge. *Deluxe.* Sun Valley Rd. 83353 (726–3344). Private balconies, fireplaces.

Bald Mountain Hot Springs. *Moderate.* 151 Main St. 83353 (726–9963). Charming rooms, Olympic-size swimming pool with natural hot water. Near restaurants and shopping.

Tyrolean Lodge. *Moderate.* Box 202, 83353 (726–5336). Cable TV, heated pool, cafe, health club. Near ski areas.

GUEST RANCHES. Idaho has many outstanding guest ranches, some specializing in pack trips for hunters or fishermen. For more information, write to the *Idaho Outfitters and Guides Association,* Box 95, Boise, ID 83701 (342–1438).

Clark-Miller Guest Ranch. Star Route, Ketchum 83340 (774–3535). Fishing haven 43 miles north of Ketchum.

Harrah's Lodge. Box 10, Boise 83720 (342–7888). A luxurious wilderness retreat on the Middle Fork of the Salmon River.

Mackay Bar Lodge. 3190 Airport Way, Boise 83705 (344–1881). Guest rooms and tent cabins on the River of No Return.

Mystic Saddle Ranch. Stanley 83340 (774–3591). In the Sawtooth Wilderness. Pack trips, fishing, big-game hunting.

Salmon River Lodge. Box 348, Jerome 83338 (324–3553). Located on the Salmon River. Fishing, float trips, primitive area pack trips, big-game hunting.

Sulphur Creek Ranch. 7153 W. Emerald Rd., Boise 83704 (377–1188). On the Middle Fork of the Salmon River, this ranch is basically for hunters and fishermen.

RESTAURANTS. Food in the Idaho Rockies tends to be plain and simple; the fancy restaurants and fern bars popular from Aspen to Jasper have gained no toehold here. This is the land of the hearty eater and the big breakfast. Beware if you are used to starting the day with only a slice of toast and a cup of coffee—they won't tolerate that sort of thing here. Our categories are for two full meals with appetizers, exclusive of drinks, tax, and tip.

Super Deluxe, over $40; *Deluxe,* $30–$40; *Expensive,* $20–$30; *Moderate,* $10–$20; and *Inexpensive,* under $10.

Coeur D'Alene Beverly's. *Expensive.* At Coeur d'Alene Resort (765–4000). Filet mignon; beautiful view of the mountains.

The Cedars. *Expensive.* Junction I-90 and Route 95 (664–2922). This floating restaurant on lake Coeur d'Alene features Hawaiian-style chicken.

Cloud Nine. *Expensive.* Atop the North Shore Motel, 115 S. Second St. (664–9241). Plush dining overlooking the lake.

Osprey. *Moderate.* 1000 W. Hubbard St. (664–2115). Salmon Wellington, fresh seafood. Entertainment, dancing.

Priest Lake. Hill's Resort. *Moderate.* At Hill's Resort (443–2551). Steak and oysters are specialties. Entertainment, dancing in summer.

Salmon. Salmon River Coffee Shop. *Moderate.* 606 Main St. (756–3521). Steaks, seafood, and home-baked pastries. Music, dancing, entertainment.

Shady Nook Lounge and Supper Club. *Moderate.* Route 93 (756–4182). Steak, seafood, shrimp in beer batter, home-baking.

Sandpoint. The Garden. *Moderate.* 15 E. Lake St. (263–5187). Charming restaurant that makes Sandpoint such a pleasant place. Outdoor dining, lakeside view; home-baked breads, seafood.

Stanley. Idaho Rocky Mountain Ranch Dining Room. *Moderate.* Nine miles south on Route 75 (774–3544). Beef, seafood, chicken. Restaurant will also prepare fish caught by guests.

River Company. *Inexpensive.* One mile south on Hwy. 75. (774–2250). Quiche, pepper steak. Outdoor dining.

Sun Valley. Christiana. *Expensive.* In Christiana Lodge, 303 Walnut St. (726–3388). Lamb, veal, seafood, homemade desserts. Outdoor dining.

Le Club. *Expensive.* 716 N. Main St., Ketchum (726–3286). Chicken Rochambeau, Kiwi trout, veal dishes. No smoking allowed.

Lodge Dining Room. *Expensive.* In Sun Valley Resort Lodge (622–4111). Medallions of veal; Entertainment, dancing; jacket required.

Creekside Bar & Grill. *Moderate.* 319 Skiway Dr. (726–8200). Seafood, lamb, pasta, home-baking. Outdoor dining.

Evergreen. *Moderate.* 171 First Ave., Ketchum (726–3888). French-American menu, lamb Madiera, roast duck, veal; outdoor dining with view of Mt. Baldy.

The Ore House. *Moderate.* Sun Valley Mall, Ketchum (622–4363). This place has attained regional fame for its do-it-yourself salads, lobster, and beef.

River Street Retreat. *Moderate.* 120 River St., Ketchum (726–9502). New York steak, fresh seafood, salad bar; outdoor dining.

Warm Springs Ranch. *Moderate.* 1801 Warm Springs Rd., Ketchum (726–8238). Outdoor dining with mountain view. Trout and barbecued ribs.

The Kitchen. *Inexpensive.* 216 N. Main St., Ketchum (726–3856). Omelets, quiche, waffles.

LIQUOR LAWS. The legal age for the consumption of alcoholic beverages in Idaho is 21. Liquor can be obtained from state liquor stores or by the glass at taverns from 10 A.M. until 1 A.M. daily. The sale of liquor is prohibited on Sundays, Memorial Day, Labor Day, until the polls close on Election Day, Thanksgiving, and Christmas.

HOW TO GET AROUND. Access to the vast primitive areas of the state is mainly by pack horse and charter plane. Guides are widely used by latter-day Hemingways. The Idaho Travel Council (see *Tourist Information* above) provides a list of wilderness outfitters.

By air. The only airlines flying between cities like Boise and Pocatello are *Horizon Airlines (Alaska Airlines)* and *Delta.*

By car. Interstate 90 crosses the Idaho Panhandle. The route followed by Lewis and Clark is paralleled by Route 12. Route 95, cutting along the western portion of the state, is the longest of Idaho's highways, and touches more than its share of splendid scenery.

Cars can be rented in most cities. In Pocatello: *Hertz* (233–2970), *Avis* (232–3244). In Boise: *Hertz* (383–3100), *Avis* (383–3350). In Idaho Falls: *Hertz* (529–3101), *Avis* (522–4225). Smaller companies serving other Idaho cities include *Budget, Dollar, National, Payless, Sears,* and *Thrifty.*

By bus. The only bus lines serving cities within Idaho are *Greyhound* and the *Boise-Winnemucca Stages* (336–3300).

INDIANS. Idaho has a rich Indian heritage. Among the major tribes in the state are the Nez Perce, who befriended the Lewis and Clark expedition, the Coeur d'Alene, the Pend Oreille, the Kootenai, the Shoshone-Bannock, and the Paiute. Idaho's Indian people have six languages and were closely identified with their neighbors in the Great Basin, the Columbia Plateau, and the Great Plains.

A little more than a decade ago, 67 Kootenai Indians living on a 12-acre reservation near Bonners Ferry declared war against the United States of America, seeking the return of some of their aboriginal lands. The "war" ended after some time without bloodshed, and the Indians getting some of what they sought but not all. The whole affair resembled *The Mouse*

That Roared; in the words of one Indian, their war was more like "Skinned Shin" than "Wounded Knee."

Of the four reservations in the state, the largest is Fort Hall, where 1.8 million acres were set aside for the Shoshone and Bannock tribes. The reservation has now dwindled to little more than a half million acres. "Indian Days" are held at Fort Hall on the last weekend in October.

NATIONAL FORESTS. Eight national forests lie entirely within the borders of the state and seven others are partly within the boundaries, giving the state about 21 million acres of national forest lands. More detailed information on the national forests is available from the *U.S. Forest Service: Intermountain Region,* Federal Office Building, Ogden, UT 84401 (801–625–5182), or *U.S. Forest Service: Northern Region,* Missoula, MT 59801 (406–329–3511).

Boise National Forest. 3 million acres. Attractions include the Sawtooth Wilderness Area, abandoned mines, and ghost towns. The Forest has 800 miles of trails suitable for foot or horse travel. Write Boise National Forest, 1750 Front St., Boise, ID 83702 (364–4100).

Challis National Forest. 2.5 million acres. The highest mountain in Idaho, Borah Peak, is here, as are the Salmon River and the towns of Salmon and Stanley. The Forest has nearly 1,600 miles of trails, wonderful for riding, hiking, or backpacking. Write Challis National Forest, Box 404, Challis, ID 83226 (879–2285).

Clearwater National Forest. 1.7 million acres. Part of the famed Lewis and Clark Trail can be found here, along with the Selway-Bitterroot Wilderness, and excellent trout and salmon fishing. Write Clearwater National Forest, 12730 Highway 12, Orofino 83544 (476–4541).

Coeur d'Alene National Forest. This forest lies in Idaho's northern Panhandle and includes the Cataldo Mission and beautiful 30-mile-long Lake Coeur d'Alene. Write Idaho Panhandle National Forests, 1201 Ironwood Dr., Coeur d'Alene, ID 83814 (765–7223).

Kaniksu National Forest. Northernmost of all the national forests in Idaho, near the towns of Sandpoint, Bonners Ferry, and Priest River, Kaniksu is home to two beautiful lakes—Pend Oreille and Priest. The forest is set within the Selkirk Mountains, with many excellent trout-fishing streams. The Schweitzer Basin Ski Resort is near Sandpoint. Write Idaho Panhandle National Forests, 1201 Ironwood Dr., Coeur d'Alene, ID 83814 (765–7223).

Nez Perce National Forest. 2 million acres. Among the attractions of this western Idaho forest are a portion of the Selway-Bitterroot Wilderness, Salmon River Breaks Primitive Area, Seven Devils Range, lake and stream fishing, horse and hiking trails, and wilderness pack trips. Write Nez Perce National Forest, Route 2, Box 475, Grangeville, ID 83530 (983–1950).

Payette National Forest. 2.4 million acres. The attractions include the Hell's Canyon-Seven Devils Scenic Area, excellent trout and salmon fishing, and wilderness hiking. Just south of the Nez Perce Forest, Payette has more than 2,400 miles of trails and includes the Payette Lakes Winter Sports Area. Write Payette National Forest, Box 1026, McCall, ID 83638 (634–8151).

Salmon National Forest. 1.8 million acres. In the sparsely settled eastern portion of the state, Salmon offers the Idaho Primitive Area, a portion of the Lewis and Clark Trail, the Salmon River Canyon, and boat trips on the River of No Return. Write Salmon National Forest, Box 729, Salmon, ID 83467 (756–2215).

Sawtooth National Forest. 1.7 million acres. Attractions here include the famed Sun Valley winter resort, the Sawtooth Wilderness Area, and beautiful views of the Snake River Valley. Sportsmen will find excellent fishing and hiking and eight winter-sports areas. Write Sawtooth National Forest, 2647 Kimberly Rd. E., Twin Falls, ID 83301 (733–3200).

STATE PARKS. The Idaho State Department of Parks and Recreation maintains 19 parks, ranging from undeveloped, natural wilderness to full-scale recreational areas. For more information, consult the *Idaho Department of Parks and Recreation,* 2177 Warm Springs Ave., Boise, ID 83720 (800–334–2154).

Bear Lake. On the north shore of Bear Lake, near the Utah border. Fishing, swimming, boating.

Farragut. On the shore of Lake Pend Oreille, with 145 sites.

Henry's Lake. Seventeen miles south of West Yellowstone on Mountain Man Lake.

Historic Missions. At Cataldo Mission.

Malad Gorge. Near Hagerman. Scenic gorge with a waterfall.

Ponderosa. At McCall, on the southern end of Payette Lake.

Priest Lake. Three camping units, boating, fishing, swimming.

Round Lake. Ten miles south of Sandpoint, near Lake Pend Oreille.

CAMPING. Idaho has campgrounds throughout the state, including more than 400 in the national forests alone and 26 recreational sites developed by the Bureau of Land Management. For specific information, write *Bureau of Land Management,* 3380 American Terr., Boise ID 83706 (334–1414)

More than 250 public recreation sites, including 8,000 campsites, have been provided by private companies in Idaho. In addition, there are numerous Kampgrounds of America (KOA) sites throughout the state. For information, write the *Idaho Travel Council,* Statehouse, Boise, ID 83720 (800–635–7820).

Camping season in Idaho runs from approximately May – Sept. There is a charge for camping, with or without hookups, in state parks (see list below). The maximum stay is 15 days out of any 30 except at Priest Lake, Farragut, and Ponderosa, where the maximum stay is 10 days.

FISHING. Fishing is good all over Idaho. Record-size trout have been taken from Lake Pend Oreille in the north, and steelhead trout and sturgeon abound in the Snake River. Fishing season generally runs from Memorial Day through November; bag limits vary with different species. Non-resident fishing licenses, available from vendors in nearly every town in Idaho, cost $36, $18 for a 10-day license, and $6 for a one-day license. For additional information, write to the *Idaho Fish and Game Department,* 600 S. Walnut St., Box 25, Boise, ID 83707 (334–3700).

HUNTING. General seasons for deer, elk, and bear extend from mid-September until November, although areas and seasons vary throughout the state. Controlled hunts are sometimes established for moose, antelope, mountain goat, and bighorn sheep. Non-resident big-game hunters should contact the Idaho Fish and Game Department (see above) by January, since licenses for the upcoming season are distributed on a quota basis. Hunting maps also are available from the Fish and Game Department after July 1. License fees for non-residents are $86; game tags range up to $236 per kill; and a deer tag is $91.

Birds. Hunting seasons of varying lengths are set for partridge, quail, and grouse, usually in September or October. Pheasant season runs from late October through November; waterfowl, from mid-October through December. Opening dates for upland birds are usually set in May. Licenses can be obtained from vendors in nearly every town in the state. Further information is available from the Fish and Game Department (see above).

RAFTING. Because of its wild western rivers, the United States is probably the best country in the world in which to go rafting—and Idaho is undoubtedly the best state.

A number of rivers in Idaho are ideal for rafting, including the Salmon, the Selway, and the River of No Return (they're just kidding, folks; don't take them seriously). But the *piece de resistance* is the Middle Fork of the Salmon River. The Middle Fork starts about 20 miles north of the little town of Stanley and then runs northeast (unusual) for about 135 miles before joining the big river and churning through one of America's deepest canyons.

A number of guides and outfitters can make it easy for you to run the Middle Fork of the Salmon even if you have never been on a river before. They provide everything you need, including accommodations and food. The trips are a little expensive but worth every penny—and they will leave you with an experience you will remember for the rest of your life. River rafting trips are popular, so it's wise to reserve a year in advance. May and June see the whitest water and the most tourists.

For more information on rafting the Middle Fork of the Salmon, consult the *Stanley Chamber of Commerce* (774–2286).

The best and safest way to see Hell's Canyon is via jetboat on the Snake River. The boats leave from Hell's Canyon Dam. A raft trip through the canyon takes six days. For information, write Hell's Canyon Chamber of Commerce, 2207 E. Main St., Lewiston, ID 83501 (743–3648).

There are boat trips of all types along the Snake River, Salmon River, and River of No Return, as well as through Hell's Canyon. For information on them, write to the *Greater Lewiston Chamber of Commerce,* 1030 F St., Lewiston, ID 83501 (743–3531). For information on jet or paddle trips on the Middle Fork of the Salmon and the Selway, write to *Idaho Outfitters and Guides Association,* Box 95, Boise, ID 83701 (342–1438).

DOWNHILL SKIING. Skiing is the fastest growing sport in Idaho. For information on tour operators serving the ski areas and prices on lodging, contact the *Idaho Travel Council,* Statehouse, Boise, ID 83720 (800–635–7820).

Bogus Basin. (336–4500). Sixteen miles north of Boise and a favorite with western Snake River fans, this is one of the major ski areas in the Pacific Northwest, with the longest illuminated slopes in the country and more than 1,000 acres. Forty-three major runs, day and night skiing, accommodations, restaurants, ski school.

Brundage Mountain. (634–5650). Seven miles north of McCall. The slopes overlook the Payette Lakes. Two double chairs, one t-bar, ski shop, rentals, ski school, cafeteria. At this high and dry level, powder snow is the rule rather than the exception.

Lost Trail. Forty-two miles north of Salmon, near the Montana border and the Continental Divide. Double chair, seven open runs, 10-mile cross-country area, ski school, rentals.

North-South Bowl. (245–4222). Sixty miles south of Coeur d'Alene. Double chair, two rope tows, ski school, rentals.

Schweitzer Basin. (263–9555). Eleven miles northwest of Sandpoint. Seven chair lifts and one t-bar, two huge bowls, almost 40 runs and trails up to three miles long, lodge, rentals, ski school.

Silverhorn. (783–1151). Six miles south of Kellogg, off I–90. Fourteen major runs, wooded and open terrain, freefall skiing, double chair lift, rentals, cafeteria, ski school, hookups for recreational vehicles.

Sun Valley. (622–4111). The granddaddy of them all, made famous by Hollywood before anyone ever *heard* of skiing. Sun Valley is the ultimate in ski resorts, with 200 ski instructors, three ice rinks, lodging, dining, and entertainment. Ketchum is the nearest town, and you can get buses from there to Sun Valley and Elkhorn.

SEASONAL EVENTS. January. *U.S. Pacific Northwest Championship Dog Sled Races,* Priest Lake. *Winter Carnival,* Sandpoint.

February. *Winter Carnival,* Salmon.

April. *River of No Return Jet Boat Races,* Salmon.

May. *Salmon River Rodeo,* Riggins. *Lake Coeur d'Alene Days,* Coeur d'Alene. *Kamloops and Kokanee Fishing Derby,* Sandpoint.

June. *Summer Theatre,* Coeur d'Alene. *International Folk Dancing,* Rexburg.

July. *Blue Grass Festival,* Sandpoint. *Old Timer Fiddlers Jamboree,* Shoshone. *Kootenai River Days,* Bonners Ferry. *Woopee Days,* Rexburg.

August. *Boundary County Fair,* Bonners Ferry.

September. *Bonner County Fair,* Sandpoint. *South East Idaho State Fair,* Blackfoot. *North Idaho Fair and Rodeo,* Coeur d'Alene. *Lumberjack Days,* Orofino. *Wagon Days,* Ketchum.

October. *Oktoberfest,* Coeur d'Alene. *Indian Days,* Fort Hall.

November. *Hunting season.*

MUSEUMS. Bonner County Historical Museum. Ontario St., Sandpoint 83864 (263–2344). The area's Indian and pioneer heritage. Closed during winter.

Boundary County Historical Museum. County Building, Bonners Ferry 83856 (267–7720). Displays relating to the ferry route across the Kootenai River, which established this little northern town.

Museum of North Idaho. 115 Northwest Blvd., Coeur d'Alene 83814 (664–3448). Local history, native Americans, and an unusual game room of animals taken from all over the world by local hunters. Open April–Oct.

Lewis-Clark State College Museum. Lewiston 83501 (799–5272). Exhibits pertaining to the famed explorers and their route across Idaho.

HISTORIC SITES AND HOUSES. Atomic Energy Site. West of Idaho Falls. The world's first nuclear power plant is now a National Historic Landmark. Guided and self-guided tours.

Cataldo Mission. This is the oldest standing building in Idaho, constructed beginning in 1846 completely without the benefit of nails. The mission is atop a low hill overlooking Interstate 90 at Cataldo, and Cataldo is between the towns of Kellogg and Coeur d'Alene. The mission was built by the Coeur d'Alene Indians under the direction of the "black robes" (as they were called by the Indians), after they abandoned an earlier mission on the shores of Lake Coeur d'Alene. There are tours of the mission from March through October daily. There is also picnicking, an information center, and a history trail. For information, contact Park Manager, Box 135, Cataldo 83810 (682–3814). Cost per vehicle $2.

Lewis and Clark Trail. Route 12 parallels the route of explorers Lewis and Clark through Idaho.

Yankee Fork Gold Dredge. This 1870 gold dredge was built on the Yankee Fork of the Salmon River. Now the mining camps are ghost towns, but reminders of this colorful era in Idaho's history still can be found.

ARTS AND ENTERTAINMENT. Dramatic groups are springing up all over Idaho, and community theater can go a long way toward relieving the "cabin fever" of Idaho's long and cold winters. The **Coeur d'Alene Summer Theatre Carousel Players** bring musical entertainment to North Idaho from June to September. Community theaters in both Sandpoint and Bonners Ferry have seasons during both the fall and winter.

Country and western music is *the* music of Idaho. Every town of size has at least one tavern with live country music on Friday and Saturday nights.

THE ALBERTA ROCKIES

by
ENA SPALDING

Ms. Spalding, originally from Scotland, is a writer and editor at the Banff Centre. She is a naturalist and a free-lance photographer.

There is something epic about Alberta, some impression of glamor and grandeur which draws tourists and—even today—droves of new settlers. The province is to the Canadian imagination what Texas is to the American, at once romantic and tacky; if *Dynasty* were a Canadian serial, it would surely be filmed in Calgary. It is the Rocky Mountains, more than anything else, which have created this romance about the state.

In the 18th and 19th centuries, the mountains were seen by British explorers merely as an obstacle to be faced en route to the Pacific. Using Indian guides, explorers like Alexander Mackenzie, David Thompson, Duncan McGillivray, and George Simpson pioneered routes through seemingly impassable barricades, making it possible for railroad engineers to contemplate uniting the Atlantic and Pacific by train.

In 1883, the railroad reached Alberta and greatly influenced the development of the national parks system. One day three railway workers chanced upon the Basin Hot Springs near Banff. So that all Canadians could enjoy the health benefits of the springs, a large area around them was set aside by the Canadian government as a park reserve in 1885. In 1887, Rocky Mountains Park, later renamed Banff, was established as

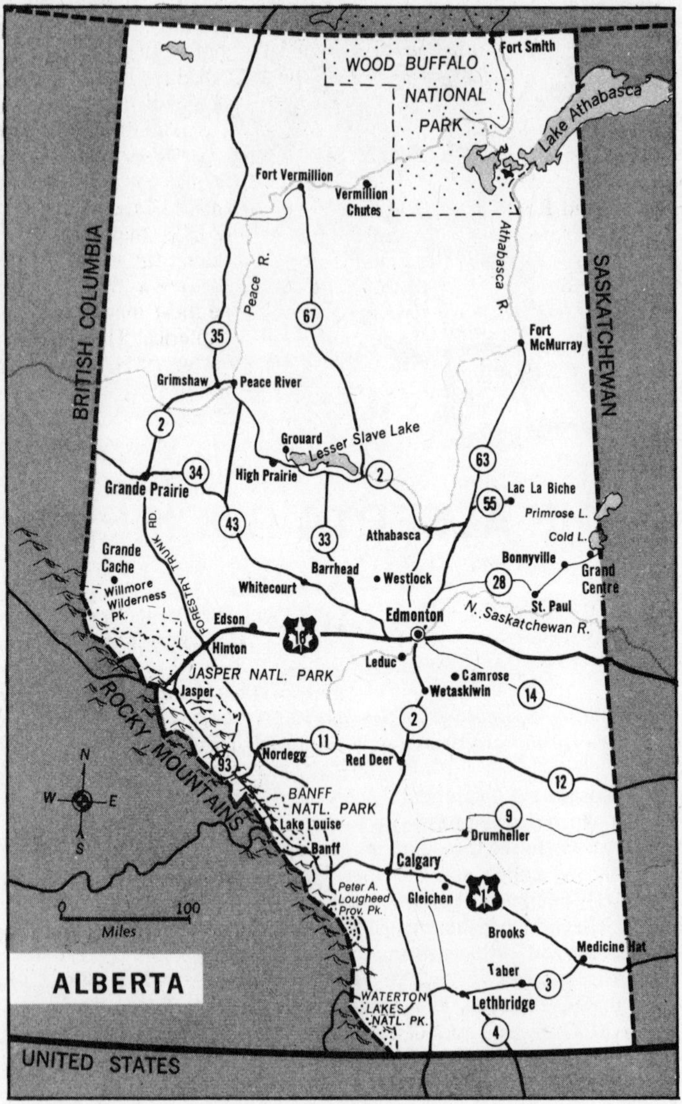

WOOD BUFFALO
NATIONAL
PARK
Fort Smith
Lake Athabasca
Fort Vermillion
Vermillion Chutes
Athabasca R.
Peace R.
BRITISH COLUMBIA
SASKATCHEWAN
35
67
Fort McMurray
Grimshaw
Peace River
2
Grouard
Lesser Slave Lake
63
34
Grande Prairie
High Prairie
2
Lac La Biche
55
Primrose L.
Cold L.
43
33
Athabasca
Grande Cache
FORESTRY TRUNK RD.
Barrhead
Westlock
Bonnyville
Grand Centre
Willmore Wilderness Pk.
Whitecourt
28
St. Paul
Edson
16
Edmonton
N. Saskatchewan R.
Hinton
Leduc
JASPER NATL. PARK
Camrose
Jasper
Wetaskiwin
14
ROCKY MOUNTAINS
2
11
Nordegg
93
Red Deer
12
N
W
E
S
BANFF
NATL. PARK
Lake Louise
9
Drumheller
Banff
Calgary
Peter A. Lougheed Prov. Pk.
Gleichen
1
0
100
Miles
Brooks
Medicine Hat
ALBERTA
Taber
3
WATERTON LAKES NATL. PK.
Lethbridge
4
UNITED STATES

Canada's first national park. Jasper became a national park in 1907, with the opening of Canada's second, more northerly, transcontinental line. Today's travelers can recreate much of the romantic history of exploration, but with considerably less hardship.

There's a lot to choose from in the Alberta Rockies. The Main Ranges, found in the two major national parks, are of limestone, sandstone, and shale, the oldest rock found in the region. They contain the highest mountains and form the Continental Divide, the watershed for North America and, for many miles, the border between Alberta and British Columbia.

The Front Ranges found in Banff and Jasper parks are composed of thick layers of limestone and shale. They often have a tilted, toothlike appearance and have been folded, like Mt. Rundle, which towers over Banff townsite, and Roche Miette, near the east entrance to Jasper Park.

In the national parks, there are foothills only in a small area in the southeast of Jasper, but the foothills extending along the eastern slopes of the Alberta Rockies—outside of the parklands—are a joy to explore.

Finally, Alberta has the Columbia Icefield, the most magnificent and largest glacier in the subarctic interior of North America. The last major glacial advance ended about 10,000 years ago, but you'd be forgiven for thinking it's still going on in Alberta. There are many active icefields and glaciers in the area, particularly in the main ranges along the Icefields Parkway.

CALGARY

Calgary lies among picturesque foothills and ranches at the edge of the Canadian Rockies. The "shining mountains" are nearly always in view from the city, as magnificent and intriguing to today's travelers as they were to the earliest explorers. To the east, rolling prairies march off into the distance, golden wheat fields waving in the breeze. To the southwest lie the "badlands" and desert areas, where dinosaurs used to roam and fossils of previously unknown species are still being found. To the north is a unique aspen parkland.

The landscape around Calgary was shaped by ice sheets and glaciers, the last of which receded a mere 10,000 years ago. Evidence of this movement is visible in the "erratics train," a series of huge rocks left behind when the ice melted. The most famous of these is The Big Rock near Okotoks, southwest of the city. Geologists say this erratic rode a glacier from Jasper, hundreds of miles away.

Though Calgary is over a hundred years old, it has only recently come of age. The North West Mounted Police are usually credited with having established Calgary by building a fort at the confluence of the Bow and Elbow rivers in 1875. Of course, Indians, most recently the Blackfoot tribes, had inhabited the area for centuries before. The Blackfoot depended on bison (buffalo) for their food, clothing, and shelter, following huge herds that used to darken the prairies. With the introduction to the native people of horses in the 1750s, bison were eventually wiped out, and along with them the nomadic lifestyle of the Blackfoot Indians.

Anthony Henday, who arrived in 1754, was the first white man to set foot in Alberta. He was an employee of the Hudson's Bay Company, which

Calgary—Points of Interest

1) Calgary Tower
2) Olympic Interpretive Center
3) Convention Center
4) Glenbow Museum
5) Calgary Centre for the Performing Arts
6) Visitors Information
7) Fort Calgary
8) Calgary Zoo and Dinosaur Park
9) Sam Livingston Fish Hatchery
10) Inglewood Bird Sanctuary
11) Olympic Saddledome
12) Exhibition Grounds and Stampede Park
13) Reader Rock Garden
14) Devonian Gardens
15) Energeum
16) Planetarium
17) Calgary Olympic Park
18) McMahon Stadium
19) Jubilee Auditorium
20) Patrick Burns Memorial Garden
21) Calgary Airport

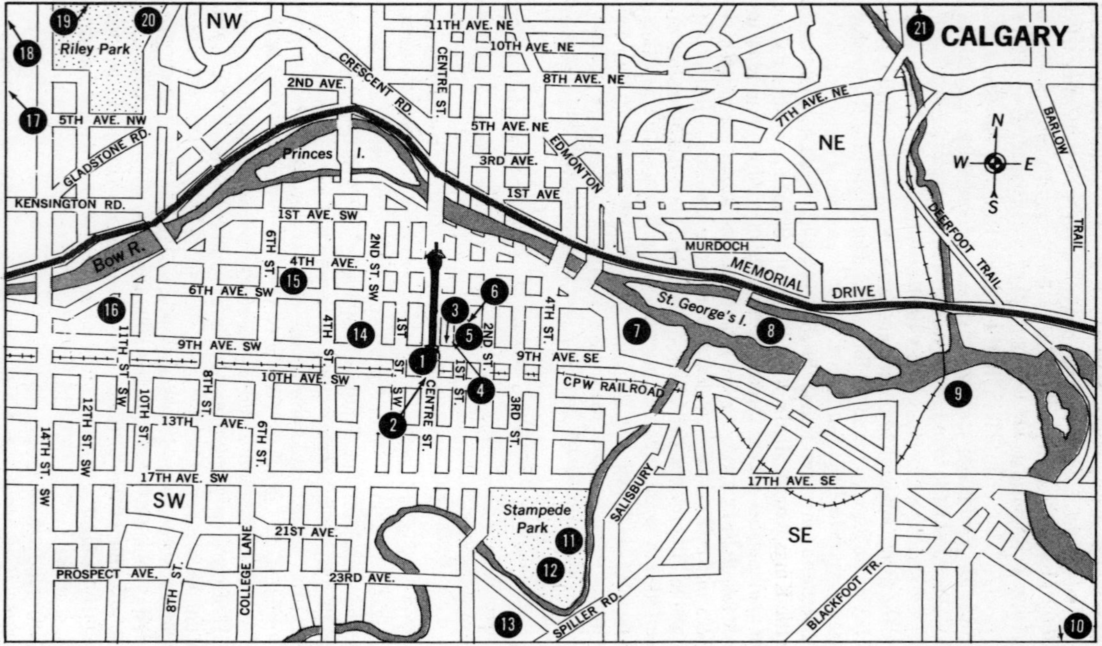

had trading rights in Rupert's Land, the name given to all the territory from the Rockies to Hudson's Bay. Trading outposts were established by both the Hudson's Bay and the rival North West Company, for gathering furs from the Indians, at a time when beaver pelts, not coins, were accepted currency.

Mapmakers and missionaries came next. Cartographer David Thompson was probably the first white man to pass through the site of Calgary, following the Bow River toward the mountains. Later came the survey teams for the Canadian Pacific Railway. Settlers and ranchers were attracted in huge numbers when the transcontinental rail tracks reached Calgary in 1883.

Alberta became cow country when the bison were gone, and the new "Cattle Kings," most of whom were of British origin, built opulent mansions and ranches which stretched to hundreds of thousands of acres. Every fall, the cattle were driven from the foothills to Calgary, which became a major meat-packing center and "cow town." Several sites from that era tell the story: Cochrane Ranch on Hwy. 1A can be visited on the way to the mountains; Bow Valley Ranche, once owned by cattle magnate Pat Burns, is in Fish Creek Park, in the south of the city; the stockyards are still in business, east of the downtown area. Nearby are the Calgary Stampede Grounds, where the first rodeo took place in 1912. American cowboy Guy Weadick managed to sell his dream of "the Last and Best Great Wild West Frontier Days Celebration" to the four most influential Calgary businessmen of the time. The willing backers are now immortalized in the name of the Big Four Building. Today, cowboys compete in rodeo events for half a million dollars worth of prizes, and the Stampede has spilled over into a two-week citywide western celebration that attracts a million visitors every year.

Early Calgary was a makeshift affair of tents and shanties, most of which were destroyed by a fire in 1886. The beautiful buildings which replaced them were largely of sandstone quarried from the Bow River valley. In more recent years these have fallen prey to bulldozers, as the fever for new and shiny skyscrapers has gripped the city.

Wealth from oil and gas discoveries has brought problems as well as people, business, and money. Today, affluence may not be as great as during the last oil boom of the late 70s and early 80s, but the quality of life has not slackened greatly, and the pace of daily existence has—mercifully—tapered off. Fortunately, all the spin-offs of more affluent days remain for Calgarians and visitors alike.

Exploring Calgary

Central Calgary is a modern affair of high rises and glass edifices, headquarters for hundreds of energy-related and computer companies. For a bird's-eye view of the city, start at the Calgary Tower on 9th Ave. at Centre St. From the top you can appreciate Calgary's location, between prairies and mountains, grasslands and forest. Absorb the scenery as you enjoy a meal or a drink in the revolving restaurant at the top.

In the same block of Palliser Square are the Via Rail station, the grand old CP Palliser Hotel, and the Calgary Olympic Centre. Cross the street to the Glenbow Museum on 8th Ave. to take in the history of the area and Western Canada.

One block east, on 8th Ave., is the Centre for Performing Arts. Two heritage buildings adjoin it: the Calgary Public Building and the Burns Building, which houses the Calgary Tourism and Convention Bureau. Take a public tour of the complex from the centre. In the block beyond is the brand-new, gleaming city hall, abutting the tiny sandstone structure it replaced. On the other side of 7th Ave. is the main public library.

Turning west on 8th Ave., wander along Stephen Avenue Mall, a pedestrian area with stores, open-air cafes, free entertainment, and lots of colorful people. At 3d St. W. is the welcome greenery of the extensive Devonian Gardens on the third floor of Toronto Dominion Square, a mall and office complex.

Calgary's most popular city park is Prince's Island, on the Bow River at the fringe of downtown. At lunch hour, it teems with joggers, cyclists, and strollers. During the summer, a series of outdoor events and festivals takes place here, among them the folk and jazz festivals in August.

Chinatown, concentrated just east of Centre St. south of the Bow River, is a stone's throw from downtown. Chinese restaurants and specialty shops abound. Calgary has the third-largest Chinese community in Canada.

Catch the light rail transit or bus on 7th Ave., which is open only to public transport. Go west to 11th St. W. to reach the Calgary Centennial Planetarium and Science Centre. Budding scientists can have a lot of fun at the nearby Energeum, a museum of energy resources, on 5th Av. at 6th St. SW.

Going east on 9th Ave. from downtown, visit the historic Mounted Police Headquarters at Fort Calgary. A little farther on is the Calgary Zoo and Prehistoric Park, situated on St. George's Island in the Bow River; it's easiest to reach the zoo by the train from 7th Ave. Continuing on 9th Ave. to 20 A St. SE, relax and walk in the natural surroundings of Inglewood Bird Sanctuary.

Heritage Park, in the southwest of Calgary, can be reached via Macleod Trail and Heritage Dr. In summer, a pleasure steamboat makes sailing trips on Glenmore Reservoir. Much further south is Fish Creek Provincial Park, of interest to both cultural and natural history. It has the Bow Valley Ranche, a great-blue-heron colony, and a man-made lake for swimming. Reach the park either by Macleod Trail and Canyon Meadows Rd. or by Deerfoot Trail to Bow Bottom Rd.

When you're leaving town to go west to the mountains, stop off at Canada Olympic Park at the city limits, where there are facilities for bobsledding, luge, ski-jumping, and downhill skiing.

PRACTICAL INFORMATION FOR CALGARY

WHEN TO GO. Alberta is dry and sunny year-round, earning it the name "Sunshine Province." In Calgary, the weather can be surprisingly pleasant in winter, especially when a welcome "chinook" blows in from the west. The "chinook" wind comes across the Rockies, the air warming dramatically as it sweeps down from the mountains, melting the snow in its path. Sometimes it's possible to cycle in shorts in Calgary parks in midwinter, when there's lots of snow only an hour away in the mountains.

Dramatic temperature changes, and, some say, emotional changes, accompany the chinook, which can cause rises of up to 45 degrees in an hour! From the city, the coming chinook announces itself as a huge grey-blue arch of cloud just east of the Rockies.

HOW TO GET THERE. By air. Calgary has a modern international airport in the northeast of the city. Airlines include: *AeroMexico* (800–237–6639), *Air Canada* (265–9555), *America West* (800–247–5692), *American Airlines* (236–8880), *Canadian Airlines* (235–1161), *Cascade Airways* (236–5863), *Continental* (800–525–0280), *Delta* (265–7610), *Eastern* (236–2833), *Lufthansa* (294–0353), *Northwest Territorial Airways* (250–3972), *Pan Am* (264–0346), *Southern Frontier* (250–3842), *Time Air* (800–552–8007), and *United* (800–265–4873).

By train. *Via Rail* passenger station is behind the Calgary Tower, 131 9th Ave. SW. For schedules of arrivals and departures, call 265–8033.

By bus. *Greyhound* has five buses daily from Banff. The bus station is at 850 16th St. SW, just off Bow Trail and 9th Av. W. Call 260–0877 or 265–9111 for schedules.

By car. Calgary is situated on Canada's TransCanada Highway (Route 1), which runs from coast to coast. Major highways radiate from the city and link easily with other provinces and the United States.

ACCOMMODATIONS. Hotels and motels in Calgary run the gamut from five-star to fleabag. Our categories for double-occupancy rooms are as follows: *Super Deluxe,* over $125; *Deluxe,* $100–$125; *Expensive,* $80–$100; *Moderate,* $50–$80; and *Inexpensive,* under $50.

Super Deluxe

Delta Bow Valley Inn. 209 4th Ave. SE, T2G 0C6 (266–1980 or 800–268–1133). Downtown, with pool, sauna, Jacuzzi, entertainment, dancing, wheelchair facilities.

Palliser Hotel. 133 9th Ave. SW, T2P 2M3 (262–1234 or 800–268–9411). Grand Canadian Pacific hotel, right next to the train station and right downtown, with dining, Boulevard Cafe, deli, wheelchair facilities. Kids under 14 free.

Skyline Hotel. 110 9th Ave. SE, T2G 5A6 (266–7331). Downtown, with rooms for handicapped, limousine service, pool, sauna, whirlpool, dining in *Trader's.*

Westin Hotel. 4th Ave. at 3d St. SW, T2P 2S6 (266–1611 or 800–228–3000). Pool, sauna, whirlpool, wheelchair facilities. Two lounges and restaurants. Children under 18 free.

Deluxe

International Hotel. 220 4th Ave. SW, T2P 0H5 (265–9600, 800–223–0888, or 800–661–8627). Downtown, with dining, lounge.

Expensive

Chateau Airport. 2001 Airport Rd. NE, T2E 6Z8. (291–2600 or 800–268–9411). Adjoining the airport, with exercise room, pool, sauna, Jacuzzi, entertainment, wheelchair facilities.

Stanley Park Inn. 4206 Macleod Trail T2G 2R7 (287–2700). This comfortable place has airport limousine service. There is no charge for youngsters under 18 sharing room. Floors are available for nonsmokers.

Moderate

Calgary Centre Inn. 202 4th Ave. SW, T2P 0H5 (262–7091 or 800–661–1463). Downtown, with pool, casino, beer hall. Children under 18 stay free.

Motel Village. TransCanada Hwy. and Crowchild Trail NW. Many motels in this small area offer competitive rates.

Sandman Hotel. 888 7th Ave. SW, T2P 3V3 (237–8626 or 800–663–6900). Fitness club, pool, Jacuzzi, sauna. Children under 18 free.

Stampeder Inn. 3828 Macleod Trail T2G 2R2 (243–5531). Pool, whirlpool, wheelchair facilities.

Westgate Motor Hotel/Flag Inn. 3440 Bow Trail SW, T3C 2E6 (249–3181 or 800–661–1460). Nightclub, large beer hall, wheelchair facilities, near big mall.

York Hotel. 636 Centre St. S, T2G 2C7 (262–5581). In the heart of downtown, with large beer hall. Children under 18 free.

Inexpensive

Regis Hotel. 124 7th Ave. E, T2G 0H5 (262–4641). Downtown, with bar. Kids under 12 free.

Relax Inn Airport North. 2750 Sunridge Blvd. NE T1Y 3R2 (291–1260 or 800–661–9563). Near airport, with pool, Jacuzzi, handicapped facilities. Hard to beat for the price.

Relax Inn South. 9206 Macleod Trail S., T2J 0P5 (253–7070 or 800–661–9563). Pool, Jacuzzi, handicapped facilities. Children under 12 free.

BED AND BREAKFASTS. For an economical trip spiced with Alberta's famous hospitality, try a bed and breakfast, or "B & B." All homes are inspected by licensed B&B agencies, and many offer babysitting, extra meals, or laundry facilities. Rates are generally in the *Inexpensive* category. For further information contact:

Alberta Bed & Breakfast. 4327 86th St., Edmonton, AB, T6K 1A9 (462–8885). The personal approach to travel in Alberta. They can book circle tours from Calgary to Banff, Lake Louise, Columbia Icefields, Jasper, Edmonton, and other mountain areas in Alberta and British Columbia. Directory of hosts costs $3.

Bed and Breakfast Bureau. Box 7094, Station E, Calgary, T3C 3L8 (242–5555). Warm Canadian hospitality in Calgary, Banff, Cochrane, Bragg Creek, and Waterton.

Welcome West Vacation Ltd. 1320 Kerwood Crescent SW, Calgary, T2V 2N6 (258–3373). Hosts are friendly and interested in having you as guests in their homes. Both city and country accommodations.

GUEST RANCHES. These offer a chance to smell new-mown hay, milk a cow, or gather fresh eggs, while enjoying real western hospitality. Price categories are the same as for hotels (see above).

Homeplace Guest Ranch. *Moderate.* Site 2, Box 6, R.R. #1, Priddis, T0L 1W0. Southwest of Calgary in beautiful foothills. Horseback riding year-round. Seasonal activities include hiking, fishing, golfing, sightseeing, sleigh rides, tobogganing, and cross-country skiing.

Mesa Creek Ranch (Dave and Lucille Glaister). *Inexpensive.* R.R. #1, Millarville, T0L 1K0 (931–3573 or 931–3610). Working cattle ranch 28 miles from Calgary in the foothills of the Rockies. Riding, hiking, fishing, and cross-country skiing. Accommodations in log ranch home, and home-cooked meals with the family.

YOUTH HOSTELS. Hostels provide a good way for young people to stay cheaply in Alberta and to meet other shoestring travelers. International Youth Hostel Federation members pay about $5 a night; non-members are charged about a dollar more.

The *Southern Alberta Hostelling Association,* 1414 Kensington Rd. NW T2N 3P9 (283–5551), is an administrative office supplying memberships, reservations, and brochures, as well as the Hostel Shop, an outdoor-equipment store with discounts for members. The **Calgary Youth Hostel,** 520 7th Ave. SE T2G 0J6 (269–8239), accommodates 112. Laundry, snack bar, cooking facilities.

RESTAURANTS. Calgary's lack of a distinctive local cuisine has made its natives very tolerant of a great variety of cooking, with the result that Calgary has far more culinary alternatives to offer than many other cities of its size. Our categories are for two meals with appetizer, exclusive of tax, tip, and drinks: *Expensive,* over $30; *Moderate,* $20–$30; and *Inexpensive,* under $20.

Expensive

Caesar's. 512 4th Av. SW (264–1222). Fine char-broiled Alberta steak, ribs, rack of lamb, and seafood.

Calgary Tower. 101 9th Ave. SW (266–7171). Revolving panorama room gives a 360-degree view of prairies and mountains.

Le Flamboyant. 4018 16th St. SW (287–0060). Hot dishes from creole to curry reflect the mixed nationalities of the French Mauritian restaurateurs.

Owl's Nest. In the Westin Hotel, 4th Ave. and 3d St. SW (266–1611). A good taste of Albertan fare.

Three Green Horns. 503 4th Ave. SW (264–6903). Well-aged, well-prepared Alberta beef.

Traders. In the Skyline Hotel, 110 9th Ave. SE (266–7331). Excellent food to satisfy a variety of tastes.

Moderate

A Touch of Ginger. 514 17th Ave. SW (228–9884). Ginger in everything. Fine Vietnamese cuisine.

Bali, 7. 5308 17th Ave. SW (242–5411). Bali *rijstafel* features 14 selections from the chef.

Boulevard Cafe. In the Palliser Hotel, 133 9th Ave. SW (262–1234). Light fare, great salad bar.

Cafe Ceres. #5, 201 10th St. NW #5 (283–0964). Mediterranean cuisine with a Turkish touch.

Cannery Row. 317 10th Ave. SW (269–8889). Great seafood. Peanut bar; live Dixieland jazz.

Da Guido. 2111 Centre St. N (276–1365). Try the Italian combination plate or the seafood with delicious sauces. Alternatively, ask Guido to fix you up something special!

4 St. Rose. 2116 4th St. SW (228–5377). Popular bar and eating place with a California-style menu. Great salads and pizza; choice of main courses.

Ile de France & Cafe de Paris. 401 9th Ave SW (233–2018). This restaurant has been acquiring a good reputation for French food, and deserves it.

Japanese Village Steakhouse. 10201 Southport Rd. SW (255–1212). Quite far south on Macleod Trail, but you'll be rewarded by the sushi and *teppan,* with impressive and entertaining displays by the chefs.

Mimo, 4909 17th Ave. SE #203 (235–3377). Good Portuguese family fare.

Moti Mahal. 507 17th Ave. SW (228–9990). Gourmet Mughlai cuisine from Northern India.

Olive Grove. Midnapore Mall, Midlake Blvd. SE (256–4610). Way down south, but if you feel like a Middle Eastern feast, worth the trip. Try the seafood pizza to take out.

Pegasus. 101 14th St. SW (229–1231). Best Greek food in town.

Sushi Hiro. 727 5th Ave. SW (233–0605). Perfect for exotic tastebuds. Flying fish eggs and sea urchin are on the menu, along with teryaki.

Yervand's. 1137 17th Ave. SW (245–4136). Chef will specially prepare Swiss or French dishes from the menu while you wait.

Inexpensive

Blackfoot Truck Stop. 1840 9th Ave. (265–5964). It's Canadian, eh! Good, plain food without the frills.

Dragon Pearl. 1223A 9th Ave. SE (233–8810). Consistently good Szechuan dining in older part of town.

Empress Garden. 301 16th Ave. NW (277–2110). Peking-style Chinese fare.

Kingfisher Seafoods and Cafe. 316 3d St. SE (294–1800). Serves only seafood, salad, and bread, but you would, too, if you made them this well.

La Trattoria d'Italia. 3927 Edmonton Trail NE (276–6026). Great pizza to eat in or take out.

Lancaster Building. 304 8th Ave. SW, Second floor (261–2615). Dozens of ethnic food outlets under one roof. Nice spot for lunch.

Mandarin. 1204 17th Ave. SW (245–8979). Hot Szechuan and Hunan dishes.

Sam's Original Deli. 2208 4th Ave. SW. (228–6696). This kosher-style, nicely quaint deli is good for post-show noshing.

Sara's Pyrohy Hut. 1216 Centre St. NE (277–2712). Famed for fresh homemade Ukranian specialities to eat in or take out.

Sizzling Wok. 203 4th St. NW (265–8818). An interesting array of Chinese and Malaysian dishes.

Taj Mahal. 4816 Macleod Trail S (243–6362). New Delhi specialties from northern India.

Ye Olde Pizza Joint. 1006 16th Ave. NW (289–9205). Enjoy pizza by a big open fire or take it out.

LIQUOR LAWS. The legal drinking age is 18. In bars, you are not allowed to drink standing up. Beer, wine, and spirits can be bought at 28 Alberta Liquor Control Board (ALCB) stores around the city. Most stores are open Tues.–Sat. noon–8 P.M.; a few stay open until 10 P.M. Beer is sold at three beer stores in town.

NIGHTLIFE AND BARS. New establishments come and go in Calgary. The area just south of downtown—10th and 11th aves. SW—is currently in vogue among evening carousers. Many establishments have live entertainment.

Body Shoppe Nightclub. 4127 6th St. NE (276–8671). Rock 'n' roll nightly.

Kensington's Deli Cafe. 1414 Kensington Rd. NW (283–0771). Folk and contemporary artists.

Clubhouse. 313 4th St. NE (269–5856). Promotes local rock and new-wave bands and live music for dancing.

Dusty's Barndance and Saloon. 502 11th Ave. SE (263–5343). This is the place to break in your new cowboy boots.

King Edward Hotel. 438 9th Ave. SE (262–1680). Coolest blues in town with blues musicians from all over North America. The action starts late and finishes in the wee hours.

Lucifer's. 609 7th Ave. SW (265–9000). A mainstay for rock-dancing enthusiasts.

Marty's Cafe. 338 17 Ave. SW (228–9227). Marty puts on everything from blues, jazz, rock, and folk to poetry workshops.

National Hotel. 1042 10th Ave. SE (265–5717). Punk, new wave, and occasional out-of-town outrages.

Snicker's Comedy Club. 510 9th Ave. SW (261–8991). Sure to keep you in the holiday spirit.

Ranchman's. 9615 Macleod Trail S (253–1100). A variety of country-music acts to warm the hearts of urban cowboys.

T & T Caribbean Club. 1120 53d Ave. NE # 101C (275–1905). For fans of reggae, steel bands, and dub poets. Authentic Caribbean food in the restaurant downstairs.

The Banke. 125 8th Ave. SW (233–7402). For movers and shakers.

HOW TO GET AROUND. The public transport system is so good that you don't need to drive to get around town. So leave your car at home and enjoy the city on foot, by bus, or by train.

By airporter bus. It runs frequently between downtown hotels and airport. The fare is $5.

By Calgary transit. This public transport system operates bus and C-Train LRT (Light Rail Transit) routes throughout the city. The C-Train routes are from downtown south along Macleod Trail to Anderson Road; northeast to Whitehorn Station, 44th Ave NE; and northwest past the University. The C-Train is free in the downtown core, but fares must be paid outside downtown and on all bus routes. Fares: adults, $1.25; juniors (6–14 years), 75¢. You need exact fare to buy train tickets from ticket vending machines on platforms; no change is given on buses. Transit timetables, maps, route information, tickets, and monthly passes are available from *Calgary Transit Information Centre,* 206 7 Ave. SW (276–7801).

By car. Companies operating from the Calgary Airport and in Banff are *Avis* (250–0763 or 800–268–2310), *Budget* (250–0760 or 800–268–8900), *Hertz* (250–0746 or 800–268–1311), and *Tilden* (250–0770 or 800–663–9822).

By taxi. Most give discounts to senior citizens. *Associated Cab* (276–5312), *Checker Cabs* (272–1111), *Co-op Taxi* (273–5759), *Mayfair Taxi* (255–6555/253–1153), *Prestige Cabs* (250–5911), *Red Top Cabs* (250–9222), *Shamrock Taxi* (248–5555), *Stampeder Cab* (250–2880), *Yellow Cab* (250–8311).

TOURIST INFORMATION. *Calgary Tourist and Convention Bureau Hospitality Centres* are located at: Burns Building, 237 8th Ave. SE (263–8510); 1300 6th Ave. SW; Calgary Tower, Centre St. and 9th Ave.; Calgary International Airport, Arrivals area.

Travel Alberta, Box 2500, Edmonton T5J 2Z4 (800–661–8888 from Canada and continental USA; 800–222–6501 in Alberta; 427–4321 in Edmonton), gives year-round information on travel opportunities, conditions, campgrounds, accommodation, ski reports, attractions, and events. For those who can make it to Edmonton, personal counseling is available daily May 9–Oct. 15, 8:15 A.M.–8 P.M.; 8:15 A.M.–4:30 P.M., Mon.–Fri. Oct. 15–May 8, 8:15 A.M.–4:30 P.M., with taped reports after hours.

TOURS AND SPECIAL-INTEREST SIGHTSEEING. Guided bus tours of Calgary's finest attractions are conducted on luxury motor coaches, with pick-up and return to major hotels. For information, call *Brewster City Tours* (237–5252).

Calgary Centre for Performing Arts. 205 8th Ave. (294–7455). Links the past and present, incorporating the historic Burns and Public buildings. Concert halls and theaters on site.

Calgary Tower. 101 9th Ave. SW (266–7171). From the observation deck or revolving restaurant of this 626-foot (191-meter) tower, you can look east across the prairies or west to the mountains. Open daily 7:30 A.M.–midnight; except Sun. until 11 P.M. only. Adults $2.75, children (12 and under) $1, seniors $1.25.

Centennial Planetarium. 11th St. at 7th Ave. SW (264–2030). Entertaining star shows blend special effects with astronomy in the 360-degree Star Chamber. Open Tues.–Sun.; for times call 264–4060. Children's matinee shows on Sat.–Sun., 2:30 P.M.

Chinatown. A 10-minute stroll north from the Calgary Tower at 9th Avenue and Centre Street Chinese immigrants who came to western Canada a century ago to work on the railroads stayed to establish restaurants, grocery, and gift shops now operated by new generations. Browse or enjoy a meal.

Sam Livingstone Fish Hatchery. 1440 17A St. SE, off Blackfoot Trail at 17th Ave. SE. Everything you might ever want to know about the fish species found in Alberta. Produces seven million fish yearly to stock Alberta's rivers. Free.

Spruce Meadows. Three miles (5 km) on Hwy. 22X off Macleod Trail (256–4977). A horse-lover's heaven, with world-class show jumping and training facilities for young riders. Tournaments held June–Sept. Visitors welcome; tours available.

Stampede Park. 17th Ave. and 2d St. SE (261–0101). The location of the Calgary Stampede every July, including rodeos, entertainment, chuckwagon races, Indian dancing and displays, carnivals, and midway fairs. During the rest of the year, the Roundup Centre and Big Four and Agriculture Buildings have regular consumer and trade shows. At the Corral and the Olympic Saddledome, there are sporting events and rock concerts, as well as Calgary Flames ice hockey.

PARKS AND GARDENS. For such a boreal metropolis, Calgary is blessed with an extraordinary variety of green spaces, large and small, indoor and outdoor. They're great places to hike, cycle, picnic, barbeque, cross-country ski, or just relax. For detailed information, call the *Parks/Recreation Department* at 268–5211; to join nature walks, call 268–4718.

The **Devonian Gardens,** (268–5207) are indoors on the third level of Toronto Dominion Square, between 2d and 3d streets SW on 8th Ave. They include 2½ acres of greenery with pathways, pools, fountains, benches, sculptures, art exhibits, and frequent entertainment during weekday lunch hours. Equipped with ramps for the handicapped. Open daily 9 A.M.–9 P.M. Free.

Parks in the downtown area include **Prince's Island Park,** where 3d St. SW meets the Bow River; **Central Park,** at 12th Ave. and 2d St. SW, site of the Muttart Gallery; **Century Gardens,** an oasis at 8th Ave. and 8th St. SW; **St. Patrick's Island Park,** connected by a footbridge to Fort Calgary, 750 9th Ave. SE; **Inglewood Bird Sanctuary,** on the Bow River pathway or east on 9th Ave. to 20A St. SE. (269–6688). All are free.

Other parks are less central, but easily reached:

Beaver Dam Flats. Take Glenmore Trail east to 18th St. SE, then follow Lynnview Rd. SE.

Bowmont Park. Take Crowchild Trail NW, then turn left on Sarcee Trail to Silverview Dr. or Silver Valley Blvd. NW.

Bowness Park. Take Bowness Road to 85th St. NW, then turn left on 48th Ave. NW.

Confederation Park. Off 14th St. NW at 24th Ave. NW.

Edworthy Park and **Lowery Gardens.** Take Bow Trail west and turn right on 45th St. SW, left on Spruce Dr.

Glenmore Park. Take Crowchild Trail south into park, or take Glenmore Trail and turn left on 37th St. SW. From the south, take 14th St. SW, right on 90th Ave. SW, right at 24th St. SW.

Inglewood Bird Sanctuary (269–6688). Take 9th Ave. east and turn right on 20A St.

Nose Hill. Take 14th St. north. Access off 64th St. NW and several streets beyond.

Pearce Estate. Follow 9th Ave. and 17th Ave. east to 17A St. SE.

Riley Park. Take 10th St. NW, turn left on 5th Ave., then right on 12th St.

Sandy Beach. Follow Elbow Dr. south and turn right on Riverdale Ave. SW.

Shouldice Park. Take Bowness Rd. west and turn left at 48th St. NW.

Stanley Park. Follow Macleod Trail south and turn right on 42d Ave. SW.

Weaselhead. Take Glenmore Trail west and turn left on 37th St. SW and right at 66th Ave SW.

ZOOS. Calgary Zoo, 1300 Zoo Rd. NE (265–9310 or 262–8144). On St. George's Island, five minutes from downtown on the northeast LRT route. One of Canada's largest and best zoos, with over 200 indoor and outdoor exhibits, children's petting zoo, tropical aviary, and many endangered species. Underwater viewing of polar bears and seals; special lighting for viewing nocturnal animals. Special events year-round. Restaurant, gift shop, picnic sites. Open daily, in summer 10 A.M.–7 P.M.; in winter 10 A.M.–5 P.M. Adults $5.50, children $1.75.

PROVINCIAL PARKS. Fish Creek Provincial Park (278–5640) is a 2,800-acre natural area in a river valley in the southern part of the city, with many recreational opportunities, but no camping. Take Deerfoot Trail south and Bow Bottom Rd. Other access from Canyon Meadows Dr., Macleod Trail S or 37th St. SW.

Two other provincial parks a short drive from the city are **Big Hill Springs** (day use only), west on Crowchild Trail towards Cochrane; and **Bragg Creek** (camping available), west on Hwy. 22X or Richmond Rd.

CAMPING. Here are some local facilities: **Bow Bend Trailer Park,** 5227 13th Ave. NW (288–2161); **Bow Ridge RV Park,** 8220 Bow Ridge Cres. NW (288–4441); **KOA,** at west city limits on Hwy. 1 (288–0411), with handicapped facilities; **Sunalta Trailer Park,** Hwy. 1 at Valley Ridge exit (288–7911), with handicapped facilities.

OUTDOOR ACTIVITIES. The Calgary area has many fine private and public **golf** courses. For information about the six City of Calgary courses, call 269–2531. Other courses in the city welcoming the public area:

Douglasdale Golf Course, 11825 24th St. SE (279–7212); *Highland Golf and Country Club,* 4304 3d St. NW (277–8681); *Inglewood Golf and Curling Club,* 34th Ave. and Barlow Trail SE (272–3949); *Shaw-Nee Golf Club,* 146th Ave. and 8th St. SW (256–1444); *Valley Ridge Golf Club,* off Route 1 at west city limits (288–9457).

Tennis courts in the city parks are free. There are also indoor courts.

There are many miles of beautiful **jogging** trails in city parks and along the rivers. For pathways map, call 268–5211.

Over 100 miles of **cycling** pathways link the parks, providing days of exploration within the city. Maps showing pathways, residential areas, and repair shops, and giving regulations and information, are available free; call 268–5211.

Calgary's rivers and dams provide excellent opportunities for **sailing, canoeing,** and **kayaking;** instruction is readily available. A boating brochure with map is available free; call 268–5211.

Befitting its cowtown image, Calgary has numerous **horseback-riding** schools and stables, as well as horse rentals, by the hour, day, and longer periods.

Cross-country skiing is available in all the city parks and along summer cycle routes, giving plenty of scope for short or day-long trips.

DOWNHILL SKIING. Lyon Mountain. Bragg Creek (949–3335). Take Route 1 or 8 to Route 22; 30 miles (50 km) southwest of Calgary. Beautiful views of prairies and mountains. Five lifts; mostly novice to intermediate runs.

Paskapoo Ski Area. Calgary (288–4112 or 288–2632). Just west of town on Route 1. The location of several Olympic events. Terrain suitable for all levels. Ski-jumping, luge, and bobsled facilities. Six lifts. Open mid-Nov–mid-March.

FISHING: People come from all over the world to fish for brown and rainbow trout in the Bow River, right within Calgary's city limits. "Catch-and-release" is encouraged. Angling permits required for all, except for children under 16. For more information on regulations, seasons, species, and licenses, contact *Alberta Energy and Natural Resources,* Fish and Wildlife Division, 200 Sloane Square, 5920 1A St., Calgary, T2H 0G1 (297–6423). Several outfitters offer guiding services:

Alberta Drift (J. Kim Dayman), 39 VanHorne Crescent NE, Calgary, T2E 6H2 (291–4162 or 289–3090).

Great Waters Alberta (John and Bethe Andreason), Box 391, Station G, Calgary, T3A 2G3 (239–2520).

Silvertip Outfitters, Box 515, Midnapore, T0L 1J0 (256–5018).

SPECTATOR SPORTS. Calgary's NHL hockey team—the Flames—is its residents' dominant obsession during the winter months. Its CFL football team—the Stampede—and its minor-league baseball team take up the slack when hockey season's over. Keep an eye out for curling competitions all year round.

SEASONAL EVENTS. May. *International Horse Show.*

July. The world-famous *Calgary Stampede* is a wild 10-day festival, starting with a parade. Highlights are the rodeo events, chuck wagon races, and Indian village events. There are concerts, shows, agricultural exhibitions, casinos, and an amusement park. Calgarians join in the Western spirit with great gusto—everyone dresses Western, from oil executives to gas-pump attendants. For information and tickets, write the Calgary Exhibition and Stampede, Box 2890, Calgary (403–261–0101).

August. *Calgary Folk Festival* and *Calgary Jazz Festival,* both open-air events at Prince's Island on the Bow River.

HISTORIC SITES AND HOUSES. Calgary's history is the history of westward expansion, gold, and the Royal Canadian Mounted Police, in the 19th century, and its historical buildings reflect and understandable pride in that period.

Alberta Historical Resources Foundation, 102 8th Ave. SE (297–7320), has information about historical buildings in the city and province, and maps with a self-guided historical walking tour of the downtown area. Open weekdays, 9 A.M.–5 P.M.

Bow Valley Ranche. Fish Creek Provincial Park (278–5640). Take Deerfoot Trail south, then Bow Bottom Rd. past Canyon Meadows Dr. Anglo-Canadian ranch house built in 1896. Interpretive tours available. Museum in Visitors' Centre covers over 8,000 years of local history. Open Mon.–Fri., 10 A.M.–noon and 1 P.M.–4 P.M.; Sat.–Sun., 10 A.M.–5 P.M. Free.

Fort Calgary. 750 9th Ave. (290–1875). On the site of an 1875 North West Mounted Police post at the confluence of the Bow and Elbow rivers. A 40-acre native prairie park on the river edge shows the outline of the fort. Open Wed.–Sun., 10 A.M.–6 P.M. Free.

Heritage Park. 1900 Heritage Dr. SW (255–1182 or 252–1858). Take #53 bus. A 50-acre reconstructed town site on the edge of Glenmore Reservoir, portraying the Canadian west before 1914. Take the old steam engine to visit the various parts of the site, including Hudson's Bay Company fort, a working grain mill, newspaper, bakery, ice cream parlor, hotel, school, and oil rig. Open daily in summer till 6 P.M. Admission: Adults $5; children, $3.25. For an extra charge, take a cruise on the reservoir in a paddlewheel steamboat.

MUSEUMS. Alberta Science Centre. Centennial Planetarium, 11 St. at 7th Ave. SW, (294–1141). 30 hands-on exhibits—holograms, zoetropes, and frozen shadows. Open Tues.–Sun., 1:30–8 P.M. Admission: Adults, $2; children over 6, $1.

Energeum. 640 5th Ave. SW (297–4293). Informative energy center established by the Energy Conservation Board shows the history of energy in Alberta through models, video games, and memorabilia—including a pink '58 Buick—from the energy exploration industry. Kids love the hands-on exhibits. Open Mon.–Fri., 10:30 A.M.–4:30 P.M. Free.

Glenbow Museum. 130 9th Ave. SE (264–8300). One of the six major museums in Canada. Visitors can trace the history of the Plains Indians, fur trappers, pioneers, Royal Canadian Mounted Police, the railroad, and the oil industry. Open Tues.–Sun., 10 A.M.–6 P.M. Closed Mon. Adults, $2; students, $1; children under 12, free. No charge on Saturdays.

Grain Academy. Roundup Centre, Stampede Park (263–4594). The story of bringing grain from the field to the table. Open Mon.–Fri., 10 A.M.–4 P.M.; Sat. in summer noon–4 P.M. Free.

Nickle Arts Museum. University of Calgary, 434 Collegiate Blvd. (220–7234). Access from 32d Ave. NW, or by bus #9 or 103 from downtown. Extensive permanent collection of coins of the ancient world. Open Wed.–Sat., 10 A.M.–5 P.M.; Sun., 1–5 P.M. Closed Mon.–Tues. Free.

Regimental Museums. Building B6, Currie Barracks, 4225 Crowchild Trail SW, (242–6610 or 240–7322). Exhibits tell the story of Lord Strathcona's and Princess Patricia's Canadian Light Infantry regiments. Open Mon.–Sat., 9 A.M.–4 P.M.; Sun., noon–5 P.M. Free.

Sarcee People's Museum. 3700 Anderson Rd. SW (238–2677). Model teepee, clothing, and artifacts from the early tribal life of the Sarcee Indians. Open Mon.–Fri., 8 A.M.–4 P.M. Donations accepted.

MUSIC. Popular, jazz, rock and alternative music are played live at many venues around town. Check the *Calgary Herald* newspaper for current events. These radio stations have concert information lines. *CKIK* (244–8882) and *CKXL* (228–9124). See *Nightlife and Bars* above for other venues.

Calgary Centre for Performing Arts. 205 8th Ave. SE (294–7455). Year-round orchestral, theatrical, and variety entertainment, with multilevel retail mall. Centrally located, convenient to downtown hotels.

Calgary Early Music Society. At Mount Royal College, 4828 Richard Rd. SW (288–8348) Gives workshops and concerts.

Calgary Opera Association, Bay 3, 6025 12th St. SE (252–9905). Regular productions yearly; in 1988, *Porgy and Bess.*

Calgary Philharmonic Orchestra. The Centre (294–7420).

Calgary Renaissance Singers and Players. University of Calgary Theatre (220–7201).

Festival Chorus. The Centre (240–6996).

Jazz Calgary. 2500 University Dr. NW (270–3609). Information on jazz in town. Hosts annual two-day outdoor festival in Aug. in Princes' Island Park.

Lyric Chamber Players. Mount Royal College (240–6864).

Mount Royal Woodwind Quintet. Leacock Theatre, Mount Royal College (240–6862). Regular concerts on campus.

Southern Alberta Opera Association. Jubilee Auditorium (262–7286). Presents three shows a year.

THEATER. Calgary has a surprising array of theater possibilities, and prices are generally lower than in most major cities.

Alberta Theatre Projects. In the Centre (294–7475). Performs five plays a year.

Glenmore Dinner Theatre. 2720 Glenmore Trail SE (236–2060). Theater and dining.

Lunchbox Theater. 205 5th Ave. SW (265–4292). Lunch-hour entertainment downtown.

One Yellow Rabbit Performance Troupe. 637 11th Ave. SW (264–8131). Nonmainstream drama and street theater.

Pleiades Theatre. In the Centennial Planetarium, 11th St. at 7th Ave. SW (264–2030). Specializes in live mystery theater and comedy. Open Wed.–Sun., with weekend matinees.

Pumphouse Theatre. 2140 9th Ave. SW (263–0079). Regular schedule of plays.

Stage West Theatre and Restaurant. 727 42d Ave. SE (243–6642). Combines drama with dining.

Storybook Theatre. 2140 9th Ave. SW (277–6195). Weekend matinees at the Pumphouse.

Theatre Calgary. The Centre (294–7440). Two series of popular and classic drama.

DANCE. The **Alberta Ballet Company** makes regular visits to the centre.

Calgary City Ballet (233–7010) has a new home in the old CN Station and a rejuvenated schedule of performances.

Sun-Ergos Theatre and Dance, 700 9th St. NW #2205 (264–4621), gives regular performances around the city.

GALLERIES. Calgary is hardly the Arles of the 1980s, but artists of ability do continue to flock here, primarily to take advantage of the area's beautiful scenery. Be on the lookout for Inuit (Eskimo) arts and crafts.

Alberta College of Art Gallery. 1407 14th Ave. NW (284–7600). Exhibits by international artists, students, and faculty. Open Tues.–Sat. 10 A.M.–6 P.M., Sun. noon–5 P.M.

Centre Eye Photography Gallery. 1717 7th St. SW (244–4816). Photographer-run gallery featuring local, national, and international artists. Open Tues.–Sat., noon–5 P.M.

Cottage Crafts Gifts and Fine Arts. 6503 Elbow Dr. SW (252–3797). Wide selection of Inuit and Indian art and Canadiana—soapstone, graphics, tapestries, and the like. Closed Mon.

Drum Dancer. 617 11th Ave. SW (263–5262). Inuit sculpture and prints.

Muttart Gallery in Central Park. 12th Ave. at 3rd St. SW (266–2764). Shows contemporary Albertan artists. Open Tues.–Fri., noon–9 P.M.; Sat., 10 A.M.–5 P.M.; Sun., 1:30–5 P.M.

Off Centre Centre. 3rd Floor, 118 8th Ave. SE (233–2399). Artist-run space always doing something different from the mainstream.

Pitavik Galleries. 919a 17th Ave. SW (245–5747). Canadian arts, crafts, jewelry, sculpture, and ceramics.

Prairie Accent Gallery. 101 10th St. NW (283–1635). Specializes in the work of wildlife artists.

Rocky Mountain Art Galleries. 821 14th St. NW (283–9432). Specializes in the art of Robert Bateman.

Westlands Art Gallery. 417 8th Ave. SE (237–5053). Near downtown. Good selection of Indian art of the Great Plains.

SHOPPING. There are many unusual stores and galleries around 17th Ave. SW and in the 10th St. NW/Kensington Rd. area. The Stephen Avenue Mall, a pedestrians-only section of 8th Ave., caters to hard-core shoppers. There are plenty of eateries along these streets to cater to those who shop until they're about to keel over. Items to look for in Calgary include western wear with a Canadian flavor.

Alberta Boots. 614 10th Ave. SW (263–4623). The place to get Canadian-made cowboy boots.

Global Village Gifts. 220 Crowchild Trail NW (270–0631). Handicrafts from many Third-World countries.

Hostel Shop. 1414 Kensington Rd. NW #203 (283–8311). Specialty store for mountain people and travelers. Rents camping and outdoor equipment. Discounts for IYHF members.

Mountain Equipment Co-op. 112 11th Ave. SE (269–2420). A nonprofit enterprise selling outdoor recreation clothes and equipment at low prices.

CHILDREN'S ACTIVITIES. Calgary has a combination of tourist and everyday facilities to keep children entertained. Remember that aside from "children's attractions" as such, the city's many parks are attractive venues for general romping about.

Bonzai Water Slide. 8306 Horton Rd., at 8500 Macleod Trail S (255–3426). Open June 15–Sept. 7. Admission: $8, full day; $5.50, half-day.

Calaway Park. (240–3822). A large amusement park, half an hour west of Calgary on Route 1. Turn off at Springbank Rd. Open late May–late Nov. Admission: $11.95 adults, $8.95 children 3–6, includes all rides; general pass with rides extra, $6.95.

Loose Moose Theatre Company, 2003 McKnight Blvd. NE (291–LMTC). Has children's matinees. Tickets $3.

Prehistoric Park. At the Calgary Zoo (see above). A fascinating reconstruction in eight landscaped acres of Alberta in the dinosaur era, with lakes, swamps, badlands, and all. Various prehistoric animals have been reproduced life-size to amaze and intrigue you at every turn. Free with zoo admission.

Storybook Theatre. Pumphouse Theatre, 2140 9th Ave. SW (234–7737 or 277–6195). Puts on evening and weekend matinee performances for kids. Tickets about $4.

Surf City Waterslide Park. Chestermere Lake (272–9200). At the intersection of routes 1 and 1A east of Calgary. Open mid-June–early Sept. Admission: $8, full day; $5.50, half day.

BANFF AND BANFF NATIONAL PARK

The town of Banff is one of the most beautiful mountain resorts in the world. Banff National Park attracts over three million visitors a year, who come to climb mountains, ski, hike, cycle, ride horses, fish, canoe, watch wildlife, take photos, look at the scenery, and breathe in the fresh mountain air. It's not surprising that Banff is geared almost totally to offering visitors a memorable vacation.

Exploring Banff

Winter or summer, the best way to see Banff is from above. An eight-minute gondola ride up Sulphur Mountain will put you among the peaks. The lift up Mt. Norquay also gives a privileged view of the Rockies. Farther afield, the gondola rides up to Sunshine and Lake Louise are highly recommended.

For more summer scenery, cruise Lake Minnewanka, then visit the mining ghost town of Bankhead nearby or get close to plains and wood bison in the Buffalo Paddock. Finish off the day with a soak in the Upper Hot Pools or take in a concert by world-class performers at the Banff Centre.

In winter, whatever else you do, go skiing. These are some of the most famous ski slopes in the world, and for good reasons. Cross-country terrain is nearly limitless.

Even if you're not staying there, you'll want to visit the Banff Springs Hotel, just to admire the architecture and location. Explore park history at the Cave and Basin Hot Springs and at the several museums in town.

Take a leisurely tour along the edge of Vermilion Lakes, on the western edge of town—a great place to see wildlife. When you're heading for Lake Louise, take the scenic route along the Bow Valley Parkway (Hwy. 1A) to Castle Junction. The turnoff is just west of Banff on the TransCanada Hwy.

PRACTICAL INFORMATION FOR BANFF AND BANFF NATIONAL PARK

HOW TO GET THERE. By air. The nearest international airport is in Calgary. The grass landing strip for small planes at Banff is to be closed down.

By bus. The bus station is at 100 Gopher St., next to the train station on the northwest side of town. Greyhound (762–2286) has 10 buses daily to Banff—five from Vancouver, Lake Louise, and the west, and five from Calgary and points east (two go to Canmore). *Brewster Transport*

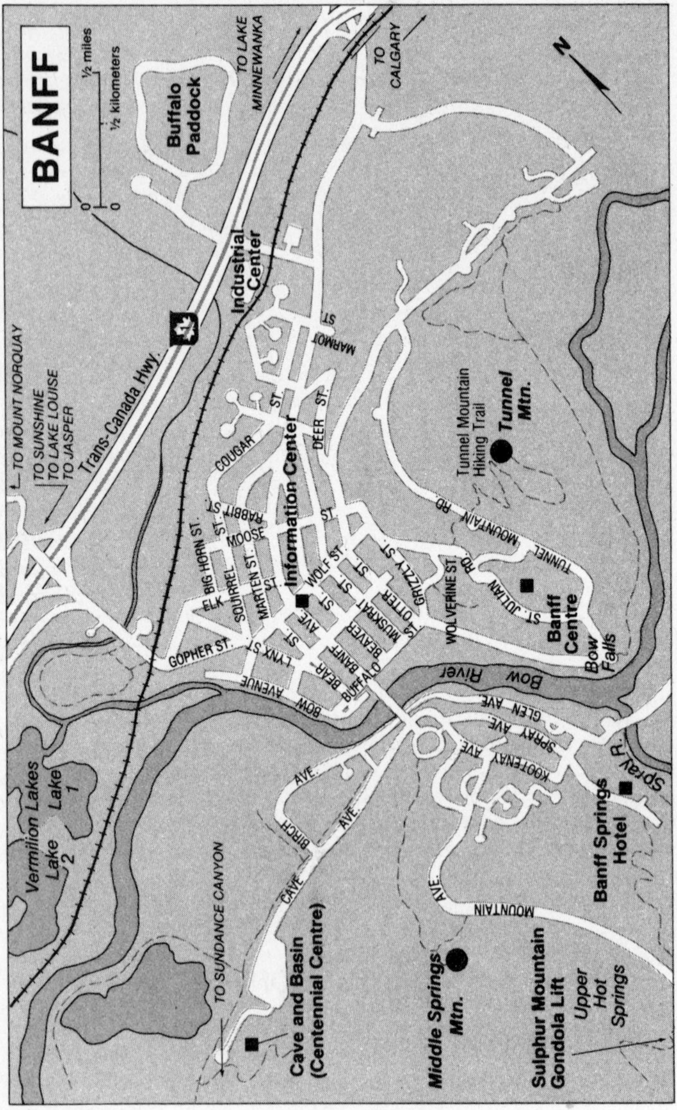
BANFF
½ miles
½ kilometers
N
Buffalo Paddock
TO LAKE MINNEWANKA
TO CALGARY
TO MOUNT NORQUAY
TO SUNSHINE
TO LAKE LOUISE
TO JASPER
Trans-Canada Hwy.
Industrial Center
Information Center
Tunnel Mountain Hiking Trail
Tunnel Mtn.
TUNNEL MOUNTAIN RD.
Banff Centre
Bow Falls
Bow River
Spray R.
Banff Springs Hotel
Vermilion Lakes
Lake 1
Lake 2
TO SUNDANCE CANYON
Cave and Basin (Centennial Centre)
Middle Springs Mtn.
Sulphur Mountain Gondola Lift
Upper Hot Springs
MARMOT ST.
DEER ST.
COUGAR ST.
RABBIT ST.
MOOSE ST.
BIG HORN ST.
ELK ST.
SQUIRREL ST.
MARTEN ST.
WOLF ST.
GOPHER ST.
LYNX ST.
BEAR ST.
BANFF AVE.
BEAVER ST.
MUSKRAT ST.
OTTER ST.
GRIZZLY ST.
CARIBOU ST.
WOLVERINE ST.
ST. JULIAN RD.
BUFFALO ST.
BOW AVENUE
GLEN AVE.
SPRAY AVE.
KOOTENAY AVE.
BIRCH AVE.
CAVE AVE.
MOUNTAIN AVE.

(762–2241) runs a bus to Calgary International Airport from the Gopher St. depot, as well as buses to Sunshine Village and Lake Louise from Calgary. *Pacific Western* (762–4558 or 276–0766) runs an airporter service and shuttle buses from Banff to Lake Louise.

By car. Banff is 80 miles (128 km.) west of Calgary on TransCanada Hwy. 1. Hwy. 1A, via Cochrane and Canmore, is a more leisurely route.

By train. *Via Rail* (800–665–8630) serves Banff daily with one train from the east (Calgary) and one from the west (Vancouver). The train station is on the northwest edge of town.

ACCOMMODATIONS. Banff fills up quickly in summer and holiday periods, so book ahead. To write, use box numbers and mailing addresses listed below, e.g., Box #, Banff, AB, T0L 0C0. Price categories for double occupancy rooms are: *Super Deluxe,* $125 and up; *Deluxe,* $100–$125; *Expensive,* $80–$100; *Moderate,* $50–$80; and *Inexpensive,* under $50.

Banff Central Reservations. Box 1628 (762–5561 or 800–661–1676). Book accommodations or a vacation package with recreational activities through their Summit Vacations service.

Super Deluxe

Banff Park Lodge. Box 2200 (762–4433 or 264–4440 or 800–661–9266). 222 Lynx St. Mini mall, fine dining at the Terrace, family dining, indoor pool, steam room, whirlpool, and nightly entertainment. Special rooms for guests in wheelchairs. No charge for children under 16.

Banff Rocky Mountain Resort, Box 100 (762–5531 or 800–661–9563), is about 1.5 miles (3 km) east of Banff on Banff Ave. at Tunnel Mountain Rd. Condo-style suites with fireplace, kitchen, and balcony set in the woods in the outskirts of Banff. Kids under 14 free. Lounge and dining in D.B. Dowling Restaurant. Squash and tennis courts, indoor pool, whirlpool, steam room, and weight room. Accommodation for guests in wheelchairs.

Banff Springs Hotel. Box 960 (762–2211 or 800–268–9411). About 1 mile from downtown at the end of Spray Ave. A majestic turret-crowned baronial hotel built in 1888. One of the original CPR hotels. 18-hole golf course, tennis courts, riding stables, exercise room, and skating rink. 35 handicraft, clothing, and souvenir stores, sports-equipment rentals, and a post office in the indoor mall. 600 rooms ranging from the simple to the sumptuous. Eat at a range of dining rooms, from the sushi bar, to family cafes to the elegant Rob Roy Supper Club. Wine bar, outdoor terrace, and dancing at the Works. Children under 14 stay free. Accommodation for guests in wheelchairs.

Deluxe

Douglas Fir Resort. Box 1228 (762–5591 or 264–2563 or 800–661–9267). On Tunnel Mountain Rd. Chalet, condo, and motel units, all with fireplaces and kitchens. Most popular feature is indoor waterslide (also open to public). Racquetball, squash, and tennis courts. Indoor pool, sauna, and whirlpool. Wheelchair facilities.

Elkhorn Lodge. Box 352 (762–2299). Only four units, and it's away from the madding crowd at 124 Spray Ave. Perfect for those seeking a rustic, restful atmosphere. Wood fireplaces and lots of privacy.

Ptarmigan Inn. Box 1840 (762–2207 or 800–661–8310) at 339 Banff Ave. Centrally located. Family units. Large open atrium lobby with bars and restaurants. Whirlpool and sauna. International cuisine in Le Jardin restaurant and open terrace cafe.

Sunshine Village Inn. Box 1510 (762–6500 or 800–661–1363). High alpine ski and summer resort at 7,200 feet elevation. Getting there takes 15 minutes by bus or car, then a spectacular 45-minute ride in a mountain gondola. Unparalleled location. Skiing from Nov.–May and hiking from July-Sept. Food plan included.

Expensive

Banffshire Inn, Box 489 (762–2201 or 800–661–8630) at 537 Banff Ave., a few blocks from downtown. Sauna and whirlpool, sun deck.

Bow View Motor Lodge. Box 339 (762–2261) at 228 Bow Ave. Right on the river and only two blocks from downtown. Family units available. Outdoor pool, steam room, and Jacuzzi.

Mount Royal Hotel. Box 550 (762–3331) at 138 Banff Ave. In the heart of downtown. Restaurant and lounge. Children under 12 free.

Rimrock Inn. Box 1110 (762–3356) on Mountain Ave. Near the hot pools and Sulphur Mountain Gondola. Presently undergoing extensive renovations and expansion.

Moderate

Banff Caribou Lodge. Box 279 (762–4041 or 762–2332). Two motels at 521 Banff Ave. They offer suites and family units. Three blocks from downtown.

Bumper's Inn. Box 1328 (762–3386) at Banff Ave. and Marmot St., on the east edge of town. Next door is Bumper's Restaurant, with bar and nightly entertainment. Rooms for guests in wheelchairs.

Cascade Inn. Box 790 (762–3311) in the heart of downtown Banff. Only half the rooms have full baths. Family restaurant, lounge, disco, cabaret entertainment, and piano-bar tavern.

Homestead Inn. Box 669 (762–4471) at 217 Lynx St. Melissa's restaurant next door. Short stroll to river or downtown.

Inns of Banff Park. Box 1077 (762–4581 or 800–661–1272) at 600 Banff Ave. Dining-room lounge, weight room, squash court, pool, sauna, and whirlpool. Visitors to the less-expensive sister motels next door—**Pinewoods** and **Swiss Village**—and **Rundle Manor Apartment Hotel,** at 384 Marten, may use the dining and recreational facilities.

Red Carpet Inn. Box 1800 (762–4184 or 762–4448) at 425 Banff Ave. El Toro restaurant next door.

Inexpensive

Johnston's Canyon Resort. Box 875 (762–2971). In a beautiful location 16 miles (26 km) west of Banff on Hwy. 1A, beside one of the most popular hiking trails in the park. Rustic motel units, groceries, and gas station. Open mid-May–mid-Sept.

King Edward Hotel. Box 250 (762–2251). Downtown Banff. King Eddy's Tavern features nightly live entertainment. Shuffleboard. Not all rooms have baths. Hostel-type accommodations also.

BED AND BREAKFASTS. These hospitable alternatives to ordinary hotel stays have become tremendously popular in Banff. You can book rooms through Alberta B&B, Edmonton (462–8885), or the B&B Bureau,

Calgary (242–5555). Price categories below are the same as those for the hotels above.

Mrs. Cowan. *Inexpensive.* Box 1436 (762–3696). Rooms at 118 Otter St.

Mrs. Colins. *Moderate.* Box 935 (762–2979). Rooms, suites, and cabins at 417 W. Cougar St. and 220 Beaver St. Open mid-June–mid-Sept.

Cougar Creek Inn. *Inexpensive.* Box 1162, Canmore (678–4751). Four rooms with private entrance.

Mrs. Horton. *Inexpensive.* Box 1623 (762–2146). Rooms with shared bath at 223 Otter. Summers only.

Mrs. Ness. *Inexpensive.* Box 6 (762–2439). Rooms with shared bath at 347 Banff Ave. Open July–mid-Sept.

Mrs. Riva. *Inexpensive.* Box 16 (762–24719). A room and cabin at 345 Marten St. Open April-Oct.

Mrs. Simpson. *Inexpensive.* Box 2763 (762–5134). Bed but no breakfast at 137 Muskrat St.

Pension Tannenhof. (Herbert Riedinger). *Expensive.* Box 1914 (762–4636). Rooms and a suite, dining room, and living rooms at 121 Cave Ave. Summers only.

YOUTH HOSTELS. Banff and environs are big on these. This is the cheapest way to sleep under a roof that's not made of canvas. Nightly rates vary, but are generally a dollar or two cheaper for members of the International Youth Hostels Federation (IYHF).

Banff International Hostel. Box 1358 (762–4122). On Tunnel Mountain Rd., two miles (three km) from Banff. Accommodation for 154 people, including families. Cafeteria, kitchen, laundry. Reservations accepted. Members, $9; nonmembers, $14.

Castle Mountain Hostel. On Hwy 1A (762–2367). A mile east of Castle Junction at the Hwy. 93 turnoff. Newly renovated; sleeps 36. Great base for hiking, skiing, climbing. Members, $5; non-members, $6.

Spray River Hostel. South of Banff, on the Spray River Fire Rd., which is closed to vehicles and begins at the Banff Springs Hotel. Accommodation for 47. Members, $6; non-members, $8. Closed Tues. nights.

RESTAURANTS. Stiff competition encourages attention to quality, and Banff abounds with decent restaurants. You can add spice to your holiday by eating at a few of these. Our price categories, for two meals with appetizer, exclusive of tax and tip, are: *Deluxe,* $50–$75; *Expensive,* $25–$50; *Moderate,* $15–$25; and *Inexpensive,* under $15.

Deluxe

Beaujolais. Banff Ave. and Buffalo St. (762–2712 or 762–5365). French cuisine with an elaborate menu.

Rob Roy. One of Banff Springs Hotel's many restaurants (762–2211). A selection of seafood, steak, and pasta to suit most tastes. Live entertainment and dancing.

Expensive

Giorgio's La Casa. Upstairs (762–5116), and **La Pasta** (762–5114), 219 Banff Ave. Authentic Italian cuisine. Intimate dining upstairs; moderately priced family dining downstairs. Homemade pasta.

Grizzly House. 207 Banff Ave. (762–4055). Specializes in fondues: cheese, meat, vegetable, seafood, Oriental, chocolate, and fruit—the "ultimate" includes most of those plus buffalo and caribou meat. Raclette and steaks, too. Unusual liqueurs. Rustic interior.

Le Jardin in Ptarmigan Inn. 337 Banff Ave. (762–4868). Interesting selection of international dishes. Outdoor patio.

Terrace. Banff Park Lodge, 222 Lynx (762–4433). A wide range of fish and seafood, as well as Alberta beef and other meats.

Tommy's. 209 Banff Ave. (762–5899). A variety of selections from grills and seafood to pasta. Music and dancing Thurs.–Sat. Lounge and stand-up bar.

Moderate

Balkan. 120 Banff Ave. (762–3454). Excellent Greek food. Try the Greek platter. Vegetarian specials and kids' portions.

Bumper's. 603 Banff Ave. (762–2622). A steak house specializing in Alberta beef and barbecue ribs. Entertainment in bar upstairs. Senior-citizens' discount.

The Caboose. In the old CPR railroad station at Elk and Lynx sts. (762–3622 or 762–2102). A steak and lobster restaurant set in old-world surroundings, depicting the history of the railroad in Banff Park.

D.B. Dowling. Banff Rocky Mountain Resort, about 1.5 miles (3 km), east of town on Banff Ave. at Tunnel Mountain Rd. (762–5531). The international menu leans towards the French, with chicken, beef, seafood, and pasta. Children's menu. Lounge with movies. Patio. Wheelchair access.

Guido's. Upstairs at 116 Banff Ave. (762–4002). Italian food, pasta, veal, and their own smoked trout.

Magpie & Stump. 203 Caribou St. (762–2014 or 762–2014). Tex-Mex food and live late-night entertainment.

Melissa's. A rustic log building at 218 Lynx St. (762–5511). Any size steak, unusual burgers, and deep-dish pizza, served by athletic waiters. Popular bar upstairs.

Paris. 114 Banff Ave. (762–3554). European menu with choices for everyone—veal, steaks, and pasta. Fresh seafood a specialty. Adjoining **Cafe de Paris** is a sidewalk bistro and wine bar.

Rose and Crown. Banff Ave. at Caribou (762–2121). British pub and Victorian restaurant. Burgers and beef dishes, draught beer and darts. Friendly.

Suginoya. Upstairs in the mall at 225 Banff Ave. (762–4773 or 762–5759). Japanese fare, including sushi bar, sukyaki, teryaki, and tempura. Try the seafood hotpot.

Ticino. 205 Wolf St. (762–3848). A Swiss/Italian restaurant specializing in cheese and meat fondues, veal dishes, and pastas. Wonderful dining in attractive surroundings. Children's menu.

The Yard. 206 Wolf St. (762–5678). Lots of room to lounge outdoors. Specialties include Tex-Mex dishes and mesquite barbecue. Half-orders for the not-so-hungry. Wheelchair access.

Inexpensive

Athena. 112 Banff Ave. (762–4022 or 762–4022). A pizza and spaghetti house that also serves steak. Open till 2 A.M. daily. Family menu.

Craigs' Way Station. In the Cascade Inn, 124 Banff Ave. (762–5958). Family meals, burgers, etc.

Joe's Diner. 223 Banff Ave. (762–5529). Light fare at reasonable prices. Senior-citizens' discount.

Picadilly Fare. 321 Banff Ave. (762–3555) Light and easy alternatives: sandwiches, salads, omeletes.

Rundle Restaurant. 319 Banff Ave. (762–3223). Both western and Cantonese food. **Sidestreet Lounge** also serves food. Wheelchair access.

TJ's. 120 Banff Ave. (762–5474). Great pizza, homemade pasta, and veal. Take-out and free delivery. Children's portions.

NIGHTLIFE AND BARS. Most of the evening action takes place in the hotels and restaurants mentioned above.

Dancing and live music: **The Clubhouse** and **The Works** in the Banff Springs Hotel; **King Edward Hotel; The Great Divide** in **Cascade Inn.** For disco dancing, try **Fast Freddie's** behind the Rose and Crown.

Lounges with live entertainment: **Buffalo Paddock** in **Cascade Inn; Bumper's Loft Lounge; Inns of Banff Park; Glacier Lounge** in **Banff Park Lodge; Les Voyageur Lounge** in the **Voyager Inn,** 555 Banff Ave.; **Rimrock Inn; Royal Express** in the **Mount Royal Hotel.**

HOW TO GET AROUND. By bus. Many hotels have private or charter bus service to the bus and train stations, ski slopes, and Calgary Airport (see above).

By rental car. Companies operating in Banff and at Calgary Airport are *Avis* (762–3222 or 800–268–2310), *Budget* (762–4565), *Hertz* (762–2027 or 800–268–1311); and Tilden (762–2688 or 800–663–9822).

By taxicab. Companies include *Banff Taxi and Sightseeing* (762–4444); *Legion Taxi* (762–3353); *Mountain Taxi and Tours* (762–3351); and *Taxi Taxi* (762–3111).

By bike. Regular and mountain bikes are available for rent at many locations in town and are a highly recommended mode of transport.

TOURIST INFORMATION. The **Travel Alberta** information number is 762–2777. The nearest information center is 10 miles (17 km) away on Hwy. 1 near Canmore (678–5277 or 800–222–6501). Write *Travel Alberta,* Box 2500, Edmonton T5J 0H4.

Banff Information Centre. (Parks Canada) 224 Banff Ave. (762–4256). Everything you want to know about the national parks. Information available by mail from *Banff National Park,* Box 900, Banff T0L 0C0.

Banff/Lake Louise Chamber of Commerce. 93 Banff Ave. (762–3777). Information on facilities and special events.

Banff Park Warden. Between Hwy. 1 and the townsite (762–4506). Open 24 hours.

Banff Recreation Department. (762–4454). Offers programs and activities.

TOURS AND SPECIAL-INTEREST SIGHTSEEING. Brewster Travel Service. Box 1140, Banff Ave. (762–3207). Runs sightseeing trips and vacations all through the Rockies. They will connect you by bus, train, horse, or raft; from Calgary and Banff to Lake Louise, Columbia Icefield, Jasper, or Vancouver.

Minnewanka Tours. Box 2189 YOL 0CO (762–3473). Cruises to Devil's Gap on Lake Minnewanka. Fishing trips. Adults, $10; children under 11, $5.

Mt. Norquay Gondola. (762–4421). Operates from mid-June–Aug. Adults, $5; children 5–11 yrs., $2.25; under 5, free.

Rocky Mountain Reservations. Sundance Mall (762–4347). For tickets and reservations.

Sulphur Mountain Gondola. Mountain Ave. (762–5438 or 762–2523). Beside the Upper Hot Pools. Take the eight-minute ride to a great view. Summit restaurant.

Sunshine Gondola. Hwy. 1 (762–6500). 11 miles (18 km) west of Banff. Takes you 7,200 feet up fragile alpine meadows to the highest resort in Canada.

Tickets. 304 Caribou St. (762–5385). Reserves tickets for sightseeing, entertainment, and adventure trips.

NATIONAL PARKS. Banff National Park is the second largest of Canada's mountain parks, covering over 80,000 square miles of mountains, valleys, glaciers, forests, alpine meadows, lakes, and wild rivers. The park has 25 peaks over 9,800 feet, scores of glacial-blue lakes, hoodoos (odd natural rock monuments), canyons, and hot springs.

CAMPGROUNDS AND HUTS. There are nine campgrounds in the Banff area, catering to everyone from the fully loaded RV driver to the hiker with his sleeping bag. Camping in the back country in designated areas only—ask for the map showing locations. **Y Mountain Lodge,** Box 520 (762–3560) is at 414 Muskrat, and accepts both single men and women, and couples.

Alpine Club of Canada, Box 1026 (762–4481) has several huts in excellent climbing/skiing areas. Members may make reservations.

Parks Canada has several huts and shelters in the back country. Call 762–4256 or ask at information centers.

HIKING. There are many good short hikes near Banff. Sundance Canyon, about a mile beyond the Cave and Basin, can be explored in about two hours. Visit the Bow Falls, a 30-minute hike along the river from the bridge on Banff Ave. It's a gradual three-hour hike till you're halfway up Mt. Rundle, but that's high enough for great views; after that it's strictly climbing. Wander out along the edge of the golf course at the Banff Springs Hotel for a two-hour loop. Several excellent routes radiate from the Mt. Norquay parking lots.

The hiking around Lake Minnewanka is just as scenic as the sailing. If art is your objective, you can get your exercise on the way up Tunnel Mountain to The Banff Centre School of Fine Arts. On the nearby Bow River, take a look at the strange hoodoos, pillars of rock formed by erosion, when unconsolidated material was carried away by the river, leaving "statues" of the harder stuff. The Fenland Trail on the west edge of town is a sure bet for a wildlife adventure.

OUTDOOR ACTIVITIES. Cycling allows you to combine exercise and sightseeing, and many local firms rent bicycles. Mountain bikes are restricted to designated trails. Guided cycle tours are available from *Rocky Mountain Cycle Tours,* Box 895, Banff T0L 0C0 (678–6770).

Horseback riding is the western way to see Banff National Park. Horses are for rent, and guided tours available, at several locations in town. Try *Martin's Stables* (762–2832) or *Brewster's* (762–5454).

Canoeing and **kayaking** are excellent on many of the lakes and rivers in the region, but power boats are allowed only on Lake Minnewanka. See *Practical Information for Canmore* for guided trips and lessons. **Windsurfing** is especially good on Vermilion Lakes, Two Jack Lake, and—for advanced sailors—Lake Minnewanka. Equipment can be rented in Banff. **Rafting** trips on local rivers can be booked through *Rocky Mountain Raft Tours,* Box 1771, Banff (762–4454) or *Maligne River Adventures,* Jasper (852–3370).

Fishing is excellent in the region. *Banff Fishing Unlimited,* Box 216, Canmore, T0L 0M0 (762–4936 or 678–2486) offers a guiding service.

The *Banff Springs Hotel* (762–2211) welcomes the public at its challenging 18-hole **golf** course. The hotel also has excellent **tennis** courts, as does the *Banff Recreation Department* (762–4454).

Some hiking trails make good **cross-country skiing** runs, but some don't. Check park authority maps and brochures. Trips are possible on every level, from a meander around the golf course to a week-long expedition on a glacier. Favorite routes close to town include the Cascade Fire Rd., Carrot Creek, the Tunnel-Hoodoos Loop, and the Spray River. For above-the-treeline adventure without the effort of getting there, ride the gondola to Sunshine and ski out into the meadows, where cover often lasts until May. Inquire at Parks Information about alpine huts and guided tours, and *never* go out without checking for avalanche danger.

Many **outfitters** offer a variety of wilderness expeditions. Among the better ones:

Savoie Mountain Adventure. Box 399, Banff T0L 0C0 (762–4728).

Banff Alpine Guides. Box 1025, Banff T0L 0C0 (762–2791).

One Step Beyond. 749 Railway Ave., Canmore T0L 0M0 (678–5255).

DOWNHILL SKIING. The two closest ski hills to town are Mt. Norquay, only four miles distant, and Sunshine, an 11-mile drive and a wonderful gondola ride away.

Mt. Norquay. Box 1258, Banff T0L 0C0 (762–4421). Six lifts; 20 trails.

Sunshine Village. Box 1510, Banff T0L 0C0 (762–6500). 12 lifts; 103 trails.

More and more skiers are using helicopters to seek the extra-special experience of a few hours or a few days in the steep and deep, the untouched back-country powder. Some companies providing heli-skiing tours in the Banff area follow.

Banff Heli-Sports. Box 2326, Canmore T0L 0M0 (678–4888).

Cariboo Helicopter Skiing. Box 1824, Banff T0L 0C0 (762–5548).

CMH Heli-skiing. Box 1660, Banff T0L 0C0 (762–4531).

Mountain Canada Purcell Helicopter Skiing. Box 1628, Banff T0L 0C0 (762–5383).

SEASONAL EVENTS. January. *Banff/Lake Louise Winter Festival* begins. **June.** *Banff Television Festival. Banff Festival of the Arts* begins.

July. *Canada Day Parade.* **October.** *Mainstage events* at the Banff Centre begin. *Banff Mountain Film Festival.*

HISTORIC SITES AND HOUSES. Cave and Basin Hot Springs and Centennial Centre. Cave Ave. (762–3324) is the site of Canada's first national park, with an original 1887 bathhouse and historical and interpretive displays. Exhibits open daily 10 A.M.–5 P.M.Admission to pool: adults, $1.50; children, $1.

A "Heritage Homes" tour, sponsored by the Whyte Museum, explores two houses and four cabins from the early days of Banff. Tours start at the Whyte Museum. Tours Wed.–Fri. and Sun. 10 A.M.–4:30 P.M.; Sat. 1:30 P.M.–4:30 P.M. Fee $1.

MUSEUMS AND GALLERIES. Banff Park Museum. 93 Banff Ave. A beautiful "museum of a museum," built in 1903, with animal exhibits dating back to 1860. Open daily 10 A.M.–6 P.M. Free.

Luxton Museum. Cave Ave. (762–2388). A fine collection of plains Indians artifacts. Open daily 10 A.M.–5 P.M. Adults, $2; students, $1; seniors, 50¢; children under 12, free.

Natural History Museum. 112 Banff Ave. (762–4747). Interesting exhibits and movies. Open daily 10 A.M.–6 P.M. Adults, $1.50; children, 75¢.

Walter Phillips Gallery. At The Banff Centre School of Fine Arts, St. Julien Rd. (762–6283). Regular exhibits of emerging Canadian and international artists. Open daily, noon–5 P.M. Free.

Whyte Museum of the Canadian Rockies. 111 Bear St. (762–2291). Contains the Archives of the Canadian Rockies, a heritage collection of local human history, and a gallery with frequently changing exhibits relating to the area. Open daily 10 A.M.–6 P.M. Admission $1; under 12, free.

ARTS AND ENTERTAINMENT. The **Banff Centre,** just above Banff town site on St. Julien Rd., is a unique institute with an international reputation. It has schools of fine arts and management, as well as conference facilities. Throughout the year, myriad art exhibitions, music, theater, opera, dance, drama, ballet, music concerts (classical, jazz, new music), readings, videos, and foreign films are open to the public. Lunchtime concerts and many other events are free. For information, call 762–6157.

SHOPPING. The mecca of shoppers is the Hudson's Bay Company on Banff Ave. But there are dozens of other gift, craft, and souvenir stores worth scouting out. Shop around.

Banff Bears. 225 Banff Ave. (762–3411). Exclusively bears and bear memorabilia for arctophiles.

Canada House. 201 Bear St. (762–3757). Large selection of prints by Canadian artists and Inuits. Carvings, jewelry, and paintings.

Creations. 204 Banff Ave. (762–4442). Local and Canadian crafts.

Marika's. 112 Banff Ave. (762–2678). Canadian handcrafted jewelry.

Nijinska's. 111 Banff Ave. (762–5006). Specializes in Canadian handmade wooden gifts.

The Quest for Handcrafts. 105 Banff Ave. (762–2722). Unique Canadian arts and crafts, including pottery, sculpture, prints, and jewelry by Canadian artists. Gallery of Eskimo art downstairs.

LAKE LOUISE

Cradled by high mountains with Victoria Glacier cascading down behind it, Lake Louise is simply breathtaking. Gliding canoes ripple across the blue water and trails wind along the lakeshore through evergreen forest. In winter, ski trails radiate across the lake towards the glacier. On shore, the huge Château Lake Louise adds to the majesty of the scene.

Known as the "Lake of Little Fishes" to the Indian people, it was renamed "Emerald Lake" for its intense color by a 19th-century rail surveyor. Later it was renamed Lake Louise to honor Queen Victoria's daughter, who married the Governor General of Canada.

The area is more than one lake alone. Only a kilometer from the château, Moraine Lake Road leads visitors eight miles (12.5 km) to another, arguably just as beautiful, scene—Moraine Lake and the Valley of Ten Peaks, which is depicted on the back of the Canadian $20 bill.

It's three miles (4.5 km) up a fairly steep road to Lake Louise, 5,600 feet from the village below. The village has been going through expansion and construction for several years and will eventually have complete services for visitors.

The scenic way to Banff is the Bow Valley Parkway (Hwy. 1A), which runs west between the village and the lake for five miles (7 km) to the Continental Divide. The Divide forms the border between Alberta and British Columbia, and between Banff and Yoho parks. Hwy. 1A is a fine place to watch wildlife, with many stopping places, picnic sites, campgrounds, and interpretive exhibits.

Route 1 leads 16 miles (27 km) to Field in Yoho Park, British Columbia, where you can visit the Spiral Tunnels, Takkakaw Falls, Emerald Lake, and the Natural Bridge.

Going west, turn after two miles (3 km) onto Route 93 to tour the Icefields Parkway, with some of the most spectacular mountain scenery in the world. The road passes the Columbia Icefield and the Athabasca Glacier, which flows 8 miles distant, on the way to Jasper.

PRACTICAL INFORMATION FOR LAKE LOUISE

HOW TO GET THERE. Lake Louise is 120 miles (190 km) west of Calgary and 35 miles (58 km) west of Banff on the TransCanada Highway. For train, bus, and taxi information, see *Practical Information for Banff.* The Via Rail Station in Lake Louise can be reached at 522–3841 or 800–665–8630.

ACCOMMODATIONS. Lake Louise has a great diversity of lodgings. Our price categories are: *Super Deluxe,* over $125; *Deluxe,* $100–$125; and *Moderate,* $80–$100. All prices are in Canadian dollars, for a one-night stay in a double room. The Canadian postal code for all establishments listed below is TOL 1E0.

Château Lake Louise. *Super Deluxe.* Box 96 (522–3511 or 800–268–9411). A huge, sumptuous CPR hotel/mansion, originally built in 1890. It burned down shortly thereafter and has been reconstructed twice. Rooms with views over the lake are at a premium. It has been expanded to 521 rooms, with three dining rooms, two lounges, coffee shop, outdoor cafe, pub, exercise room, swimming pool, Jacuzzi, steam room, and many shops and boutiques. Definitely worth a visit even if you don't stay.

Lake Louise Inn. *Deluxe.* Box 209 (522–3791). In the village. Sauna, whirlpool, big pool, exercise room, dining room, lounge with entertainment, pub with disco.

Post Hotel, Box 69 (522–3989/3877), in the village on Pipestone Creek has, undergone extensive reconstruction. The main log building is one of the original ski lodges built in the 1940s. Outpost lounge bar and fine dining.

Expensive

Deer Lodge. *Expensive.* Box 100 (522–3788 or 800–661–1367). A few minutes' walk from the lake. Built in the '20s, a beautiful old lodge, dining room, hot tub, sauna, outdoor patio.

Moderate

Paradise Lodge and Bungalows. Box 7 (522–3595). Available here are 21 cozy bungalows, six lodge rooms, and family rooms. The facility is a short walk from lake. Barbecue, groceries, playground are available.

CHALETS AND MOUNTAIN LODGES. These establishments combine the amenities of better hotels with the outdoor ambience of ski huts. Price categories are the same as for *Accommodations* above.

Baker Creek Bungalows. *Moderate.* Box 66 (522–3761). In a quiet forested area nine miles (15 km) from Lake Louise. Open May.–Sept.

Deluxe.

Castle Mountain Village. Box 1655, Banff T0L 0C0 (762–3868). 18 miles (29 km) from Lake Louise and 20 miles (32 km) from Banff on Hwy. 1A. There are cedar and log chalets for two to six people, with fireplace.

Moraine Lake Lodge and Cabins. *Expensive.* Box 70 (522–37B3). Access above Lake Louise village eight miles (13 km) along Moraine Lake Rd. Open June–mid.-Sept. Superb location far from the throng. Dining room.

Paradise Lodge and Bungalows. *Deluxe.* Box 7 (522–3595). On the road up to the lake above the village. Grocery store. Open mid-May–Sept.

Skoki Lodge. *Expensive.* c/o Skiing Louise, Box 5 (522–3555). Accommodates 22 guests in a beautiful log lodge and cabins nine miles into the backcountry. Built in 1930 by alpine enthusiasts, it's in a great location for hiking, climbing, skiing, trail-riding, and fishing. Rates include three delicious home-cooked meals a day. Open Christmas–April for skiing; June–Sept. for summer activities.

HUTS. The Alpine Club of Canada has several huts in Banff National Park which can be booked by members. These are ideal bases for climbing and ski-touring. The huts are: **Abbot Pass,** above Lake Louise; **Castle**

Mountain; and **Neil Colgan,** above Moraine Lake. Write to: *ACC,* Box 1026, Banff TOL 0C0 (762–4481).

Parks Canada has several huts and shelters in the area. Reservations must be made at Banff Information Centre (762–4256); backcountry use permits are required.

YOUTH HOSTELS. These spartan facilities, affiliated with the International Youth Hostels Federation (IYHF), offer bunks to shoestring travelers. Despite their name, not all of them are restricted to young travelers. Rates for IYHF members range from $4.50–$5. Non-members pay $5.50–$6.

Castle Mountain. Route 1A (762–2367). Just east of Castle Junction. Sleeps 36. Closed Wed.

Corral Creek. Route 1A. Three miles east of Lake Louise. Sleeps 50. Closed Mon.

Mosquito Creek. Icefields Parkway. 16 miles (26 km) north of Lake Louise. Sleeps 38, sauna. Closed Tues.

CAMPING. There are numerous campgrounds along hwys. 1 and 1A from Banff, most of which are near the railway track. The one at Lake Louise has over 400 sites. Facilities range from primitive to full-service.

RESTAURANTS AND NIGHTLIFE. Lake Louise's restaurants tend to be on the upscale end of things. Our categories, for a dinner for two, including appetizer, but exclusive of drinks, tax, and tip, are as follows: *Deluxe,* over $50; *Expensive,* $25–$50; and *Moderate,* under $25.

Lake Louise's hotels all have lounges and bars with a variety of nightly entertainment, ranging from live folk music to disco dancing.

Tom Wilson Dining Room. *Deluxe.* In the Château Lake Louise (522–3511). A glass-enclosed rooftop dining room serving fine Continental and western cuisine. Spectacular mountain view. Summer only.

Post Hotel. *Expensive.* Lake Louise (522–3989). Dining room specializes in Swiss cuisine, especially trout and beef. High tea is served in the sitting room. Great breakfast buffet.

Victoria Dining Room. *Expensive.* In the Château Lake Louise (522–3511). Serves steak, salmon, chicken, lamb. Breakfast buffet. Nightly entertainment; great view.

Cafe Louise. *Moderate.* In the Deer Lodge (522–3788). Innovative dishes including reindeer, salmon, trout, veal, pasta and Alberta beef.

Heritage Restaurant. *Moderate.* In the Lake Louise Inn (522–3791). Interesting specialties like bison and reindeer, as well as prime rib, in large dining room with informal atmosphere.

TOURIST INFORMATION. Avalanche Report. 762–3600/3324 (24 hours).

Parks Canada Information Centre. 522–3833. Open mid-June–Aug. 8 A.M.–10 P.M. May–mid-June and Sept. 10 A.M.–6 P.M.

Park Warden Office. Lake Louise 522–3866 or 762–4506 (24 hours) in Banff.

OUTDOOR ACTIVITIES. There are many **hiking** trails within walking distance of the Château Lake Louise, all offering outstanding views. A recommended route goes along the lake shoreline, Fairview Mountain lookout, Saddleback, Plain of Six Glaciers, Mirror Lake, and Lake Agnes. There are rustic teahouses at Plain of Six Glaciers and Lake Agnes, a relaxing reward for your efforts.

Other popular trails are around Moraine Lake, the Valley of the Ten Peaks, Consolation Lakes, and Paradise Valley, all reached via Moraine Lake Road, just below Château Lake Louise. From Moraine Lake, longer routes lead up to Larch Valley, Eiffel, and Sentinel Pass.

To get a head start on the climb, take the gondola up, and then hike in the high valleys behind the ski area to Boulder Pass or on down to Skoki Valley. There are self-guiding interpretive trails along the Bow River and at Moraine Lake.

Horseback riding is available from the establishments listed below at hourly and daily rates. All are near the lake and all rent guides: *Brewster Stables* (522–3872); *Guided Saddle Horse Trips* (522–3770); *Timberline Tours* (522–3743).

Canoeing is available at several rental facilities at Lake Louise and Moraine Lake. The Bow River has some excellent white water, but calls for an experienced guide.

Cycling is an excellent way to take advantage of the scenery—as well as the excellent hostels and campgrounds—along the Bow Valley Parkway and the Icefields Parkway.

Skating is excellent on the lake in winter.

Lake Louise is one of the prettiest places in the world to go **cross-country skiing.** Excellent trails run near the village; the Upper Lake Louise trails run nearer the lake. Many lead from the Château Lake Louise. A favorite route leads around the lake to Moraine Lake Road, which is track-set, and from there up Paradise Valley. From the downhill ski area, the day trip to Skoki Lodge is excellent for those of intermediate ability.

Many of the hiking trails make excellent ski trails, but some are dangerous, so take only recommended routes. Check the avalanche danger by calling 762–3600/3324 before you set out.

DOWNHILL SKIING. Lake Louise Ski Area. Box 5, Lake Louise T0L 1E0 (522–3555, 256–8473, or 800–661–1158). Thirty-six miles (60 km) west of Banff on Route 1. One of the largest ski areas in Canada. 9 lifts; 46 trails.

CANMORE

In a spectacular setting on the floodplain of the Bow River, snow-capped ranges towering on all sides, Canmore is a paradise for the outdoors enthusiast. Noble mountain landmarks surround the town: the Three Sisters, just to the east; Chinaman's Peak beyond; and the Rundle Range, which stretches all the way to Banff.

Once passed over by tourists bound for the better-known mountain parks, Canmore is now chosen by more and more people as a quiet, cheap alternative to the busy Banff town site. With a population of just over 4,000, and accommodations for more than 12,000, it's just a 20-minute drive from Banff along a beautiful stretch of highway. Canmore makes a great base for exploring both Banff National Park to the west and Kananaskis Country to the east and south.

Tourist interest in the town has grown with the addition of the Canmore Nordic Site—specially equipped for cross-country skiing and biathlon events, and a new recreation complex. In recent times, Canmore has experienced boom growth, making it a less sleepy town with more attractions for more visitors year-round.

Exploring Canmore

Established as a mining town in 1883, Canmore hasn't preserved a great deal from its past. A few old shafts can be seen in the area, and a few of the small railcars that carried coal are displayed around town. Stroll the back streets to see a few of the original miners' cabins.

You can thoroughly explore the entire town in half a day. On foot or bicycle, take the pathway system that winds through Canmore. The Outdoor Adventure Centre, Deadman's Flats (678–2000), rents bikes.

A few artists and artisans live in Canmore. Their work is often exhibited in the Guild Gallery of the Public Library, 700 9th St. (678–2468). Downstairs is a collection of photographs depicting the demise of the local coal-mining industry.

PRACTICAL INFORMATION FOR CANMORE

HOW TO GET THERE. By car. Follow Hwy. 1 west 111 km from Calgary. Alternatively, take Hwy. 1A (from Crowchild Trail North) through Cochrane, Morley, Seebe, and Exshaw to Canmore. This is a beautiful, more leisurely route with interesting stops along the way; the prairies gently unfold into the mountains as the road passes through the Stoney Indian Reserve and many historic sites.

By bus. There are two *Greyhound* buses from Calgary to Canmore per day: one in the morning and one in the early evening (403–260–0877 or 265–9111). The Briggs Pharmacy (678–5288), 705 8th St., functions as the town bus station.

By train. *Via Rail* has a daily train through Canmore from Calgary, but it doesn't stop till it gets to Banff (see *Calgary* and *Banff* above).

ACCOMMODATIONS. Some of the accommodations listed are in Harvey Heights, the small community about half a mile (1 km) west on the TransCanada Hwy. Many places offer kitchenettes. More than 20 families in Canmore have opened their homes for B&Bs, which can be booked through bureaus listed under Bed and Breakfasts (see *Calgary*). Mailing addresses are the box numbers listed in the entries, followed by Alberta, TOL OMO. Price categories, for double-occupancy room, exclusive of tax and tip, are: *Expensive,* \$80–\$100; *Moderate,* \$50–\$80; and *Inexpensive,* under \$50.

Expensive

Rocky Mountain Chalets. Box 725 (678–5564). On Hwy. 1A at 17th St. Condo units with kitchenettes. Some with fireplace. Restaurant and lounge adjoining.

Rundle Ridge Chalets. (678–5387). Individual cedar chalets with kitchen and fireplace. Quiet location.

Moderate

Cee-Der Chalets. Box 525 (678–5251). Individual log cabins in a quiet forested setting.

Rundle Mountain Motel. Box 147 (678–5322). At 1815 Mountain Ave., right on Hwy. 1 service road. Kitchenettes and wheelchair facilities.

Skiland Motel. Box 696 (678–5445). On Hwy. 1 service road. Cozy family apartments plus smaller units. Wheelchair facilities.

Sundance Inn. Box 755 (678–5528). On Hwy. 1 service road. No charge for children under 12. Restaurant, disco, and bar.

Tatranka Lodge. Box 421 (678–5131), 909 Railway Ave. Practically downtown but with balconies overlooking the creek and mountains. Restaurant, bar, and open terrace. Owners speak five languages. Wheelchair facilities.

Inexpensive

Akai Motel. Box 687 (678–4775 or 678–4664). On the service road to Hwy. 1. Kitchenettes.

Canmore Clubhouse. Alpine Club of Canada, Box 1026 (678–5855). About two miles (3 km) east of town off Hwy. 1A. Very pleasant, cheap, clean dormitory accommodations and self-catering facilities in a beautiful location.

Haus Alpenrose. Box 723 (678–4134). A Bavarian-style lodge at 629 9th St. Cheap, with clean dormitory-style and private rooms. Nonsmoking outdoor enthusiasts characterize the clientele. Base for Canadian School of Mountaineering.

MOUNTAIN LODGES. One of the unique experiences of the area, promising a memorable visit to the backcountry.

Kranabitter Lodge. Currently under construction in Spray Lakes Valley, just off Spray Lakes Rd. (Hwy. 742) from Canmore, will provide inexpensive hostel-style accommodations for hikers and skiers.

Mount Assiniboine Lodge. Operated by Sepp and Barbara Renner, Box 1527, Canmore T0L 0M0 (678–2883 or 762–5075). Southwest of Canmore in Mount Assiniboine Provincial Park on an alpine plateau of the Great Divide at 7,200 feet elevation. The lodge is most easily accessible from Spray Lakes Valley, outside of Canmore. Built in 1928 by the Canadian Pacific Railway, it is a magnificent log building: rustic, old world, and charming. Interiors and furnishings are hand-hewn. It's an excellent area for cross-country skiing in the winter and for hiking and wildflowers in the summer. The mountain slopes flanking the meadow are ideal for telemark skiing, and there's often 10 feet of snow, which lasts till May. Lake Magog is one of several nearby fishing lakes. Hikers, climbers, and skiers return each evening to homemade bread, gourmet meals, and a sauna.

The 15-minute helicopter flight in is spectacular, as Mount Assiniboine and the circle of peaks overlooking the lodge come into close view. Hike or ski in and out if you want, but be prepared to get an early start because it's 16 miles (26 km) by the Spray Lakes route and about 17.5 miles (28 km) by the alternative route via Sunshine Village. Rates are high but include meals and guide service. Bring your own alcohol. Helicopter costs $50 each way: flights on Wednesdays, Fridays, Sundays, and holiday Mondays.

RESTAURANTS. For such a small town, Canmore has a surprising number of very good restaurants. Price categories for two meals with appetizer, exclusive of tax and tip, are: *Moderate,* $15–$25; and *Inexpensive,* under $15.

Moderate

Boccalino. 1000 7th Ave. (678–6424). Great pasta and pizza. The homemade desserts are delicious.

Gallagher House. 637 8th St. (678–5370). Fine dining and a tea room. Appeals to the more discerning palate. Everything loving homemade. Reservations recommended.

Pepper Mill. 726 9th St. (678–2292). Specializes in adventurous European cuisine and Alberta beef. Patio restaurant. Children's menu.

Rose and Crown. 8th St. and Railway Ave. (678–5168). Meet the locals in the British-style pub over a pint and a game of darts. Or choose from a varied menu in the dining room. Garden terrace on edge of creek. Children's menu.

Sherwood House. 738 8th St. (678–5211). Well-prepared seafood, pasta, and steaks. The saloon has many beers on draught, darts, and live entertainment. Outdoor patio.

The Village Green. 837 8th St. (678–5995). Brasserie and stand-up bar. Cosmopolitan cuisine in a relaxing atmosphere. Char-broiled burgers and champagne brunch on weekends and holidays.

Inexpensive

Bing's. 629 8th St. (678–6232). Szechuan and Mandarin Chinese food.

Craig's Way Station. On the Hwy. 1 service road (678–2556). Family fare; drive-thru and mini-golf.

Lone Star Cafe. 8th Ave. and 8th St. (678–4901). A favorite with locals. Burgers, salads, omelets. Children's menu.

Three Square Meals. Kendall Mall on 8th St. (678–4485). Clean, pleasant, and no frills.

Tiger Take Out. 704 8th St. (678–5992). Cheap and fast pizza, chicken, ribs, and burgers. They deliver, too.

NIGHTLIFE AND BARS. Canmore is the kind of place to enjoy a stroll on a brilliant night in the clear mountain air, while a distant coyote bays at the moon. Otherwise, nightlife in town is restricted pretty much to hotels and bars. There's usually live entertainment on weekends in the **Canmore Hotel, Sherwood House,** and the **Rose and Crown,** as well as disco dancing in the **Sundance Inn.**

HOW TO GET AROUND. By taxi. *Korridor Kabs* (678–5426). Also provides a port-a-van and sightseeing service.

By bike. Local firms rent touring and trail bicycles.

TOURIST INFORMATION. Canmore Chamber of Commerce. Information booth is at the east edge of town on Hwy. 1A.

Canmore Recreation Department. Box 460, Canmore, T0L 0M0 (678–5593). Information on recreation events and facilities.

Travel Alberta. New information center at the west entrance of town between hwys. 1 and 1A. Open year-round (678–5277, 800–222–6501 or 800–661–8888). Write **Travel Alberta,** Box 2500, Edmonton, T5J 0H4.

TOURS AND SPECIAL-INTEREST SIGHTSEEING. Assiniboine Heli Tours (678–5459) will show you the Rockies by helicopter. Located just east of town on Hwy. 1A. Flights start at $20 per person

Hoodoos. Visit these strange "earth pillars" carved out of the cliffs by the Bow River centuries ago. Made of glacial silt and calcium carbonate, they have managed to resist the forces of erosion. Located behind the cemetery on Benchlands Trail.

Pictographs. See the ancient markings made by native people on rocks at Grotto Mountain, a few miles east of Canmore on Hwy. 1A.

NATIONAL AND PROVINCIAL PARKS. Banff National Park. Only 10.5 miles (17 km) away. The Park gate is 2.5 miles (4 km) west of Canmore. See *Banff* for more information.

Bow Valley Provincial Park. Just 17.5 miles (28 km) east of Canmore. Part of Kananaskis Country, which starts on the edge of Canmore and stretches south and east. For more information see *Kananaskis Country.*

CAMPING. Bow Valley Provincial Park. 17.5 miles (28 km) east of Canmore on the edge of Hwy. 1. Camping for tents, trailers, and RVs. Reservations encouraged (678–3363).

Pigeon Mountain Resort. Box 1537 (678–5962). At Deadman's Flats just east of Canmore. Campsites, hookups, and showers.

Restwell Trailer Park. Box 388 (678–5111). Right in Canmore on the creek. Tents, RVs, and cabins.

Spray Lakes Valley (592–7222). Has several campsites off Spray Lakes Road (Hwy. 742) (see also *Kananaskis Country*).

OUTDOOR ACTIVITIES. The lakes and rivers near Canmore provide plenty of diversion for those who enjoy water sports. The *Whitewater Institute,* Box 1050 (678–4102), offers instruction in **canoing** and **kayaking,** and several firms in town rent boats and equipment. Anglers will have a field day **fishing** on the Bow River and the other local streams and lakes. Licenses and information are available in many stores, or contact the Canmore *Fish and Wildlife Office* (678–2373) in the Provincial Building, 800 Access Rd.

Lac des Arcs, 12.5 miles (20 km) east of Canmore, is renowned for challenging **windsurfing** conditions. And *Outdoor Adventure,* Deadman's Flats (678–2000), rents boards and equipment.

Johnny's Riding Stables (678–4171) rents horses by the hour or day. Just east of town off Hwy. 1, riders will find the stables convenient to trail heads.

Some of the best scenery a golfer will ever encounter is to be glimpsed from the 18-hole *Canmore Golf Course* on 17th St. and 8th Ave. The public is invited to take advantage of rentals, pro shop, restaurant, and club house. For greens reservations, call 678–5959.

Tennis buffs are welcome to use the public courts in *Lions' Park* on Fairholme Dr. at 15th St.

If **guided trips** and **mountaineering instruction** are what you're after, Canmore is the place for you. The Canmore-based *Canadian School of Mountaineering,* Box 723 (678–4138), conducts hikes, ski excursions, and climbs over rocks, ice, mountains, glaciers, and any other treacherous terrain you can think of.

As if that isn't enough, *The Ultimate in Rocky Mountain Adventures,* Box 1537 (678–2000), offers one- to five-day adventures combining whitewater rafting, trail riding, helicopter sightseeing, windsurfing, mountain bike touring, and canoeing.

World-class guides lead students of the *Yamnuska Mountain School,* Box 7500 (678–4164), on backpacking, rock, snow and ice climbing, self-rescue, wilderness training, mountaineering, and ski-touring trips of various lengths. They emphasize developing confidence and new friendships, as well as new wilderness skills.

HIKING. There are many fine day hikes around Canmore and back-country trips into Kananaskis Country, the Front Ranges, and the south end of Banff National Park. The Spray Lakes Rd. (Hwy. 742) in Spray Lakes Valley is the starting point. To get there, follow the signs through town to the Canmore Nordic Site and continue up the steep gravel road.

Bow River. Hike along the river in either direction.

Goat Creek. Take Spray Lakes Rd. past the upper reservoir. Parking lot and trail sign are on the right. This trail leads to the Banff Springs Hotel.

Grassi Lakes. On the left of Spray Lakes Rd., soon after the Nordic Site. The rustic trail was blazed by Lewis Grassi, a famous alpinist who lived in Canmore.

CROSS-COUNTRY SKIING. Canmore Nordic Site, on Spray Lakes Rd. (678–2400). Custom-built to the demands of world-class cross-country, nordic, and biathlon skiers. Extensive recreational trail system leading from the day lodge. A lighted 1-mile (1.5-km) trail for night skiing. Maps available.

Outstanding cross-country and telemark terrain surrounds Canmore. Often you can follow someone else's trail; sometimes, you get to blaze your own. Always inquire locally before you attempt an unfamiliar trail, and check on avalanche conditions. Carry a map, emergency food, clothing, and equipment.

DOWNHILL SKIING. The closest ski slopes are east in Kananaskis Country, **Fortress Mountain** and **Nakiska** at Mount Allan; and west in Banff National Park, **Mt. Norquay** and **Sunshine.**

SEASONAL EVENTS. January. *Winter Festival.* **February.** *Winter Sports Festival.* **July 1.** *Canada Day Celebration.* **August.** *Heritage Day Folk Festival. Canmore Oldtimers Rodeo.* **November.** *Arts and crafts fair.*

HISTORIC SITES AND HOUSES. Heritage Walk. Take an hour to relive 100 years of history. Starting at the North West Mounted Police barracks on 8th St., tour the Ralph Connor United Church, Cascade Insurance Co. Building, Canmore Hotel, Canmore Youth Centre, St. Michael's Anglican Church, Canmore Model School, the old hospital, and the Mine Shareholder's Cabin. Map available from Town of Canmore office (678–5593).

MUSEUMS. Passing of the Legends Museum. Rafter Six Ranch, Seebe (678–3622). Turn off on Hwy. 1, 17 miles (28 km) east of Canmore. Pioneer and Indian artifacts. Open 10 A.M.–9 P.M. summer, 10 A.M.–6 P.M. off-season.

Nakoda Institute/Lodge, between Seebe and Morley, on Hwy. 1A east of Canmore (881–3949). Artifacts, an A/V show on Stoney Indian history, and Indian art and handicrafts for sale.

SHOPPING. Local artisans sell handicrafts, ceramics, prints, glass, bronze, photographs, and clothing at these locations:

Mountain Aven Gallery. 730 9th St. (678–4471).

Settler's Cabin. 829 8th St. (678–5966).

Stonecrop Studios. 8th St. and 8th Ave. (678–4151).

THE ICEFIELDS PARKWAY

The Icefields Parkway between Lake Louise and Jasper is one of the world's greatest mountain high roads, named for the chain of huge icefields that lies among the peaks of the Rockies. Not long ago this journey took two weeks or more by pack train. Now you can cover the entire stretch in a day, but there's enough terrain here to last a lifetime of exploring.

Sprawling across Banff and Jasper parks and into British Columbia, the Columbia Icefield is the largest in the Rockies, covering 125 square miles. It feeds six large glaciers, three of which you will see on the Parkway—Athabasca, Dome, and Stutfield. It reaches depths of over 900 feet, and its meltwaters drain into three oceans, the Arctic, Pacific, and Atlantic. Underneath the ice is an extensive system of caves which may be even older than the icefield itself. The most famous is Castleguard Cave.

In the early 19th century, the Athabasca Glacier reached to where the road is, and it has since receded nearly a mile. Markers show the historical positions of the "toe," which is now four miles long and a half-mile wide. On its surface, you can walk on ice formed from snow that fell hundreds of years ago.

In the early 1800s local Indians and fur traders used parts of this route to cross the mountains. Surveyors, mountaineers, and early tourists followed in their footsteps, and place names along the way commemorate those hardy souls. The first road was built as a relief-work project during the Great Depression. The present road was finished only in the early 1960s.

ICEFIELDS PARKWAY

Northern Section **Southern Section**

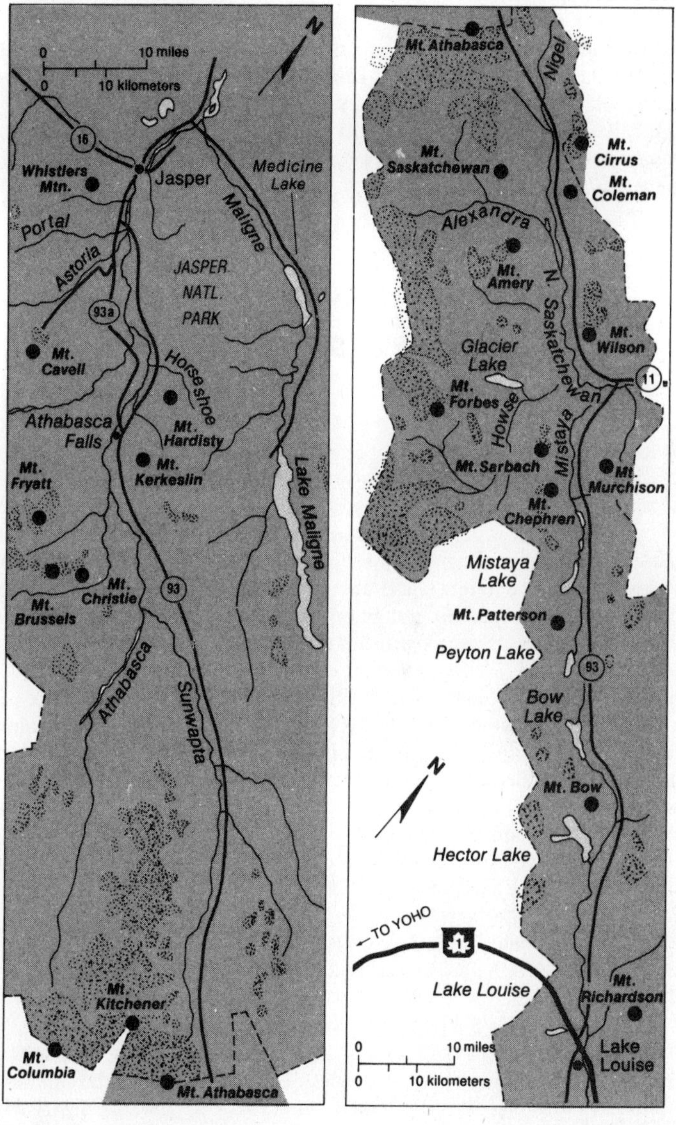

EXPLORING THE ICEFIELDS PARKWAY

If you're traveling from Lake Louise, you'll get your first look at the icefields at Crowfoot Glacier.

Bow Summit, 24 miles (40 km) north of Lake Louise, is the highest point on the road at 6,850 feet. Hike up to the viewpoint over Peyto Lake, where wildflowers abound in summer.

Athabasca Falls, 20 miles (32 km) south of Jasper, is an impressive example of the sculpting power of water, as is Sunwapta, 13 miles (22 km) further on.

PRACTICAL INFORMATION FOR THE ICEFIELDS PARKWAY

HOW TO GET THERE. By car. From Lake Louise, Jasper, or Rocky Mountain House, take Hwy. 11. The parkway (Hwy. 93) is built for leisurely sightseeing rather than high-speed travel. It winds around lakes and mountains and climbs through passes. You can travel the 143 miles (230 km) in a day but it is better to plan taking a few days. You'll want to stop frequently for views, photos, and wildlife. Gas, food, and accommodations are available only at a few places along the route, so it's important to plan well. The route is open all year but often closes after snowstorms. It can snow on the high passes even in mid-summer.

ACCOMMODATIONS AND RESTAURANTS. There's very little in the way of lodging along the Icefields Parkway, but those planning to make a thorough exploration of the area should consider staying in one of the establishments listed below, so as not to have to day-trip from Lake Louise and Jasper. All listings below fall into the *moderate* price range of $50–$80 for one night, double occupancy.

There are no restaurants to speak of on the parkway, other than those connected with the lodgings below. Of these, the Num-ti-Jah has excellent cuisine.

Columbia Icefield Chalet. Box 1140, Banff T0L 0C0 (762–2241). Incredible views of Athabasca Glacier. 22 rooms, restaurant, gift shop. Open May–Sept.

The Crossing. Bag Service 333, Lake Louise T0L 1E0 (721–3290). Located at junction of hwys. 93 and 11 at Saskatchewan River Crossing. 66 units, cafeteria, dining room, groceries, gas station. Open March–Nov.

Num-ti-Jah Lodge. Box 39, Lake Louise T0L 1E0 (phone Calgary Mobile Operator). Located 21 miles (34 km) north on the parkway at Bow Lake. Beautiful rustic lodge on lakeshore with 26 rooms and breathtaking views. Dining room, bar, coffee shop.

HOSTELS AND HUTS. There are several International Youth Hostels Federation (IYHF) establishments operating near the parkway, charging members $4–$6 and nonmembers $5–$7.

Rampart Creek. 12 miles (20 km) north of Saskatchewan River Crossing, 23 miles (34 km) south of Columbia Icefield Centre. Sleeps 30. Sauna. Closed Wed.

Hilda Creek. Five miles (8 km) south of Columbia Icefield Centre and 72 miles (120 km) north of Lake Louise at Parker's Ridge. Sleeps 21. Closed Thurs.

Beauty Creek. 48 miles (78 km) south of Jasper and 18 miles (30 km) north of Columbia Icefield Centre. Sleeps 20. Open May–mid-Sept., otherwise key system. Closed Wed.

Athabasca Falls. 18 miles (30 km) south of Jasper, 42 miles (68 km) north of Columbia Icefield Centre. Sleeps 40. Closed Tues.

Mt. Edith Cavell. 8 miles (13 km) off Hwy. 93A alternate. Sleeps 32. Road closed in winter; ski in. Closed Thurs. Key system mid-Sept.–April.

The Alpine Club of Canada runs the **Lloyd McKay Hut** on the remote Freshfield Glacier. Inquiries to *Alpine Club of Canada,* Box 1026, Banff, T0L 0C0 (762–4481).

Three Parks Canada huts—**Balfour Hut, Bow Hut,** and **Peyto Hut**—are popular but dangerous to get to. Reservations and permits from *Banff Information Centre,* 224 Banff Ave. (762–4256).

TOURIST INFORMATION. The **Icefield Information Centre,** 64 miles (103 km) south of Jasper town site, has exhibits on the Columbia Icefield and Athabasca Glacier. Open daily 9 A.M.–7 P.M., mid-June–Aug.; 9 A.M.–5 P.M., late May–mid-June and Sept.–mid-Oct.

TOURS. One-hour **Snocoach** Tours on the Athabasca Glacier operate daily, late-May–Sept. Huge, specially designed vehicles go out to the middle of the glacier, where you can walk on the ice, while the driver-guide explains glacial/geological features. Good footwear and warm clothes are recommended. Buy tickets at the Visitors Center, or for reservations contact *Columbia Icefield Tours,* Box 1140, Banff T0L 0C0 (762–2241).

HIKING. The hiking trails leading off the parkway provide some of the most beautiful and unusual of Rocky Mountain adventures. We can list only some of the most popular short trails; the nine mostly unserviced campgrounds along the parkway make good bases for those who seek longer sojourns into the wilderness.

There is a short river hike to Hector Lake. The four-mile Helen Creek trail leads to alpine meadows with summer wildflowers. Bow Lake picnic site has a short lake walk, and at Bow Summit a 400-yard walk will take you to an outstanding vista of Peyto Glacier and Lake. A 300-yard nature trail in Mistaya Canyon cuts through the gorge of the Mistaya River (*Mistaya* is Cree for grizzly bear; watch out).

A six-mile trail through a pine and spruce forest leads to exquisite Glacier Lake, with the tumbled ice-fall of Southeast Lyall Glacier beyond.

At Parker's Ridge, a steep mile-and-a-half ascent to 7,000 feet affords an expansive view over the massive Saskatchewan Glacier. This is a tongue of the Columbia Icefield and the source of the North Saskatchewan River, which flows east through Edmonton.

There are short walks around Athabasca Glacier and Athabasca Falls and, further on, a two-mile trail through burned-out areas of Wabasso Lake. Cavell Lake can be reached on a short trail from alternate Hwy. 93A.

A two-mile trail across alpine meadows leads to close views of Angel Glacier. The Valley of the Five Lakes trail runs a mile and a half through jade-green lakes. The Geraldine Lakes and Fryatt Valley trails are for day- and longer trips into the backcountry.

OUTDOOR ACTIVITIES. Cycling is a wonderful way to explore the Icefields Parkway at just the right speed. Hostels and campgrounds are located to suit fairly slow progress. (See *Practical Information for Banff* for ways of renting a bike or joining a cycle tour.)

Some of the best **cross-country skiing** in the Rockies can be found along the parkway. Only the remoteness and the cold should deter the adventurous—always notify the park warden office of your planned route, and never travel alone.

JASPER AND JASPER NATIONAL PARK

Jasper is the largest of Canada's Rocky Mountain national parks, 4,200 square miles of broad valleys, rugged mountains, majestic glaciers, lakes, forests, and alpine meadows along the eastern slopes of the Rockies.

This park is one of the last great wildlife refuges in the Rockies and a playground for naturalists and photographers. Elk, bighorn sheep, and mule deer abound. Black bears are often seen along roadways and near campgrounds, though chances of getting mauled by one are slim. Mountain goats, marmots, and pikes, and even a few grizzly bears inhabit the remote alpine elevations.

The town of Jasper has a population of 4,000. Unlike Banff, it manages to retain its small town provinciality—if not friendliness.

History

Amerindians, fur traders, geologists, railroad workers, mountaineers, naturalists, and prospectors all have played a part in the history of the area. In prehistoric times, a quarry near the park was the source of a flint-like quartz which the Amerindians used to fashion tools and arrowheads. Ancient artifacts made from this stone have been found several hundred miles away from the mine.

The first European explorers ventured into the region in the early 1800s in search of a fur trade route across the mountains. They established a local trading post and called it "Jasper's House," after the North West Company clerk, Jasper Hawse.

Exploring Jasper

Jasper Park is full of natural wonders that intrigue as well as impress. Medicine Lake, 19 miles (32 km) southeast of Jasper town on the Maligne

Lake Rd., actually disappears for part of the year! The water level varies seasonally due to underground drainage.

Seven miles (11 km) en route to Maligne Lake is Maligne Canyon, a spectacular limestone gorge with a maximum depth of 165 feet. A dramatic criss-crossing trail leads visitors back and forth over the deep and violent waters that tumble down the gorge. You get some idea why it was named the "wicked" river.

Thirty miles (48 km) southeast of Jasper on the same road lies Maligne Lake, at 13 miles long, the largest glacier-fed lake in the Canadian Rockies. Take a two-hour boat tour to the legendary Spirit Island or break out your fishing tackle—a 21-lb. rainbow trout was caught here in 1980!

There are paved trails for bikes and wheelchairs around lakes Edith and Annette, only 3.5 miles (6 km) from town on Jasper Lodge Rd. The lakes have the warmest water of any in the park and nice beaches for picnics and sunbathing.

Thirty miles east of town on the Miette Hot Springs Rd., is an unusual rock formation at Punchbowl Falls. Take a bathing suit. You are welcome to take a dip in the hot mineral waters of the nearby springs.

A winding road northwest of town leads to two sparkling lakes, Patricia and Pyramid. Only 5 miles (8 km) away, this is a place where the whole family can enjoy boating, windsurfing, horseback riding, fishing and, of course, hiking and skiing.

A trip to the top of Whistlers Mountain, named for the whistling marmots who live there, will afford you a glimpse of Mt. Robson to the west, the highest peak in the Canadian Rockies. Turn to the south and view the vast Columbia Icefield.

PRACTICAL INFORMATION FOR JASPER AND JASPER NATIONAL PARK

HOW TO GET THERE. By air. The closest major airports are in Edmonton and Calgary. Small planes and charter flights land on a paved runway at Hinton, 40 miles east (64 km).

By car. Jasper is 225 miles (362 km) west of Edmonton and 265 miles (450 km) northwest of Calgary, at the intersection of the Yellowhead Route (Hwy. 16) and the Icefield Parkway (Hwy. 93). It's 178 miles (287 km) from Banff and 143 miles (233 km) north of Lake Louise.

By bus. *Greyhound* has daily service to Edmonton (421–4211) and connections from there to Calgary (265–9111). *Brewsters,* Box 400, Jasper, T0E 1E0, has an express bus service to Banff, with connections to Calgary (852–3332 or 762–3207).

By train. *VIA Rail* has one eastbound and one westbound train daily. Edmonton is the first stop on the eastbound line. The westbound train stops in Valemount, Blue River, Clearwater, and Kamloops en route to Vancouver. The station is in downtown Jasper on Connaught Dr.; for information call 800–665–8630.

ACCOMMODATIONS. From modern hotels with all the amenities in the town of Jasper, to rustic bungalows in the wilderness, the park boasts a wide range of lodging options. Accommodations at B&Bs can be booked through bureaus listed under *Calgary* (above). Mailing addresses are Box #, Jasper, AB, T0E 1E0. Price categories for double occupancy rooms, excluding tax and tip are: *Super Deluxe,* $125 and up; *Deluxe,* $100–$125; *Expensive,* $80–$100; and *Moderate,* $50–$80.

Super Deluxe

Château Jasper. Box 1418 (852–5644 or 800–661–9323). 96 Geikie St. Beauvallon dining room, piano bar, indoor pool, whirlpool, gift shop, and rooftop sun deck. Wheelchair facilities.

Jasper Park Lodge. (852–3301 or 800–268–8136). Sits in splendor on the edge of Lac Beauvert, on the east side of the Athabasca River. Guests have the benefit of a golf course, fishing, boating, riding, pool, tennis, exercise room, sauna, and whirlpool. Wheelchair facilities. Open year-round.

Deluxe

Jasper Inn Motor Lodge. Box 879 (852–4461 or 800–661–1933). At Bonhomme and Geikie sts. Whirlpool, sauna, pool, and dining room.

Sawridge Hotel. Box 2080 (852–5111 or 800–661–6427). 82 Connaught Dr. Dining room, pool, steam room, Jacuzzi, and two outdoor hot tubs. Wheelchair facilities.

Expensive

Andrew Motor Lodge. Box 850 (852–3394). 200 Connaught Dr. Steamroom and restaurant. Wheelchair facilities.

Lobstick Lodge. Box 1200 (852–4431 or 800–661–9317). Juniper and Geikie sts. Optional kitchenettes, restaurant, pool, sauna, whirlpool, and game room. Under 15 free.

Moderate

Astoria Hotel. Box 850 (852–3386). 404 Connaught Dr., one block from the train station. Sauna, and bar.

Athabasca Hotel. Box 1420 (852–3386). 510 Patricia St. Not all rooms are equipped with bathrooms. Dining room, lounge, and popular tavern with disco dancing.

Black Cat Guest Ranch. Box 976 (865–3084). 12.5 miles (20 km) northwest of Hinton. 43 miles of trails for riding and hiking. Skiing and barbecues. All meals included.

Marmot Lodge. Box 687 (852–4471 or 800–661–6521). 92 Connaught Dr. Restaurant, lounge, and evening entertainment. Pool, sauna, and whirlpool.

Mt. Robson Motor Inn. Box 88 (852–3327). 901 Connaught Dr. Kitchenettes available.

Overlander. Box 960, Hinton, T0E 1B0 (866–3790). 15 miles (24 km) west of Hinton outside Jasper Park. Lodge rooms, chalets, and cabins. Hiking, skiing, skating, and fishing.

Pyramid Lake Bungalows. Box 388 (852–3536). 3.5 miles northwest of the Jasper town site on Pyramid Lake Rd. Kitchenette bungalows. Beach, restaurant. and rentals of boats, canoes, and windsurfers. Open April–mid-Oct.

Tekarra Resort. Box 669 (852–3058). Off Hwy. 93A, one mile south of the Jasper town site on the Athabasca and Miette rivers. Lodge rooms and cabins.

Tonquin Motor Inn. Box 658 (852–4987 or 852–4436) at the east end of town at Connaught Dr. and Juniper St. Whirlpool and restaurant.

Tonquin Valley Camp. Box 550 (852–3909). On the north shore of Amethyst Lake. High in the Tonquin Valley with the peaks of the Ramparts towering above, this is in one of the most beautiful places to stay in the Rockies. Built in the 1930s, the camp comprises a lodge and five rustic cabins, heated by wood-burning stoves. Hearty home-cooked meals are included. Accessible via a 15.5-mile (25-km) hike or cross-country ski. Open from late Jan. to mid-April and July through Sept.

Whistlers Motor Hotel. Box 250 (852–3361). Opposite the train station at 105 Miette Ave. B&B available during off-season. Sauna and whirlpool. Check out "The Den" wildlife museum down in the basement.

YOUTH HOSTELS. Hostels accept travelers of all ages and provide warm, dry accommodations in picturesque settings. Nightly rates for members of International Youth Hostels Federation (IYHF) are $4–$6; nonmembers, $6–$9.

Maligne Canyon. 9 miles (15 km) east of Jasper town site on the Sky Tram Rd. Sleeps 24. Family rooms. Closed Wed.

Whistler's Mountain. At the base of Whistler's Mt., 4.5 miles (7 km) south of Jasper on Hwy. 93. Sleeps 50. Showers.

RESTAURANTS. Not quite up to Banff standards, the restaurants in Jasper are more likely to please eaters with big appetites than those with cultivated palates. Price categories for two meals including appetizers, exclusive of tax and tip are: *Deluxe,* $50–$75; *Expensive,* $25–$50; *Moderate,* $15–$25; and *Inexpensive,* under $15.

Deluxe

Jasper Park Lodge main dining room and **Henry House.** Good Alberta steaks and great views.

Expensive

Beauvallon Dining Room. Château Jasper, 96 Geikie St. (852–5644). International menu with a European emphasis. Steak, chicken, and rabbit, as well as vegetarian dishes.

Inn Restaurant. Jasper Inn, corner of Bonhomme and Geikie St. (852–3232). Seafood and chicken specials nightly. Specialties include West Coast clams, oysters, crab, and pasta. Children's menu.

Moderate

Amethyst Dining Room. Andrew Motor Lodge, 200 Connaught Dr. (852–3394). Specializes in Italian food.

Lobstick Lodge Dining Lounge. Juniper and Geikie St. (852–4431). Canadian and Italian food. Steaks, ribs, and trout. No lunch served.

Marmot Dining Lounge. Marmot Lodge, 94 Connaught Dr. (852–4544). Continental menu with steak and seafood. No lunch.

Red Dragon. Athabasca Hotel, Patricia and Miette sts. (852–3386). Chinese and Canadian food.

Something Else. 623 Patricia St. (852–3850). Specializes in Greek and Italian food. Souvlaki, baklava, donairs, and pizza.

Tokyo Tom's Place. 1491 Geikie St. (852–3780). Run by a Japanese ski instructor who swears by the authenticity of the Japanese fare. Sushi bar, sukiyaki, sashimi, tempura, and teriyaki. Dinner only.

Tonquin Prime Rib Village. 1216 Juniper St. (852–4966). Seafood specialties include arctic char, salmon, and prawns. Children's menu. No lunch served.

Villa Caruso. 628 Connaught Dr. (852–3920). Alberta prime rib, pizza, and pasta. Dinner only.

Inexpensive

Jasper Pizza Place. 402 Connaught Dr. (852–3225). Burgers, chicken, and pizza. Free delivery to hotels.

L&W Takeout. At the corner of Hazel and Patricia St. (852–4114). Great burgers, ribs, souvlaki, and pizza—all homemade.

NIGHTLIFE AND BARS. Nightlife in Jasper usually means a quiet romp in the woods or drinks with pals in a bar. But for more conventional evening entertainment, try:

Dancing and live music at **Astoria Hotel, Athabasca Hotel, Marmot Lodge,** and **Sawridge Hotel.** Live entertainment also at **Château Jasper** and other hotels and bars.

HOW TO GET AROUND. By bike. Rent one in town. Some motels provide them for guests free.

By bus. *Brewsters* runs service between the ski hill and major hotels (852–3332).

By rental car. Companies with offices in both Jasper and Banff are *Avis* (852–3970 or 800–268–2310), *Hertz* (852–3793 or 800–268–1311) and *Tilden* (852–3978 or 800–663–9822).

By taxi. *Jasper Taxi* (852–3146).

TOURIST INFORMATION. Jasper Chamber of Commerce. (852–3858) Box 98, Jasper, T0E 1E0, is at 634 Connaught Dr. Open 9 A.M.–5 P.M., weekdays.

Jasper Park Information Centre. (852–6176). Box 10, Jasper, T0E 1E0, is at 500 Connaught Dr. Open mid-June–Sept. 1, 8 A.M.–9 P.M.; the rest of the year 9 A.M.–5 P.M.

Park Warden Office. (852–6156). 5 miles east of the town site. Open weekdays, 8 A.M.–4:30 P.M.

Travel Alberta. (800–222–6501). 632 Connaught Dr. Open May–Oct., 9 A.M.–9 P.M.

CAMPING. The two biggest campgrounds in the park are just south of town on the Icefields Parkway: **Whistlers** and **Wapiti** have a total of 1,100 sites. In addition, there are two campgrounds off Hwy. 16 going east, **Snaring River** and **Pocahontas.** The latter and **Wabasso,** 10 miles (16 km) south on the Icefields Parkway, have facilities for visitors in wheelchairs. Of course, there are many fine camping sites in the backcountry that can be reached by hiking.

HIKING. With over 600 miles of trails that vary in challenge, from gentle strolls to arduous uphill treks, Jasper Park is a hiker's nirvana. Rewarding day hikes start within Jasper town limits and along the Icefields Parkway. Guide books and trail maps are available at local shops, tourist centers, and park service offices.

The most famous—and most frequented—overnight backpacking routes are the Skyline, Tonquin Valley, Fryatt Valley, and Maligne Pass trails; each takes at least three days. Geraldine Lakes and Watchtower Basin make for pleasant overnight trips. Those seeking high-country adventure rather than just a few days away from the hustle and bustle of modern life should check out the Athabasca Pass Trail, which takes a week to traverse, and the North Boundary and South Boundary trails, which each take at least 10 days to cover and should be undertaken only by experienced packers who are skilled in wilderness survival.

The park service restricts the number of backpackers using the trails at any one time. For more information, or to pre-book yourself for a trail, write to Park Superintendent, Box 10, Jasper, T0E 1E0. Brewsters Bus Lines runs service to trailheads along the Icefields Parkway.

OUTDOOR ACTIVITIES. Many of the motels in Jasper provide bicycles for guests who want to **cycle** around town. Local firms rent the more hardy mountain bikes for people who want to try hiking on two wheels. For cycle tours, see *Banff* above.

For sightseeing on **horseback,** the *Jasper Park Riding Academy* (852–3301) and *Pyramid Riding Stables* (852–3562) feature hourly and daily horse rentals.

In the spring and summer months, several firms offer organized **trail rides** which can last anywhere from an afternoon to several days, with meals included. Contact *Miette Trail Rides* (693–2157), General Delivery, Jasper, T0E 1E0; *Skyline Trail Rides* (852–4215), Box 207, Jasper, T0E 1E0; *Tonquin Valley Amethyst Pack Trips* (865–4417), Box 508, Jasper, T0E 1E0; *Ward's Guiding and Outfitting* (852–3717), Box 717, Jasper, T0E 1E0.

River adventure buffs will want to take advantage of the abundant **rafting** opportunities in the area. Half-day, full-day, and longer trips along the Athabasca River are available through *Jasper Mt. River Guide* (852–4721), Box 362, Jasper, T0E 1E0; and *Jasper Raft Tours* (852–3613), Box 398, Jasper, T0E 1E0.

Tomahawk Canoe Trips, 11035 64th Ave., Edmonton, T6H 1T4 (436–9189), offers **canoeing** lessons and trips of a few hours to several days. But if you just want to paddle around for fun in a row boat or canoe, many of the lodges on the local lakes offer boat-rental services to guests and non-guests.

If, for some reason, you would rather play **golf** than enjoy the natural splendor, the *Jasper Park Golf Club,* beside Jasper Park Lodge, is a challenging 18-hole course (852–3301).

The high altitude will add a new dimension to your **tennis** game. There are public courts at the *Recreation Centre* in town and courts at the *Jasper Park Lodge.*

Guided adventure trips are offered year-round. *Camp Apa Cheesta* (865–7877 or 800–661–1924), Box 803, Hinton, T0E 1B0, is an isolated camp 12 miles north of Brule on the Jasper Park boundary. In the winter, native guides take small parties on overnight cross-country ski trips in the Willmore Wilderness. Don't worry—sled dogs carry the food supplies and gear. In summertime, parties of 10 people can stay in a tipi camp and receive instruction in native culture and handicrafts.

Clarey/Bush Outfitting and Guiding (852–4078), Box 84, T0E 1E0, leads **guided packing trips** for all ages and skill levels. *Jasper Climbing School* (852–3964) offers courses on ice trekking, mountaineering, climbing, and ski-touring.

CROSS-COUNTRY SKIING. The vast wilderness of Jasper Park provides many opportunities for excellent and challenging backcountry skiing trips. But only those experienced in winter survival skills should undertake these expeditions. Always consult the park office for avalanche reports.

Many visitors prefer the tamer, marked, and groomed trails. Four areas near the town site feature the track-set trail system:

Maligne Lake area, 30 miles (48 km) from town, has five trails. Additional trails at **Beaver-Summit Lakes** at Medicine Lake, 16 miles (26 km) from Jasper.

Athabasca-Whirlpool area, about 20 miles (30 km) south of town.

Pyramid Bench areas along Pyramid Lake Rd., just north of town.

DOWNHILL SKIING. Marmot Basin Ski Lifts. Box 1300, Jasper, T0E 1E0 (852–3816 or 800–222–6501). The ski hill is 12 miles (19 km) from Jasper. 33 runs, three double and one triple chair, three t-bars, two day lodges, three restaurants. Open Dec.–May.

SEASONAL EVENTS. January. *Ice sculpting contest.* **February.** *Jasper Winter Festival.* **February-April.** *Ski races* at Marmot Basin. **Mid-June.** *Jasper/Banff relay road race.* **July 1.** *Canada Day* celebrations. **Mid-August.** *Jasper Indoor Rodeo.* For information, call 852–3858.

TOURS. *Brewster Transportation and Tours.* (762–2241) Box 1140, Banff, T0L 0C0. Bus tours from Jasper to explore the park, Lake Louise, the Columbia Icefield, and Maligne Lake. Raft tours on the Athabasca River are also offered.

Jasper Tramway. (852–3093) Box 418, Jasper, T0E 1E0. Two miles (3.5 km) south of the town site on Whistlers Mountain Road. Whisks visitors over 8,000 feet up Whistlers Mountain for views that extend 60 miles west to Mt. Robson and 47 miles south to the Columbia Icefield. Operates from mid-April–mid-Oct.

Maligne Tours. (852–3370) Box 280, Jasper, T0E 1E0. Office at 626 Connaught Dr. Scenic boat cruises on the beautiful Maligne Lake from June–Sept. Row- and motor-boat rentals. Tackle and fishing guides. Horseback riding and river rafting are also available. In winter, Maligne gives tours of the frozen labyrinth of canyon.

HIGHWAY 40: THE EASTERN SLOPE (NORTH)

Highway 40, the Forestry Trunk Road parallel to the Rocky Mountains, provides access to an area of the Eastern Slopes until recently seen only by trappers. If you're an intrepid tourist who likes to wander in undeveloped backcountry, if your idea of a fine meal is fresh-caught pan-fried fish, if watching the flames of a campfire and listening to owls hoot is your idea of nightlife, then this route is for you. For the most part, you're on your own. There's little in the way of services, food, or accommodations for hundreds of miles at a time. So fill up with gas, stock up the icebox, and prepare for a memorable adventure.

The Eastern Slopes are forested foothills stretching from Grand Prairie to the U.S. border. The 35,000 square miles of forest is mostly white spruce and lodgepole pine, with alpine fir and larch lining meadows higher up. In the lowlands and along rivers, poplar and willow create a quite different scene.

Wildlife is plentiful. Rocky Mountain bighorn sheep, mountain goat, and grizzly bear roam this wild country. Elk and deer forage in the open, moose feed in the marshes, and black bear can be found in berry patches.

North of Highway 1

This is unparalleled country to travel on horseback. There are many local guides and outfitters providing trips into the wilderness (see *Trail Riding* below). But even if you stick only to the road, you'll still travel through remote and untouched terrain.

Grande Cache is named for huge piles of furs kept there for spring trading in the 1800s. Its "new town," population 9,000, was built out of the bush in 1968 to service the mining and forestry industries. It now relies more on tourism and is a major gateway to the Willmore Wilderness.

Willmore Wilderness is a vast 1,700-square-mile park with about 450 miles of trails. It lies northwest of Hinton and west of Grande Cache, along the remote northern boundary of Jasper National Park, with the Continental Divide to the west. Hunting and fishing are allowed in Willmore in season with licenses, but motorized vehicles are prohibited. The main trailheads are at Rock Lake, Big Berland, and Hell's Gate (see *Camping*).

From Grande Cache to Hinton, the route rolls through muskeg forest and "kettle holes" left behind by retreating glaciers, typical of Northern Alberta landscape. Watch out for caribou in the area. Stop at one of the many lakes to fish, picnic, or camp.

Between Hinton and Nordegg, the road passes through many small mining ghost towns. The Luscar Cardinal Mine, however, is still active, and providing an interesting look at a typical open-face works.

Hwy. 40 crosses the David Thompson Highway (Hwy. 11) at Nordegg, once a thriving mining community. If you have time to go west towards Banff National Park, the route has many rewards. It is named after the trader and surveyor for the Northwest Company, who came this way, crossed the Rockies via Howse Pass, and established the first fur-trading post in the Columbia Valley in British Columbia.

Crescent Falls is worth a visit. Big Horn Dam, 17 miles (28 km) west, has created Abraham Lake, Alberta's longest.

Kootenay Plains

Kootenay Plains is a unique natural area 42 miles (70 km) west of Nordegg; its grasslands stand sharp contrast to the surrounding mountains. There are Indian ceremonial grounds and hiking trails to the impressive Siffleur Canyon and Falls. For those who really want to get away from it all, there is access nearby to two wilderness areas.

Siffleur and White Goat wilderness areas, together with the Ghost River area farther south on Hwy. 40, were set up to protect the unspoiled beauty of the region's mountains, valleys, and streams. They offer visitors the challenge and solitude of an undisturbed natural setting. Visitors travel on foot only. Horses, hunting, fishing, and trapping are prohibited.

At Ram River Falls, 30 miles (50 km) south of Hwy. 11, the South Ram River plunges into a dark ravine. At Corkscrew Mountain, 40 miles (66 km) northwest of Ricinus, you get an excellent view of the meandering Clearwater River. Big Horn Falls are 48 miles (80 km) NW of Cochrane near Ya Ha Tinda Ranch. Providing a landmark on the horizon, the distinctive black cliffs of "Devil's Head" appear to the west. The peak lies six miles (10 km) north of Lake Minnewanka in Banff National Park.

When you reach Hwy. 1A, near Cochrane, drive west along the scenic Bow Valley Trail to rejoin Hwy. 40 about 18 miles (30 km) east of Canmore.

PRACTICAL INFORMATION FOR HIGHWAY 40

HOW TO GET THERE. By air. The nearest airports are Edmonton and Calgary. **By car.** The towns on or near Hwy. 40 for access at various points are Grande Cache, Hinton, and Nordegg.

ACCOMMODATIONS. There are plenty of accommodations along Hwy. 40, all of them predictably new, and all of them, predictably, in Grande Cache (postal code T0E 0Y0), Hinton (T0E 1B0), and Nordegg (T0M 2H0). Our price categories for one night double-occupancy, exclusive of tax and tip, are: *Expensive,* over $80; *Moderate,* $50–$80; and *Inexpensive,* under $50.

Grande Cache

Moderate

Grande Cache Hotel. Box 600 (827–3731). Some water beds and executive suites; some with whirlpool. Restaurant, lounge, tavern.

Inexpensive

Alpine Lodge Motel. Box 1379 (827–2450). 36 units, cafeteria.

Big Horn Motor Inn. Box 20B (827–3744). 36 units, restaurant, and lounge.

Mountain Village Motel. Box 659 (827–2453). 48 units. Sauna.

Hinton

Expensive

Overlander Lodge Resort. Box 960 (866–3790). A mile east of Jasper Park. 26 lodge, bungalow, and motel units. Riding, hiking, cross-country skiing, restaurant, pool.

Moderate

Crestwood Hotel. Hinton (865–4001). Has 98 rooms, including suites with whirlpool. Sauna, pool, restaurant, lounge, tavern, laundry.

Green Tree Motor Lodge. Box 938 (865–1924). 101 rooms, some suites. Movies, restaurant, lounge, pool, and sauna. Kids under 16 free.

Twin Pine Motor Inn. Box 1035 (865–2281 or 800–232–9412). 54 rooms, some with water beds. Restaurant, lounge. Wheelchair facilities.

Inexpensive

Alpine Park Motor. Box 1125 (865–5099). On Hwy. 16, with 40 units; no charge for kids under 12. Store, laundry.

Athabasca Valley Hotel. Box 2300 (865–2241). In the shopping center, 50 rooms, some with bath. Restaurant, lounge, tavern.

Folding Mountain Cabins. Box 608 (866–3737). Two miles east of Jasper Park. 18 cabins. Restaurant. Open mid-April–mid-Oct.

Tara Vista Motel. Box 187 (865–3391). 28 units.

Timberland Hotel. Box 1250 (865–2231). 35 rooms, some with bathroom. Restaurant and tavern.

Nordegg

Inexpensive

Nordegg Resort Lodge. Nordegg (721–3757). 38 units. Restaurant, lounge, groceries, gas.

GUEST RANCHES. Bar Cee Guest Ranch. *Moderate.* Box 184, Cochrane T0L 0W0 (932–2665). Nine miles (14 km) west of Cochrane on Hwy. 940. Guest cabins, riding, barbecues, hayrides, sleigh rides, cross-country skiing, hiking, camping.

Black Cat Guest Ranch. *Moderate.* Box 976, Hinton (865–3084). Two miles (3 km) west of Hinton—go north on Hwy. 40, then west on Brule Rd. Sleeps 32. Trail rides, hiking, barbecues, cross-country skiing.

YOUTH HOSTELS. Shunda Creek (721–2140). Two miles north of Nordegg. Sleeps 39. Some family rooms. Closed Tues. and Wed. nights. IYHF members, $6; nonmembers, $9.

RESTAURANTS. Places to eat aren't all over the place in the wilderness. With a few trivial exceptions, restaurants along Hwy. 40 are all either service-station cafeterias or hotel-affiliated. See *Accommodations* above for dining rooms and restaurants. Most of the hotel restaurants fall into the price category designated *Moderate* elsewhere in this chapter.

HOW TO GET AROUND. By car. It's 90 miles (144 km) from Grande Cache to Hinton; 118 miles (192 km) from Hinton to Nordegg; 164 miles (264 km) from Nordegg to Hwy. 1A near Cochrane.

By bike. The road is paved between Grande Cache and Hinton and west from Nordegg on Hwy. 11 to Saskatchewan River Crossing.

TOURIST INFORMATION. Alberta Forest Service, Recreation Section, 9915 108th St., Edmonton TK5 2C9 (427–3582) is a useful source of pre-trip information on all of Alberta's wilderness areas. Local forest headquarters include:

Bow/Crow Forest. 8660 Bearspaw Dam NW, Calgary T9H 4P1 (297–6261).

Edson Forest. Box 1420, Edson T0E 0P0 (723–3391).

Rocky-Clearwater Forest. Box 1720, Rocky Mountain House T0M 1T0 (845–8250).

Travel Alberta. Box 2500, Edmonton T5J 2Z4 (800–222–6501 or 800–661–8888).

Local tourist offices:

David Thompson Country Tourist Council. 4811 48th Ave., Red Deer T4N 3T2 (342–2032).

Evergreen Tourist Association. Box 2548 Edson, T0E 0P0 (723–4711).

NATIONAL AND PROVINCIAL PARKS. Rocky Mountain House National Historic Park (845–2412), three miles (5 km) southwest of Rocky Mountain House on Hwy. 11A, tells the story of 18th-century fur-trading posts. Open daily May–Sept., 10 A.M.–8 P.M.; Sept.–May, weekdays 8.30 A.M.–5 P.M., weekends 10 A.M.–6 P.M. Free admission.

William Switzer Provincial Park, 12 miles (19 km) north of Hinton, has 207 campsites with wheelchair facilities, and lots of fishing, hiking, and boating.

See text above for information on **Ghost, Siffleur, White Goat** and **Willmore Wilderness** areas.

CAMPING. For most of the Hwy. 40, there are no commercial accommodations, only forest-service campgrounds with pit toilets. All roadside and backcountry sites are designated. Get a map of the sites from the Forestry Service. This is ideal country for tents and campers, though some sites are unsuitable for RVs.

Grande Cache–Hinton:

Big Berland. 43 miles (70 km) northwest of Hinton. 20 sites. Trail head for Willmore Wilderness.

Blue Bridge. A mile west of Grande Cache. 22 sites. Pretty basic facilities.

Hell's Gate. Six miles (10 km) north of Grande Cache. 10 sites. Trail head for Willmore Wilderness.

Pierre Grey's Lakes. 74 miles (120 km) northwest of Hinton, beautiful lake scenery.

Rock Lake. 53 miles (86 km) northwest of Hinton. 70 sites near lake trail head for Willmore Wilderness.

William Switzer Provincial Park (865–7504). 207 sites. Trailer hookups, showers, fishing on lakes.

Hinton–Nordegg (north):

Cardinal River. 56 miles (91 km) south of Hinton. 11 sites near an outstanding viewpoint.

Coalspur. Six miles (10 km) south of Robb. Eight sites.

Fairfax Lake. 65 miles (105 km) of Edson. 15 sites.

Hinton Campground. At Hinton Valley turn-off. 50 sites.

Lovett River. 18 miles (30 km) southeast of Coalspur. 17 sites.

Mountain Park. 45 miles (75 km) southeast of Hinton. 12 sites.

Pembina Forks. 68 miles (109 km) south of Edson. 20 sites.

Watson Creek. 69 miles (112 km) southwest of Edson. 39 sites.

Whitehorse Creek. 75 miles (122 km) southwest of Edson. 13 sites.

Nordegg:

Blackstone. 19 miles (30 km) north of Nordegg. Seven sites.

Brazeau River. 45 miles (72 km) north of Nordegg. 10 sites.

Brown Creek. 28 miles (45 km) north of Nordegg. 12 sites.

Thompson Creek. 54 miles (87 km) southwest of Nordegg. 55 sites.

Upper Shunda Creek. Two miles (3 km) northwest of Nordegg. 21 sites.

Nordegg–Hwy. 1A:

Burnt Timber. 40 miles (65 km) southwest of Sundre. 30 sites.

Fallen Timber. 48 miles (80 km) northwest of Cochrane. 59 sites.

James-Wilson. 24 miles (40 km) west of Sundre. 15 sites.

North Ghost. 42 miles (70 km) northwest of Cochrane. 173 sites.

Waiparous Creek. 39 miles (65 km) northwest of Cochrane. 59 sites.

Wildhorse. 42 miles (70 km) west of Sundre. Four sites.

OUTDOOR ACTIVITIES. Hiking trails in the country around Hwy. 40 are neither as well-defined nor as well-traveled as elsewhere in the Rockies. Always travel with a compass and a detailed map here. Leave a note on your vehicle dashboard describing your route and the estimated time of your return, or notify a park or forest warden about your plans.

Hunting and **fishing** are excellent in the region, but remember that hunting is illegal in national and provincial parks. You will need a fishing license ($5–$12, depending on citizenship; available at stores locally) in order to try Hwy. 40's excellent rivers and streams. Hunting and fishing information from *Alberta Fish and Wildlife,* 9945 108th St., Edmonton, AB T5K 2C9.

The terrain is ideal for **cross-country skiing** in winter, but take the same precautions mentioned above for hiking if you're thinking of venturing into the wilderness.

TRAIL RIDING. Trail riding trips can recapture some of the romance and adventure of the pioneer days in the wilderness, with of course lots of luxuries. Outfitters abound in this part of the province.

Willmore-Grande Cache area.

Athabasca Trail Trips. Entrance Ranch, Box 951, Hinton, T0E 1B0 (865–7549). Trips into Willmore Wilderness.

High Country Ride and Fish. Box 354, Wildwood T0E 2M0 (325–3961). Summer trips into Willmore Wilderness.

High Country Vacations. Box 818, Grande Cache T0E 0Y0 (827–3246). Five-day or custom-length trips into Willmore Wilderness, June–Aug.

Sherwood Guides and Outfitters. (Peter McMahon). 1 Birch Village, 22322 Wye Rd., Sherwood Park T8A 2S9 (922–2266). Longer trips into

Willmore Wilderness. Hearty home-style meals, roomy tents. Mid-June–mid-Aug.

Tom Vinson Horseback Adventures. Brule T0E 0C0 (865–2641 or 865–4777). Longer trips into Willmore Wilderness or Jasper Park. June–Aug.

Washy Creek Outfitters. Box 6, Grande Cache T0E 0Y0 (827–2699 or 827–3520). Summer and winter trips in the Grande Cache and Willmore Wilderness areas. Trail riding, cross-country skiing, winter camping.

Nordegg-Hinton area.

Diamond Jim's Mountain Rides. Box 394, Rocky Mountain House T0M 1T0 (845–6859 or 845–6920). Hourly and daily rides in the Eastern Slopes near Nordegg, mid-June–Aug.

McKenzie's Trails West. Box 971, Rocky Mountain House, T0M 1T0 (845–6708). Trips to the Eastern Slopes, northwest of Nordegg.

Sam Sands Summer Pack Trips and Trail Rides. Box 568, Rocky Mountain House T0M 1T0 (845–6487, 845–4190 or 845–6676). Longer trips along the Ram and Saskatchewan rivers. June–Sept.

Hwy. 1A-Nordegg.

Holmes Outdoor Recreation. c/o Holmes Mountainaire Lodge, Box 570, Sundre, T0M 1X0 (call Calgary Mobile Operator and ask for lodge). Short and long rides along Red Deer and Panther rivers. Everything included.

Panther Valley Packtrips. Elnora T0M 0Y0 (773–2442). Longer trips along Panther and Dormer rivers. Includes meals and pick-up in Calgary. June–Sept.

Saddle Peak Trailrides. Box 1463, Cochrane T0L 0W0 (932–3299). Three- to five-day trips into Ghost River area, with white-water rafting. May–Sept.

MUSEUMS. Alberta Forestry Museum. In the Alberta Forest Technology School, 1176 Switzer Dr., Hinton (865–8211). Open Mon.–Fri., 8:30 A.M.–4:30 P.M. free admission.

KANANASKIS COUNTRY: THE EASTERN SLOPE (SOUTH)

Kananaskis Country offers astounding scenery and a whole range of outdoor activities. Its boundaries encompass more than 1,600 square miles of foothills, mountains, forests, valleys, lakes, and rivers. And the provincial government pushes this as an alternative to the crowded Banff and Jasper parks.

The name *Kananaskis* comes from an Indian term for "the place where the two rivers meet." An ancient Indian legend also has it that there was once a warrior named Kananaskis who survived a terrible axe blow in a skirmish between the Stoney and Kootenai tribes over control of the valley.

Wild animals are plentiful and should be allowed to remain so. Bighorn sheep, elk, deer, moose, squirrel, and beaver, as well as many species of birds, are commonly seen. Black and grizzly bears and mountain goats are around if you know where to find them.

Exploring Kananaskis

Four miles (seven km) south of Hwy. 1, turn east along Sibbald Trail for a scenic backroad tour of the foothills area. The road loops round to meet Hwy. 1 at the Sibbald Flats turn-off. The Kananaskis Forest Experiment Station here has a pleasant trail that will introduce you to the local flora and fauna and forestry-management techniques. It was used as a POW camp in World War II (see *Historic Sites* below).

Mt. Allan and the Nakiska ski resort lie to the west, 16 miles (26 km) south of the TransCanada. The Fortress Mountain Ski resort is only 12 miles (19 km) away. Nearby, a new alpine village has taken shape at Ribbon Creek. Until recently a small youth hostel was virtually the only accommodation available in the valley. Now three hotels await skiers, hikers, and golfers.

The scenic Lougheed Provincial Park, 35 miles (56 km) south of Hwy. 1, offers enough outdoor pursuits to keep most people occupied for a week or two. Explore the Spray Trail/Smith-Dorrien Rd. towards Canmore in Spray Valley. The road is open year-round.

Highwood Pass, 51 miles (82 km) south of Hwy. 1 on Hwy. 40, is the highest drivable pass in Canada. You can see snow in July here. The views are beautiful anytime, but try to visit in fall when the trees change color. The steep Ptarmigan Cirque trail will take you up to a fragile alpine world. A boardwalk trail from the parking lot runs across equally fragile marshland.

From Highwood Junction—last gas station—it's 69 miles (112 km) to Crowsnest Pass along Hwy. 940 (Kananaskis Road). Beware: it has a graded gravel surface and is used by logging trucks. You'll find beautiful scenery, solitude, and quiet campgrounds if you can cope with poor road conditions and fast-moving trucks.

Wild Water

It's worth a short detour along Hwy. 517 for the Gap, a dramatic break in the Livingstone Range, where the Oldman River plunges through a narrow gorge from the mountains in to the surrounding prairies.

Take a break at Livingstone Falls 40 miles (65 km) north of Hwy. 3, where the Livingstone River rushes over the rock face, creating picturesque falls.

The Oldman River recreation area is ideal for hiking and camping. Along the edge of the Rockies watershed are some 400-year-old trees among the oldest in Alberta.

Several places in the Crowsnest Pass area relate to its often disastrous mining history, among them the Leitch collieries, and Hillcrest and Frank slides (see *Historic Sites* below).

PRACTICAL INFORMATION FOR KANANASKIS COUNTRY

HOW TO GET THERE. To the Hwy. 40 turn-off, also called Kananaskis Trail, on TransCanada Hwy. 1, it's 45 miles (73 km) from Calgary, 20 miles (33 km) from Canmore and 35 miles (56 km) from Banff. To Highwood Junction (Hwy. 40) it's 25 miles (37 km) from Longview and 65 miles (107 km) from Calgary, via hwys. 2 and 540. It's 27 miles (48 km) from Pincher Creek and 60 miles (96 km) from Fort Macleod to Hwy. 40 at Crowsnest Pass on Hwy. 3.

ACCOMMODATIONS. Major hotel-building has been going on here for several years, and the range and opulence (in some cases) of Kananaskis's hotels would shock someone who hasn't been here since the 1970s. As well as the obvious five-star *nouveau* resorts, Kananaskis offers a good number of alternative lodgings. Our price ranges for one night, double occupancy, exclusive of tax and tip, are: *Super Deluxe,* over $125; *Deluxe,* $100–$125; *Expensive,* $80–$100; *Moderate,* $50–$80; and *Inexpensive,* under $50.

Super Deluxe

Hotel Kananaskis. Box 6666, Kananaskis Village TOL 2HO (591–7711) or 800–268–9411). This new five-star Canadian Pacific hotel is the most expensive in a three-hotel complex in the new alpine village near Nakiska at Mt. Allan. It has 70 rooms, a 125-seat dining room, lobby lounge, health club with sauna and Jacuzzi, and a pool.

The Lodge at Kananaskis. Kananaskis Village TOL 2HO (591–7711 or 800–268–9411). Five minutes from Nakiska at Mt. Allan, with 255 guest rooms and suites; dining room, lounge, sushi bar, nightclub, tennis, squash and racquetball courts, several shops, swimming pool.

Expensive

Kananaskis Inn. Kananaskis Village TOL 2HO (591–7500). 96 rooms, some suites with fireplaces, are offered at this comfortable inn.

Moderate

Fortress Mountain Lodge. Box 7220, Station E, Calgary T3C 3M1 (264–5825 or 591–7108). Three suites at the ski hill. Also inexpensive dormitory accommodations. Restaurant. lounge, bar. Open Nov.–April.

Inexpensive

Cedar Inn. Box 129, Blairmore, TOKOEO (562–8851). Two blocks south of Hwy. 3. Suites, water beds, whirlpool, sauna, restaurant, and lounge.

Cosmopolitan Inn. Box 609, Blairmore, TOK 0E0 (562–7321). Restaurant and tavern.

Stop Inn. Box 595, Coleman, TOK 0M0 (563–3492). Family units and kitchenettes extra.

GUEST RANCHES. Western hospitality and an unhurried pace characterize these unique ranches. Find out the meaning of the word *dude.*

Kananaskis Guest Ranch. Box 964, Banff, T0L 0C0 or Seebe, T0L 0X0 (673–3737 or 762–5454). Rustic lodge and cabins. Dining room, lounge. Open May–Sept. Riding, hiking, and fishing. Rates are moderate and include meals, but bring your own booze.

Rafter Six Ranch Resort. Seebe, T01 0X0 (673–3622 or 264–1251). Eighteen miles (30 km) east of Canmore, close to Kananaskis Country. Beautiful countryside on the Kananaskis River. From Calgary it's 44 miles (71 km) east on Hwy. 1 to the turn-off. Impressive log lodge and cabins. Dining room, lounge, coffee shop, games room, gift shop, dance hall, whirlpool, outside pool, petting zoo, rodeo grounds, hay- or sleigh rides, horseback riding, and skiing. Passing of the Legends Museum gives history of native people and white pioneers. Inexpensive for room rental, expensive with meals.

YOUTH HOSTELS. Ribbon Creek. 60 miles (97 km) from Calgary, 14 miles (24 km) from Hwy. 1 on Hwy. 40. Sleeps 40. Family rooms, showers, cooking facilities. Closed Tues. night. Members, $5; nonmembers, $7.

RESTAURANTS. The following price categories are based on the cost of two meals with appetizer, exclusive of tax and tip; *Deluxe,* $50–$75; *Expensive,* $25–$50; *Moderate,* $15–$25; and *Inexpensive,* under $15.

Deluxe

Hotel Kananaskis dining room. At the new alpine village. International dining, attentive service.

Expensive

Lodge at Kananaskis. At Mt. Allan. Continental menu and leisurely dining. Japanese sushi restaurant and other less expensive eateries in neighborhood.

Moderate

Kananaskis Golf Club House. (591–7070). Steaks, burgers, pasta, and quiche. Open May 1–mid-Oct.

Inexpensive

Cafeterias and fast food in Kananaskis Country at **Fortress Mountain Lodge** (winter), **Boulton Creek Trading Co.** and **Mt. Kidd RV Centre.**

LIQUOR LAWS. Liquor is allowed only within campsites in the provincial parks.

HOW TO GET AROUND. By car. From Hwy. 1 in the north or Hwy. 3 in the south. **By cycle.** Only paved routes are recommended. Trails designated for mountain bikes exist; get a map from Visitor Centre (591–7222).

By horse. Several areas are designated for equestrian use, and there are three equestrian campsites in the Highwood area.

TOURIST INFORMATION. Alberta Forest Service and Bow/crow Forest (see above).

Barrier Lake Travel Information Centre. (673–3985). 5 miles (8 km) from Hwy. 1. Open 8 A.M.–8 P.M., May–Oct., 9 A.M.–5 P.M., Nov.–April.

Kananaskis Country. Suite 412, 1011 Glenmore Trail SW, Calgary, T2V 4R6 (297–3362) or Box 280, Canmore, T0L 0M0 (678–5508).

Kananaskis Park Ranger Office. (591–7222).

Kananaskis Visitor Centre. (591–7222). Interpretive displays on history and geography. Slide shows. Information on recreation and advice on trail conditions. Open year-round, 9 A.M.–5 P.M. and weekends in summer till 8 P.M.

Travel Alberta. Box 2500, Edmonton, T5J 0H4 (800–222–6501).

HISTORIC SITES AND MUSEUMS. **Colonel's Cabin** is the Visitor Centre of the Forest Management Interpretive Trail, five miles (eight km) from Hwy. 1 on Hwy. 40. The cabin was used by the colonel in charge of the prisoner-of-war camp during World War II. The trail gives an enlightening hour-and-a-half walk in the forest, showing forest management techniques. Open daily, mid-May–early Sept. Call Alberta Forest Service at 239–0004.

Crowsnest Museum, in the old Coleman High School, Coleman, has exhibits on the community and heavy-duty mining.

Frank Slide, is 17 miles (27 km) east of the British Columbia borders. Here, in 1903, 90 million tons of rock crashed down Turtle Mountain, covering much of the town of Frank and killing 70 people. For more information, visit the Frank Slide Interpretive Centre, east of Frank off Hwy. 3. It orients visitors to the history of the coal-mining community and its tragic slide. Dramatic views of the slide and pass area with a multi-media presentation. Open mid-May–Aug. 10 A.M.–8 P.M. Sept.–mid-May 10 A.M.–4 P.M. mid-May. Free. Call 562–7388 or 427–5708 for information.

Volcanic Rocks, west of Coleman on Hwy. 3, are the only evidence found to date of volcanic action in Alberta. They are 100 million years old, older than the Rockies. Watch for the roadside signs.

SIGHTSEEING FOR THE DISABLED. Many of the facilities in Kananaskis Country have been designed specifically for use by those confined to wheelchairs. Mount Lorette Fishing Ponds have been made accessible for handicapped people.

The William Watson Lodge has been specially designed for people who use wheelchairs, have limited mobility, are deaf or blind, or have mental or physical handicaps. Their families and friends are welcome, too. Albertan senior citizens 65 and over may also use the Lodge. It is 41 miles (66 km) south of Hwy. 1 on Hwy. 40. Main lodge, dining room, duplex cottages, campsites, picnic sites, and paved trails. Fishing and interpretive programs are offered.

The lodge was named for an Albertan who was born with both arms paralyzed, yet learned to write, swim, and ski. After earning a law degree in the 1920s, he traveled extensively to learn about rehabilitation methods for the disabled, helped establish vocational schools, and wrote several books on rehabilitation. Reservations are advised up to four months in advance. Contact: *William Watson Lodge,* Kananaskis Provincial Park, General Delivery, Seebe T0L 1X0 (591–7227). Open year-round.

PROVINCIAL PARKS. **Bow Valley Provincial Park,** 3 miles (5 km) east of the Hwy. 40–Hwy. 1 junction, is popular for fishing and riverside camping, and has unusually rich displays of wildflowers. Call 673–3663 for information.

Lougheed Provincial Park is renowned for its mountain scenery, lakes, and recreational facilities. Call 591–7222.

CAMPING. If you want to venture farther than the auto-accessible campsites listed below, then you've come to the right place. There are many backcountry sites designated; ask at the Visitor Centre (591–7222) for map.

Kananaskis Country and the Eastern Slopes are prime camping areas. There are close to 3,000 campsites accessible by car in Kananaskis Country alone. Popular roadside campgrounds regularly fill up on the weekends. You can usually find a site by just driving a bit farther.

Kananaskis:

Bow Valley Area, three miles (five km) west of Hwy. 1–Hwy. 40 junction. Two campgrounds in the Provincial Park and three others nearby. Facilities for RVs, hookups, showers. For reservations call 673–3663.

Kananaskis Valley, 21 miles (33 km) south of Hwy. 1. One drive-in and four backcountry campgrounds, plus *Mt. Kidd RV Park.* Mt. Kidd RV Park (591–7700) is open year-round. Hookups, whirlpools, saunas, showers, laundry, groceries, and tennis.

Loughheed Provincial Park, 35 miles (56 km) south of Hwy. 1. Six drive-in and six backcountry campgrounds. Showers, groceries, and restaurant. For reservations call 591–7226.

Cataract Creek, 75 miles (120 km) south of Hwy. 1. Four drive-in campgrounds. Two have equestrian facilities.

South of Kananaskis:

Bellvue Campground, at east entrance to Bellvue. 16 sites.

Chinook, 7 miles (12 km) northwest of Crowsnest. 74 sites.

Dutch Creek, 19 miles (30 km) northwest of Crowsnest. 42 sites.

Livingstone Falls, 37 miles (60 km) north of Crowsnest. 22 sites.

Lost Lemon Campground, in Blairmore (562–2932). 110 sites.

Oldman River, 25 miles (40 km) north of Crowsnest. 10 sites.

Racehorse Creek, 15 miles (25 km) north of Crowsnest. 37 sites.

OUTDOOR ACTIVITIES. There are many self-guided interpretive hiking trails throughout Kananaskis Country and an extensive network of other trails in the countryside.

The **fishing** is excellent. Provincial licenses are required and are available for \$5–\$12, depending on citizenship, at various local stores. *Mount Lorette Fishing Ponds,* 11 miles (17 km) south of Hwy. 1, are designed for wheelchair anglers, with paved trails and barbecue sites. Ponds are stocked. Watch for beaver at dusk and dawn. *Kananaskis Lakes* provide a lot of opportunity for anglers. Convenient fish-cleaning stations and boat launches.

Hunting is not allowed in the Provincial Park, but it is excellent in parts of the Highwood area.

There are many miles of paved **cycling** trails in Kananaskis Country, linking campgrounds and scenic outlooks.

There are two 18-hole **golf** courses—Mt. Lorette and Mt. Kidd—at the *Kananaskis Country Golf Course,* Box 1710, Canmore T0L 0M0 (591–7070 or 800–372–9201). Mountains tower over the fairways. Some walk-on tee-offs may be available. Open May–mid-Oct.

Canoeing and **kayaking** are popular on the region's placid lakes and rushing rivers.

CROSS-COUNTRY SKIING. There are over 150 miles of nordic skiing trails in Kananaskis Country, many of which are track-set and groomed regularly. You can make your own tracks in the backcountry, but check first for avalanche conditions at the Visitor Centre.

The Smith-Dorrien Cross-Country Ski Trail systems at Sawmill and Mt. Shark, between Canmore and the Kananaskis Visitor Centre, are available for racing and training.

At Ribbon Creek there are 29 miles of recreational trails; Lougheed Provincial Park has 55 miles. On the east side of the front Ranges, nearer Calgary, there are 28 miles at Bragg Creek and 23 miles at Sandy McNabb's.

DOWNHILL SKIING. Fortress Mountain. Box 7220, Station E, Calgary T3C 3M1 (591–7108 or 264–5825). 32 miles (53 km) south of Hwy. 1. Six lifts; 31 trails.

Nakiska at Mount Allen. Box 1718, Canmore, T0L 0M0 (591–7777). 18 miles (30 km) south of Hwy. 1. Site of the 1988 Winter Olympics. Three chairs; 30 trails.

WATERTON LAKES NATIONAL PARK

A billion years of geological history are recorded in the richly colored mountains of the southwestern corner of Alberta, and some of the oldest rock in the Canadian Rockies can be seen here. The land was sculpted by glaciers that left behind lakes, waterfalls, and hanging valleys. Upper Waterton Lake is the deepest in the Canadian Rockies at 485 feet, and is home to some unique water creatures, including the pygmy whitefish and opossum shrimp.

Driving into the park from the east, visitors are surprised by the sudden change from rolling prairies to the spectacular towering mountains of the park.

Wildlife

Waterton's varied habitats—prairies, aspen groves, alpine meadows, marshes, and evergreen forest—support a richness of plants and animals. The park is on a major bird migration route, so spring and fall are especially interesting times for visiting ornithologists. There are many wildflowers here unique in Canada's parks, such as the elegant beargrass.

Elk ("wapiti"), mule deer, squirrels, bighorn sheep, and black bears are common. It would be unusual to visit the town site and *not* see elk and deer browsing among the houses or around tents in the campground.

Black bears are often seen crossing the roads or foraging on hillsides. Grizzly bears are sometimes seen, preferably from a distance.

History

Archeological finds show that the area was heavily used in prehistoric times. When Europeans first reached here, it was shared by the Blackfoot and Kootenai tribes. In the 19th century, white adventurer Kootenai Brown and others started a movement to preserve the land. In 1911 Waterton National Park was established and Kootenai became its first superintendent. A memorial to him is just north of the town site. In 1932, the park was joined to Glacier National Park in Montana to form Waterton-Glacier International Peace Park, the first park in the world to represent peace, goodwill, and shared values, along the longest undefended border in the world.

Oil City, the site of western Canada's first producing oil well, is only five miles (eight km) from the park town site along the Akamina Parkway. It was producing about 300 barrels a day in 1902, but soon ran dry. Nonetheless, the find encouraged a widespread search for oil in Alberta that led to the discovery of the Turner Valley oilfield in 1914.

Exploring the National Park

Waterton, with only 203 square miles of area, is relatively small, and its attractions are quite accessible. The cascading Cameron Falls is right on the edge of the town site, and the old Prince of Wales Hotel is worth a visit, if only for the view.

It's only a 22-mile (36 km) round-trip to Red Rock Canyon, a dramatic, water-carved gorge. The rock gets its color from iron deposits that are literally rusting. You're bound to meet some bighorn sheep or deer around the canyon.

Nineteen miles (32 km) along the Akamina Parkway lies Cameron Lake, in a beautiful alpine setting. A 12-mile (20 km) excursion takes visitors to the Buffalo Paddocks where there is a small herd of plains bison.

Farther afield, take a trip to Montana is famous Going-to-the-Sun Highway, which crosses Logan's Pass in Glacier National Park. See the *Montana* chapter for more information on this thrilling drive.

If you're traveling north to Calgary, stop for a couple of hours at Head-Smashed-In Buffalo Jump, 10 miles (16 km) west of Hwy. 2 between Fort Macleod and Claresholm on the Spring Point Rd. (Hwy. 516). It is the largest and best-preserved buffalo jump in North America, used by Indians for more than 5,600 years to drive bison to their deaths. Open daily 8 A.M.–8 P.M., mid-May–Aug.; 10 A.M.–5 P.M., Sept.–Oct. Call 553–2030 for information.

PRACTICAL INFORMATION FOR WATERTON LAKES NATIONAL PARK

HOW TO GET THERE. By air. The closest major international airport is Calgary. Lethbridge, Alberta, has a smaller airport. Cars can be rented at both airports.

By train. The nearest *Via Rail* station is Calgary. The nearest *Amtrak* stations are East Glacier and Belton, Montana.

By bus. *Greyhound* serves nearby Pincher Creek daily in summer, with connections to Calgary and Lethbridge. Depot at Itussististukiopi (that's how it's spelled) Laundrette on Windflower Ave.

By car. The park is 165 miles (266 km) southwest of Calgary, via hwys. 2, 3, and 6; or hwys. 2 and 5. It's 86 miles (138 km) southwest of Lethbridge via Hwy. 5. From Glacier National Park, use Hwy. 6 from Chief Mountain. The park is 40 miles (67 km) northwest of St. Mary, Montana on hwys. 89 and 17.

ACCOMMODATIONS. Waterton has a surprising range of accommodations for its size, but all depend on tourism, and there is virtually no place to stay here between November and March. For off-season information, phone 859–2445. Our price categories for a double-occupancy room, exclusive of tax and tip, are: *Expensive,* over $80; *Moderate,* $50–$80, and *Inexpensive,* under $50.

Addresses for all establishments listed are box number, Waterton Park, AB T0K 2M0.

Expensive

Bayshore Inn. Box 38 (859–2211, 800–552–8008 or 800–661–8080). On Waterton Ave. 70 lakefront units, some with whirlpool. Restaurant, lounge, pub. Open May–Sept.

Moderate

Aspen-Windflower Motels. Box 64 (859–2255 or 800–552–8018). Across from the pool off Main St., with 53 motel and bungalow units, wheelchair facilities, whirlpool, playground, and picnic area. Open mid-March–Oct.

Crandell Lodge Motel. Box 114 (859–2288). 11 units, including family units, at 102 Mount View Rd. Open May–mid-Oct.

El Cortez. General Delivery (859–2366). Two- and three-bedroom units at 208 Mount View Rd. Open May–Sept.

Emerald Bay Motel. Box 7 (859–2620). Overlooking bay and marina. Open mid-May–Sept.

Kilmorey Lodge. Box 124 (859–2334 or 239–1129) A rustic establishment right on the lake at the entrance to town. Rooms and family suites, some with fireplaces. Restaurant. Open April–Oct.

Prince of Wales Hotel. c/o Glacier Park Inc. East Glacier Park, Montana 59434 (859–2231 or 406–226–5551). A magnificent, much-photographed castle-like building overlooking the lakes and town site. Built in 1926, it has 81 rooms, and a restaurant, and lounge. No charge for kids under 12. Open June–Sept.

Inexpensive

Northland Lodge. General Delivery (859–2353). In the residential area, with a variety of rooms, most with bath. Lounge with fireplace. Open mid-May–mid-Oct.

GUEST RANCHES. Gladstone Mountain Guest Ranch. *Moderate.* Box 2170, Pincher Creek, AB, T0K 1W0 (627–2244). Log lodge and cabins for 20 people, 20 miles west of Pincher Creek. Sauna, trail riding, fishing, hiking, wildlife observation, snowmobiling, cross-country skiing, and snowshoeing.

RESTAURANTS. There are plenty of good-quality restaurants in Waterton. Our categories for two meals with appetizer, exclusive of tax and tip, are: *Expensive,* over $25; *Moderate,* $15–$25; and *Inexpensive,* under $15.

The Prince of Wales Hotel and the Bayshore Inn have lounges.

Expensive

Kootenai Brown Dining Room. In the Bayshore Inn, Waterton Ave. (859–2211). Western fare; try the British Columbia salmon and Alberta beef. Right on the lake. Cocktail lounge.

Prince of Wales Hotel (859–2231). For fans of salmon and prime rib. Fantastic view. Cocktail lounge.

Tourist Cafe. 110 Waterton Ave. (859–2393). Home-cooked pies and steak.

Moderate

New Frank's Restaurant. 106 Waterton Ave. (859–2240). Varied family fare.

Pearl's Pantry. 305 Windflower Ave. (859–2284). Tasty homemade meals.

Inexpensive

Zum Burger Haus. 116 Waterton Ave. (859–2365). For burger fanatics.

HOW TO GET AROUND. By boat. Boat rentals are available from boat tour operators (see *Tours*) and at Cameron Lake.

Waterton Shoreline Cruises (859–2362) provides boat taxi service to Crypt Landing and other destinations.

By taxi. *Mountain Sunset Tours,* in the Tamarack Mall on Mount View Rd. (859–2612), provides taxi and hiker shuttle service.

TOURIST INFORMATION. The **Chinook Country Tourist Association,** 2805 Scenic Dr., Lethbridge, AB T1K 5B7 (329–6777) is the best source of general information on southern Alberta. More local sources, helpful in planning hikes and trips, include:

Heritage Centre. Box 145, Waterton Park T0C 0M0 (859–2691 or 859–2624). Run by the Waterton Natural History Association on Waterton Ave. Bookstore, exhibits, family activity center, outdoor heritage education programs. Information on natural and cultural history of the park and southwest Alberta. The centre runs a *Heritage Education Program,* with a diverse schedule of activities exploring local peoples and landscapes. Open daily May–mid-Sept., 9 A.M.–9 P.M.

Park Information Bureau. Waterton Park TOK, OMO (859–2445). Open daily late May–early Sept., 8 A.M.–10 P.M. Reduced hours in late Sept. Phone lines are open all winter.

Park Administration Office. Waterton Park, TOK OMO (859–2262). Open year-round, Mon.–Fri. 8 A.M.–4 P.M.

Waterton Lakes Chamber of Commerce. Waterton Park TOK OMO.

TOURS. Two-hour **boat tours** are the best way to see the true beauty of the area on both sides of the border. Trips run mid-May–mid-Sep. and include a stop in Montana. Companies offering boat tours include *Adventure Boat and Rental,* Box 55 (859–2455), at the boat dock in the bay area; and

International Scenic Cruise Tours, at the international dock.

In summer you can take **coach tours** of the park in a 1936 bus. For reservations call *Glacier Park Inc./Waterton Transport Co.* (226–9311; 602–248–2600 off-season).

CAMPING. There are backcountry campsites, reachable by the most popular hiking trails, at Crypt Lake, Alderson Lake, Rowe Lakes, and Twin Lakes. You don't need to restrict yourself to Canada—many lead in to the United States. Backcountry camping permits must be obtained at one of the Parks Canada offices.

Crooked Creek Provincial Campground has 75 sites on Hwy. 5, three miles (five km) east of the park boundary.

Parks Canada (859–2262 or 859–2445) has three campgrounds. The 240 sites in the town site have facilities for wheelchair campers, and fill up rapidly. There are 24 sites at Belly River, 16 miles (26 km) south of Waterton on Hwy. 6; and 129 sites at Crandell Mountain, five miles (eight km) from town on Red Rock Canyon Rd.

Waterton Homestead Campground (859–2247) has 250 sites on Hwy. 6, two miles (three km) north of the park gates.

Waterton Riverside Campground, Box 1451, Cardston, AB TOK OKO, (653–2888), has 65 sites on Hwy. 5, a mile north of the park gates.

OUTDOOR ACTIVITIES. There are over 100 miles of **hiking** trails winding through Waterton's mountains and valleys. Popular destinations which make good day-hikes from the town site include Bear's Hump, Linnet Lake, Bertha Lake, and Lakeshore.

The most bizarre and renowned trail in the region, reachable by crossing Waterton Lake by boat, leads to Crypt Lake. The trail leads up a narrow valley past several waterfalls before reaching a stream that springs suddenly from the ground. In the course of this six-mile hike, you will have to crawl through a 65-foot tunnel and cross the border into the United States.

Horseback riding is the traditional way to see the backcountry, and there are corrals along some of the popular trails. Rentals are available from *Alpine Stables,* Box 53 (859–2462), a mile north of town.

Many outfitters offer **trail rides,** which are both expensive and exciting. *Diamond Hitch Outfitters,* Box 2316, Pincher Creek, AL T0K 1W0 (627–2949 or 627–2773), offers trips of two to eight days from Waterton Park north into wilderness areas. *Timbermountain Packtrain,* Box 511, Claresholm, AL T0L 0T0 (625–2931), offers trips into the southern Rockies.

Fishing is excellent for rainbow, brook, and cutthroat trout; Dolly Varden, pike, and whitefish. Fifty-pound lake trout have been caught in the region. Licenses ($10) are available at the Parks Information Bureau. Hunting is prohibited in Waterton and other national parks.

The 18-hole **golf** course at the *Waterton Park Golf Club* (859–2383), two miles northeast of the town site, has rolling fairways with the surrounding peaks a spectacular backdrop. There are **tennis** courts in the town site.

Boats and **windsurfers** can be rented on the lake. Scuba diving is also popular; one popular dive is to the wreck of a paddle-steamer scuttled in 1918 in Emerald Bay.

Swimming is available in the town site at a public pool open 11 A.M.–7 P.M. in summer. Adults, $1.75; children, $1. Try the lake for a free dip.

In winter, many of the hiking trails and lakes make ideal **cross-country skiing** terrain. There is winter camping at the Blakiston Creek Bridge picnic area. Call 859–2262 weekdays or 859–2445 weekends for trail and road conditions.

THE BRITISH COLUMBIA ROCKIES

by
ENA SPALDING

British Columbia is at its most spectacular in the mountainous eastern regions. From the High Country that stretches to Canada's loftiest peak to the Okanagan with its lush green orchards, from the pristine lakes of the Kootenay Country to the interior mountain ranges, there is too much to see here for one visit.

Along the Continental Divide, which describes the border between British Columbia and Alberta, the Rocky Mountain range narrows to about 50 miles. Couched between the Rockies and the western coastal ranges, the rugged and luxuriant Columbia Mountains beckon for side trips. High precipitation in British Columbia makes for a luxuriant and diverse growth of plant and animal life: "Rain-forest" growth exists only a few miles from Canada's highest mountains. It is no wonder that tourist brochures refer to the province as "super, natural B.C."

The history of eastern British Columbia is closely linked to fur trading. In 1806, the Northwest Trading Company commissioned David Thompson to explore the upper reaches of the Columbia River. His enthusiastic reports led to an onslaught of trapping and trading. Soon competing companies and rival countries were vying for control of the market. As the

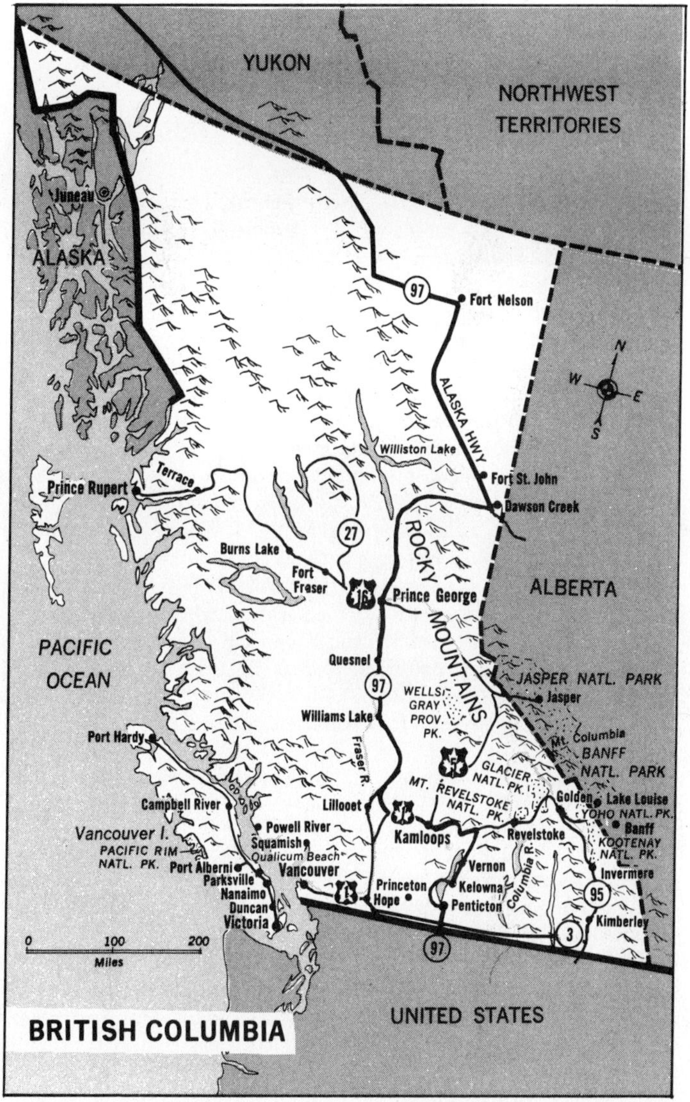
YUKON
NORTHWEST TERRITORIES
Juneau
ALASKA
97
Fort Nelson
ALASKA HWY
N
W
E
S
Williston Lake
Fort St. John
Terrace
Prince Rupert
Dawson Creek
27
ROCKY MOUNTAINS
Burns Lake
Fort Fraser
16
Prince George
ALBERTA
PACIFIC OCEAN
Quesnel
97
JASPER NATL. PARK
Jasper
WELLS GRAY PROV. PK.
Williams Lake
Port Hardy
Fraser R.
Mt. Columbia
BANFF NATL. PARK
GLACIER NATL. PK.
MT. REVELSTOKE NATL. PK.
Campbell River
Lillooet
Golden
Lake Louise
YOHO NATL. PK.
Banff
Powell River
Vancouver I.
Kamloops
Revelstoke
Squamish
KOOTENAY NATL. PK.
PACIFIC RIM NATL. PK.
Qualicum Beach
Port Alberni
Vancouver
Vernon
Columbia R.
Invermere
Parksville
Nanaimo
1
Princeton
Hope
Kelowna
95
Duncan
Penticton
Victoria
Kimberley
3
97
0 100 200
Miles
UNITED STATES
BRITISH COLUMBIA

area's fame mounted, merchants, miners, and others were inspired to seek their fortunes in this ruggedly beautiful area. The British Columbia Rockies have still not been tamed, and even on a brief tour visitors will experience the same thrill of conquest the early settlers felt.

THE WESTERN SLOPE: KOOTENAY, YOHO, MOUNT ASSINIBOINE

The three contiguous parks—two national, one provincial—on the Western Slope of the Continental Divide offer Rocky Mountain scenery as awesome as that across the border in Alberta, but with far fewer crowds—and fewer amenities. This is not a haven for mock-Swiss coffeehouses or summer-stock theaters.

Since prehistoric times, this land of startling contrasts has served as a major north-south travel route. The Kootenai Indians settled in the region and crossed the mountains twice a year to hunt bison on the prairies. Pictographs found near the region's hot springs indicate that the western slope was a meeting place for plains and mountain tribes. "Kootenay" comes from the Indian *K'tunaxa,* meaning "strangers" or "people from beyond the mountains."

Fur traders and explorers arrived in the 1800s, seeking good routes through the mountains. George Simpson, governor of the Hudson's Bay Company, passed by on his way to the Columbia River in the 1840s. Dr. James Hector and his comrades on the Palliser Expedition became the first white men to conquer Vermilion and Kicking Horse passes in 1858. Later came homesteaders and entrepreneurs anxious to develop the hot springs around Radium. Railway track was laid through the pass in 1884, and the TransCanada Highway followed the same route in 1927.

Kootenay National Park

Kootenay stretches through 63 miles of Rocky Mountains, encompassing Vermilion and parts of Sinclair and Kootenay valleys. Within its 543 square miles are towering summits, hanging glaciers, narrow chasms, and color-splashed mineral pools.

Every mile of the Banff-Windermere Highway reveals something interesting to explore. Marble Canyon is actually a limestone gorge, but has never left visitors disappointed. The nearby Redwall Fault has awesome red cliffs and shattered rocks. The famous Radium Hot Springs at the southern end of the park are natural mineral springs heated deep inside the Earth to about 207 degrees Fahrenheit. The northern end of the park is all high peaks and glaciers.

Sinclair Canyon is of geological interest, and the animal lick near Simpson River is a good place to look for wildlife. Vermilion Pass Burn, on the Continental Divide, was the site of a huge forest fire in 1968. The blaze took four days to peter out, and burned 6,000 acres. The area now gives visitors an insight into how life reasserts itself after such devastation.

ROCKY MOUNTAIN PARKS
Monkman Provincial Park
Continental Divide
Grande Cache
Scale 0 10 20 30 Miles
0 10 20 30 40 Kilometers
N
Willmore Wilderness Park
Athabasca River
Yellowhead Hwy.
16
Edmonton
Cariboo Mountains
Hinton
40
Jasper National Park
Mount Robson
Jasper
ALBERTA
Wells Gray Provincial Park
Mount Robson Provincial Park
Mt. Edith Cavell
Forestry Trunk Road
2
Columbia Icefield
Hamber Provincial Park
11
5
93
Rocky Mountains Forest Reserve
Kirbashel Lake
Peyto Lake
Bow Lake
Banff National Park
Monashee Mountains
Glacier Natl. Park
Yoho National Park
Lake Louise
Iona
Thompson River
Mt. Revelstoke National Park
Kicking Horse Pass
Bow Valley Pkwy.
Banff
Canmore
Kamloops
1
Revelstoke
Kootenay National Park
Calgary
Upper Arrow Lake
95
Radium Hot Springs
Mt. Assiniboine Provincial Park
Peter A. Lougheed Provincial Park
BRITISH COLUMBIA
97
Purcell Mountains
Kooteray Lake
Lower Arrow Lake
Vancouver
Kimberley
3
Crowsnest Hwy.
6
Waterton Lakes National Park
WASHINGTON
395
IDAHO
MONTANA
Glacier National Park (US)

Yoho National Park

East of Banff and north of Kootenay National Park, Yoho, with only 547 square miles, is the smallest, but by no means the least significant, of the Rocky Mountain parks. The name *Yoho* is Cree for "awe-inspiring." It is a land of waterfalls and glacial lakes, snow-topped mountains, and silent forests.

Yoho contains several impressive waterfalls, including Laughing, Wapta, Twin, and—one of Canada's highest—Takakkaw Falls. There is a natural rock bridge over the Kicking Horse River, where torrents have worn a hole through the middle of a solid rock bed. Perhaps the park's most famous phenomenon, the "hoodoos," are pillars of glacial silt with nodal boulders balanced precariously on top. Also not to be missed are the Burgess Shale fossil beds, which contain the fossilized remains of 120 marine animal species dating back 530 million years.

EXPLORING YOHO

There are a variety of sights on the TransCanada Highway as you travel west from the Alberta border. The Kicking Horse Pass was chosen in 1881 as the route for Canada's first transcontinental railway. Further along is an avalanche path where years ago a snow slide reached the highway from half a mile above, devastating the forest in its wake. Avalanches are nowadays released artificially to avert snow build-up and destruction.

On Hwy. 1A, the Great Divide marks the North American watershed. A stream here demonstrates the principle by bifurcating and flowing in opposite directions. This road provides access to Lake O'Hara Lodge, which, at 6,700 feet, is one of the highest resorts in the Canadian Rockies. At the Spiral Tunnel viewpoint you can find out about the building and operation of spiral tunnels.

Take the detour up Yoho Valley Road for some of the park's finest scenery. In summer, the road takes visitors to within a short walk of the magnificent 1,000-foot Takakkaw Falls, among the world's highest.

The side road to Emerald Lake is another that can be done in an hour, but would take days to do well. First, take a look at the natural bridge on the Kicking Horse River, then continue on to the lake.

Further west on the TransCanada Highway, Field is a quiet little railroad town popular with mountaineers and ice climbers. Two nature trails farther along on the highway pass a number of avalanches and hoodoos. Leanchoil Marsh, near Wapta Falls Road, is a good place to look for wildlife.

Mount Assiniboine Provincial Park

Mount Assiniboine is a wilderness park of 158 square miles, lying on the Continental Divide and bordered by Banff and Kootenay National parks. There is no road access, but hiking and skiing trails lead in from Spray Valley in Kananaskis Country, Sunshine in Banff Park, and routes along the Simpson and Mitchell rivers off Hwy. 93 in Kootenay Park. Access routes are subject to avalanche danger in winter. There are more than 35 miles of hiking trails in the park as well as four alpine shelters, a beautiful old mountain lodge, campsites, and summer park ranger cabins. Since it takes a long day of hiking to get into the park, it would take at least four days to make a visit to Mount Assiniboine worthwhile.

The park is as scenic a spot as any in the Rockies. Its most famous landmark is the eponymous mountain, a distinctive triangular peak resembling the Matterhorn in Switzerland. At 11,571 feet, it is seventh-highest in the Canadian Rockies. The park is dotted with lakes, the largest being Lake Magog, at the foot of Assiniboine. Alpine wildflowers grow in profusion in the meadows, and the larch trees put on a golden show every autumn.

PRACTICAL INFORMATION FOR THE WESTERN SLOPE

HOW TO GET THERE. By air. The nearest airports are at Calgary, 137 miles (220 km) east of Yoho and 164 miles (264 km) east of Radium; and at Cranbrook, 90 miles (145 km) south of Radium.

By train. The nearest major *Via Rail* stations are at Banff and Lake Louise. One eastbound and one westbound train stop daily at Field.

By bus. *Greyhound* buses stop daily at Radium and Banff, and several buses a day travel through Yoho National Park.

Dewdney Trail Stages, 135 Bay St., Trail V1R 4A7 (368–5555 or 800–332–0282), operates between Golden and Cranbrook, stopping at Radium.

By car. Kootenay National Park is 17 miles (29 km) west of Banff on Hwy. 1; turn west on Hwy. 93. From Lake Louise, travel 16 miles (27 km) west on hwys. 1 and 93. Kootenay is 90 miles (145 km) north of Cranbrook; take Hwy. 93/95 north, then turn east on Hwy. 93.

Yoho is 51 miles (82 km) west of Banff and 32 miles (52 km) east of Golden on the TransCanada Hwy.

ACCOMMODATIONS. Accommodations on the Western Slope are not common, but they do offer a good deal of variety. Most of the traditional lodgings are in the town of Radium. "Chalets," or detached bungalows, are popular; many of them are self-catering. Many of the hotels have amenities like golf and fitness facilities. Our price categories for one night in an average room are *Moderate,* $50–$80; and *Inexpensive,* under $50.

Moderate

Alpen Motel. Box 6, Radium V04 1M0 (347–9823). A mile from the Hot Springs. 14 units and wheelchair facilities.

Big Horn Motel. Box 176, Radium V04 1M0 (347–9522). Whirlpool, sauna, minigolf.

Mount Farnham Bungalows. Box 160, Radium V04 1M0 (347–9515). A block from the Hot Springs. Two-bedroom units, with fireplaces, kitchenettes, sun decks.

Radium Hot Springs Golf Resort. Box 310, Radium V04 1M0 (347–9622). Overlooks the hot pools, with 66 units, recreation room, dining, lounge, health center.

Vermilion Crossing Bungalows. Box 958, Banff T0L 0C0 (no phone). 43 miles (69 km) south of Banff on Hwy. 93, with 10 units, showers, kitchen, gas station, store. Open May–Sept.

West Louise Lodge. Box 9, Lake Louise T0L 1E0 (604–343–6311). Seven miles (11.2 km) west of Field, with 50 units, sauna, pool, dining room, lounge.

Inexpensive

Blakeley's Bungalows. Box 190, Radium V04 1M0 (347–9918). Two blocks from the Hot Springs, with barbecues, playground.

Crystal Springs Motel. Box 218, Radium V04 1M0 (347–9759). Jacuzzis, kitchenettes, sun deck, barbecues, wheelchair facilities.

MOUNTAIN LODGES. The Canadian Rockies are the home of the opulent, back-to-nature retreat, and the Western Slope has as heavy a concentration of such establishments as anywhere. Despite their names and rustic surroundings, they're anything but ramshackle. All have excellent restaurants, and most would fall in our *Super-Deluxe* price category for accommodations.

Beaverfoot Lodge. Box 1560, Golden V0A 1H0 (346–3205 or 346–3216). Just south of Yoho's east gate, eight miles (13 km) from Hwy. 1, this big old log lodge overlooks marvelous meadows and mountains. Three remote cabins are within skiing or hiking range, with 12 rooms and a few cabins. Sauna, dining, homemade meals.

Emerald Lake Lodge. c/o Canadian Rocky Mountain Resorts, Box 1598, Banff T0L 0C0 (800–663–6336). Built by Canadian Pacific Railroad in 1902, the lodge combines splendid isolation with easy access. Hand-hewn timber and stone fireplaces. Two- and four-unit cabins with fireplace and balcony. Clubhouse with exercise area, sauna, sun deck, and hot tub. Day lodge with restaurant. Dining, lounge, saloon, entertainment, lectures.

Lake O'Hara Lodge. Box 1677, Banff T0L 0C0 (604–762–2118 Oct.–June; 604–762–6418 July –Sept.). A beautiful 1920s log lodge, built by Canadian Pacific and perfectly situated. Open-beamed dining lounge with large stone fireplace. Trails provide access to six alpine valleys and 16 alpine lakes. The lodge has eight rooms and 11 lakefront summer cottages. Summer access for guests by Parks Canada bus (call 604–343–6324); winter access by ski only.

Mount Assiniboine Lodge. Box 1527, Canmore T0L 0M0 (604–678–2883). A magnificent rustic log building built in 1928 by Canadian Pacific. Access is available by helicopter from Spray Valley, above Canmore. For more information, see *Practical Information for Canmore.*

Storm Mountain Lodge. Box 670, Banff T0L 0C0 (604–762–4155). On Vermilion Pass on Hwy. 93. For details, see *Practical Information for Banff.*

HUTS AND HOSTELS. Fay Hut is a small alpine hut in Prospector's Valley overlooking Tokuum Creek. It's an excellent base for climbing the peaks of Kootenay or for skiing on the icefields. Contact the Kootenay Park Superintendent.

Surprise Creek and **Mitchell River Cabins** are small huts between Hwy. 93 and Mount Assiniboine. Contact the *British Columbia Parks Branch,* Regional Director for Parks and Outdoor Recreation, 101–1050 W. Columbia St., Kamloops, BC V2C 1L4.

In Mount Assiniboine Park, the **Naiset Cabins** accommodate 29 and are available Dec.–May by reservation. Contact the *Parks Division,* Box 118, Wasa V0B 2K0 (422–3212).

The *Alpine Club of Canada,* Box 1026, Banff, AL T0L 0C0 (403–762–4481) operates three huts in Yoho National Park. They are: **Abbott Pass,** between Lake O'Hara and Lake Louise, with room for 40; **Elizabeth Parker,** near Lake O'Hara and many major peaks; and **Stanley Mitchell,** in Little Yoho Valley above Laughing Falls, with great skiing, mountaineering, and climbing terrain.

The **Whiskey Jack Hostel** is eight miles (13 km) along Yoho Valley Road from Kicking Horse Campground, and 13 miles (22 km) west of Lake Louise on Hwy. 1. Sleeps 27. Showers. Open mid-June–mid-Sept. IYHF members, $5.50, nonmembers $7.

RESTAURANTS. Eating is a necessity in the wilds, but dining isn't, and there are practically no restaurants on the Western Slope not connected in some way with hotels or lodges. Check our listings under *Accommodations* and *Mountain Lodges,* the former for good grub, the latter for more *haute cuisine.* Especially recommended is the **Burgess Dining Room** in the Emerald Lake Lodge (343–6321). Seafood, reindeer, rabbit, pasta, and steaks are featured.

TOURIST INFORMATION. The *Rocky Mountain Visitors Association of British Columbia,* Box 10, Kimberly V1A 2Y5 (427–4838), has information pertaining to all British Columbia national and provincial parks.

For specific information on Kootenay: *The Superintendent, Kootenay National Park,* Box 220, Radium Hot Springs V0A 1M0 (347–9615).

For information on Yoho: *Park Superintendent, Yoho National Park,* Box 99, Field V0A 1G0 (343–6324). The *Yoho Park Warden Office* is just west of Field. The *Yoho Visitor Information Centre* issues permits and fishing licenses and gives information.

TOURS. *Brewster Transportation and Tours,* Box 1140, Banff (403–762–2241), has bus tours along Hwy. 1 from Calgary, Banff, and Lake Louise. They stop at the major points of interest in Yoho, including Takakkaw Falls, Kicking Horse Pass, and Emerald Lake.

In Kootenay, self-guiding trails lead to special features in the park, including Marble Canyon and some ancient Indian paint pots.

CAMPING. To camp in Kootenay, you will need a permit, available at the park information center at Marble Canyon or through the park superintendent. There are three campgrounds: *McLeod Meadows* and *Marble Canyon* are on Hwy. 93. *Redstreak,* the only one with serviced sites, is two miles (three km) south of the Hwy. 93/95 junction, south of Radium.

Sunnyside Trailer Court, Box 37 (347–9564), has 65 sites with showers and hookups. *Canyon Camp,* Box 279 (347–9564), has 83 sites, hookups, showers, and playground.

Yoho has five campgrounds. *Hoodoo Creek, Chancellor Peak,* and *Kicking Horse* are all accessible by car. Getting to *Takakkaw Falls* involves a short hike, and *Lake O'Hara* can be reached either by hiking or private bus in summer. In addition, there are primitive sites on most backcountry trails. There is winter camping at Finn Creek. Permits for all camping must be obtained from the park warden.

OUTDOOR ACTIVITIES. There are more than 100 miles of **hiking** trails in Kootenay National Park. Many full-day and half-day trips are near the highway, among them Dog and Comb lakes, Stanley Glacier, and Kindersley Pass. The northern end of the park is ideal for longer trips. Some of the best are between the highway and the Vermilion Range—by Floe Lake and Numa, Tumbling, and Helmet creeks. The Kaufmann Lake Trail takes hikers to the other side of the Valley of Ten Peaks, also accessible via Moraine Lake Rd. near Lake Louise. The Simpson River Trail is another way into Mount Assiniboine Park, also accessible from Kananaskis Country.

Yoho National Park has about 200 miles of trails. The most popular summer routes radiate from Yoho Valley, Lake O'Hara, and Emerald Lake.

Fishing is excellent in all three parks; remember to get a national parks fishing license before setting out. Dolly Varden, char and trout run in the rivers and lakes of Yoho. In Kootenay, try your luck in the Vermilion, Simpson, and Kootenay rivers, and in the lakes. Remember that **hunting** is illegal in the national parks.

Boating is allowed on all waters, but power boats are prohibited.

There is **swimming** all year at the Radium Hot Springs Aquacourt. The hot pool and cool pools are both outdoors. Adults, $1.75; children, $1.

The section of Hwy. 93 that runs through Kootenay National Park is a popular **cycling** route. At the southeastern end of the park you can continue south through the Columbia Valley on Hwy. 93/95; at the northeastern end, follow Hwy. 1A to Lake Louise or Banff.

Horseback riding is restricted in some parts of Yoho; check at the park warden office for details. There are horses for rent at Emerald Lake.

Most of the hiking trails make good **cross-country skiing** trails. In Kootenay, Stanley Glacier and Boom Lake are favorites with Calgarians. In Yoho, the Emerald Lake area has some track-set trails. Yoho Valley and Little Yoho Valley are popular multi-day trips. In the spring, many skiers descend from the Wapta Icefields into the Yoho Valley. The Lake O'Hara Lodge has excellent touring terrain and reliable snow. As always, check avalanche conditions before heading out, and never ski alone.

THE YELLOWHEAD HIGHWAY: MOUNT ROBSON AND WELLS GRAY PROVINCIAL PARKS

In the 1800s, the "Overlanders," following the Yellowhead Route from the prairies to Fort Kamloops, suffered many hardships. Modern visitors can enjoy the same wilderness scenery without such privations. The Yellowhead Highway, made up of parts of routes 5 and 16, is surely one of the most scenic drives in Canada. The name "Yellowhead" comes from the French *Tête Jaune,* the nickname of a blond trapper who worked for the Hudson's Bay Company in 1814. He apparently kept a cache of furs in the area.

Exploring the Yellowhead Highway

The Yellowhead Highway, Route 5 north of Kamloops, leads to many exciting wilderness experiences. The road follows the North Thompson River to Tête Jaune Cache, then on to 3,760-foot Yellowhead Pass, before crossing the Continental Divide into Alberta and Jasper National Park.

Clearwater is the gateway to Wells Gray Provincial Park, the third largest park in the province. This is a land of dense forests, lakes, waterfalls, icefields, and even extinct volcanoes. Most of the park is wilderness, except for a few accessible campsites and a road to the spectacular Helmecken Falls, which plunge 450 feet into a foam-and-mist-filled gorge. The Clearwater River also attracts white-water-paddling enthusiasts.

Farther north, Blue River is a base for heli-skiing trips. At Valemount—uniquely located at the meeting of the Rocky, Cariboo, and Monashee mountain ranges—Route 5 enters the Rocky Mountain Trench. This is the last stopping-off place for those exploring Mt. Robson Provincial Park.

Passing right through Mount Robson Park, the Yellowhead Highway allows visitors a close-up view of one of the highest mountains on the continent. That's if Robson isn't shrouded in cloud, which, unfortunately, it often is. Hikers will want to follow the trail to Berg Lake, where the impressive Berg Glacier rumbles and groans as it "calves" huge chunks of ice into the turquoise glacial waters.

PRACTICAL INFORMATION FOR THE YELLOWHEAD HIGHWAY

HOW TO GET THERE. By train: *VIA Rail* stops at Jasper, Valemount, Blue River, and Clearwater, with one eastbound and one westbound train daily.

By bus: *Greyhound* runs daily east and west on Hwy. 16. Ask for a flag stop at Yellowhead Pass or Mount Robson Viewpoint. Valemount, Clearwater, and Blue River are served by Greyhound from Kamloops and Jasper.

By car: Mount Robson is 180 miles (290 km) east of Prince George and 54 miles (87 km) west of Jasper on Yellowhead Highway 16. Valemount is 195 miles (320 km) north of Kamloops and 55 miles (90 km) north of Blue River on Hwy. 5 and 12 miles (20 km) south of Tête Jaune.

TOURIST INFORMATION. The following offices in British Columbia are very generous with information and should definitely be consulted by anyone considering heading into the wilderness without a guide.

Blue River Community Association. Box 7, Blue River V0E 1J0.

Clearwater Chamber of Commerce. Box 518, Clearwater V0E 1N0.

High Country Tourism Association. Box 298, Salmon Arm V0E 2T0 (832–8028).

Mount Robson Park Supervisor. Box 579, Valemount V0E 2Z0 (566–4325).

Valemount Tourist Information. Box 168, Valemount V0E 2Z0.

ACCOMMODATIONS. There's not much to choose from in this neck of the woods, though what is here is both comfortable and friendly. By our rating system, the establishments listed below as *Moderate* cost $50–$80 for one night in a double-occupancy room, exclusive of tax and tips. *Inexpensive* rooms are under $50.

Helmecken Falls Lodge. *Moderate.* Box 239, Clearwater V0E 1N0 (674–3657). On the edge of Wells Gray Park. 11 chalets, sauna, campground with 21 sites, dining and wheelchair facilities. Ski, canoe, and snowshoe rentals. Open May–Oct. and Dec.–Mar.

Mount Robson Guest Ranch. *Moderate.* Hargreaves Rd., Box 301, Valemount V0E 2Z0 (566–4370). Six log cabins. Hiking, horseback riding, fishing, and climbing. Impressive view of Mt. Robson. Open June–mid-Sept.

Mountaineer Flag Inn. *Moderate.* Box 217, Valemount V0E 2Z0 (566–4477). 30 units. Squash court, indoor pool, sauna, and cross-country ski rentals.

Venture Lodge. *Moderate.* Box 37, Blue River V0E 1J0 (673–8384). 22 suites. Kitchenettes, dining, sauna, and wheelchair facilities.

Blue River Motel. *Inexpensive.* Two blocks off Hwy. 5, turn right at Spruce St.; Box 47, Blue River VOE 1JO (673–8387). Housekeeping units, some one- and two-bed. Winter plug-ins, free coffee.

Dutch Lake Resort and Campground. *Inexpensive.* Box 2160, R.R. 2, Clearwater V0E 1N0 (674–3351). 16 cottage and motel units, plus 69 campsites on the lake. Dining, patio, B&B, and wheelchair facilities. Fishing and winter sports.

RESTAURANTS. Though gourmet cuisine is not the standard on the Yellowhead Hwy., the hearty western fare can be delicious and satisfying. The following restaurants are *Inexpensive:*

Old Caboose. On the Yellowhead Hwy. in Clearwater (674–2945). Enjoy fresh seafood, steaks, and barbecued ribs in covered patio overlooking gardens. Wheelchair facilities.

Wells Gray Flag Inn. On the Yellowhead Hwy. in Clearwater (674–2214). Steak and seafood lounge, coffee shop, and dining room. Wheelchair facilities.

PROVINCIAL PARKS. British Columbia's provincial parks offer a range of seasonal accommodations from the very basic to the most luxurious. In this area, facilities are fairly standard. Though many parks are not officially open in winter, they *are* open for skiing and other winter recreation.

Mount Robson Provincial Park is on Hwy. 16, just east of its junction with Hwy. 5. Its facilities are open from May to Oct., and include 177 campsites at three campgrounds, two boat launches, 125 miles of hiking trails, nature trails, and adventure playground, fishing, boating, paddling, mountaineering, swimming, horseback riding, ski touring, ice fishing, snowshoeing, and dog sledding.

Mt. Robson Park is over 500,000 acres of mountainous wilderness, adjacent to Jasper National Park, Alberta. It contains the headwaters of the Fraser River and the highest peak in the Canadian Rockies, 12,972-foot Mt. Robson. The massive Berg Glacier nearby is one of the few living, advancing glaciers in the Rockies.

Robson poses an ever-present challenge to alpinists, and its extreme conditions claim lives regularly. First climbed in 1913, it was one of the last major Canadian mountains to be scaled. Keen hikers now make the popular 12-mile pilgrimage past Kinney Lake, through the beautiful Valley-of-a-Thousand Falls, and up to Berg Lake, to be rewarded, with luck, by a fleeting glimpse of the towering summit. Keener hikers continue over Robson Pass to the North Boundary Trail, leading to the remote parts of Jasper National Park.

The plant life in the park varies from lush rain forest just before Kinney Lake, to high alpine tundra. There are many wild mammals: moose, beaver, black bear, squirrels, and chipmunks at lower levels; grizzly bears, marmots, mountain goats, and pikas higher up.

Local Indians called Robson *Yuh–hai–has–hun,* meaning "Mountain of the Spiral Road." The eponym of Robson was probably an employee of the Hudson's Bay Company in the 1820s.

Mount Terry Fox Provincial Park comprises about 5,000 acres, six miles (10 km) north of Valemount. It was named in honor of Terry Fox, who set out to run across Canada to raise money for cancer research, after losing a leg to cancer. He died of bone cancer before completing his heroic journey. A primitive hiking trail provides the only access into the park.

North Thompson River Provincial Park, 300 acres just south of Clearwater on Hwy. 5, has 61 campsites, hiking, skiing, ski-touring, fishing, canoeing, kayaking, and archeological sites. Open June–Sept.

Rearguard Falls Provincial Park, three miles (five km) east of Tête Jaune on Hwy. 16, is a lookout over the Upper Fraser River. Salmon migrate 700 miles upriver from the Pacific and meet their last barrier here. They can be seen leaping the 30-foot stepped falls in August.

Spahats Creek Provincial Park is 750 acres off Hwy. 5, nine miles (15 km) north of Clearwater. It has 20 campsites, picnicking, hiking, fishing, and many nature trails. It also has a 400-foot-deep canyon, carved by the creek through layers of lava, and falls that drop 185 feet over a volcanic precipice. *Spahats* is the native word for "bear." So watch out. Open June–Sept.

Wells Gray Provincial Park, reachable on a gravel road off Hwy. 5, is 25 miles (40 km) north of Clearwater and 16 miles (26 km) west of Blue River. The park has 129 vehicle campsites, 25 wilderness sites, four overnight shelters, and a developed beach with boat launches at Mahood Lake. It is cut by 176 miles of hiking trails, 33 miles of ski trails, and 33 miles of gravel roads.

The park covers 1.25 million acres of precipitous mountains and glaciers, upland plateaus, lakes, rivers, waterfalls, extinct volcanoes, lava beds, and mineral springs. The northern part has many icefields and small glaciers. Among them, the Rausch Glacier is a hanging glacier with a great icefall. Ancient glacial sculpting has left many U-shaped valleys with large lakes—the Clearwater, Azure, Hobson, Murtle, and Mahood—that are ideal for paddling. Helmecken Falls, where the Murtle cascades 450 feet with a great roar, is the most impressive of the park's many waterfalls.

Wells Gray has been the site of almost continuous volcanic activity for the past half million years, and extinct volcanic cinder cones, lava flows, and explosion craters cover the landscape. Other curious volcanic phenomena, such as Pyramid Mountain and Dragon Cone, can be seen at close range on short hikes.

The park boasts over 170 species of birds, 50 kinds of mammals, and a great variety of fish. There are also 35 archeological sites and Indian pictographs belonging to the cultures of the Salish, Shuswap, and Chilcotin peoples. From more recent times, there's evidence of mining, gold-digging, logging, and farming. There are two commercial resorts on the park boundary.

CAMPING AND HUTS. There's plenty of choice between roadside, resort, forest, and backcountry sites in the parks. Consult *Provincial Parks* above to figure out which of their many attractions you'd like to position yourself closest to. For information on camping in Mt. Robson Provincial Park, write: *Mount Robson,* Box 157, Valemount V0E 2Z0 (566–4821). Among their sites:

Emperor Ridge. Beside Kinney Lake, close to Mt. Robson. 37 sites. Open mid-May–mid-Oct.

Robson Shadows. On the Fraser River, near Mt. Robson. 45 sites. Open mid-May–mid-Oct.

For those with recreational vehicles, the **Yellowhead Campsite and Trailer Park,** General Delivery, Valemount V0E 2Z0 (566–4227), has 40 creekside sites with hookups. Open May–Sept.

Ralph Forster/Mount Robson Hut, a good base for attempts on Robson, is 10 hours from the trailhead overlooking Kinney Lake on the mountain itself. It sleeps eight. For more huts in the Robson area, contact *British Columbia Parks Branch,* Regional Office, Regional Director Parks and Outdoor Recreation, 101–1050 W. Columbia St., Kamloops, BC V2C 1L4.

OUTDOOR ACTIVITIES. Hundreds of miles of **hiking** trails are available to area visitors.

Canoeing, rafting, and **kayaking** are popular on the Clearwater River. *Interior Whitewater Expeditions,* General Delivery, Celista V0E 1L0 (955–2447 or 675–4620), offers raft trips on the Clearwater in Wells Gray Park. *Headwaters Outfitting Ltd.,* Box 818, Valemount V0E 2Z0 (566–4718), offers guided wilderness trips in Mt. Robson and Jasper parks, Willmore Wilderness, and the Valemount area, with boating, riding, canoeing, backpacking, telemark skiing, photo safaris, outdoor artists workshops, and fishing.

W.J. Duncan, Box 202, Valemount V0E 2Z0 (566–4584), leads wilderness pack trips on horseback.

There are **cross-country skiing** trails near each of the towns in the area and unlimited opportunities in the wilderness sections. A specialty of the Columbia Range is ski touring from remote mountain huts (see *Camping and Huts* above).

DOWNHILL SKIING. Clearwater has a ski hill with a 1,000-foot vertical drop; it has two primitive lifts and offers night skiing. Open April–Dec.

Helicopter skiing has become extremely popular in this part of the Rockies. Blue River is a taking-off point for heli-skiing in the Cariboo and Monashee mountains. Contact **Mike Weigele Helicopter Skiing,** Box 249, Banff, AB T0L 0C0 (762–5548 or 800–661–9170). Other outfitters include:

CMH Heli-Skiing. Box 1660, Banff, AB T0L 0C0 (762–4531). Flights into the Bugaboos, Cariboos, Monashees, Panorama, Revelstoke, and Valemount.

Yellowhead Helicopter. Valemount, BC V0E 1J0 (566–4401). Flights into the Monashees for heli-skiing and other activities.

SEASONAL EVENTS. February. *Sno Drifters Race, Figure Skating, Ice Capades, Snowarama,* Clearwater.

March. *Winter Carnival,* Blue River and Valemount. **July.** *Strawberry Festival,* Clearwater. **August.** *Swift Creek and Fraser River Salmon Run, Beer Garden, Demolition Derby, Softball Tournament,* Blue River.

REVELSTOKE AND THE NATIONAL PARKS ROUTE

Known as the "national parks route," the TransCanada Hwy. 1 between Revelstoke and the Alberta border winds its way through three national parks: Revelstoke, Glacier, and Yoho. It's an awe-inspiring route, as it cuts through sheer rock, past giant trees, vast snowfields, and cascading mountain rivers to mount the treacherous Rogers Pass.

EXPLORING REVELSTOKE

Revelstoke is the gateway to this route, lying between the majestic Selkirk and Monashee mountain ranges at the point where the Illecillewaet River joins the noble Columbia River. West from Revelstoke on Hwy. 1 towards Sicamous is a pioneer village called "Eagle Pass." Families enter a world of fantasy in the "Enchanted Forest" and can tour Miniatureland inside Beardale Castle at Craigellachie. Canyon Hot Springs is east on Hwy. 1 towards the Selkirks. Down the road is Glacier National Park.

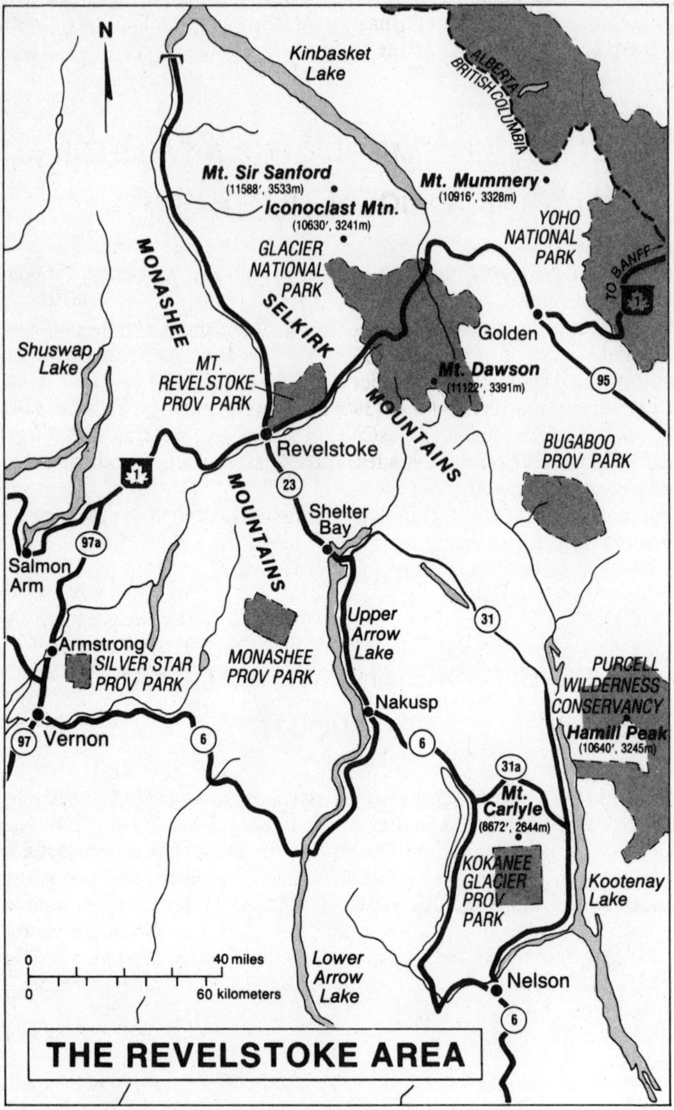
N
Kinbasket Lake
ALBERTA
BRITISH COLUMBIA
Mt. Sir Sanford
(11588′, 3533m)
Iconoclast Mtn.
(10630′, 3241m)
Mt. Mummery
(10916′, 3328m)
YOHO NATIONAL PARK
TO BANFF
1
GLACIER NATIONAL PARK
MONASHEE
SELKIRK
MOUNTAINS
Golden
Mt. Dawson
(11122′, 3391m)
95
Shuswap Lake
MT. REVELSTOKE PROV PARK
Revelstoke
1
23
MOUNTAINS
BUGABOO PROV PARK
Shelter Bay
97a
Salmon Arm
31
Upper Arrow Lake
Armstrong
SILVER STAR PROV PARK
MONASHEE PROV PARK
PURCELL WILDERNESS CONSERVANCY
Hamill Peak
(10640′, 3245m)
Nakusp
97
Vernon
6
6
31a
Mt. Carlyle
(8672′, 2644m)
KOKANEE GLACIER PROV PARK
Kootenay Lake
0
40 miles
0
60 kilometers
Lower Arrow Lake
Nelson
6
THE REVELSTOKE AREA

You can enjoy Mt. Revelstoke National Park from magnificent lookouts right along the highway. The highest point is 6,500 feet. Wildflowers are everywhere in July and August—a rewarding time of year to go hiking through the alpine meadows. Families and nature lovers can learn more about the national parks at interpretive programs with park staff. Rogers Pass, in Glacier National Park, has an interpretive center, dining room, and guest accommodations at the summit.

PRACTICAL INFORMATION FOR REVELSTOKE AND THE NATIONAL PARKS ROUTE

HOW TO GET THERE. By air. From Calgary or Kamloops. Revelstoke and Golden have small airstrips for light planes.

By bus. *Greyhound* has buses stopping in Revelstoke, Golden, and at Rogers Pass several times daily. *Golden* has bus service to Cranbrook on Hwy. 93/95 (Dewdney Trail Services: 800–332–0282).

By car. Revelstoke is 250 miles (390 km) west of Calgary, 65 miles (148 km) west of Golden on the TransCanada Hwy. and 130 miles (209 km) east of Kamloops; Golden is 84 miles (135 km) west of Banff and 160 miles (258 km) north of Cranbrook.

By train. *VIA Rail* has one train each way daily, stopping in Revelstoke and Golden.

ACCOMMODATIONS. The following listings are for Revelstoke, Golden, and Rogers Pass. Address letters to motels by box number, town, BC, postal code. The postal code for Revelstoke and Rogers Pass is V0E 2S0; for Golden, V0A 1H0. Rates for a double-occupancy room, exclusive of taxes and tips, are categorized as follows: *Moderate,* $50–$80; and *Inexpensive,* under $50.

Moderate

Best Western Glacier Park Lodge. Rogers Pass (837–2126). Dining, cafeteria, lounge, sauna, and pool.

Columbia Motel. 1601 2d St. W., Box 421 (837–2191) in Revelstoke. Family units and restaurant adjacent.

Golden Rim Motor Inn. Box 510 (344–2216) in Golden. Sauna, indoor and outdoor pools, waterslide, and whirlpool. Gorgeous mountain views.

McGregor Motor Inn. 2d St. at Connaught Ave. in Revelstoke, Box 530 (837–2121). Dining, lounge, pub, pool, sauna, and whirlpool. Wheelchair facilities.

Revelstoke TraveLodge. 601 1st St. W, Box 650 (837–2181). Pool and restaurant.

Inexpensive

Mary's Motel. Box 322 (344–7111). Right on the river in Golden. Indoor and outdoor pools, whirlpool, sauna, spa, and playground. Wheelchair facilities.

Swiss Village Motel. Box 765 (344–2276). Rooms, campground, and RV park in Revelstoke. Wheelchair facilities.

MOUNTAIN LODGES. Rustic or modern, mountain lodges combine a complete escape from city life with wilderness sports and adventure. Rates for each lodge vary greatly, depending on the room, meal plan, and extras you choose. Call or write for more information.

Blanket Glacier Chalet. Contact the Schaffers, Box 1050, Canmore, AB TOL 0M0 (403–678–4102). A 12-minute helicopter ride will land you at the chalet, located within an hour's hike, or ski from Blanket Glacier on Lake Claudia in the Monashees. Ski touring, telemarking, ice and rock climbing, mountaineering, canoeing, and fishing. Instruction available. Sauna and lounge.

Durrand Glacier Chalet. Contact *Golden Alpine Holidays,* Box 1932, Golden, BC V0A 1H0 (604–348–2341 or 348–2285). A short helicopter hop from Revelstoke. Chalet overlooks the Monashees and offers excellent hiking, skiing, and climbing terrain. Guide service. Sauna.

Esplanade Lodges. Contact *Golden Alpine Holidays,* Box 1932, Golden, BC V0A 1H0 (604–348–2341 or 348–2285). A helicopter will carry you to these rustic lodges, nestled in the Esplanade Range of the Selkirk Mountains, just north of Rogers Pass and Glacier. Skiing, hiking, and climbing. Sauna and private washrooms.

RESTAURANTS. Price categories, based on cost of dinner for two with appetizer, exclusive of tax and tip, are: *Moderate,* $15–$25; and *Inexpensive,* under $15.

Moderate

112 Room. Regent Inn, 112 1st St. E (837–2107). Seafood, salmon, crepes, veal, and lamb.

Roma Restaurant. 306 Mackenzie St. (837–4106). Traditional Italian pizza, crab legs, and steaks.

Zala's. 1601 W 2d St. (837–4996). Steak, lobster, barbecued ribs, pasta, and pizza.

Inexpensive

Burger Junction. 1601 Victoria Rd. (837–2724). Burgers and Columbia fried chicken.

Frontier. on Hwy. 1 at 122 Big Bend Hwy. (837–5119). A family place featuring western fare. Children's menu.

HOW TO GET AROUND. By bus. Frequent service by *Greyhound* to and from Revelstoke, Rogers Pass, and Golden.

By helicopter. Several firms offer heli-skiing, heli-hiking, and sightseeing services (see *Cross-country Skiing* below).

By train. Service between Golden and Revelstoke.

By rental car. *Tilden* has offices in Revelstoke.

TOURIST INFORMATION. Glacier and Mount Revelstoke National Parks, Box 350, Revelstoke, V0E 2S0 (837–5155).

High Country Tourism Association, Box 962, Kamloops, BC (372–7770).

NATIONAL PARKS. Mount Revelstoke National Park. This is a majestic and unspoiled park. Take the 16-mile (21 km) gravel-surfaced Summit Road from town—a slow, scenic drive through several plant zones, from dense rain forest up to alpine meadows. You can drive to the top of a 6,140-foot (1,938-mile) high mountain and step out for a picnic in flower-filled meadows, with the spectacular ice-capped Monashees and sharp-peaked Selkirks looming in the distance. Hike one of the trails from the parking lot deeper into the park.

The park is east of town on Hwy. 1 and is open from July–Sept. There is no roadside camping, just day-use facilities, hiking trails, and a few back-country campsites.

Glacier National Park. The park sits in the northern Selkirks with the Purcells on its east boundary. Sharp peaks, avalanche-scarred valleys, and vast fields of ice and snow make for extraordinary sightseeing and scenery. Glacier is aptly named. Heavy yearly snowfall feeds more than 400 glaciers in the park, and about one-eighth of the park is permantly covered with ice and snow.

Harsh conditions deter the proliferation of most species, but the black and grizzly bears thrive here. Glacier has the highest concentration of grizzlies of any Canadian national park. The bears forage on the avalanche slopes that harbor their favorite plants. Ground squirrels, marmots and varieties of birds also inhabit the park.

Rogers Pass was discovered in 1881, and four years later the railway through it was laid. In 1910 a 5-mile (8-km) tunnel through Mt. Macdonald was constructed after a series of tragic avalanches. The challenge continues. Recently the CPR accomplished another engineering feat, the building of a new tunnel through Mt. Macdonald. In 1886 the government designated the area as a park.

This rugged, ice-covered terrain daunts even the most adventurous of outdoor enthusiasts. Sightseeing for most visitors is done from the highway or on the 87 miles of trails that switchback up the mountains and glaciers. Climbers and overnight hikers must procure permits and register at the park warden office. There are three accessible summer campsites, at Illecillewaet, Loop Brook, and Mountain Creek. Illecillewaet is also available for winter use.

The risk of avalanches renders ski-touring a hazardous venture and all slopes along Hwy. 1 are closed to winter recreation.

PROVINCIAL PARKS. Around Revelstoke Reservoir and along Hwy. 23 are many provincial parks, with camping, hiking, fishing, swimming, and paddling. There are campgrounds in Victor Lake and Yard Creek parks on Hwy. 1.

CAMPING. The national and provincial park service offices provide information about campgrounds and maintain several remote alpine huts in Glacier and Revelstoke parks, which serve as base-camps for avid climbers and skiiers. Hermit, Glacier Circle, Arthur Wheeler, and Sapphire Col huts are all in Glacier, and Eva Lake Shelter lies in Revelstoke Park. For information, contact the parks office in Revelstoke. There are two huts in the Northern Selkirks: Fairy Meadow, near the Granite Glacier of the Adamant Group, and Sir Sandford (Great Cairn) at the west corner of Sir Sandford Glacier. They are operated by the Alpine Club of Canada, Box 1026, Banff, AB T0L 0C0 (762–4481).

HIKING. Trails run throughout the national and provincial parks. Take a glacier-viewing hike in Glacier Park or one of the trails leading off from the parking lot at the summit of Mt. Revelstoke. The Giant Cedars Trail, off Hwy. 1 heading east from Revelstoke, winds through a stand of 1,000-year-old cedars.

OUTDOOR ACTIVITIES. If you didn't bring your own **boat,** you may feel an irresistible urge to rent one and travel some of the 200 miles (320 km) of navigable Colombia River in the area. A few firms operate boat rentals on the local lakes, too, for **fishing** or just paddling around.

If you crave an intense winter wilderness experience, consider *Adventure Bound* (344–2639), Box 811, Golden V0A 1H0. They run a base-camp consisting of spacious yurts, accessible via a 12-minute helicopter ride. Great for cross-country skiing and telemarking mavens.

A 50-mile (80-km) flight northeast from Golden will land you in Hamber Provincial Park. You can stay in the summer tent camp called *Fortress Lake Lodge* (344–2683), Box 1560, Golden V0A 1H0. Guiding and meals are included in the price.

CROSS-COUNTRY SKIING. Be extremely cautious about avalanche danger in Revelstoke and Glacier parks. Some of the best ski-touring is from the mountain lodges and chalets, accessible only by helicopter, and blissfully deep powder has made the area famous. Most helicopter operators transport sightseers and hikers in summer. *Canadian Mountain Holidays,* Box 1660, Banff, AB T0L 0C0 (762–4531) flies to the Bugaboos, Cariboos, Monashees, Panorama, Revelstoke, and Valemount. *Mountain Canada Purcell Helicopter Skiing,* Box 1628, Banff, AB T0L 0C0 (762–5383) services the Purcells from Golden. *Okanagan Helicopter,* Banff (762–4082) flies out of Banff and Golden. *Selkirk Tangiers Heliskiing,* Banff (762–5627 or call collect 604–344–5016) flies to the Selkirks and Monashees from Revelstoke and Golden.

DOWNHILL SKIING. Mount Mackenzie, Box 1000, Revelstoke, V0E 2S0, has a vertical drop of 2,000 feet. 20 runs; 4 lifts. (837–5268).

HISTORIC SITES AND HOUSES. Recapture the past at the *Eagle Pass Pioneer Village.* This living museum, west of Revelstoke at Three Way Gap, is a replica of a western town of the 1880s.

Railroad buffs will want to visit Craigellechie, west of Revelstoke, where in 1885 railway and government officials gathered to drive the last spike of Canada's transcontinental railroad.

MUSEUMS. **Revelstoke Museum and Art Gallery** (837–3067).

SEASONAL EVENTS. **February.** *Snow Festival.* **May.** *Lord Revelstoke Day.* **June.** *Elks Rodeo.* **July 1.** *Canada Day* celebrations. **August.** *Annual Pilgrimage* to Eva Lake. **September.** *Revelstoke Fair.*

Index

Map pages are in **boldface.**

Fodor's Travel Guides

U.S. Guides

Alaska
Arizona
Atlantic City & the New Jersey Shore
Boston
California
Cape Cod
Carolinas & the Georgia Coast
The Chesapeake Region
Chicago
Colorado
Dallas & Fort Worth
Disney World & the Orlando Area
Florida
Hawaii
Houston & Galveston
Las Vegas
Los Angeles, Orange County, Palm Springs
Maui
Miami, Fort Lauderdale, Palm Beach
Michigan, Wisconsin, Minnesota
New England
New Mexico
New Orleans
New Orleans (Pocket Guide)
New York City
New York City (Pocket Guide)
New York State
Pacific North Coast
Philadelphia
The Rockies
San Diego
San Francisco
San Francisco (Pocket Guide)
The South
Texas
USA
Virgin Islands
Virginia
Waikiki
Washington, DC
Williamsburg

Foreign Guides

Acapulco
Amsterdam
Australia, New Zealand, The South Pacific
Austria
Bahamas
Bahamas (Pocket Guide)
Baja & the Pacific Coast Resorts
Barbados
Beijing, Guangzhou & Shanghai
Belgium & Luxembourg
Bermuda
Brazil
Britain (Great Travel Values)
Budget Europe
Canada
Canada (Great Travel Values)
Canada's Atlantic Provinces
Cancun, Cozumel, Yucatan Peninsula
Caribbean
Caribbean (Great Travel Values)
Central America
Eastern Europe
Egypt
Europe
Europe's Great Cities
Florence & Venice
France
France (Great Travel Values)
Germany
Germany (Great Travel Values)
Great Britain
Greece
The Himalayan Countries
Holland
Hong Kong
Hungary
India, including Nepal
Ireland
Israel
Italy
Italy (Great Travel Values)
Jamaica
Japan
Japan (Great Travel Values)
Jordan & the Holy Land
Kenya, Tanzania, the Seychelles
Korea
Lisbon
Loire Valley
London
London (Great Travel Values)
London (Pocket Guide)
Madrid & Barcelona
Mexico
Mexico City
Montreal & Quebec City
Munich
New Zealand
North Africa
Paris
Paris (Pocket Guide)
People's Republic of China
Portugal
Rio de Janeiro
The Riviera (Fun on)
Rome
Saint Martin & Sint Maarten
Scandinavia
Scandinavian Cities
Scotland
Singapore
South America
South Pacific
Southeast Asia
Soviet Union
Spain
Spain (Great Travel Values)
Sweden
Switzerland
Sydney
Tokyo
Toronto
Turkey
Vienna
Yugoslavia

Special-Interest Guides

Health & Fitness Vacations
Royalty Watching
Selected Hotels of Europe
Selected Resorts and Hotels of the U.S.
Shopping in Europe
Skiing in North America
Sunday in New York